Michael Moore

CLASS : CULTURE

SERIES EDITORS
Amy Schrager Lang, Syracuse University, and Bill V. Mullen, Purdue University

TITLES IN THE SERIES:

The Syntax of Class: Writing Inequality in Nineteenth-Century America
Amy Schrager Lang

Vanishing Moments: Class and American Culture
Eric Schocket

Let Me Live
Angelo Herndon

Workin' on the Chain Gang: Shaking Off the Dead Hand of History
Walter Mosley

Commerce in Color: Race, Consumer Culture, and American Literature, 1893–1933
James C. Davis

You Work Tomorrow: An Anthology of American Labor Poetry, 1929–41
Edited by John Marsh

Chicano Novels and the Politics of Form: Race, Class, and Reification
Marcial González

Moisture of the Earth: Mary Robinson, Civil Rights and Textile Union Activist
Edited by Fran Leeper Buss

Grassroots at the Gateway: Class Politics and Black Freedom Struggle in St. Louis, 1936–75
Clarence Lang

Natural Acts: Gender, Race, and Rusticity in Country Music
Pamela Fox

Transcribing Class and Gender: Masculinity and Femininity in Nineteenth-Century Courts and Offices
Carol Srole

An Angle of Vision: Women Writers on Their Poor and Working-Class Roots
Edited by Lorraine M. López

Michael Moore: Filmmaker, Newsmaker, Cultural Icon
Edited by Matthew H. Bernstein

Michael Moore

Filmmaker, Newsmaker, Cultural Icon

MATTHEW H. BERNSTEIN
Editor

The University of Michigan Press
Ann Arbor

Published in the United States of America by
The University of Michigan Press
Manufactured in the United States of America
♾ Printed on acid-free paper

2013 2012 2011 2010 4 3 2 1

A CIP catalog record for this book is available from the British Library.

Library of Congress Cataloging-in-Publication Data

Michael Moore : filmmaker, newsmaker, cultural icon / Matthew H. Bernstein, editor.
p. cm. — (Class, culture)
Includes bibliographical references and index.
ISBN 978-0-472-07103-6 (cloth : alk. paper) — ISBN 978-0-472-05103-8 (pbk. : alk. paper)
1. Moore, Michael, 1954 Apr. 23—-Criticism and interpretation. 2. Motion picture producers and directors—Political activity—United States. 3. Documentary films—Political aspects—History and criticism. 4. Motion pictures—Political aspects—United States. I. Bernstein, Matthew.
PN1998.3.M665M53 2010
791.4302'33092—dc22 2010014036

In honor of my mother, Elayne P. Bernstein

From women's eyes this doctrine I derive:
They sparkle still the right Promethean fire;
They are the books, the arts, the academes,
That show, contain, and nourish all the world.

—*Love's Labour's Lost,* act 4, scene 3

Acknowledgments

I thank the excellent scholars who contributed to this volume. They, along with University of Michigan Press Senior Acquisitions Editor LeAnn Fields, and series editors Amy Schrager Lang and Bill Mullen, have displayed extraordinary patience while I assembled it. I also wish to thank Leo Braudy, Horace Newcomb, Tom Rosteck, Sheila Tefft, and Brian Winston for their assistance, as well as Gary Crowdus of *Cineaste* for permission to reprint two essays from that esteemed publication: Christopher Sharrett and William Luhr's "*Bowling for Columbine*" originally appeared in *Cineaste* 28, no. 2 (2003): 36–38, and Richard Porton's *Sicko* appeared in *Cineaste* 32, no. 4 (2007): 44–46. I thank the University of California Press for permission to reprint Miles Orvell's essay "Documentary Film and the Power of Interrogation: *American Dream* and *Roger and Me*," *Film Quarterly* 48, no. 2 (1994–95): 10–18. Finally, I thank Rowman and Littlefield for the right to reprint Jeffrey P. Jones' chapter on Michael Moore in his *Entertaining Politics: Satiric Television and Political Engagement,* 2nd edition (2009).

I thank my colleagues in Film Studies at Emory University—Karla Oeler, Michele Schreiber, Eddy von Mueller, Dave Pratt, Bill Brown, Annie Hall, Aby Parsons, and Cecelia Shannon—for their general collegiality. As always, I am deeply indebted to Natalie, Justin, and Adam Bernstein for their affection, high spirits, and sharp sense of humor.

I dedicate this volume to my mother: for her indefatigable energy, her dedication to true communication, her unfailing sense of compassion and understanding, her faith in people, and her optimism in the face of life's challenges. And especially, for instilling in me a love of education and of the performing arts.

Contents

I. OVERVIEWS

Introduction
MATTHEW H. BERNSTEIN 3

The Left's Biggest Star: Michael Moore as Commercial Auteur
SERGIO RIZZO 27

Class, Gender, Race, and Masculine Masquerade in the Documentaries of Michael Moore
GAYLYN STUDLAR 51

II. MOORE AND THE DOCUMENTARY TRADITION

Michael Moore and the Aesthetics and Politics of Contemporary Documentary Film
DOUGLAS KELLNER 79

"Everything Is Personal": Michael Moore and the Documentary Essay
PAUL ARTHUR 105

III. THE MAJOR FILMS

Roger & Me
Documentary Film and the Power of Interrogation: *American Dream* and *Roger & Me*
MILES ORVELL 127

Bowling for Columbine
Bowling for Columbine: A Review
CHRISTOPHER SHARRETT AND WILLIAM LUHR 141

Fahrenheit 9/11

Prelude to Moore: A Comparison of Rhetorical Techniques in Frank Capra's *Why We Fight* Series and Michael Moore's *Fahrenheit 9/11*
RICHARD R. NESS 149

Truth and Rhetoric in Michael Moore's *Fahrenheit 9/11*
CHARLES MUSSER 167

Dystopia Now: *Fahrenheit 9/11*'s Red Pill
DAVID TETZLAFF 202

Sicko

Sicko Movie Review
RICHARD PORTON 223

IV. BEYOND THE AMERICAN MULTIPLEX: MOORE IN THE MEDIA MARKETPLACE

Moore Muckracking: The Reinvention of TV Newsmagazines in the Age of Spin and Entertainment
JEFFREY P. JONES 231

The British Take On Moore
RICHARD KILBORN 255

MoveOn, Michael Moore, and the Summer of '04: Marketing Online Political Activism
CARY ELZA 278

Contributors 307

Index 311

I. OVERVIEWS

Introduction

MATTHEW H. BERNSTEIN

With the premiere of his popular debut film *Roger & Me* in late 1989, Michael Moore proved himself an astonishingly successful nonfiction filmmaker. Thirteen years later, *Bowling for Columbine*'s extraordinary box office performance and its Academy Award for Best Documentary confirmed Moore's standing as a cultural commentator to be reckoned with. In the intervening years, Moore diversified his output: he became a best-selling book author, TV show producer, and media personality. When *Fahrenheit 9/11* premiered in June 2004, following its winning the Palme D'Or at Cannes, Moore certified his status as a filmmaker, newsmaker, icon, and political celebrity larger than any one of the films, books or TV shows he produced or the website established and maintained in his name.

For 20 years and counting, Moore has served as a comic, unofficial, harried, and harrying spokesperson for the disenfranchised working class and liberal and leftist Americans—a single-handed critic of corporate America and an answer to the rise of Fox News. He had also become a lightning rod for conservative criticism and personal attacks long before he attempted to influence the outcome of the 2004 American presidential election with *Fahrenheit 9/11*. And while 2007's *Sicko* was not nearly so ambitious as the 2004 opus—and it's worth recalling that no other theatrical nonfiction film has ever tried to dethrone a sitting American president—Moore's 2007 movie inaugurated a more intensive phase in America's ongoing efforts at healthcare reform that the Obama administration and Congress have begun to address through legislation.

In his essay for this volume, Douglas Kellner explains concisely Moore's phenomenal success:

> He is a populist artist who privileges his own voice and point of view, inserting himself as film narrator and often the subject of his film's action. Moore plays the crusading defender of the poor and oppressed, who stands up to and confronts the powers that be. He uses humor and compelling dramatic and narrative sequences to engage his audiences. He deals with issues of fundamental importance, and convinces his audience that the problems he presents are highly significant and concern the health of U.S. democracy. Moreover, despite the severity of the problems he portrays, the films and filmmaker often imply that the problems are subject to intervention, and that progressive social transformation is possible and necessary.

It's worth noting how powerfully Moore has broken box office records for theatrical nonfictional films using his strategic and idiosyncratic combination of irreverent humor and personal provocations of corporate and political leaders. According to www.boxofficemojo.com, four of the six top grossing theatrical political documentaries are Moore's: *Roger & Me* ($6.7 million domestic, $7.7 million worldwide), *Bowling for Columbine* ($21.6 million domestic, $58 million worldwide), *Sicko* ($24.5 million domestic, $35.7 million worldwide), and, of course, *Fahrenheit 9/11* ($119.2 million domestic, $222.4 million worldwide). Among documentaries in general, *Fahrenheit 9/11, Sicko,* and *Blowing for Columbine* still rate in the top six highest grossing nonfiction theatrical films (political or otherwise) of all time.

Moore's box office record has been uneven, however. Moore's only effort at fictional filmmaking—the political satire *Canadian Bacon* (1995), starring John Candy and Alan Alda—was a flop (a limp $163,971 domestic gross). *The Big One* (1997) performed modestly, but better than *Canadian Bacon* at the box office ($720,074 domestic). This picaresque account of Moore's book tour (47 cities in 50 days) to promote his 1996 best seller *Downsize This!* featured bits of Moore's stand-up comic corporate critique interspersed with frequent detours in which Moore learned about and intervened in local unionizing efforts or corporate layoffs. Indeed, Moore did not hit his cinematic stride again until *Bowling for Columbine* in 2002. *Slacker Uprising* (made in 2007 but released in September 2008) is another minor effort: it most resembles *The Big One* as a rambling account of Moore's five-week tour of college campuses (joined by various celebrities and rock stars) during the fall 2004 presidential election. It went direct to

DVD and downloadable video on the Web. As I write this, Moore's latest film, *Capitalism: A Love Story,* has earned well over $14 million in 11 weeks of domestic release, placing it eighth on the all-time list of documentary releases, and fifth among political documentaries. Given Moore's popularity in foreign markets, the film's $3 million gross from its international distribution is disappointing. Still, it is hard to imagine another documentary filmmaker whose films will gross over $330 million.

Box office aside, Moore's creativity and popularity cannot be denied. His first television series, *TV Nation* (1994–96) won an Emmy. His second, *The Awful Truth* (1999–2000), received an Emmy nomination.[1] Indeed, Paul Arthur suggests in this volume that it was the short-form journalism of his TV work that enabled Moore to regain his prominence and success as a filmmaker with *Bowling for Columbine.* In the meantime, Moore's books, many of them bestsellers, allowed him to stay near if not in the spotlight of America's political culture. In addition to Moore and Kathleen Glynn's *Adventures in a TV Nation* (HarperCollins, 1998), there were two more books published in succeeding years, *Stupid White Men* (Regan Books, 2002) and *Dude, Where's My Country* (2003, Warner Books), as well as *Mike's Election Guide* in 2008.

All of these texts draw upon Moore's experience in activist politics. In 1972, he became the youngest officeholder in Michigan history due to his teenage service on the Flint public school board. Moore's cultural output also grew from his work in left-wing muckraking journalism: he founded the *Flint Voice,* which became the *Michigan Voice*: he had a very brief stint as editor of *Mother Jones;* and he held an even shorter tenure as the editor of a media watchdog newsweekly for Ralph Nader.

Throughout his several careers, Moore recognized that putting himself in the middle of social issues would command more attention from a general audience. Beyond his own work, before the fall 2002 premiere of *Bowling for Columbine,* Moore made guest appearances in TV series such as *Mad About You* and *The Simpsons,* and visited the talk show circuit—including appearances on *The Late Show with David Letterman* and *Late Night with Conan O'Brien,* as well as at least one appearance on a TV show politically hostile to his views, *The O'Reilly Factor.* Moore even appeared as an expert talking head in the 2003 documentary *The Corporation.* He has also turned up on liberal-leaning comedy shows such as *The Daily Show* and *Real Time with Bill Maher* that, as Jeffrey P. Jones argues in his volume, Moore's brand of political humor helped to inspire. Often Moore appeared to promote his latest film or book; often he did not.

Several weeks in advance of the premiere of *Sicko,* the June 1, 2007, issue of

Entertainment Weekly featured a photo of Moore on the cover with the headline "Here Comes Trouble." Before this, and well before Moore made the rounds of the talk shows to promote the film in late June, Bill Maher in May 2007 could boast that Moore had granted *Real Time with Bill Maher* his first TV interview in over two years. More recently, Moore appeared on *Larry King Live* from late spring 2008 through spring 2010 with no film to promote; he was simply there as a prominent celebrity. In fall 2008, he appeared as a commentator on the Republican National Convention, along with "Plumbers for Obama," or on *Larry King Live* to discuss the financial and Detroit automakers' bailouts. (Of course, he made the rounds of talk shows when *Capitalism: A Love Story* premiered in fall 2009, even singing "The Times They Are A-Changing" on the new *Jay Leno Show.*) Clearly, the American media have discovered that they can attract readers and viewers when Moore shows up. Even Moore's occasional public utterances are reported in the press, as when he, in early 2004 as Democratic presidential primaries were under way, accused George W. Bush of being a deserter during his service in the National Guard in Alabama; the Bush administration took the accusation incredibly seriously, scrambling to refute this charge made well in advance of the June premiere of *Fahrenheit 9/11.* Since the premiere of that film, Moore has inspired several books and feature documentaries devoted purely to attacking him.[2] The ferocity of the onslaught against Moore, even the dismissive use of his name and persona as a synonym for liberal extremism, only testify to his considerable presence on the American scene. Moore is, quite simply, an instantly recognizable national figure who commands national attention. Put another way, Moore is impossible to ignore.

Within the realm of American cinema, Moore's impact is equally undeniable. *Roger & Me* alone represents a transformative milestone in the history of documentary filmmaking. Courtesy of a distribution deal (for $3 million, less than half of the film's eventual gross) with Warner Bros., *Roger & Me* brought its unique alchemy of Moore's filmmaking tendencies—ironic self-presentation, humorous social commentary on the woes of the unemployed working class, and a laser-beam focus on corporate indifference to the communities where people work—into the mass media marketplace. There, it also received searing examination for certain alterations of chronology in delineating Flint's troubles.

More recently, reports have surfaced that Moore deliberately left out of his film the undeniable fact that politically active groups were feverishly at work protesting General Motors's layoffs; as a result, Moore appears to fight the good fight against GM's inhumane policies alone. Even more devastating to the film's

Michael Moore with cinematographers Shermer and John Prusak in a widely-seen publicity shot for *Roger & Me* that emphasizes his small crew and Moore's own inexperience as a first-time filmmaker. Copyright 1989 Warner Bros., Inc.

reputation is the recent revelation that Moore had actually landed an interview with GM CEO Roger Smith for the film but chose not to include it. Moore chose to omit both these facts so that *Roger & Me* would be more personal and more humorous. The film's extraordinary box office performance affirmed Moore's decision. Still, the revelation of Smith's availability to Moore undercut a crucial premise of the film and has further damaged its credibility.[3] The controversies and debates that greet each of Moore's films, however, have not diminished his or their impact on American culture and politics. Indeed, as the stage-managed refusal of Disney to allow Miramax to distribute *Fahrenheit 9/11* demonstrates, they only enhance his films' impact and enable Moore to thrive.

Furthermore, Moore's films have played a major role in film history, specifically by helping to transform theatrical documentaries into viable commercial properties more frequently than they ever had been in the past—even when they take the form of an extended PowerPoint presentation, as did *An Inconvenient Truth* (2006). Moore has also inspired a new generation of filmmakers who use his personalized, humorous, quickly cut combination of archival footage, found films, home movies, and newly shot scenes to explore problems in American society and politics. To take just one example, Morgan Spurlock's *Supersize Me* (2004) is clearly in the tradition of Moore's highly personal brand of muckraking, here accomplished amiably and somewhat masochistically, but definitely framed as an incisive critique of a fast-food industry that can destroy Americans' health.

Moore's films can also be seen as anticipating the work of more recent cinematic exposés of corporate greed. Alex Gibney's *Enron: The Smartest Guys in the Room* (2005) detailed one company's jaw-dropping greed and malfeasance in the energy markets in such detail that it made the General Motors of *Roger & Me* almost seem compassionate by comparison. Several of the issues raised in *Fahrenheit 9/11* have been elaborated by a string of documentaries critical of the Iraq war and its catastrophically incompetent execution: Eugene Jarecki's *Why We Fight* (2005), Charles Ferguson's *No End in Sight* (2007), and on the subject of torture, Alex Gibney's *Taxi to the Dark Side* (2007), as well as Errol Morris's *Standard Operating Procedure* (2008). In retrospect, we can see that Moore's films, particularly *Fahrenheit 9/11*, provided a sketchy overview of various flaws in American politics and society that subsequent nonfiction films have explored with greater intensity and focus—and, quite appropriately, with considerably less humor.[4]

Given Moore's importance in American political culture, a broad assessment of Moore's work is overdue. True, countless reviews of his books, films, and TV shows are not hard to find. Recent years have seen the publication of three informative trade press biographies of Moore, as well as one scholarly book on the impact of, and firefights over, *Fahrenheit 9/11*.[5]

Still, this volume fills an important gap. It examines individual films but also Moore's filmmaking as a whole, which remains his most influential form of personal expression, and his most important contribution to cultural and political debates in this country. We offer analysis of his populist approach to American politics, in particular, and his eclectic method of critiquing America, its media, and most of all, its politicians. We look closely at the cinematic techniques Moore uses to convey his ideas, his views of gender and class among the latter.

We also consider Moore's ambivalent relationship with documentary filmmaking traditions. Moore has tried to distance himself and his films from documentaries. At the same time, the ways in which Moore has shaped his films have often been greeted with cries of propaganda. He is indeed commonly and casually described in talk shows and the news media as a left-wing propagandist, a view that reflects a highly limited understanding and the history of the documentary form and an extremely naive view of the documentary's relationship to reality. The authors in this volume recognize that the nonfiction film represents the filmmaker's revelation of and response to events that occur in the world. The controversies that have arisen over Moore's films—their strong point of view or their misleading use of facts—do not compromise their status as nonfiction works, nor do they invalidate the documentary form as a whole.

Moreover, in this volume we look beyond the American movie theater, with considerations of Moore's status as a celebrity, his forays into TV production, the reception of his films and TV shows in the United Kingdom, and an analysis of Moore's development of a website relative to the lightning-fast development of American political activism on the Internet, a movement that grew after 2004 to become an essential tool of political organizing during the 2008 election cycle and into the present day.

We begin with two general overviews of Moore's filmmaking career. Sergio Rizzo examines Moore's celebrity persona. Few people think of Moore as an auteur, but Rizzo argues persuasively that Moore thrives in an era when the auteur functions as a marketing brand. Rizzo examines those elements of Moore's personal biography that his films emphasize to make him a distinctive figure. Key among them is Moore's close identification with Flint, Michigan, as a true locus of average American life and, as Rizzo puts it, "a symbol of his personal authenticity." There was also Moore's all too brief sojourn at *Mother Jones*, a humiliation Moore blamed on the intellectual liberal elite from which Moore stridently distinguished himself. Rizzo then examines the star persona created in Moore's "commercial performance" of himself as a muckraking reporter, appealing to a class-based identity politics that ignores the film business. In Rizzo's hands, the contradictions of Moore's persona multiply: Moore's prominence in the brand-name marketing for his films is at odds with the traditional stance of the documentary filmmaker as oppositional artist; like any working-class movie icon, Moore's status as "the left's biggest star" complicates Moore's everyman persona (a "schlump in a ball cap").

Gaylyn Studlar's essay also considers Moore's Flint-based, white, working-class image as part of her examination of the class, gender, and race politics of Moore's major films. Flint, she finds, is essential to Moore's on-screen "masquerade of working-class masculinity" (his persona as "an apparently unsophisticated, class-bound white man"). From this position, Moore develops what Studlar calls a "solidarity strategy": Moore appears to enjoy a genuine connection with the powerless victims whose plights he explores in his films, a rapport that disguises the cultural power he exercises as a filmmaker. Moreover, Studlar finds, with very few exceptions (such as Lila Lipscomb in *Fahrenheit 9/11* and the former health insurance executive Linda Peeno in *Sicko*), that women rarely occupy an important role in Moore's analysis of the social, political, or economic problem at issue in his films. More typically, they are victims pure and simple, with whom Moore displays extraordinary, almost feminine empathy. At the same time, Moore neglects to provide in his films the kind of gender analysis that might show, for example, in *Bowling for Columbine,* that the American man's assertion of masculinity is responsible for so much of the gun violence he dissects in the film. Moore prefers instead to point at class inequalities, ruthless capitalism, and inhumane government programs ("Welfare to Work") as the primary causes of these school shooting tragedies. While the centrality of class to Moore's films has been apparent since *Roger & Me* and continues in *Capitalism: A Love Story,* Studlar's essay is the first to consider its function and meanings in Moore's films and its intersections with gender and race in a systematic way.

Of course, lower-class victims figure prominently throughout the history of social documentary. This is just one tradition of documentary filmmaking that Moore's film work takes up. Part 2 of this volume examines Moore's uneasy engagement with such legacies. Douglas Kellner focuses in particular on the workings of Moore's three major political documentaries (*Roger & Me, Bowling for Columbine,* and *Fahrenheit 9/11*) in contrast to the pioneering, highly influential work of another left-wing documentary filmmaker, Emile de Antonio. Kellner argues that Moore employs three crucial strategies: "personal witnessing" (apparent even in the title of *Roger & Me*), "exploratory and confrontational quest dramas" (apparent in all of Moore's films, but best exemplified by *Bowling for Columbine*), and "agit-prop political interventions" (typified by *Fahrenheit 9/11* and, we can now add, *Slacker Uprising*). The similarities Kellner finds between de Antonio and Moore are striking: both eschew claims of documentary objectivity, and both make their points by using a mix of found and shot footage, contrasting editing strategies and ironic humor. But their differences are fascinating as well: de Antonio left it to his viewers to interpret the meanings of his films, while Moore favors a more "viewer-friendly" method that relies heavily on voice-over narration. While critics—indeed, several contributors to this volume—continue to debate Moore's relationship to other films and filmmakers, Kellner's invocation of de Antonio proves highly illuminating. He reminds us that Moore's films carry on a tradition of partisan documentary filmmaking whose existence is denied or dismissed by so many of Moore's critics.

Like Douglas Kellner, Paul Arthur examines Moore's films relative to the nonfiction film tradition. As Arthur notes, the most commented-upon features of Moore's film work are "the director's first-person presence and a structural propensity for segmentation, digression, and clashing rhetorical tones." But where previous commentators have disagreed as they sought to characterize Moore's work in terms of well-established documentary categories (and notably, Bill Nichols' categories of documentary modes[6]), Arthur proposes that Moore's films are best understood as progressively assuming the form of the documentary essay film, exemplified by films ranging from Alan Resnais's seminal *Night and Fog* of 1955 to Ross McElwee's *Sherman's March* of 1986. Essay films emphasize in equal measure the subjectivity of the filmmaker (her memory and personal experience) with commentary on the world the filmmaker inhabits. Arthur argues that the essay framework allows us to account for so much of what makes Moore's films distinctive: their emphasis on Moore himself, but also his recourse to a rhetorical framework in which his faux naïf character raises his consciousness (and the viewer's) as he sets out to learn more about the topic of his investigations. The essay film framework also encompasses Moore's use of diverse kinds of footage (original, found, home movies, TV news clips, commercials, newsreels) and music, and the highly idiosyncratic, sometimes free-association logic that informs his approach to the subjects he explores—as well as the documentaries made attacking him. Unfortunately, Paul Arthur passed away before he could revise his essay to incorporate comments on *Sicko* and *Capitalism: A Love Story*. The implications of his insights on Moore's film work in general and for those films in particular, however, remain clear. Moreover, his essay is but one more example of his rich and enriching legacy of erudite, insightful writing on all aspects of film culture.

Part 3 of this volume offers an array of essays on Moore's four major theatrical films, *Roger & Me, Bowling for Columbine, Fahrenheit 9/11,* and *Sicko.* Miles Orvell's essay, published in 1994, compares *Roger & Me* with Barbara Kopple's Oscar-winning *American Dream* (1991), a sober account of the defeat of a workers' strike at Hormel meat plant in the 1980s. While both films chart the diminished power of labor unions to win concessions for their members in a postindustrial and global age—particularly after eight years of business-friendly policies enacted by the Reagan administration—Orvell notes how distinctly different these films are. As Kopple follows the efforts of union leaders and members to succeed and even survive during the strike, she takes a traditional approach to depicting the labor struggle, pairing (in Bill Nichols' terminology) expository and observational modes. Moore by contrast creates a "documentary satire," one that questions the tradition in which Kopple works by taking a free-wheeling, satiric approach to his account of Flint's devastation at the hands of GM. Each film, Orvell concludes, "bears witness" to the struggles of laboring Americans in distinct ways: "Kopple's camera reveals the nature of powerlessness and gives it a voice, but it conceals the awful silence of the powerful. And that silence, absurd in its pomposity, infuriating in its Kafkaesque reticence, is exactly what Moore shows us."[7]

Christopher Sharrett and William Luhr's review of *Bowling for Columbine* (originally published in *Cineaste* in 2003) offers a concise, insightful assessment of Moore's most acclaimed work. Noting Moore's unusual combination of comedy and social and political criticism, Sharrett and Luhr hail his ability to show his audience "the grotesque, almost incomprehensible features of American life" and note that Moore's obvious revamping of found footage and handling of staged scenes provide a robust reply to the criticisms that he does not make every trick of his trade apparent to the viewer. At the same time, Sharrett and Luhr duly note that while Moore persuasively presents the Columbine killers as "logical products of American life," Moore's analysis of America's love affair with the gun can appear "confused and confusing." For example, the dramatic moment in which Kmart agrees to stop selling the ammunition with which the Columbine killers attacked the school is surprising, moving, and powerful—but it is ultimately ephemeral. Moreover, Moore's final interview with Charlton Heston, whatever it reveals about the late National Rifle Association leader, likewise seems ultimately pointless. Earlier, when Moore engages in cross-cultural comparisons (gun violence in the United States versus Canada), Sharrett and Luhr assert, his argument appears to lose focus and coherence.

Fahrenheit 9/11 remains the milestone event in Moore's career and cultural production; accordingly, this volume offers three essays on the film. Richard R. Ness examines its use of cinematic techniques by comparing the film's protest against the Iraq war with Frank Capra's pro–World War II indoctrination films, the Why We Fight series (1943–45). There are some striking similarities, some of which arise from the fact that both Capra and Moore offer viewers a populist view of America and its place in the world. Thus, like the narration in the Capra series, Moore's narration strikes an intimate, informal tone relative to the audience. Moreover, both Capra and Moore recontextualize documentary or factual footage (Capra working with Leni Riefensthal's *Triumph of the Will* [1934], Moore with television news feeds of the Bush administration). Both filmmakers also incorporate footage from studio films—used as reenactments of actual events in Capra's work, and ironically so in Moore's. Most broadly, Ness uses this comparison to challenge the notion that propaganda and documentary are absolutely opposed, or even that there is consensus on the definitions of documentary and of propaganda. These were central terms in the debate over *Farhenheit 9/11*'s merits, value, and achievements. In fact, as Ness shows, Capra's work inspired precisely the same debates when it premiered 60 years earlier.

Charles Musser's essay considers *Fahrenheit 9/11* in terms of the notion of documentary "truth." He first compares Moore's film with the more "sober" documentary work of Robert Greenwald (exemplified by his 2003 *Uncovered: The Whole Truth About the Iraq War*), which presents its case against the Bush administration as if at a courtroom trial. Musser then zeroes in on the competing assessments in different documentary films and press journalism of what actually transpired and for how long during Bush's seven-minute sojourn on September 11, 2001, in the Sarasota elementary school classroom after he was informed that a second plane had hit the second tower of the World Trade Center. Whereas Moore claims "nobody did anything" for those seven minutes, Alan Peterson's *FahrenHYPE 9/11: Unraveling the Truth About Fahrenheit 9/11 & Michael Moore* asserted that Moore was absolutely wrong. By meticulously showing that no filmmaker or newsmaker had access to an uninterrupted seven-minute clip of Bush's stay in the classroom, Musser is able to demonstrate that Peterson's claims are inconclusive and create a sideshow that distracts from the larger issue of the Bush administration's inattentiveness to the threat of Osama bin Laden. By situating Moore's film within an understanding of documentary film truth that is relational—in particular, seeing the film as an account of recent American history designed to counter the version put forward by the Bush administration and the major American news media—Musser argues for a new way of appreciating Moore's achievement in this film.

David Tetzlaff also argues for seeing *Fahrenheit 9/11* as an alternative account of American history since 2000. Yet Tetzlaff advances an unusual and compelling understanding of the film: that it is best appreciated not as a bona fide or distorted documentary, but as a dystopian vision, akin to *Brazil* (1985), *The Matrix* (1999), or George Orwell's novel *1984*. Moore's film, Tetzlaff argues, "is more about social control through the manipulation of imagery and information than it is about the Iraq war. It is more a cautionary tale about the construction of false consciousness in general than an attack on George W. Bush in particular." Tetzlaff proceeds to discuss the conventions of the dystopian narrative and shows how they inform Moore's strategies. Beyond *Fahrenheit 9/11*'s recasting of the 2000 presidential election as a dream and a nightmare, both Moore's personal narration and Lila Lipscomb's journey to political awakening are akin to that of the dystopian protagonist, such as Montag in *Fahrenheit 451*, who lives unreflectively within this society gone wrong and slowly comes to realize that something is amiss. As our guide to the new American political order in which the image is all powerful and used effectively for political ends, Moore offers a counternarrative about the Bush administration. He deploys images and events not reported by the mainstream media, which basically followed the Bush White House's version of events.[8] Tetzlaff's essay offers a bold and original thesis about *Fahrenheit 9/11.* Other commentators have noted the film's quotations from Orwell; no one has previously taken the dystopian vision to be the keynote of the film.

We offer a reprint of Richard Porton's characteristically perceptive analysis of 2007's *Sicko.* Noting the remarkable praise the film earned across the political spectrum, Porton argues that Moore's response to the Americans denied health care is more empathetic than ever before; and that he "attempts to explain why Americans, perfectly content with government-run post offices and public libraries, have been brainwashed to believe that nationalized health care . . . is akin to a communist conspiracy." Porton refers to sober studies that agreed with, if they did not inspire, Moore's thesis in the film, and he points out its various blind spots (letting Bill Clinton off the hook for sharing Bush's faith in private industry's ability to provide adequate health care). Porton also takes due account of Moore's narcissism, which results in his continuing centrality to his films, and argues that the stronger part of the film is the first half, where Moore documents the dire straits into which insurance companies have placed hapless citizens, as opposed to the second half, where he visits other countries for terms of comparison (a strategy Moore first deployed in *Bowling for Columbine*). Porton reasonably characterizes the visit to Cuba as a "closing gambit and a dubious polemical ploy," concluding, "With Moore, alas, it is necessary to swallow some of films' reflexive gimmickry and admire his generally good political instincts and intentions." Porton's observation here, in fact, holds good for all of Moore's work.

Part 4 of this volume turns to that work beyond the American movie theater. Jeffrey P. Jones examines Moore's two TV series, *TV Nation* and *The Awful Truth,* as satires of the newsmagazine show typified by CBS's *60 Minutes.* Jones further situates them as early instances of the "politico-entertainment" that surrounds us now in fake news shows best typified by *The Daily Show with Jon Stewart.* While post-1960s American satirical fake news goes as far back as at least *Saturday Night Live's* "Weekend Update," Moore's programs featured special reports in the field that continued his movies' populist anticorporation, anticonservative crusades. Jones's analysis also reveals Moore's mixing and matching stories and methods from television in his films: one of Moore's pro-gun control reports, following a school shooting, features a kiddy sing-along with Pistol Pete; in *Bowling for Columbine,* Pistol Pete's place is taken by the talking bullet who narrates America's violent history. (These kinds of examples support Paul Arthur's claim that the TV show episodes facilitated Moore's return to theatrical documentary filmmaking in the 2002 film.) Most broadly, the hallmark of Moore's TV work, in Jones's terms, is his "unruly" approach to investigative journalism, combining traditional reporting methods with an "anything goes" muckraking spirit that Moore justifies as necessary to explore the systematic nature of the pervasive unfairness of American economics and politics—and a necessary alternative to traditional news organizations that do not give Americans the information and analysis they should. The result, as with *The Daily Show with Jon Stewart,* is a truly alternative, highly critical form of news reporting.

Richard Kilborn demonstrates that those key aspects of Moore's TV work, such as his refusal to respect or even recognize the properties of documentary filmmaking so revered in the United Kingdom, have generated his considerable popularity in Great Britain, where documentary is closely associated with TV. Moore's TV shows echoed earlier British TV comic political reviews, such as *That Was The Week That Was,* or the Monty Python shows. At the same time, Kilborn shows how influential Moore has been on British documentary culture, as measured by the growth of fake news shows there and the willingness of certain TV creators (Louis Theroux, Chris Morris, and Mark Thomas) and the documentarian Nick Bloomfield to put themselves on screen. Kilborn concludes by tracing Moore's impact on British media studies, which has debated whether Moore's films exemplify the dumbing down of documentary practice, a question perhaps answered in part by Douglas Kellner's comparison of Moore's films with those of de Antonio. Another possible answer is that Moore's films are revitalizing the form in ways we are still beginning to appreciate.

Kilborn's much-needed account of Moore's considerable impact outside the United States also notes the importance of his ability to use old and new technologies, including the Web. This is the very subject of Cary Elza's essay, which examines Moore's partnership with MoveOn.org in summer 2004 as "a turning point in the intersection of political action and Internet community-building." Moore's website, www.michaelmoore.com, has often consisted only of two blogs (one by Moore himself) and links to the websites of other sympathetic groups, and Moore is also able to use it as a supplement to his films, providing documentation for a number of their claims. Yet as Elza shows, Moore's and MoveOn.org's websites thrive because they redact (collate and select) the most pertinent news stories for the political community they help to create. They thus create a public sphere where citizens can argue and strategize to change a nation's politics. Elza argues that Moore's films also perform redaction, selecting little-known or overlooked (by the mainstream media) bits of information (banks giving away guns, George Bush lingering in the Sarasota classroom) for our consideration as examples of an America gone awry. She also traces out the various initiatives MoveOn.org proposed to its members to promote *Fahrenheit 9/11*—to hand out flyers of the film's poster (Moore and George W. Bush holding hands on the White House lawn), and to attend "National Town Meeting" house parties before the film opened, at which Moore and MoveOn founder Eli Pariser spoke via a live web broadcast not just about the film but about voter registration—a key goal of the Moore-MoveOn alliance.

Elza is thus able not only to explain the mechanics of Moore's web presence, but the ideals and new political culture the Internet has generated since 2004. Much as Sergio Rizzo discusses Moore as a commercial auteur, a brand name, so Elza identifies Moore's web presence as a commercial brand, one that allows fans to feel they are part of a desirable community by appealing to their ideal, activist selves. Even if the desire to be politically active is an advertised commodified product, it still has political impact, in terms of how we define ourselves online, which constitutes a new "public sphere."

Elza thus situates Moore's and MoveOn.org's web presence from 2004 going forward as a crucial marker of the transformative role the Internet has played in national politics—a fitting observation, given that Moore began his career as a political activist before becoming a journalist or filmmaker. Indeed, the role of bloggers, Internet sites, redactors, and activist groups like MoveOn.org multiplied during the 2008 election cycle, providing almost instant alternative commentary to campaigns' claims and attacks, with MoveOn.org's website equaled if not eclipsed by the Huffington Post and politico.com. Still, MoveOn.org remains a premiere organizing entity on the Web, as was seen during the 2008 presidential election. Indeed, political campaigns will continue to study and copy the online campaign and fund-raising strategies the Obama campaign used so successfully.

Moore himself continues to send out e-mails to those registered at his site: announcing appearances on TV, celebrating Obama's victory and inauguration (November 5, 2008, and January 20, 2009), rejoicing when Obama compelled the head of General Motors to step down (April 1, 2009); asking supporters who work in the financial industry to step forward and reveal what they know about the Wall Street meltdown and financial bailout for use in *Capitalism: A Love Story* (February 11, 2009); and to urge fans to attend his latest film during its opening weekend (October 2, 3, 4) and the following weekend (October 9). Moore's multimedia presence is just one more hallmark of his success in the marketplace and his impact on American popular culture.

SINCE *FAHRENHEIT 9/11*

Moore's career reached its peak of influence with *Fahrenheit 9/11*, but he remains a crucial figure in American political culture and film history. Certainly, Moore has inspired a great deal of thought, some of it angry, since he emerged on the scene. Perhaps the most striking development in this regard is the premiere of *Manufacturing Dissent*, a 2007 documentary by Canadians Rick Caine and Debbie Melnyk, filmmakers who—unlike Moore's previous cinematic critics—are sympathetic to Moore's politics and aims, but ultimately grew disillusioned as they learned more about his methods. The film reveals Moore's omission of his interview with Roger Smith for *Roger & Me*.[9] Moore's critique of GM's devastation of Flint remains undiminished, however. Even if Smith met with Moore, GM did not reopen plants and rehire Flint residents.

Sicko, which premiered in late June 2007, resembles many of Moore's previous films. As Richard Porton notes, Moore is still the center of the film—he narrates it, and he is on camera a good bit. As in *Roger & Me*, he blames American industries—here those of health insurance and pharmaceuticals—for putting profits above human health and welfare. As he has always done, Moore uses ironic humor constantly, as when he faux naively asks a British couple in a London hospital how much they paid for the newborn they are carrying. He inserts brief satirical sequences, such as the *Star Wars* music and opening credits crawl to list the vast array of preexisting conditions that insurance companies use to justify denying coverage—much like the *Bonanza* sequence mocking the Bush administration in *Fahrenheit 9/11*. He continues to report in unruly fashion, using diverse materials (home video footage of a man suturing his own knee at the start of the film, for example). As he ponders why American health care is in such a sorry state, Moore also explores the universal health care systems in Canada, Great Britain, and France—a type of comparative reasoning he employed in *Bowling for Columbine*. The film certainly fits the parameters of the documentary film essay film Paul Arthur describes.

The segment of the film that provoked the greatest criticism is that in which Moore stages a visit to Guantánamo Bay and then Cuba in search of health treatment for medical personnel who have suffered various serious ailments since their voluntary work at Ground Zero, and who have received no coverage for treatment or even a diagnosis in the United States. While Guantánamo Bay's authorities don't respond to his loudspeaker requests from a speedboat to enter, Cuban doctors provide for free the medical treatment the American health industry has denied them, and Cuban firefighters salute the American volunteer heroes. This is a stunt that would be perfectly at home on one of Moore's TV series episodes, as Jeffrey Jones describes. Here, it is as if Moore has taken the few seconds of footage of happy pre-war Iraq in *Fahrenheit 9/11* and fabricated an entire, penultimate sequence from it about Cuba as a paradise of compassion. Indeed, it is highly possible, and extremely likely, that the Cubans who participated in Moore's film saw this as an opportunity to put the country's best foot forward and so may have acted with unusual largesse. But as David Tetzlaff might remind us, Moore need not show us the devastating poverty in Cuba or the repressive cruelty of the Castro regime; we've heard all about it from the American news media and several presidential administrations. Moore's footage gives us a side of Cuba that exists, however marginally, and that we haven't seen before, and it is frankly quite moving to see Cuban firefighters salute the American lifesavers. We might even be tempted to frame *Sicko* as a dystopian narrative, much as David Tetzlaff argues for *Fahrenheit 9/11*—an outraged perspective on the American health system. This view is encapsulated when Moore—while contemplating the fate of a woman without health coverage who has been dumped by a South Los Angeles hospital, like so much garbage, at a shelter—asks of his American audience, "Who are we?" How could we allow such things to happen in our country?

Beyond the film itself, we could note that Moore has used the government's harassment of him—on the grounds of his illegal visit to Cuba—as a means of promoting the film before its premiere, although this did not get nearly the attention that greeted the alleged refusal by Disney/Miramax to distribute *Fahrenheit 9/11* after it won the top prize at Cannes. And, as Cary Elza observes, MoveOn.org did send e-mails to its members encouraging them to attend *Sicko* during its opening weekend to boost its box office.

But *Sicko* also shows Moore shifting gears in significant ways. In part because he solicited stories of health care run amuck, he builds the film on the accounts of Americans denied insurance and medical care, people who tell their own stories as he listens. If this replicates the time-honored documentary practice of focusing sympathetically on the victim that the John Grierson British documentary movement pioneered, Moore also includes among those interviewed not only widows (such as the hospital worker) who indict the insurance companies who denied their family members coverage, but also Becky Malke, a whistle-blower who displays an aroused conscience the rest of the insurance industry has yet to demonstrate. It is Malke who explains that she was paid to keep people from getting treatment, and that in health insurance lingo, a "medical loss" refers to money spent on a patient to help her get well. (One widow raises the specter of racism in the denial of treatment to her African American husband.) There are fewer ambush interviews with corporate representatives than we expect in a Moore film, largely because the insurance and pharmaceutical companies were wary of speaking with Moore once they learned of the film's creation.

Another departure resides in the fact that *Sicko*'s critique of health care in America is less partisan than Moore's previous films. Though its first clip contains Bush's celebrated campaign misspeak, "Too many ob-gyns aren't able to practice their love with women all across this country," this footage is more of a quick reference back to *Fahrenheit 9/11*, which ended with Bush's struggle with the "Fool me once / fool me twice" adage. The opening with Bush is also the kind of satiric appetizer that opens *Bowling for Columbine* with a few seconds from an NRA campaign film ("The NRA has produced the following film. Let's have a look at it"). True, a subsequent sequence astoundingly replays a recording of President Nixon conferring with Bob Erlichman about Robert Kaiser's proposal to set up health care businesses (HMOs) that maximize profits for insurance companies; Moore then shows footage of Nixon announcing the new policy the following day. Moore also briefly shows the Bush administration's indifference to the issue, and highlights former, "mother-loving" Congressman Billy Tauzin's advocacy for the health insurance industry while in Congress, and then taking a job as its chief lobbyist when out of Congress. But another sequence shows how Hillary Clinton failed to create health care reform in the early 1990s and subsequently accepted contributions from the health care industry. In other words, Moore takes pains to point out that legislators of both parties have failed to reform the health industry. We might also note that there have been several commentaries from health industry experts who report, barely concealing their surprise, that Moore's treatment of the issue was overwhelmingly accurate.[10] The Cuba sequence aside, at first blush, *Sicko* seems to be Moore's most mature film yet; it is certainly his least comical.

In publicizing *Sicko* prior to its June 2007 premiere, Moore commented at a press conference that he is now part of the mainstream, not because he has changed his positions on various social and political issues, but because America has caught up with him.[11] He listed each of his major films and their fierce critique of America's politics, economic system, and cultural values. Indeed, GM and the entire automotive industry still struggle for viability (now two decades after *Roger & Me*'s premiere); Larry King invited Moore on his show in spring 2008 to discuss the automotive industry's bailout based on his expertise as a longtime Flint resident and the maker of *Roger & Me.* The April 2007 shootings at Virginia Tech and the all-too-many shootings since, only renew the sense of urgency about gun violence that inspired *Bowling for Columbine.* The Wall Street meltdown and bailouts of fall 2008 through spring 2009, including GM's declaration of bankruptcy, demonstrate the ongoing endless greed and conservative-inspired lax government regulation of America's banking and investment sectors that Moore mocked in his TV series.

As this list shows, the more liberal branch of the American mainstream has only further endorsed many—certainly by no means all—of the views Moore expressed in his films through June 2007. During the 2008 presidential primaries and the general election, candidates took health care reform seriously—even if few candidates advocated the kind of government-directed, universal coverage Moore advocated in *Sicko.*[12] (The fall 2009 story of Rocky Mountain Health Plan's denial of insurance to 17 pound, 4-month-old Alex Lange on the grounds that he was "too fat" is another example of the health insurance absurditites Moore examined in that film.) Most powerfully, of course, after 2005's Hurricane Katrina, a majority of Americans embraced the view of George W. Bush advanced in *Fahrenheit 9/11*—as an arrogant, incompetent, warmongering, out-of-touch president who had damaged the core principles of American democracy and the worldwide reputation of the United States. Major books such as Frank Rich's *The Greatest Story Ever Sold,* as well as countless journalistic exposes of the Iraq war, corroborate the 2004 film's accusations against the Bush administration.[13] Moore is not *the* or even *a* primary reason for this shift in American attitudes—the changing demographics of eligible voters is a far more forceful factor—yet the prescience of Moore's views remains striking: i.e., his undeniable assertions that major problems abide and flourish in American society, as do the all-too-numerous ways in which the United States fails to live up to its ideals.[14]

In this light, *Capitalism: A Love Story* seems to be a step backwards for Moore. One might argue that economic and social conditions in the United States have not changed enough since Moore's debut in 1989 with *Roger & Me* for him to change tactics and move away from a reliance on what are by now very familiar strategies and rhetorical tropes in his films. In fact, Richard Porton put it best when he wrote that the film "recapitulates (perhaps unwittingly) Moore's Greatest Hits" and that it is "the most poorly structured of all of Moore's features" (http://www.cineaste.com/articles/toronto-international-film-festival-daily-update).

Moore does raise many valuable points in *Capitalism: A Love Story*, which is best characterized as an essay film, along the lines Paul Arthur describes in this volume (highly digressive and with emphasis on Moore himself). The film reminds the viewer of the rampant cronyism that pervaded the federal government in the second half of the twentieth century and continues under President Obama: Donald Regan, President Reagan's Secretary of the Treasury, was Chairman of Merrill Lynch before being tapped for government service and led the massive deregulation of the financial markets of the 1980s that led to the Savings and Loan scandals. Moore brings to light current, obscure examples of predatory business practices: the "dead peasant" life insurance policies taken out by major corporations on young employees that make the employer the sole beneficiary; the "condo vultures" who swoop down on devalued real estate and buy it for half or less of its original value; the juvenile court judge who accepted kickbacks from a private juvenile detention center for sentencing teens guilty of minor offenses to lengthy imprisonment. Moore dwells on the cut wages paid to major airline pilots (courtesy of Congressional testimony by national hero Captain "Sully" Sullenberger) and the low wages paid to regional airline pilots.

There are more familiar rhetorical moves from Moore's previous films. Once again, Moore plays the faux naïve, wondering: "How are these companies able to get away with this?" Or, "I didn't understand how any of this could be legal." There is his use of found footage, in this case scenes from an old Encyclopedia Brittanica film on "Life in Ancient Rome" that Moore uses to suggest that America is an empire in decline; or when Moore speculatively dubs business speak into the mouth of Jesus Christ in a campy educational film ("Go forth and make profits"; "I cannot heal your pre-existing condition"). The film also features Moore's knowing use of film and TV musical references, for example, the theme from Nino Rota's score for Federico Fellini's *Il Bidone* ("The Swindle") when Moore describes his own Flint, Michigan, childhood, and Bernard Herrmann's credit music for Alfred Hitchcock's *Vertigo* (1958) when describing over an assortment of found 1950s footage how victimized Americans were "hypnotized" into believing that capitalism is right.

More seriously, it is striking when Moore visits the Flint AC Spark Plug plant with his dad, who recalls his delight in his co-workers, and when two

Catholic priests tell Moore that capitalism as currently practiced in America is a sin. It is inspiring to see Jonas Salk explain why he never sold the polio vaccine to a pharmaceutical company ("Would you patent the sun?," he asks Edward R. Murrow in an interview). It is heartening to see how Isthmus Engineering is owned by its employees or how Republic Windows and Doors employees recently struck inside their plant until the company's boss agreed to pay them the back pay owned to them. It is powerful to hear FDR speak of a "second bill of rights" (a decent job, a livable wage, an adequate pension, a paid vacation, a good education) before his death. These few exceptions to the rule constitute the only countervailing visions of proper corporate conduct in the film.

Yet Moore provides no serious analysis of what exactly has happened on Wall Street, and his vague appeals to historical strikes or more recent assertions of employee rights prove as ephemeral as getting Kmart to stop selling a certain kind of bullet or as uncertain as his comparisons with health systems abroad. Moore's ironic street theater antics now look tiresome. Anyone knowledgeable about Moore's body of work (particularly his routines about corporate crime in his TV shows or in *Bowling for Columbine*) could predict that he would stage a visit to the New York Stock Exchange, or AIG and Citibank's Manhattan headquarters and try to tape the sidewalk as a crime scene, or try to make a citizen's arrest of the CEOs, or demand a refund of the Federal government's bailout money from late 2008 and early 2009. Unlike *Roger & Me*, *Capitalism: A Love Story* tries to address capitalism as a system; but moments such as these show him reverting to the more personal targets (corporate heads, Charlton Heston) in previous films.

The "greatest hits" strategy in *Capitalism: A Love Story* really hits home when Moore references *Roger & Me* and he reuses his infamous interview in which GM spokesperson Tom Kay admitted that GM would cut thousands of jobs to stay competitive. Referring to GM's June 2009 bankruptcy, Moore comments, "Maybe now they'd listen," and Moore heads to GM headquarters where security officers won't let him come through the main entrance. Corporate America knows who Moore is now, as was powerfully demonstrated when, in *Sicko*, Cigna insurance, threatened by Moore's potential interest, agreed to provide previously denied coverage for two cochlear implants for a child.

Is Moore past his prime? Has he exhausted his ideas for comic documentary filmmaking? Only his future films will provide the answer. Of course, any study of a filmmaker in midcareer cannot pretend to be comprehensive, and this volume is not exhaustive. For example, it does not examine Moore's books. No contributor considers *Canadian Bacon* or *The Big One* in a sustained way, reflecting the critical consensus that these are minor works in the Moore filmography, though not without interest.[15] Rather, in this volume, we pause to assess through a multifaceted lens the Michael Moore phenomenon. His importance to American filmic, political, and social culture simply cannot be denied; neither can the importance of understanding his work so far—and the work that is to come in an increasingly divided America.

Notes

1. http://www.boxofficemojo.com/genres/chart/?id=politicaldoc.htm (accessed April 20, 2010).

2. For some of the attacks on Moore, see David T. Hardy and Jason Clark, *Michael Moore Is a Big Fat Stupid White Man* (New York: ReganBooks, 2004); the trio of 2004 films: Alan Peterson's *Fahrenhype 9/11*, Kevin Knoblock's *Celsius 41.11: The Temperature at Which the Brain Begins to Die*, Bruce Wilson's *Michael Moore Hates America;* and Steven Greenstreet's *This Divided Nation* (2005). The year 2007 saw a cinematic liberal critique of Moore, Rick Caine and Debbie Melnyk's *Manufacturing Dissent*, discussed in the text.

3. These revelations have been reported in the news media but also appear in the film *Manufacturing Dissent* and in Roger Rappaport's *Citizen Moore* (Muskegon, MI: RDR Books, 2007). It is surprising that Roger Smith never revealed this fact before his death in 2008. For some discussion of Moore's impact on the marketplace for theatrical documentary, see Anonymous (roundtable discussion), "The Political Documentary in America Today," *Cinéaste* 30, no. 3 (Summer 2005): 29–37.

4. Participant Productions creates both fictional and documentary films; their 2005 slate included *Murderball, Syriana, North Country;* in 2007, *Jimmy Carter: Man from Plains, Darfur Now, The Kite Runner*, and *Charlie Wilson's War;* in 2008, *Standard Operating Procedure;* and in 2009, *Food, Inc.*

5. For biographies of Mooore, see Emily Schultz, *Michael Moore: A Biography* (New York: ECW, 2005), Jesse Larner's *Forgive Us Our Spins: Michael Moore and the Future of the Left* (New York: Wiley, 2006), and Rappaport's *Citizen Moore.* See also Sergio Rizzo, "Why Less is Still Moore: Celebrity and the Reactive Politics of *Fahrenheit 9/11*," *Film Quarterly* 59, no. 2 (Winter 2005/2006): 32–39. Robert Brent Toplin's *Michael Moore's* Fahrenheit 9/11: *How One Film Divided a Nation* (Lawrence: University Press of Kansas, 2006) is a well-reasoned examination of the controversies Moore's film stirred in 2004.

6. Bill Nichols has formulated and revised his notion of documentary modes of representation in several publications. See his "Voice of Documentary," *Film Quarterly* 36, no. 3 (Spring 1983): 17–30; his chapter "Documentary Modes of Representation" in *Representing Reality: Issues and Concepts in Documentary* (Bloomington: Indiana University Press, 1991), 32–75; the "Performing Documentary" chapter in *Blurred Boundaries: Questions of Meaning in Contemporary Culture* (Bloomington: Indiana University Press, 1994), 92–106; and his "What Types of Documentary Are There?" chapter in his *Introduction to Documentary* (Bloomington: Indiana University Press, 2001), 99–138.

7. For reasons of space, I have omitted my "Documentaphobia and Mixed Modes: Michael Moore's *Roger and Me.*" This essay situates Moore's first film in terms of Bill Nichols's typology of documentary modes of representation, exploring how *Roger & Me* partakes of a variety of established documentary practices—at times appearing highly personal and interactive, at other times presenting a very straightforward analysis of GM's policies and their impact on Flint. I also show why Moore's filmmaking caused so many critics to feel misled by its handling of chronology and uncomfortable with its treatment of on-camera subjects. Interested readers can find the original essay in *The Journal of Film and Video* 46, no. 1 (Fall 1994): 1–17; it was reprinted and abridged in *Documenting the Documentary,* ed. Barry K. Grant and Jeanette Sloniowski (Detroit: Wayne State University Press, 1998), 397–415.

8. Tetzlaff's reading of *Fahrenheit 9/11* is congruent with Moore's own statements about the film at the time of its release. When asked, as he repeatedly was, whether the film was propaganda, Moore gave some variation on the following answer shown in *Slacker Uprising* (2008):

> How much were we propagandized by the Bush administration? And by our mainstream national media? Over and over and over again. What if you had done your real job? What if you had asked the hard questions and demanded the evidence about this war? . . .
>
> My movie exists to counter the managed, manufactured news which is essentially a propaganda arm of the Bush administration. My movies are the antipropaganda. The only thing sad about that is that people have to pay eight or nine dollars to come to a movie theater, get a babysitter, to learn things they should be getting for free sitting on the couch and eating Tostitos.

Moore made similar remarks in June 2004 on the CBS morning news talk show, much to the delight of Jon Stewart, who admiringly excerpted the clip on *The Daily Show* that month.

9. See film producer Jon Pierson's open letter to Moore occasioned by both the release of *Sicko* and the availability of *Manufacturing Dissent;* see "Indiewire First Person: Jon Pierson, An Open Letter to Michael Moore," June 29, 2007, http://www.indiewire.com/people/2007/06/‹rst_person_jo_1.html. Thanks to Paul Arthur for alerting me to its existence. Pierson's criticism of Moore is notable especially because it was Pierson who secured Moore's distribution deal with Warner Bros. for *Roger & Me.*

10. See, for example, Jonathan Cohn, "Schticko; It's no fun to agree with Michael Moore," *New Republic* 237, no. 4816 (July 2, 2007):18–19; and A. Chris Gajilan, "Analysis: 'Sicko' Numbers Mostly Accurate; More Context Needed," Friday, June 29, 2007, http://www.cnn.com/2007/HEALTH/06/28/sicko.fact.check/index.html.

11. See S. James Snyder, "Michael Moore: 'I'm Mainstream Now,'" Wednesday, June 20, 2007, http://www.time.com/time/arts/article/0,8599,1635192,00.html.

12. See for example, Robin Toner, "2008 Candidates Vote to Overhaul U.S. Health Care," *New York Times,* July 6, 2007, sec. 1, A7.

13. *The Greatest Story Ever Sold: The Decline and Fall of Truth in Bush's America* (New York: Penguin, 2007).

14. See Paul Krugman, "Disaster and Denial," *New York Times,* December 14, 2009:

A29, on the failure of the federal government to pass effective regulations for the financial markets in 2009, one year after the many meltdowns of a year before.

It's worth briefly considering *Slacker Uprising*, a decidedly minor effort from Moore, in light of his claims that he is now part of the American mainstream. The film follows Moore on his five week old-style barnstorming tour of college campuses prior to election day 2004. As an early title explains: "Fearing four more years of George W. Bush, a cadre of rock musicians, hip-hop artists and citizen groups went out on the road with their own 'shadow campaigns.' To save John Kerry and the Democrats from themselves. This the story of one filmmaker's failed attempt to turn things around."

The film contains some very humorous moments. Michigan's Republican Party tried to sue Moore for bribery for handing out "a change of underwear" and ramen noodle packets at rallies to any "slackers" who promised to vote in the election. Moore created some mock campaign ads for the Republican Party (if Max Cleland was a true patriot, he would have sacrificed his one remaining limb while serving in Vietnam; if John Kerry were, he would have died in Vietnam). He offered pretend compassion for the Republicans who protest his campus appearances ("Here's the bonus, my Republican brothers and sisters . . . even though many of us in here see you as a deviant form of behavior, Republicanism, right-wingism, we'll still let you marry each other"). Moore's campus rallies are often enhanced by the presence of major rock stars and bands (R.E.M., Eddy Vedder, and even Joan Baez) who perform. Yet, the tone of *Slacker Uprising* is such that if a viewer did not know the outcome of the 2004 election, one would think George W. Bush was removed from office. This is perhaps one key reason why the film never gained a theatrical release. Another is that even before the 2008 election, the film was old news. A third would be that most of *Slacker Uprising* is simply very boring.

15. *Canadian Bacon*'s satire of American politics and militarism combined elements of Stanley Kubrick's 1964 *Dr. Strangelove* (Rip Torn as a power mad general; absurd dialogue in the War Room; Alan Alda as an ineffectual, shallow, unpopular, and opportunistic president) with Moore's own signature themes and characters. Here, his *Roger & Me* persona is assumed by comedian John Candy in one of the latter's final films. *Canadian Bacon* also features Moore's ironic use of a mix of songs, such as Tex Ritter's "God Bless American Again," which plays over the opening credits, and Candy and friends singing the repetitive refrain (which is all they can remember) of Bruce Springsteen's "Born in the U.S.A" as they drive to rescue a friend in Canada. Also typical of Moore, the film begins by focusing on unemployment before moving on to dramatize the impact of the military-industrial complex on blue collar residents of Niagra Falls and the nation as a whole (anticipating the focus of *Bowling for Columbine*). Shot by master leftist cinematographer Haskell Wexler of *Medium Cool* (1968) fame and featuring countless jokes about Canada's pacifism and irrelevance, as well as cameos by comedians such as James Belushi and Dan Ackyroyd, *Canadian Bacon* was a box office flop, with an over-the-top final sequence in which characters race to prevent a nuclear launch.

Yet *Canadian Bacon* does have its share of authentically funny scenes and lines of dialogue. It is also worth recalling that its scenario of a president using unprovoked war to raise his approval ratings anticipates that of Barry Levinson's *Wag the Dog* (1997). Here, an American president used a Hollywood producer and the media to create an Albanian war to distract Americans' attention from his recent sex scandal, revealed just days before an election. Levinson's film was itself released in January 1998 as Americans first learned of Bill Clinton's sexual encounters with Monica Lewinsky. Moreover, 1999's *South Park: Bigger, Longer and Uncut* would more successfully riff on American disdain for—and aggression against—its neighbor to the North. If Moore did not spoof these subjects with success, he certainly created scenarios that other cinematic satirists would develop more fully and profitably.

The 1997 release *The Big One* reiterates *Roger & Me*'s pro-labor politics in the face of the very unemployment his book *Downsize This* protested. It also includes Moore's persistent confrontations with corporate press relations people who command his crew to turn off their cameras and leave the grounds and who refuse to give Moore access to CEOs (of the Leaf Corporation [makers of the Payday candy bar], Johnson Controls, Pillsbury, and Proctor and Gamble) as well as then Wisconsin governor Tommy Thompson. Interspersed with his book talks are conversations with celebrities (Garrison Keillor, Cheap Trick's Rick Neilsen) and excerpts of his funny observations about Republican candidates ("Steve Forbes must be an alien since he never blinks"); corporate America ("We need to turn crack over to General Motors, 'cause they'll really screw it up. We'll eliminate crack in five years if we just turn it over to General Motors"); and giving America a makeover, renaming it "The Big One." As in *Roger & Me*, Moore is front and center in the film and often self-mocking (not least through his use of dramatic theme music such as the *Peter Gunn* theme song as he approaches a corporate headquarters or paranoid workers). The rapport Moore creates with working class Americans, as discussed by Gaylyn Studlar in her essay, is on full display here, as are the enthusiastic crowds who greet Moore in many cities. While the efficacy of Moore's actions can be questioned, the newly unemployed or struggling employed whom he encounters in the film clearly appreciate his sympathy and his public stance against corporate America. Moreover, unlike the hapless residents of Flint, Michigan, in *Roger & Me*, a film that emphasizes the obsolescence of the labor movement, employees of several Borders Books branches in *The Big One* celebrate their unionization in the course of the film.

The most discussed aspect of *The Big One*, however, was Moore's climatic and unanticipated meeting with Phil Knight, CEO of Nike Shoes. Moore insists that Knight shut down the Indonesian factories that employ and woefully underpay Indonesian teenage girls and open a factory in Flint, Michigan, instead. While Knight ultimately agrees to contribute $10,000 to Flint's schools, he refuses to be Moore's "man of conscience," different from other CEOs, by opening a factory in Flint (Knight remains unconvinced that Americans, even unemployed Flint residents, will really take jobs making shoes). Here we see not only the reiteration of Moore's efforts, dating back to *Roger & Me* and continued in his TV shows, to meet with corporate leaders who usually shun him but also the prototype for Moore's confrontation with Charlton Heston in *Bowling for Columbine*. As in *Slacker Uprising*, the film is self-congratulatory at the same time that it aims to empower workers throughout America.

The Left's Biggest Star: Michael Moore as Commercial Auteur

SERGIO RIZZO

Like no one else before him, Michael Moore has managed to turn documentary filmmaking into Hollywood gold. Warner Bros. paid him $3 million for his first film, the pathbreaking documentary *Roger & Me* (1989), which set box office records for a documentary film. During the 1990s Moore continued to successfully market the persona he introduced in *Roger & Me* through print and television: penning three best-sellers and producing an Emmy-winning television series. This success was dwarfed, however, by the Academy Award–winning *Bowling for Columbine* (2002), which became the highest grossing documentary of all time, $21 million, only to be surpassed by *Fahrenheit 9/11* (2004), which earned the staggering figure of $119 million domestically and a little over $100 million internationally. After the reelection of George W. Bush in 2004, some commentators wondered if Moore's star would start to dim. However, the financial and critical success of the Oscar-nominated *Sicko* (2007) would suggest otherwise. His most recent film, *Capitalism: A Love Story* (2009), while not matching *Sicko,* did well at the box office and with the critics, giving further proof of the filmmaker's enduring popularity and bankable reputation.

Despite the fame and fortune Moore has earned as a director, it is difficult to take him seriously as an auteur—the notion sounds like an invitation to one of his trademark pranks. On rare occasions he tries to cast himself in an auteurish light. One example comes from an article on his website responding to Pauline Kael's negative review of *Roger & Me.* After claiming indifference to her opinion—"It was OK with me that she didn't like the film, and it didn't bother me that she didn't like the point I was making, or even how I was making it"—

he attacks her as a "deadly serious historical revisionist"[1] and attempts to explain away her criticisms as the result of her personal pique caused by his refusal to send a videotape of the film for her to preview. For all her flaws, though, Moore still wants the famous—and by now dead—critic's approval:

> She saw herself as the champion of the independent filmmaker, and always wanted to be the one to take the risk and be first in endorsing a brave new work like *Nashville* or *Taxi Driver.* Had she been treated with the respect she deserved and been shown *Roger and Me* early on, it's clear from her writings that mine was EXACTLY the kind of film she would have been behind a hundred percent.[2]

It is hard to tell which is more graceless, his response to Kael's review or his attempt to insert himself into the pantheon of American auteurs, represented by the works of Robert Altman and Martin Scorsese. Luckily for Moore, his awkward assertions of artistry are overshadowed by his easy recognition as, in his words, the "schlump in a ball cap"[3] whose political filmmaking eschews any aesthetic pretensions.

Ironically, it is Moore's political opponents who have had the most success in highlighting his craft as a filmmaker, if a "disingenuous" one, as the Republican senator and 2008 presidential candidate John McCain memorably labeled him during the 2004 presidential campaign. For some of Moore's supporters, he inspires comparisons to Charlie Chaplin or is appreciated in terms of innovative documentary filmmakers such as Ross McElwee, Kevin and Pierce Rafferty, or Errol Morris. However, his polemical antics with a camera discourage many from seeing his work in terms of the auteur, with its connotations of artistry and careful craftsmanship. For Moore, the camera as sword is still mightier than *la camera stylo.*

Moore's style has much more to do with television than film, satirically bringing to the big screen the pioneering tele-journalism of shows like *60 Minutes* and its bastardized offspring.[4] A common distinction made about film and TV is that film elevates its subject matter with an audience that gazes up at its larger-than-life figures, while TV's "candid camera" cuts everyone down to size, especially the rich and powerful. Despite his reputation as a filmmaker, Moore's ethos is much more suited to TV's way of seeing the world. But the medium Moore uses is almost irrelevant to many of his fans on America's beleaguered liberal Left. For them, the most relevant comparison is not to Chaplin or more contemporary star directors, but to media personalities like Rush Limbaugh who succeed, by whatever means necessary, in getting their message out. As Chris Lehane, the Democratic strategist hired by Moore to handle the publicity for *Fahrenheit 9/11*, expressed it, "'There's a tremendous appetite among Democrats to have someone say the things that have been bothering them for the last couple years . . . [Moore] and this movie have come along at a time when people are looking for someone to get up there and say something interesting. He's filled that void.'"[5]

THE BUSINESS OF BEING AN AUTEUR

Before passing judgment on Moore as failed auteur, though, the concept of the auteur itself should be examined. Part of the reason for the difficulty of thinking of Moore in terms of the auteur can be traced to a romantic sense of moviemaking as art, canonized by the *politiques des auteurs* and the French New Wave.[6] Radical in its day, the conception of the director as the source of artistic coherence and meaning in a film seems increasingly conservative in the face of poststructuralism and its deconstruction of the author. Furthermore, the notion of the director as an artist able to imprint his or her personal vision on films in spite of the commercial and popular interests of filmmaking has been overtaken by a new economy of the image whereby the auteur becomes, in the words of Timothy Corrigan, "a commercial strategy for organizing audience reception."[7]

Corrigan traces the commercialization of the auteur to the film industry's reliance upon the blockbuster along with the new spectator-oriented technologies it uses to distribute its product, namely VCRs and cable television. One could now add DVDs and the Internet. The new technologies diminish the critical status of the auteur as expressive artist who fights (un)successfully either within or outside the system. The new spectator-oriented technologies unite both the blockbuster and the independent film as the industry strives for "shareablility"[8] between movie theater and TV. "Within this climate and under these conditions," Corrigan argues, "the different, the more peculiar, the controversial enter the marketplace not as an opposition but as a revision and invasion of an audience market defined as too large and diverse by the dominant blockbusters."[9] Far from the death of the auteur, the commercialization of the auteur has made the concept more important than it ever was before. As part of a corporate production and marketing strategy of "decentralized control,"[10] a film company—whether it is a major studio or a lesser satellite—uses the concept of the auteur to hail its audience, much as the genre concept has done and continues to do, thereby spreading the risk of investment and enhancing the illusion of consumer choice.

Within the new "business of being an auteur," Corrigan further distinguishes between two types of the star director: the "commercial auteur and the auteur of commerce."[11] The commercial auteur includes a wide range of director-stars, from Sylvester Stallone at one end to Lina Wertmüller at the other. Corrigan passes over this group in favor of a select few auteurs of commerce, represented by Francis Ford Coppola, German theorist and filmmaker Alexander Kluge, and exiled Chilean filmmaker Raoul Ruiz. While I don't intend to argue that Moore is an auteur along the lines of Coppola, Kluge, or Ruiz, he can be usefully examined in terms of Corrigan's first group, the commercial auteur, whom the critic ignores as a less "intriguing variation"[12] of the auteur of commerce. Like other commercial auteurs, Moore's celebrity as an auteur "produces and promotes texts that invariably exceed the movie itself, both before and after its release."[13] According to Corrigan's main thesis, these texts work to prepackage the film, as in "a Michael Moore movie," helping it to address its segment of the viewing audience across various distribution methods: movie theater, cable, home video, and Internet. However, some of these texts that work to advance Moore's commercial auteurism seem to have their own inherent instability that threatens to, if not shatter, at least unsettle the coherence of his authorial expression and stardom.

THERE'S NO PLACE LIKE HOME

The first text to examine, then, is Michael Moore before he became "Michael Moore." One of the major motifs in Moore's public biography is his hometown of Flint, Michigan. Using his personal ties to Flint, Moore not only attempts to reclaim, for the Left, middle-American turf that had been abandoned by the antiwar and counterculture movements of the sixties. Soon after *Roger & Me* came out, in an article written for the *New York Times*, "'Roger' and I, Off to Hollywood and Home to Flint," Moore displays some of the key elements in his identification with Flint. As he recounts his 110-city tour to promote his film, the archetypal contrast of self-obsessed and wealthy L.A. with Midwestern and depressed Flint helps him depict himself as a man of the people and the ultimate Hollywood outsider. "All of these events seemed to point to an obvious conclusion," he says, "I should have stayed in Flint, Michigan, my hometown and the subject of my 1989 film, *Roger and Me.*"[14] Despite his better judgment, and against his will, it seems, he leaves the terra firma of his native Flint only because "four studios wanted to distribute [his] movie."[15] His identification with Flint helps Moore present himself as an "independent filmmaker." Toward this end, he relates two conversations with studio executives. One says to Moore, "I'm surprised GM hasn't had you shot!" But then, as if to prove that he is not afraid to bite the hand that pets him, Moore tells another executive who brags about his studio's top quality films, "'C'mon . . . ninety percent of the stuff you guys make is just junk.'"[16] Opposed to the financial interests of both General Motors and Hollywood, Moore defines himself as noncommercial while seeking Hollywood's approval and money.

Conservative critics attack Moore's attempt to establish a personal link with Flint by pointing out that he actually grew up not in Flint, but nearby in the more suburban Davison, as though catching him in the Big Lie. However, considering the facts of Moore's upbringing and early career in the area, this criticism is, at best, rather pedantic. His father worked on the line at the AC Spark Plug factory, and his uncle, as Moore proudly mentions in *Roger & Me,* participated in the historic GM Flint Sit-down Strike of 1936. Even in high school, Moore was interested in local politics, winning a seat on the school board, making him the youngest member ever to sit on the Flint City Council. After high school, he remained in the area, organizing antinuclear protests and rock concerts, and briefly worked as a public radio correspondent. At the age of 22, he started a left-wing paper, the *Flint Voice,* where he worked for 10 years as its editor and effectively increased its circulation and scope as it grew to become the *Michigan Voice.* It was also at the *Voice* where Moore met a figure who would play an important role in the working-class persona he would develop, a "shop rat" at the GM auto-assembly factory by the name of Ben Hamper. Hamper, featured in *Roger & Me,* with Moore's encouragement wrote a series of articles for the *Voice* that went on to become a best seller, *Rivethead: Tales from the Assembly Line.* In it he describes Moore's local celebrity: "I was familiar with the guy. So was anyone in Flint who had one eye half open. Moore was constantly hurling himself into the midst of some trenchant uproar. You would see him on television, hear him raisin' hell on the radio, read about him causin' a ruckus down at a meeting of City Council."[17] Given his history of activity in the community, if anyone has the right to claim herself or himself a citizen of Flint, it would be Moore.

However, Moore's years as a journalist in Flint are easily overlooked. One doubts he is bothered by this fact, but if he were, he would have himself to blame. More often than not, when he mentions his prior work as a journalist, it is his dismissal after a brief four-month stint as the editor of *Mother Jones* in San Francisco, and not the successful years at the *Michigan Voice.* In response to being fired from *Mother Jones,* Moore filed a suit charging wrongful termination and asking for $2 million in damages; he eventually settled with the magazine's insurance company for $58,000, some of which was used as seed money for *Roger & Me.* The role of *Mother Jones* in his move from left-wing journalist to commercial auteur is a standard part of his biography, although Moore's account uses different terms and misses the full irony of the situation. In his version, his apparent defeat at *Mother Jones* lays the foundation for a comedic peripeteia that ends with his personal and political redemption—*Roger & Me.*

From his vantage point as a successful filmmaker and emerging spokesman for America's liberal Left, he can look back on his dismissal from *Mother Jones* as a point of pride. "'I was too left for *Mother Jones,*'" he told one reviewer for the *New York Times.* "'Can you imagine being too left for *Mother Jones?*'"[18] This assertion of a leftism to the left of *Mother Jones* is at odds with denials like the following: "But I didn't come from the left. I never read anything by Karl Marx—I'm embarrassed to admit that. My politics were formed from sitting in Flint, Michigan, in the shadow of General Motors."[19] In fact, however, the two claims are just different sides of the same working-class coin minted in Flint. On the one hand, he uses his working-class identity to position himself to the left of his educated and well-heeled opponents in the alternative liberal press—people like the owner of *Mother Jones,* Adam Hochschild, who fired Moore and whom Moore characterized as a "liberal millionaire."[20] On the other hand, he uses his working-class identity to avoid the label of liberalism, or at least the negative connotations it evokes in the popular imagination: intellectualism, effeminacy, privilege, elitism, and so on.

Moore's dismissal from *Mother Jones* and his lawsuit in response to it caused such a stir in the alternative liberal press that it landed him briefly on the mainstream pages of the *New York Times.* The *Times* article, "Radical Magazine Removes Editor, Setting Off a Widening Political Debate,"[21] comes with a picture of Moore that provides striking visual evidence of his persona before he became the Left's lovable "schlump in a ball cap." He takes the picture *sans chapeau,* and his hair is cut at a respectable medium length. Glaring into the camera, he sits at his desk behind an electric typewriter. A desk lamp above his shoulder throws an austere light onto the right side of his face and body, leaving the room behind him in the shadows, with his right elbow on the desk and his hand covering his mouth and chin. He looks every bit like an angry young man fully engaged in the sectarian warfare of the left wing's version of Grub Street. As he tells the reporter, he has "no intention of backing down."[22]

This picture can be usefully contrasted with the one he took for the *New York Times* article mentioned earlier, "'Roger' and I, Off to Hollywood and Home to Flint," in which he describes his promotional tour for his new film *Roger & Me.* Gone is the editor of a "radical" magazine posing as an angry young man. In the latter picture, taken four years later, he exhibits all the charismatic and irreverent humor that becomes his trademark. He wears a baseball cap that, like his plaid shirt underneath, is too casual for the jacket he wears. His hair is longer and sticks out messily from underneath his cap. With the city of Flint in the background, he poses looking at and casually leaning on the statue of a bowler-hatted W. C. Durant, the founder of General Motors. Together they resemble a Laurel and Hardy comedy team. In his earlier picture as the radical editor at his typewriter, his glasses connote seriousness and journalistic professionalism. Here, as he pokes fun at GM's monument to its founder, they add to his humorous appearance. While the professionalism and anger of the radical editor disappear from view, it is important to remember that the anger, at least, is not far from the surface. Critics frequently mention the anger that is behind Moore's political humor, as does Moore himself: "The best comedians used to be the people who were the angriest. Their humor was the flip side of their anger. Chaplin, the Marx Brothers, Lenny Bruce, Mort Sahl."[23]

In his metamorphosis from radical editor to "working-class clown,"[24] a central prop is his ever-changing baseball cap. Moore's account of its eponymous origin—found in his foreword to *Rivethead,* the book written by his autoworker friend Ben Hamper—connects the cap's discovery to his dismissal from *Mother Jones.* The version of his dismissal in the book's foreword, one that he gives elsewhere, pits him as a defender of the working class against the owner of *Mother Jones,* a limousine liberal who fires him for publishing some of Hamper's proletarian "smut."[25] To be sure, Moore's account is not uncontested by Hochschild and others at *Mother Jones.* In fact, even Hamper points out problems with Moore's account.[26] However, the main point here is that Moore portrays himself as a defender of what he calls, quoting the owner of *Mother Jones,* "'working class reality.'"[27]

After losing his job as editor of *Mother Jones,* Moore returns to Flint in a funk. While at Hamper's home, he discovers a ball cap that "summed up [his] life at that moment" and that goes on to become his auteurial signature: "During the first day of shooting, I happened to wear Hamper's 'Out for Trout' hat while on camera. To maintain consistency in the filming during the following days, I had to keep wearing that damned hat. That ball cap soon became the symbol for the film [*Roger & Me*], and Hamper was not to have it on his balding head again."[28] One might wonder about the consistency of a film that depends on whether or not its director wore a cap. Among other things, it confirms the centrality of Moore's image to the conception of *Roger & Me*. Furthermore, as "the symbol for the film," it becomes a talisman that neither the cap's lender nor borrower can own. It represents Moore's indebtedness to Hamper for the working-class persona he adopts, an authorial "borrowing" Moore can't fully acknowledge or repay. The cap, along with its many reiterations, also becomes one of those texts that precedes and follows Moore's films—a powerful metonym for the totalizing and reductive image of the working class that Moore promotes and that, in turn, promotes "Michael Moore."

Writing for *Time* magazine, Richard Schickel was one of the few reviewers of *Roger & Me* in the popular press to take note of Moore's professional background. In addition, he uses it to question Moore's persona as well as the premise of the film: "But wait a minute! Far from being a hick, Moore is an experienced professional journalist who knows perfectly well that getting in to see the chairman of anything without an appointment is virtually impossible."[29] It is true that Moore mentions early on in the film that he returns to Flint because he lost his job as the editor of a magazine in San Francisco that found his slant too working class. But this acknowledgment (whose premise in itself is debatable) is embedded in the regional stereotype of California's surreal café politics versus the "real" working-class politics of the Midwestern rust belt. Furthermore, his journalistic background fades from view as his lost job merges with the plight of the many others who have lost their (working-class) jobs in Flint. The filmmaker's lost job becomes part of the film's "reflexive abnegation," as Paul Arthur terms it in his essay "Jargons of Authenticity (Three American Moments)."[30] Through Moore's "trope of technical awkwardness, feigned inadequacy and victimization defined against the ruthless instrumentality of General Motors—and, by extension, Hollywood,"[31] Arthur argues, he creates the film's sense of social solidarity. However, the sense of solidarity one finds in *Roger & Me*—the kind one finds in a movie theater—is significantly different from the kind of community involvement and political engagement Moore sought to establish as editor of the *Flint Voice*.

Moore has two general ways of asserting his personal connection to Flint. One is casual and humorous, stressing the all-American quirkiness of his upbringing there. So, for example, on his website advertising *The Official Fahrenheit 9/11 Reader,* under a heading entitled "About the Author," it says: "He was an Eagle Scout, a seminarian, the first eighteen-year-old elected to public office. He has never bowled over 200."[32] The other way uses an angry tone and a sense of injustice, which at times can sound preachy and overdramatic, making one wonder if there isn't something to the questions Moore's critics raise about his blue-collar identity. Moore displays just how overwrought he can get in an article entitled "Letter from Flint, Michigan," written for a small left-wing publication, *Peacework,* in which he relates the tragic story of Kayla Rolland, a six-year-old girl shot to death in her first-grade classroom in the Flint Beecher School District by a six-year-old boy with a semiautomatic gun:

> How much more can my hometown take? How much more do the people we love have to suffer? How much? How much?? HOW MUCH!
>
> Isn't it enough that thousands of lives in Flint have been wrecked, destroyed by the greed of General Motors? Isn't it enough that my wife and I and thousands of others who love our home—love it more than any of you will ever know—have had to leave Flint in the past 20 years to find work far from family and friends.[33]

There is no doubting the sincerity of Moore's outrage, but equating his and his wife's decision to leave Flint, which was essentially a career move, with the desperate exodus of laid-off autoworkers—so memorably depicted in *Roger & Me*—seems farfetched. This sort of exaggeration has less to do with Moore's concern to rebut critics who question his authenticity, although the assertion that he and his wife love their town "more than any of you will ever know" certainly does that as well. It stems from the role of Flint in the construction of Moore as an auteur-star.

In his blockbuster *Bowling for Columbine,* Moore returns to the story of Kayla Rolland, and, as in the article for *Peacework,* she becomes part of Moore's use of Flint as symbol of his personal authenticity.[34] In particular, he uses her story in his confrontation with the iconic actor and National Rifle Association spokesman Charlton Heston. Through Rolland's story, Moore brings Flint into direct confrontation with Heston. He introduces Rolland's story in the film by saying, "Just as he did after the Columbine shooting, Charlton Heston showed up in Flint at a big pro-gun rally."[35] In this way, Rolland's death allows Moore to symbolically confront Heston on Moore's home turf. Moore uses Flint in this manner in other films. In the *Big One,* he urges Nike's chairman Phil Knight to open a factory in his depressed hometown. Although he doesn't get the factory, he succeeds in twisting Knight's arm, as he puts it, to match his own $10,000 contribution to "the kids of Flint."[36] More recently in *Fahrenheit 9/11,* Moore uses his hometown to illustrate the domestic impact of the war with Iraq, comparing the effect of the auto industry's abandonment of Flint to terrorism. In one of the movie's more effective scenes, high school students talk about the efforts of military recruiters to enlist them, and cameras follow two marine recruiters as they work a strip mall hustling low-income residents. Moore's return to Flint also introduces Lila Lipscomb, the mother who loses her son in the war and serves in some ways as the emotional climax of the film. In his following film, *Sicko* (2007), Flint all but disappears, and its greatly diminished role seems to relate to the less adversarial persona Moore adopts in the film. Flint does, however, return with a vengeance in *Capitalism: A Love Story,* most notably as Moore reuses his *Roger & Me* interview with GM spokesperson Tom Kay about cutting thousands of jobs to keep competitive. Moore also visits with his father the grounds of the AC Spark Plug factory where Mr. Moore speaks lovingly of the solidarity he felt with his co-workers during his more than 33 years of work there. Moore's dependence on Flint goes beyond the essentially opportunistic and narcissistic function that some critics ascribe to it. Rather, Flint is a product of Moore's commercial auteurism—one of those texts, with a life of its own, that personalizes the politics of his movies.

"THE LEFT'S BIGGEST STAR"

Up to this point, I have used Corrigan's notion of the commercial auteur but ignored his privileging of the "directorial interview" as a space where the auteur "can engage and disperse his or her own organizing agency as auteur."[37] Instead, under the more prosaic rubric of autobiography—and, more narrowly, Moore's use of his hometown of Flint—I have examined a variety of cinematic and noncinematic texts Moore has created to "disperse" his authorial biography. Now I would like to draw upon Richard Dyer's important work *Stars* in order to consider Moore's persona in terms of stardom per se—beyond his designation as a *director*-star.[38] Like Dyer, I will develop a closer reading of Moore's persona in his films, and I continue to use a variety of "extra-cinematic" texts (publicity, speeches, interviews, his other writings, etc.) to construct a holistic critique. In addition, with a star like Moore whose "being" in front of the camera as a director is so crucial to his stardom, the distinction between his celebrity as director and on-screen personality or "actor" is difficult, if not impossible, to make. Nonetheless, while I recognize that the sources of his celebrity are fluid and often hard to distinguish, his stardom seems to conform to some of the ideological rules that empower and constrain all stars.

Stardom divides Moore, like other stars, into two people that are simultaneously the same and different—the person Moore was before stardom, and who he is after stardom. One may also distinguish the private Moore from the public Moore. The star's paradoxical identity dramatizes the paradox of identity in general. Using the star's biography, we try to "make sense" of the star (and ourselves) in two ways. The star is either viewed in terms of how much she or he has changed or hasn't changed because of stardom or how much her or his private life is in accord with the public image she or he projects. Since he is "the left's biggest star,"[39] however, the details of Moore's biography and personal life are immediately political. So the signs of his success—living on the Upper West Side of Manhattan, sending his daughter to private school, preferring limos to taxis, flying first class, hiring spokespeople and, even, bodyguards—become matters of concern to political commentators on both the right and the left, although for different reasons. And Moore's own attempts to answer questions about the apparent contradictions of left-wing stardom are less than satisfactory. Annoyed by those on the left who question how he spends his money, Moore claims the lofty desire to "bring back to the left the sense that pleasure is O.K., that self-indulgence isn't always evil."[40]

By and large, but with significant exceptions, the mainstream and liberal press has been less motivated than Moore's conservative critics to examine his working-class persona. Besides the usual testimonials from friends that success hasn't changed him, reviewers of his movies validate his filmmaking in terms of his working-class authenticity. Stuart Klawans, for example, writing a review of *Bowling for Columbine* for *The Nation*, talks of Moore's "skill at uncovering people's attitudes" that is "embedded in his working class bearing."[41]

In contrast to positive assessments and testimonials about Moore's "working class bearing," there are persistent rumors and criticisms questioning his working-class image. Jon Ronson, writing for *Sight and Sound*, reports the rumor that when visiting London, Moore would insist on being put up at the Ritz, but also required his hosts to book him a cheaper hotel nearby so that when he met journalists they would believe he was staying in humbler circumstances.[42] Throughout Moore's career his working-class background and lifestyle have come under close scrutiny by conservative critics eager to paint him as a poseur or limousine liberal. While his conservative critics are seeking to blunt his message, one shouldn't dismiss their evidence out of hand. Matt Labash, writing for

The Weekly Standard, provides a wry and well-researched exposé that quotes people Moore grew up with, coworkers, business associates, and former friends to good effect, debunking Moore's working-class image.[43] However, like media stars on the right who have suffered scandals exposing them to charges of hypocrisy—Rush Limbaugh (abusing painkillers) and Bill O'Reilly (sexual harassment) are two notorious examples—Moore's detractors, from either the Right or the Left, seem to make little headway in diminishing his popularity. Instead, his detractors and defenders fall into antistar and prostar camps that can only see him as either "fake" or "real." Neither point of view disturbs his commercial performance as an auteur-star; if anything, they reinforce it.

Both the negative and positive views of Moore's "working class bearing" are a function of the star's charisma. In Dyer's reading of a political star, Jane Fonda, he shows how the star's charisma acts as a "reconciler of contradictions."[44] In Fonda's case, her charisma—"which evokes extremes of hate as well as love"[45]—allows her to simultaneously signify radical politics and feminism on the one hand and all-American virtues and normalcy on the other. Likewise for Moore—who no less than Fonda provokes extremes of hate as well as love—his charisma allows him to reconcile his contrasting roles as left-wing social critic and all-American regular guy.

More so than in his films, the tension between the two roles becomes apparent in the medium of print. In *Downsize This!* he responds to the right wing's demonizing of Hillary Clinton with a satire that tries to combine feminism with the sexism of a good-old-boy vernacular: "Oh, I can hear the groans now from you guys out there who think I'm nuts for finding Hillary attractive. Well, fuck you. Get some glasses. HILLARY RODHAM IS ONE HOT SHIT-KICKIN' FEMINIST BABE."[46] (A fleetingly brief version of this homage to Hillary's politically informed sex appeal is less awkwardly made in *Sicko* when Moore first begins to recount her efforts to reform health care in the early 1990s.) In *Stupid White Men,* after claiming America is the "Dumbest Country on Earth," he adds the corny and unconvincing disclaimer, "I hate writing these words. I *love* this big lug of a country and the crazy people in it."[47] In contrast to the popular conception of Moore as a star who galvanizes feelings about him—"You either love him or you hate him"—the full ideological utility of his stardom may be its ability to, seemingly, reconcile America's contradictory feelings of love and hate toward itself.

In considering the star's function as a reconciler of contradictions, Dyer discusses Barry King's work on the social significance of the star. King asserts that one of the functions of a star is to reconcile the contrary interests of an industry that seeks to produce films with enough social commentary and controversy to interest and engage viewers while not offending them. King explains that stars help the film industry solve this problem because the star "'converts the opinion expressed in the film to an expression of his [or her] being.'"[48] The star's enactment of the experiences and feelings represented on the screen shifts the question from why such things happen or why people feel that way to the question of what it must be like to have such experiences and feelings. Identifying the political issues raised by a film with a particular star helps both the film's producers and viewers to individualize and depoliticize those issues. Dyer applies King's argument to John Wayne and Jane Fonda, "both stars with obvious political associations, [who] act unavoidably to obscure the political issues they embody simply by demonstrating the life-style of their politics and displaying those political beliefs as an aspect of their personality."[49] While King and Dyer are speaking of fiction film stars, the same argument could be made of Moore's postmodern documentaries, wherein the film becomes as much about the filmmaker as it is about its ostensible subject. Consequently, like other Hollywood stars, Moore absorbs politics as an aspect of his "unique" personality.

A commonplace criticism, especially among conservative commentators, is that Moore's on-screen persona is just shallow egoism and opportunistic self-promotion. Labash is able to put it more humorously than most:

> To pull off such a pose, it takes a relentless breed of self-promoter. While most venerated directors pay homage to those from whom they take their inspiration (Woody Allen: Bergman; DePalma: Hitchcock; Scorsese: Godard), Moore gives his work a self-referential synergy that should have him suing himself for copyright infringement or paying himself for product placement. (Even his wedding invitation contained a guide to *Roger & Me* landmarks.)[50]

Even among those sympathetic to Moore's message and goals are those who complain that his on-screen persona distracts the viewer from the political message of his films. Gary Crowdus, for example, pithily complains that *Roger & Me* could have been focused a "little more on 'Roger' and some what less on 'Me.'"[51] Kevin Mattson goes further in diagnosing the political pitfalls of Moore's presence in his films: "What's odd about [Moore's] sort of engagement, though, is that it avoids the hard work of forming movements that could press for change. No need when Michael Moore, with just his camera, microphone, and baseball cap, can come to the rescue."[52] Along these lines, Larissa

MacFarquhar usefully contrasts Moore's guerrilla filmmaking with the guerrilla theater of the 1960s. She points out that the activism of the 1960s was aimed at changing or getting rid of oppressive institutions, while Moore's activism is aimed at humiliating, and rarely with the hope of actually defeating, specific individuals.[53] In effect, the confrontations Moore sets up with various authority figures inverts the catchphrase of the preceding political era, *The personal is political:* For Moore, enacting what is already implicit in stardom, the political is personal.

In an attempt to counter the charge that his films are too much about him, Moore uses his unglamorous appearance as a defense: "Who thinks that someone like me wants to see himself blown up 40 feet on a movie screen? I cringe when I see myself in the movies. I have a sign on the door for the editors to read when they walk in: 'When in doubt, cut me out!' Nobody likes to have their picture taken, especially someone like me."[54] Of course, despite his effort to declaim his stardom, Moore's weight and slovenly appearance are essential to what make him a star, just as the hypermasculinized bodies of the Hollywood "hunks" who preceded him in the 1980s made stars of Sylvester Stallone and Arnold Schwarzenegger. Moore's reminder to his editors only reinforces the centrality of the very thing it pretends to be diminishing. If we bear in mind Jean-Luc Godard's maxim, "Every edit is a political act," Moore's direction of his editors tells them that, more importantly, every edit is his *personal* act—which puts the film's emphasis on his act*ing,* rather than the viewer's act*ion.* The personalizing of the political results from Moore's status as an auteur-star. The signpost reminds the editors they are working on a "Michael Moore film," a fact that they and the audience already know.

Many contend that Moore's political agenda in *Fahrenheit 9/11* is more successfully advanced than in his earlier films because we see less of him. Moore's comments about his on-screen role in *Fahrenheit 9/11* endorse this idea. In fact, when he responds to a question put to him by Gavin Smith in *Film Comment* about the role of his on-screen persona in *Fahrenheit 9/11,* he seems to have critics like Mattson in mind:

> . . . and that's part of why I don't think I need as much of me in the film. I don't want the public to think that I'm the one who's going to correct the problem. I am not going to correct it. I'm asking them to do that. I'm asking them to join with me and I'll join with them. I don't want them to sit there passively and watch me and vicariously live through me, sort of a, "Yeah, go get 'em Mike!" Nuh-uh. I'm sorry. I'm not going to get them for you.[55]

Moore's response to Smith's question at least acknowledges that his on-screen persona might interfere with his filmmaking's political objectives. But the larger claim that *Fahrenheit 9/11* avoids this fate because there is not "as much of [him] in the film" is misleading. Like Moore's other films before it, *Fahrenheit 9/11* personalizes its politics through its auteur-star. While there isn't the focus on a big showdown interview with Bush, as there is with principal figures in his other films whether or not he actually interviews them,[56] he conveys the sense of a personal confrontation with Bush through more subtle means.

Throughout the film, Moore reminds the viewer of his personal involvement in the film's subject matter. For example, in his dramatization of the terrorist attacks on the World Trade Center, he mentions that a colleague of his, Bill Weems, was among those killed in "the largest foreign attack ever on American soil."[57] Or in discussing the Patriot Act with Congresswoman Tammy Baldwin, who stops to consider the people it might label a "terrorist," Moore interjects asking, "Like me?"[58] A more dramatic enactment of the personal occurs when Moore stages a "confrontation" between himself and Bush. It occurs as he details Bush's performance as president prior to September 11. Depicting him as an ineffective leader who responds to his problems by going on vacation, Moore includes some footage of himself at a Bush-for-President event during Bush's first presidential campaign. Among a crowd of people separating the two of them, Moore gets the candidate's attention by shouting out, "Governor Bush . . . it's Michael Moore." As Moore assumes, and Bush's response acknowledges, the filmmaker's reputation precedes him. Bush wisecracks, "Behave yourself, will you? Go find real work." As the film cuts to a photo-op of President Bush serving grits, Moore sarcastically responds, "And work was something he knew a lot about."[59] With the photo-op serving as another image of the president pretending to work, Moore's sarcastic response comes from his authorial position as the film's narrator and undercuts Bush's jibe about "real work"—turning it into a sign of hypocritical privilege that contrasts with Moore's persona as a working-class filmmaker.

Another significant enactment of the personal comes in the film's credit sequence that is intercut with Bush and his cabinet ministers preparing for television addresses and interviews. To the sound of ominously repetitive musical notes a sense of expectation builds as the viewer watches their unflattering outtakes. The final image of the sequence is of President Bush in the Oval Office preparing for a TV address. Moments before going live, Bush mugs in front of the camera, shifting his eyes from side to side. He smiles and nods, giving someone off camera a thumbs-up sign. The film cuts to its final credit. In large white block letters on a black background it reads: "Written, Produced and Directed by Michael Moore."[60] Contrary to Godard's opinion that Moore doesn't know the difference between text and image[61]—given at *Fahrenheit 9/11*'s premier at Cannes—the juxtaposition of Bush's image with Moore's name shows that, in at least one sense, he does. The image of Bush affirms what everyone in an image-dependent society intuitively knows, "The media lie." The untrustworthy image of the president is contrasted with Moore's "signature" as a filmmaker—the author of The Word. As the auteur-star, Moore assures the viewer that he will expose the truth behind this "fictitious president," as he famously called Bush in his acceptance speech at the Academy Awards.

Whether Moore likes it or not, and one suspects he likes it, such political acts as his Oscar speech are always already publicity.[62] Moore's speech illustrates that, in Corrigan's terms, the celebrity of the auteur-star's agency "produces and promotes texts that invariably exceed the movie itself, both before and after its release."[63] As Frank Rich of the *New York Times* observed, "Mr. Moore's boorish Oscar night yelling, far from relegating him to obscurity, seems to have enhanced not only his movie's box office but his own magnitude of stardom."[64] Whatever Moore's intention was in speaking out at the Academy Awards—whether it was a calculated publicity stunt or spontaneous overflow of emotion—what he says in his speech becomes secondary to the performance of his saying it and how that performance affects his "magnitude of stardom," as Rich puts it.

However, the speech pales in comparison to the publicity coup he managed with two distributors of the film, Michael Eisner, then CEO of Disney, and Harvey Weinstein at Miramax, a subsidiary of Disney. As Edward Jay Epstein explains in *The Big Picture: The New Logic of Money and Power in Hollywood*, Moore used Eisner's veto of the film to stir up controversy by alleging censorship.[65] Epstein refers to a front-page *New York Times* article, headlined "Disney Is Blocking Distribution of Film That Criticizes Bush," that included the allegation, attributed to Moore's agent Ari Emanuel, that Eisner was afraid of distributing Moore's film because it would endanger tax breaks for its theme park and other businesses in Florida, whose governor, Jeb Bush, is, of course, the president's brother and who was widely seen by Democrats as a principal player in the political chicanery that allowed Bush to win Florida and the 2000 presidential election. Epstein maintains that the Cannes jury, believing Moore to be the victim of censorship, awarded his film the Palme d'Or, providing the filmmaker with "more free publicity than any Hollywood studio could afford to buy."[66] Epstein goes on to detail how Eisner and Weinstein finagled the appearance of outside distribution, thereby allowing Disney to keep most of the profits, without appearing to backtrack on its earlier opposition to the film and paying Moore $21 million.

Moore is quite adept at playing the outsider on the inside, presenting himself as the radical filmmaker at odds with the studio system: "There're six studios. I burned my bridges at two of them, Fox and Disney. So, you know, four to go!"[67] But Epstein's account of the financing for *Fahrenheit 9/11* suggests we should view Moore's claims with a good deal of skepticism. Furthermore, despite Moore's professed concerns about finding a distributor for *Fahrenheit 9/11*, a *Time* article reports Harvey Weinstein, who had given Moore $6 million from Miramax's loan account to complete the film, did not share Moore's anxiety. On the night of the film's premier at Cannes, *Time* says, Weinstein "paced nearby and chortled, 'They say I've lost my edge? Have I lost my edge?' He had not. He spent the rest of the week negotiating with a flock of U.S. distributors hoping to profit from the film's marketable notoriety."[68] Far from showing him to be an outsider, Moore's success indicates someone who works the system as only an insider can.

The question of how Moore's own self-interests interfere with his political objectives is pointedly raised by Daniel Wolff's examination of the ethical issues involved in Moore's decision not to go public before the release of *Fahrenheit 9/11* with the footage he used in the film documenting the abuse of Iraqi detainees by U.S. troops. He gives Moore's explanation: "'I wanted to come out with it sooner, but I thought I'd be accused of just putting this out for publicity for my movie. That prevented me from making maybe the right decision.'"[69] Wolff derisively dismantles Moore's excuse that his concern about his reputation—being seen as a self-promoter—prevented him from "making maybe the right decision." He points out this is particularly ironic, if not two-faced, given Moore's criticisms of Disney for being more concerned about its image than getting out the truth. Indeed, Wolff concludes, Moore's justification suggests that *being* antiwar was less important than making an antiwar movie. Or, in terms of Moore's role as a commercial auteur, one could say his commitment to making a "Michael Moore movie" interfered with his antiwar commitment.

Even if Moore's success is a product of the auteur-star's celebrity furthering the film industry's "commercial strategy for organizing audience reception," one can fairly ask if there aren't political effects that might exceed this strategy. Before *Fahrenheit 9/11*, Moore is vague about the political effect of his filmmaking, saying that after the film is over he hopes the audience will go out and do something, "whatever that something might be."[70] He is far less vague about the effect *Fahrenheit 9/11* will have on the audience. The result, Moore proclaims, "'will be like Toto pulling the curtain back so the [American] people can see what is really going on, and they're going to be shocked, and they're going to be in awe, and they are going to respond accordingly.'"[71] Amply documented in the articles and cartoons Moore includes in *The Official Fahrenheit 9/11 Reader,* his representation of the 2004 presidential election as a showdown between himself and Bush caught the popular imagination. Without a doubt, in very concrete ways, the film had a positive impact on the Democratic campaign, helping its efforts to organize voters and raise funds.[72] However, the results of the 2004 presidential election suggest Moore oversold his ability to translate his filmmaking into political victory, which would deliver Bush's head on a platter to the Democrats. Arguments about voter fraud in Ohio notwithstanding, Bush's victory indicates that either many viewers of the film didn't "respond accordingly," or that the film's audience did not cross over from blue states into red states, as Moore and the popular press suggested.[73] In either case, the film's political agenda could not transcend the commercial organization of the audience's response into pro-star/anti-star camps.

POST–*FAHRENHEIT 9/11*

Since the Democrats won a majority of the Congress in the 2006 midterm elections, Moore's political fortunes have improved. Given the unpopularity of Bush and the Iraq war, it would be hard not to see both Moore and *Fahrenheit 9/11* as vindicated in some way. Understandably, Moore is eager to make that argument. In an interview with Wolf Blitzer on *The Situation Room* about Moore's film *Sicko,* the filmmaker took the opportunity to lash out at CNN and the mainstream media for their acquiescent role in the Iraq war, claiming, "It turned out everything I said in *Fahrenheit* was true."[74] While one could quibble with the sweeping nature of this statement, his blasting of the media felt more than a little satisfying. Blitzer seemed overwhelmed by Moore's accusations, and, furthermore, his attempt to maintain an aura of journalistic objectivity by framing the discussion of *Sicko* with a "Reality Check" segment by Dr. Sanjay Gupta was effectively undermined.

Despite the combative nature of his exchange with Blitzer, *Sicko* signals a new shift in Moore's on-screen persona. Unlike his previous films, *Sicko* is not premised upon the filmmaker's antagonistic relationship with some authority figure, like Roger Smith, Phil Knight, Charlton Heston, or George Bush. Instead, the viewer's attention focuses squarely on the health-care system in all of its dysfunctional inhumanity. Moore is still an active presence in the film, effectively narrating scenes and using his appearances to underscore humor or sympathy in his for the most part friendly interviews. This new "nonpartisan" Moore is appreciated by the movie reviewers, as Moore illustrates with the press releases he provides on his website, MichaelMoore.com. For example, the first excerpt on the site's long list of positive reviews, from Steven Snyder of *Time-Out,* proclaims the film "a triumph of a filmmaker setting aside personal politics for the larger crisis [of health care]."[75] Perhaps it is coincidental, but in "setting aside personal politics," *Sicko* also sets aside the filmmaker's hometown of Flint and the prominent role it has had in his previous films as the source of his working-class authority. Through *Sicko* Moore finds a way to be what President Bush once promised to be—a "uniter."

While Moore relies heavily on Flint in his most recent film, *Capitalism: A Love Story,* his hometown is presented in such a nostalgic light that it is more in line with *Sicko*'s new non-partisan tone than his earlier films. However, whether or not Moore can or wants to continue down this path is another question. In an interview with Larry King, Moore showed he has some way to go in mastering the rhetoric of nonpartisanship. In explaining his support of Barack Obama for the Democratic nomination, he praised the candidate for not being a "partisan person."[76] Shortly after this assertion, however, King displayed an excerpt from a recent article Moore had written for his website in which he chastised Obama for not being partisan enough. Moore, without explaining the apparent contradiction, responded by saying that in order for Obama to beat McCain he needed to "put [his] game face on"[77] and stand up to the Republican Party.

Like Rush Limbaugh and Bill O'Reilly to his far right, one suspects that Moore can't be a uniter for too long. This isn't a personal flaw. It is a function of his commerce as a political star within our infotainment culture. If we are to learn from Moore's example, we have to start rethinking the question of stardom and its relation to politics. As Corrigan observes in his discussion of Alexander Kluge, the question should not be, as it is now in American politics, how a star can "absorb the political" (whether it is Al Franken as a Democrat or Arnold Schwarzenegger as a Republican); instead, the question to ask is, "How does a star reactivate a materialist politics within his or her commercial agency."[78] Clearly, we are a long way off from anything like a "materialist politics"—if such a thing is even possible—in American politics and celebrity culture. But perhaps in smaller or more local ways Corrigan's question can help us think more critically about the stardom of politics and the politics of stardom.

Notes

1. Michael Moore, "Pauline Kael, the Truth, and Nothing but . . . Brought to You by AOL Time Warner," http://www.michaelmoore.com/words/message (accessed October 15, 2004).

2. Ibid.

3. Joshua Hammer, "Phil and Roger and Me," *Newsweek,* March 30, 1998, http://firstsearch.oclc.org.flagship.luc.edu/images/WSPL/wsppdfi/HTML/01450 (accessed May 15, 2006).

4. Moore once described his show *TV Nation* as "*60 Minutes* if it had a sense of humor and subversive edge." Chip Rowe, "A Funny, Subversive *60 Minutes,*" *American Journalism Review,* July–August 1995, http://firstsearch.oclc.org/images/WSPL/wsppdfi/HTML/04615 (accessed October 6, 2004). See also Kevin Mattson's characterization of Moore: "Add to Chaplin and Hoffman the newsmagazine tradition of Edward R. Murrow and *60 Minutes* (muckraking brought to television), mix in a heavy dose of postmodern irony, and you've pretty much got Michael Moore." "The Perils of Michael Moore: Political Criticism in an Age of Entertainment," *Dissent* 50 (Spring 2003), http://firstsearch.oclc.org/images/WSPL/wsppdfi?HTML/03550 (accessed October 6, 2004).

5. Chris Lehane, quoted in Jason Zengerle, "Crashing the Party," *New Republic,* July 19, 2004, http://firstsearch.oclc.org/images/WSPL/wsppdfi/HTML/01486 (accessed October 6, 2004).

6. Helen Stoddart, "Auteurism and Film Authorship Theory," in *Approaches to Popular Film,* ed. Joanne Hollows and Mark Jancovich (Manchester: Manchester University Press, 1995), 39.

7. Timothy Corrigan, *A Cinema without Walls* (New Brunswick, NJ: Rutgers University Press, 1991), 103.

8. Ibid., 13.

9. Ibid., 26.

10. John Sedgwick and Michael Pokorny, "The Characteristics of Film as a Commodity," in *An Economic History of Film,* ed. John Sedgwick and Michael Pokorny (London: Routledge, 2005), 6–23.

11. Corrigan, *A Cinema without Walls,* 107.

12. Ibid., 107.

13. Ibid.

14. Michael Moore, "'Roger' and I, Off to Hollywood and Home to Flint," *New York Times,* July 15, 1990, A1.

15. Ibid.

16. Ibid.

17. Ben Hamper, *Rivethead: Tales from the Assembly Line* (New York: Warner Books, 1991), 84.

18. Cyde H. Farnsworth, "If America Needs an Enemy, Muses Michael Moore, Why Not Canada?" *New York Times,* December 14, 1993, C19.

19. Brian D. Johnson, "Working-Class Clown," *Maclean's,* April 13, 1998, http://firstsearch.oclc.org/images/WSPL/wsppdfi/HTML/01812 (accessed October 6, 2004).

20. Hamper, *Rivethead,* xiii.

21. Alex S. Jones, "Radical Magazine Removes Editor, Setting off a Widening Political Debate," *New York Times,* September 27, 1986, 7.

22. Ibid.

23. Dan Georgakas and Barbara Saltz, "Michael and Us: An Interview with Michael Moore," *Cineaste* 23 (1998): 4–7, http://firstsearch.oclc.org/WebZ (accessed October 6, 2004).

24. Johnson, "Working-Class Clown."

25. Hamper, *Rivethead,* xiii.

26. Hamper recounts that Moore told him he was fired from *Mother Jones* because he insisted that the publisher let Hamper have his own column. A few days after this, Hamper was contacted by the managing editor of *Mother Jones,* who tried to convince Hamper to keep writing for the magazine despite Moore's dismissal. Hamper says, "Not knowing who to believe, nor really caring, I opted to stay out of the matter." *Rivethead,* 220.

27. Hamper, *Rivethead,* xiii.

28. Ibid.

29. Richard Schickel, "Imposing on Reality," *Time,* January 8, 1990, 77.

30. Paul Arthur, "Jargons of Authenticity (Three American Moments)," in *Theorizing Documentary,* ed. Michael Renov (London: Routledge, 1993), 133.

31. Ibid., 130–31.

32. "Press Resources, the Official Fahrenheit 9/11 Reader," http://www.michaelmoore.com/press/reader.php (accessed October 15, 2004).

33. Michael Moore, "Letter from Flint, Michigan," *Peacework,* April 2000, 9.

34. See in this volume Gaylyn Studlar's insightful essay "Class, Gender, Race, and Masculine Masquerade in the Documentaries of Michael Moore," which discusses the race and gender assumptions at work in Moore's use of Rowland's story in *Bowling for Columbine.*

35. David T. Hardy, a conservative critic who has dedicated himself to exposing Moore's "deceptive" practices, argues that Moore manipulates the viewer into thinking that Heston comes 48 hours after the shooting for a "pro-gun rally," when in fact Heston showed up eight months after the shooting for a get-out-the-vote rally. One could concede Hardy's point that Moore does skew the chronology of Heston's visit to Flint, while still granting Moore's larger claim that Heston's appearance, given his outspoken defense of gun ownership, even eight months after the event and at a get-out-the-vote rally would still be seen by some as a provocation. Nonetheless, one can't help but feel that Kayla Rolland's story gets lost in the untangling of facts. "*Bowling for Columbine:* Documentary or Fiction," http://www.hardylaw.net/Truth_About_Bowling.html.

36. Moore, "Letter from Flint, Michigan," 9.

37. Corrigan, *Cinema without Walls,* 108.

38. Richard Dyer, *Stars* (London: British Film Institute, 1979). Dyer's book provides a brief "note" on the auteur theory in which he considers stars as authors (e.g., Patrick McGilligan's *Cagney, the Actor as Auteur*) and the relationship of auteurs to stars (e.g., Howard Hawks and Marilyn Monroe in *Gentlemen Prefer Blondes*). But the category of the director-star is inexplicably removed from his discussion: "In the case of stars as au-

thors of the films they starred in, we must begin by excepting those cases where stars directed (or scripted) themselves in films. . . . In these cases, we have to make a theoretical distinction between their role as star and their other role in the production" (175). Dyer's refusal to theorize someone who has *both* a role as a star in the movie *and* some "other role in the production" is puzzling. It seems to reflect an attachment to notions of authorial coherence and control behind the star's image that his study otherwise questions and takes apart.

39. "Bowling for Columbine," *Time,* October 7, 2002, http://firstsearch.oclc.org/images/WSPL/wsppdfi/HTML (accessed October 6, 2004).

40. Larissa MacFarquhar, "Michael Moore's Art and Anger," *New Yorker,* February 16 and February 23, 2004, 137.

41. Stuart Klawans, "License to Kill," *Nation,* October 28, 2002, 44.

42. Jon Ronson, "The Egos Have Landed," *Sight & Sound,* November 20–23, 2002, http://wwwfirstsearch.oclc.org/images/WSPL/wsppdfi/HTML/00691. Along these lines, it is worth noting the flip-flop on Moore's working-class bona fides by the filmmaker's one-time friend Alexander Cockburn. Cockburn came to Moore's defense when he was fired from *Mother Jones,* supporting Moore's version of the affair that depicted him as the working-class boy from Flint up against the wealthy liberal Hochschild from San Francisco. Sometime after Moore became the Left's fastest rising star, Cockburn had a change of heart, writing a vitriolic piece that denounced Moore as an egotistical opportunist and poser. "Letter to Michael Moore, TV Nation," *New York Press,* November 12–18, 1997, 22.

43. Matt Labash, "Michael Moore, One-Trick Phony," *Weekly Standard,* June 8, 1998, http://www.weeklystandard.com (accessed October 27, 2004).

44. Dyer, *Stars,* 95.

45. Ibid., 98.

46. Michael Moore, *Downsize This!* (New York: HarperCollins, 1997), 170.

47. Michael Moore, *Stupid White Men* (New York: HarperCollins, 2004), 93.

48. Dyer, *Stars,* 31.

49. Ibid.

50. Labash, "Michael Moore, One-Trick Phony."

51. Gary Crowdus, "Michael Moore and His Critics," *Cineaste* 17, no. 4 (1990): 30.

52. Kevin Mattson, "The Perils of Michael Moore: Political Criticism in an Age of Entertainment," *Dissent* 50 (Spring 2003), http://firstsearch.oclc.org/images/WSPL/wsppdfi/HTML/03550 (accessed October 6, 2004).

53. MacFarquahar, "Michael Moore's Art and Anger," *New Yorker,* 139–40.

54. Daniel Fierman, "Michael Moore Under Fire," *Entertainment Weekly,* October 25, 2002, http://firstsearch.oclc.org/images/WSPL/wsppdf1/07208/W6UWN/9SO.HTM (accessed October 6, 2004).

55. Gavin Smith, "The Ending Is up to You: Michael Moore Interviewed by Gavin Smith," *Film Comment* 40, no. 4 (July–August 2004): 26.

56. In his *Film Comment* interview with Moore, Smith questions the political effectiveness of the filmmaker's showdown interview with Charlton Heston in *Bowling for Columbine.* Moore responds: "That's right. If I had somehow gotten an interview or a few moments with Bush—I sort of didn't want to end the movie with the audience in a

collective Bronx cheer toward Bush on the screen as he gets his comeuppance. Catharsis can be a good thing, and I think at points in this film you may feel that, but I'm not going to let you have the ultimate high [laughs] and then just go home. The catharsis has to happen on November 2," 26.

57. Michael Moore, *The Official Fahrenheit 9/11 Reader* (New York: Simon and Schuster Paperbacks, 2004), 17.

58. Ibid., 65.

59. Ibid., 13.

60. Ibid., 17.

61. Armond White, "Film of the Fascist Liberal," *New York Press*, http://www.nypress.com (accessed March 7, 2006).

62. There was some debate in the press comparing Moore's high-profile protest with the more low-key antiwar sentiments expressed by Adrien Brody in his acceptance speech for the Best Actor award for his role in *The Pianist.* Another form of protest was exercised by Aki Kaurismaki (a Finnish director whose film, *Man without a Past*, was nominated for best foreign-language film), who expressed his opposition to the war by staying away from the Oscar ceremony altogether. His publicist said of the filmmaker's refusal to attend, "There's no agenda, there's no speeches. He just felt uncomfortable in attending." (Rick Lyman, "With an Eye on the War, Oscar Plans Proceed," *New York Times*, March 21, 2003, E1.) One doubts that this Bartlebyesque protest, with its own radical implications, was even considered by Moore.

63. Corrigan, *A Cinema without Walls*, 107.

64. Frank Rich, "Bowling for Kennebunkport," *New York Times*, April 6, 2003, AR1.

65. Edward J. Epstein, "How Disney and Michael Moore Cleaned up on *Fahrenheit 9/11*," May 3, 2005, http://www.slate.com (accessed May 15, 2006).

66. Ibid.

67. Smith, *Film Comment*, 25.

68. "The Art of Burning Bush," *Time*, May 31, 2004, http://firstsearch.oclc.org/images/WSPL/wsppdf1/HTML/00360/P44YR/6F4.HTM (October 6, 2004).

69. Daniel Wolff, "Why Iraqi Detainees Should Sue Michael Moore," *Counterpunch*, June 16, 2004, http://www.counterpunch.org (accessed March 7, 2006).

70. Georgakas and Saltz, *Cineaste* 23, no. 3: 5 (1998).

71. Zengerle, "Crashing the Party."

72. Zengerle, for example, reports that despite the Kerry campaign's initial distance toward the film, it was warmly embraced by such diverse groups as the National Education Association, the NAACP, the Congressional Black Caucus, and MoveOn.org to rally their members. And in an article for *Time*, reporters speculated that the film could have been behind a two-day fund-raising record of $5 million for the Kerry campaign. Desa Philadelphia, Jeffrey Ressner, Jackson Baker, Betsy Rubiner, John F. Dickerson, and Adam Zagorin, "The World According to Michael," *Time*, July 12, 2004, http://firstsearch.oclc.org/images/WSPL/wsppdf1/HTML/00360 (accessed October 4, 2004).

73. Byron York, using a "source in the movie business," who made available to him audience information studios normally don't divulge, went behind *Fahrenheit 9/11*'s impressive box office numbers. He makes the case that while the film did perform well in "America's top eight markets" it "underperformed" in red and swing states, contradict-

ing claims by Moore and the popular press about the movie's crossover success. "The Passion of Michael Moore," *National Review,* April 25, 2005, 49.

74. "'Sicko' Reality Check," Wolf Blitzer, *The Situation Room,* CNN, July 10, 2007. CNN.Com, Transcripts, http://transcripts.cnn.com/TRANSCRIPTS/0707/10/ywt.01.html.

75. Steven Snyder, *Sicko* Press Room, MichaelMoore.com, http://www.michaelmoore.com/sicko/pressroom.

76. "Michael Moore on the 2008 Election," *Larry King Live,* CNN, April 30, 2008. CNN.Com, Transcripts, http://transcripts.cnn.com/TRANSCRIPTS/0804/30/lkl.01.html.

77. Ibid.

78. Corrigan, *A Cinema without Walls,* 118.

Class, Gender, Race, and Masculine Masquerade in the Documentaries of Michael Moore

GAYLYN STUDLAR

The importance of Michael Moore's major documentaries, including *Roger & Me* (1989), *Bowling for Columbine* (2002), *Fahrenheit 9/11* (2004), and *Sicko* (2007), cannot be overestimated.[1] And it is probably saying the obvious to state that Michael Moore is likely better known by the majority of the American public than are his films. Moore says the right wing in the United States has become "obsessed with him."[2] Certainly, conservatives have become the source of a veritable cottage industry of websites, print articles, books, and at least three 2004 films, *Celsius 41.11, FahrenHYPE 9/11,* and *Michael Moore Hates America,* seeking to unmask what is characterized in this discourse as the hypocrisy of the filmmaker and the lies and distortions that supposedly underscore his films.[3] However, it is likely that the broader spectrum of American citizens on the political right have never seen Moore's films: buying tickets to see them might be regarded an act of ideological masochism contributing to the filmmaker's coffers and his presumed ability to make more films of the same political ilk.

Nevertheless, even those who have not seen these films are trained by this political discourse to know Michael Moore when they see him. For example, Moore made an unexpected appearance on Republican campaign literature related to the November 2006 midterm election in his home state of Michigan. On an oversized postcard mailed to voters to encourage Republican turnout, Moore joined Hilary Rodham Clinton and Ted Kennedy to form an unholy trinity of liberalism. These images did not require identification, but were presented as being sufficiently familiar (and frightening) to spur Republicans to scurry straight from their mailboxes to the nearest polling place. This suggests that Moore's construction of his iconic public persona has made identification of him quite easy. Similarly, Moore's films, especially, *Fahrenheit 9/11* and *Bowling for Columbine,* are so well known and so often discussed that they have become part of the contemporary political landscape and touchstones of ideological meaning to a large number of Americans beyond those who form the audience for his films. Actual analysis of Moore's documentaries, however, remains scattered and by no means comprehensive.

As many commentators have noted, Moore's iconic status rests, at its core, on his presence as a central "character" in each of his films, although that status is somewhat softened in *Sicko,* where Moore appears on-screen only after the first 45 minutes of the film. He then moves front and center in that film when he travels to Canada, Great Britain, and France to investigate their health systems. He then organizes a trip to Guantánamo Bay, Cuba, for several boatloads of sick Americans, including three 9/11 responders and those "who needed to see a doctor but couldn't afford one," in hopes of acquiring medical attention at the U.S. Naval Station prison.[4] In all his films, Moore presents himself as a progressively minded investigative "journalist" who seeks answers to pressing national problems, but does so within a format as much associated with comedy and satire as with the "truth-telling" function associated most frequently with the documentary mode. All the topics of Moore's documentaries—whether capitalism and factory closure in *Roger & Me,* violence and U.S. gun culture in *Bowling for Columbine,* the consequences of the abuse of the truth in the invasion of Iraq in *Fahrenheit 9/11,* the dysfunctionality of the American health insurance system in *Sicko,* or the abuses of the American finance system and the economic meltdown of 2008 in *Capitalism: A Love Story* (2009)—are filtered, in varying degrees, through the on-screen visual presence and dual-layered (diegetic and voice-over) vocal comments of Moore, who has been accused of inserting himself too much in his films.[5]

The construction of Moore's film persona is more complicated than generally acknowledged. Because it is also so central to his films, it is the necessary starting place of my analysis of the intersection of class, gender, and race within Moore's documentaries. In a roundtable published in 2005 in *Cinéaste,* Philippe Diaz describes Moore's character within his films as "remarkable, but certainly not altogether admirable. Although he has a fine sense of moral outrage, he is also a self-important, self-righteous bully with an overweening sense of entitlement and little intellectual refinement."[6] While right-wing political commentaries tend to go after Michael Moore as a filmmaker, Diaz, himself a filmmaker and supporter of alternative production and distribution for independent documentaries, acknowledges that he is talking about a persona: "Moore the filmmaker is not this character."[7]

The distinction between Michael Moore the filmmaker and his on-screen persona may be irrelevant both to the majority of his enemies and to his fans; this conflation is no doubt due (in large part) to the efforts of Moore himself. However, delineating the characteristics of Moore's on-screen presence has great relevance to an understanding of the representation of class, race, and gender in his films, especially as these intersecting social categories cut across the stereotypical binarisms of American power relations that tend to hold sway in Moore's films: rich and poor, white and black, male and female. If we are to understand the representation of class, race, and gender more generally in his films, we must first understand how Moore's screen persona situates him in relation to the subject category he ostensibly represents—Midwest America's white, working-class masculinity—as well as the relation to those subject categories of U.S. society he seeks to illuminate or interrogate.

While political conservatives regularly denounce Moore's major film documentaries as blatant socialist propaganda, virulently anti-American in tone and irresponsibly distorting in content, we should not forget that they also have stirred controversy among left-leaning academics, film critics, and media-makers. Many of these liberals have not only expressed ambivalence about Moore's film persona (as Diaz does), but also criticized his films on a wide range of issues, from their lack of structure and manipulation of chronology, to their failure to create coherent sociopolitical analysis. In 1993, film scholar Linda Williams went so far as to accuse Moore in *Roger & Me* of not being radical enough, of being too locked into conventional methods of documentary practice.[8] A pattern of negative reactions may be traced to representational strategies in the documentaries that have led to Moore's "unwitting alienation of even those viewers who applaud his film's politics," as Matthew Bernstein observes in reference to *Roger & Me.*[9]

Moore's films have also been taken to task by a number of progressively minded commentators for the ways in which they represent class. The opening salvo of this attack was launched by film critic Pauline Kael, who, in her 1990 review of *Roger & Me,* accused Moore of making a film that "uses its leftism as a superior attitude" and encourages the audience to "laugh at ordinary working people and still feel they're taking a politically correct position."[10] General Motors officials distributed her scathing review as a counterattack against the film's indictment of GM's decision to close factories and lay off thousands of workers in Flint, Michigan, even as company chairman Roger Smith pursued his plan to open automobile assembly plants in Mexico.[11] In interviews Moore rebutted criticism of the depiction of the working class in *Roger & Me* by arguing that the left wing had lost its sense of humor by severing its connections to the working class and that laughter at a tough situation, like the one in Flint, was a better response than crying.[12]

Moore's frequent extratextual and textual references to Flint, Michigan, once prosperous, but by the late 1980s a rust-belt city wracked by unemployment and crime, suggests a man who is rooted in a specific and quite ordinary place. Sergio Rizzo discusses the centrality of Flint to Moore's identity at some length in his essay in this volume, but it is worth emphasizing here that through an emphasis on Flint as his "hometown," the social and political meaningfulness of Moore's on-screen appearance as an apparently unsophisticated, class-bound white man is reinforced. While Flint is the central focus of *Roger & Me*, it also figures in *Bowling for Columbine* in the extended sequence dealing with the fatal shooting of Flint first-grader Kayla Rolland. In *Fahrenheit 9/11* it comes into play in the depiction of military recruiters attempting to sign up poor teenagers. (*Sicko*, in not featuring a single sequence set in Flint, is the exception that proves the rule, but even here, one of the mothers interviewed about health care in relation to her sick daughter is briefly identified as a Flint native.) In *Capitalism: A Love Story*, Moore returns to Flint often, going so far as to reuse footage from *Roger & Me*.

Perhaps Moore's most poignant reliance on the testimony of a Flint resident as the epitome of plainspoken, earnest American Midwesternness occurs in *Fahrenheit 9/11* in the sequence detailing the response of Lila Lipscomb, a Flint social services administrator who herself was once on welfare. Lipscomb copes with the death of her son in the Iraq war and its impact on her mixed-race, working-class family. Moore responds in his voice-over commentary: "I'm tired of seeing people like Lila Lipscomb suffer."

Such comments are part of what we might call Moore's "solidarity strategy." The emphasis on Flint, not just as an ordinary place in the Midwest, but more specifically as a locus of working-class suffering, increases a sense of Moore's on-screen persona as being "authentic" and "of the people" rather than inauthentic (i.e., "false") and of the elite (whether of Hollywood or in the form of college-educated filmmakers). Moore justified his comedic or ironic approach in *Roger & Me* to the many down-and-out working-class subjects he depicted by reminding critics that he was addressing the problems, not only of his own class, but of his fellow citizens in Flint: "Our politics were not defined by going to [college in] Ann Arbor, Berkeley, or Madison. They were defined by living in the hometown of the world's largest corporation and living in an environment created by the corporate culture that dominated that town."[13] Moore is reputed to sometimes sign his e-mails, "The Man from Flint."[14] In this respect, his connection to Flint grants him license to use his own life story as the strategic "hook" for many of his films' investigation of issues that he and, by implication, we should take personally.

Brian Winston, in analyzing the highly influential Grierson documentaries of the 1930s, has referred to the "victim tradition" of revealing social problems in which the filmmaker plays the "traditional journalistic role as protector of the powerless and fearless confronter of the powerful."[15] Moore's films depart radically from the tone of sentimentality that saturates the Grierson documentaries' treatment of the working class, but not with the "victim tradition" itself. In spite of Moore's heavy reliance on humor rather than sentimentality, the prevailing strategy of representing social class in his films draws from the Grierson tradition.

Yet at the same time Moore complicates this strategy by personalizing the differences between the classes through the filmmaker's assumption of a constructed filmic persona in which he "masquerades" not only as a journalist but also as a very particular kind of masculine subject. Through his on-screen identity, Moore diverges from the Grierson model by aligning his on-screen "self" with the victimized subjects he films. This occurs primarily through Moore's assertion of his everyman status as an outsider representing ordinary citizens, someone who, like them, just wants to know the truth. As a result, Moore's on-screen persona is represented as a subject who, without the privilege of the insider's pass, is forced to go about getting answers to his questions in sometimes unexpected and unorthodox ways.[16]

The outsider status of the Moore persona is particularly evident in his films when he barges into the environs of the rich and powerful. In *Roger & Me*, Moore attempts to ride the elevator up to CEO Roger Smith's penthouse office in the GM building; security personnel halt him. In *Sicko*, Moore uses a bullhorn to call out from a fishing boat to the U.S. naval facility at Guantánamo Bay in a comically futile effort to gain entry for several boats of sick Americans to the prison where superior health-care facilities are reputedly available to enemy combatant detainees. In *Bowling for Columbine*, he and two teenage boys who were wounded in the Columbine High School massacre wait for hours in the lobby of Kmart's headquarters in Grand Rapids, Michigan. A moderately sophisticated viewer of *Bowling for Columbine* would realize that this unannounced visit to headquarters to ask the company to stop selling handgun ammo would almost inevitably be met by a changing cast of noncommittal corporate public relations personnel, just as the filmmaker certainly would have known in advance the likely outcome of his attempt to access a corporate CEO like Smith in *Roger & Me*.[17]

Moore never gets Roger Smith to come to Flint. However, Moore's camera visit to Kmart corporate offices leads to a company spokeswoman's on-camera announcement that Kmart stores will no longer sell handgun ammunition. This change is an unexpected victory in making corporate America take responsibility for the consequences of its policies. It makes Moore's intervention—as a "fearless confronter of the powerful"—even more remarkable. According to the film's logic, this moment of victory is a positive step to reducing school shootings. The announcement seems to surprise even Moore, who reveals how savvy he really is when he slyly presses the spokeswoman to more precisely articulate before the microphones and camera exactly what ammunition will be banned from the shelves.

The film viewer may admire the power of Moore's advocacy but also suspect that this sudden change in corporate policy depends upon the company's fear of negative publicity, perhaps in reaction to the presence of the camera and the poignant physical testimony of the two Littleton victims who accompany Moore.[18] This speaks to Moore's use of the solidarity strategy. In voice-over, Moore credits the two teenagers, one wheelchair bound and the other terribly scarred, with the idea of going to corporate headquarters to "return" the bullets lodged in their bodies. Moore's presentation of these two victims of gun violence in relation to his on-screen working-class persona also suggests the relevance of the Griersonian model of the role of the filmmaker. As explained by Winston, the filmmaker is the "more powerful partner" to powerless victims of society. While the latter may be allowed to express their views within the film, their comments ultimately must serve the documentarian's predetermined political purpose.[19]

Moore's control of these kinds of scenes or situations in his films must be acknowledged, but Moore's appearance undermines the presumptive notion that he is the "powerful" partner: his baseball cap, windbreaker, jeans, sneakers, stubbly beard, and even his obesity work to suggest an obliviousness to appearance, a lack of caring for anything more than comfort and functionality, associated stereotypically with working-class males. As Christopher Sharrett and William Luhr have stated (and Sergio Rizzo discusses at length elsewhere in this volume), Moore's persona is as "a big, potbellied slob from the American heartland in a baseball cap who looks like he buys his clothes in Kmart and sleeps in them."[20] Moore's exterior manifestation of a blue-collar, proletarian male self suggests a resistance to a cultural feminization associated with consumerism and an elitist overattention to appearance. These connotatively resonant strategies of self-presentation may even link his screen persona to older masculine values, those of uncultivated American manhood exalted in the image of the pioneers, the humble nation-builders whose truthfulness and simplicity stood against the contrivances and complexity of eastern civilization.[21] Thus, Moore's careful construction of his on-screen persona as a "simple working-class man" from Flint is offered as *undominating* (in manner and visual alignment with the working class) yet paradoxically *dominating* (being the film's central authoritative voice in determining moral values and searching for political justice).

Because of his obesity, Moore's alliance with the working class seems more authentic, more real. In an interview following the release of *Roger & Me*, Moore described himself as "overweight" and blamed his eating of chocolate croissants in reaction to his firing from *Mother Jones*.[22] While clothes and demeanor may be assumed to be taken up in passing as a temporary "masquerade," weight seems more permanent, less subject to being "faked." Working this aspect of his appearance to his advantage in his films, Moore's "soft" obesity compromises his character's potential alignment with class privilege because obesity has class and gender connotations as well as negative social connotations of immaturity and lack of discipline. Studies have shown that in every major Western country, weight is strongly correlated to class difference, with the fewest percentage of overweight citizens, of either gender, belonging to the highest social class, and the most belonging to the bottom social classes.[23] Women have more body fat as a consequence of their physiology, and fat men are sometimes regarded as being feminized, made unmanly (and sexually handicapped) by virtue of their weight. By virtue of this constellation of connotations, Moore's obesity prevents him from being associated with a dominating masculinity linked in popular culture to athletic, hard, muscular physicality.

That physicality achieved its height of popularity in Hollywood movies of the 1980s; Sylvester Stallone and Arnold Schwarzenegger were the exemplars of its star embodiment.[24] These stars and their characters, according to Susan Jeffords, represented the external spectacle of musculature combined with weaponry that formed the screen equivalent of the political persona of President Ronald Reagan.[25] The hardbody hero was eclipsed in Hollywood but found an extended life in political culture long after Reagan left office. Schwarzenegger's election as governor of California may be one indication of its sustained appeal in the political arena, as is the cult of masculine toughness represented by George W. Bush through his public identification with assertions of infallible masculine authority in the conduct of Iraq war as well as his manly physical exertions of brush clearing staged against the backdrop of his Crawford, Texas, ranch.

By way of contrast, Moore attempts to undermine his association with masculine authority and macho assertions of physical power. His shambling, overweight, working-class appearance disassociates the filmmaker's on-screen masculinity from the covertly aggressive, crafty, and sometimes downright deceptive techniques he uses to "ambush" some of his interviewees. As John Corner has observed, Moore participates in an "investigative verite" approach in which "the line of questioning is designed to 'wrongfoot' the interviewee," making the person feel uncomfortable and look foolish—or worse.[26] An oft-cited example occurs in *Roger & Me,* when Moore waylays blonde, beauty-queen-perky Miss Michigan, Kaye Lani Rae Rafko, at a Flint parade. He rattles her by asking what she thinks about the dire economic situation in the city caused by the GM layoffs. "How does it feel? I feel like a big supporter. . . . I'm just trying to stay neutral here," she sputters before, pressed again by Moore, she asks everyone to support her efforts as she goes to the national beauty competition. This kind of scene has been discussed as creating a sense of bad faith in which Moore's approach to his interviewees places "unfair pressure" on them, justified, it would seem, by the filmmaker's view that they are "part of the problem" or that their strangeness or comic silliness deserves to be uncovered.[27] Moore's interview of Miss Michigan in *Roger & Me* is one model for the kind of "investigative verite" approach that—sans racial tiptoeing—saturates comedic "current news" television programs like Comedy Central's *The Daily Show with Jon Stewart* and its spin-off, *The Colbert Report.* Moore uses this technique with middle- and working-class people, male and female, who are "just doing their job," but rarely with anyone who is not white. In this respect, a racial divide seems to exist in Moore's films because rarely, perhaps never, does he employ this kind of "wrongfooting" interview approach with black subjects, contrary to the television programs that have imitated him.

Moore's masquerade of working-class masculinity has an important role to play in this interview approach that "wrongfoots" his subjects. Sharrett and Luhr compare the filmmaker's shambling appearance to the constructed persona of Tom Smothers, who did not look like a counterculture threat even if he ended up being just that to CBS in particular and to network television in general.[28] Like Smothers' childish persona, Moore's undominating working-class persona gives him latitude to be both disarming and deceptive. His class-structured appearance becomes a mechanism for his faux naïf milking of class differences in the spaces (like corporate headquarters or stockholders' meetings) in which members of the working class usually are not expected to appear except as receptionists, maintenance workers, food servers, or security guards.

This approach to advocating for "his class" is foregrounded in his on-screen interactions with the rich and powerful, as in the final scene of *Bowling for Columbine* when he gains access with surprising ease to Charlton Heston. Moore punches the driveway intercom at the actor's Coldwater Canyon home. Heston answers himself and an interview time is set for the next morning. Representing hard, heroic, muscular masculinity in mainstream films of the 1950s and 1960s, Charlton Heston becomes the obese and sloppy Moore's perfect foil in *Bowling for Columbine* for reasons that extend beyond Heston's role as president of the National Rifle Association.[29] In its masquerade of constructed, performed masculinity, Moore's shambling, overweight appearance allows his on-screen persona to take on qualities of insufficient manliness, of softness, and almost feminine sympathy that contrast to figures of hard masculinity like Heston. Moore humorously plays on this antagonism, as well as his shared background with Heston as native Michiganders and hunting enthusiasts, through a brief comic montage sequence early in the film of the two men hunting in the woods, with crosscutting establishing each as the other's intended prey.

In the interview that ends *Bowling for Columbine,* Moore describes himself to Heston as a fellow NRA member. He appears to agree with Heston on a number of issues concerning the origins of violence in the United States. Then he suddenly asks Heston to apologize to the people of Columbine and Flint for staging NRA rallies in those cities after school shootings.[30] Dumbfounded by the request, Heston gets up to walk away. As a reminder of Flint's and the country's trouble with guns, Moore holds a photograph of Kayla Rolland in front of him and calls out, "Mr. Heston, this is who she is—or was." Heston then continues to walk away, and Moore props the photo of the dead child of the working class against a pillar of Heston's patio enclave. Moore's voice-over coda reinforces the sense that the working class, through Moore, has been justified in infiltrating the insulated and class-indifferent world of the rich to unsettle the masculine certainty of the hard (and hard-hearted, he implies) actor turned gun lobby spokesperson: "I left the Heston estate . . . [and] walked back to the real world."

It was announced in August 2002 that Heston was suffering from Alzheimer's disease (an illness to which the actor succumbed in April 2008).

One might argue that Heston's mildly confused state as displayed in the film mitigates the actor's long-standing image of hard, strong masculinity. It may also work against Moore's aims to compromise our automatic tendency to side with Moore. While the final scene of *Bowling for Columbine* appears to juxtapose Moore's caring advocacy of Kayla's humanity against Heston's refusal to acknowledge the role of the gun lobby in sustaining the gun violence that killed her, we may be left wondering if Moore has been unfair to Heston. It is interesting to observe that even when he is upset, Heston does attempt to be gracious to Moore. When he gets up to leave, he touches Moore on the shoulder, as if he cannot bring himself to just "close the door" on a guest, which is what Dick Clark's assistants literally do to Moore in the same film, when Moore stages an ambush interview to question Clark (who sits in the back of a minivan) about his restaurant's employing former welfare recipients to garner tax breaks in Michigan.

In spite of the dramatic effectiveness of such scenes, Moore's on-screen persona does not spend all the time in his films unsettling the rich and powerful through reminders of the victimized working class. Moore's masculine masquerade is equally effective in making him seem absolutely unthreatening within the environs of the class he purports to represent personally. In *Roger & Me, Bowling for Columbine, Fahrenheit 9/11, Sicko,* and, of course, *Capitalism: A Love Story,* Moore constructs himself as part of a community of those who cannot escape their class and who, indeed, choose to embrace their class identity and regional origins. Perhaps this is part of why he enjoys such amazingly sympathetic rapport with many of his interviewees, whether they are Michigan militia members out for maneuvers, truant teenagers hanging out at a Taco Bell restaurant in Sarnia, Ontario, or a middle-age security-door salesman in Littleton, Colorado, who chokes up at the thought of the "viciousness" of the massacre at Columbine High School, or Dawnelle Keyes, the African American mother whose young daughter develops a fever and dies in her arms, in spite of emergency hospital treatment.

Moore's identification with the working class, as sustained through his visual persona, is amplified by his films' rather simplistic but often powerful view of class relations: Moore is aligned with those who work to survive and who often have a limited understanding of why things are the way they are. As Lila Lipscomb says in *Fahrenheit 9/11,* "I thought I knew but I didn't know." In this respect, *Sicko* focuses not on those millions of Americans who don't have health insurance, but on the millions who do, or who at least think they do—until they get sick. Throughout the film, middle-class Americans are propelled into destitution or even death—by a health system that values profit over people. Characteristic of those who appear to be in shock because they never thought it could happen to them are Donna and Larry Smith. Bankrupted by the costs of fighting cancer and heart disease, they must sell their house to pay for hospital bills. With what is left of their possessions, they journey by car cross country to move in with a grown daughter who obviously doesn't want them and whose husband is leaving to work in Iraq to supplement their income. In spite of being on Medicare, a gnarled and spent seventy-nine-year-old, "Frank," works as a janitor just to pay for his and his wife's medicines. The GSMPA Medical Group denies a middle-class California woman, Maria Watanabe, an MRI to detect a brain tumor that is confirmed only when the procedure is performed, not in the United States, but in Japan, where she falls ill. She is among the lucky ones. Moore shows many other Americans in *Sicko* who die because they lack the necessary treatment for conditions that their insurance carriers tell them they don't have, couldn't have, or will not be given the diagnostic procedures to find out whether they do have.

Contrasted with his films' portrait of working- and lower-middle-class Americans at the mercy of a system designed not to help them live a decent life is Moore's unflattering picture of the privileged and the powerful. In *Sicko,* George H. Bush is shown in a jocular mood when he praises a woman at a "town meeting" campaign event for having three jobs. He smiles broadly in happy obliviousness and characterizes her desperate attempts to keep afloat as "uniquely American." The upper classes in Moore's films generally have a steadfastly held sense of superiority over and indifference to the suffering of their fellow citizens. This commingling of superiority and indifference is expressed in *Roger & Me* by the Flint's upper class at a society gala, a "Great Gatsby Party," where one man suggests that those who are out of work should "get up in the morning and do something"; another attempts to counter the negative view of the city implied in Moore's emphasis on layoffs: "Ballet, hockey. It's a great place to live."[31] Another scene in the film shows Flint's elite cavorting at a "Jail House Rock Party" in which they pay money to stay overnight in the county's brand-new jail facility. This kind of scene is contrasted with life in Flint outside the confines of the upper class through Moore's shots of a black deputy sheriff serving out the eviction of a poor black family from their home in a city that has become a crime-invested wasteland for the working class.

While Moore never singles out a specific race or gender in his films for sympathy, there is the tendency in Moore's documentaries to suggest that ethnic and racial identities, as well as gender differences, are subsumed by the commonality of class exploitation, victimization, or suffering. In other words, class designation trumps racial or gender differences in Moore's films. His films play for the "underdog" and against the American mythology of success. What do average Americans, men and women, black and white, work for? Moore suggests that the blue-collar social class he represents works to survive in "the kind of place I'm from" (as he says in *Bowling for Columbine*).

Otherwise, the mythology of American success appears in Moore's films as nothing more than greed, which accrues exclusively within a culture of white success. *Fahrenheit 9/11* articulates this attitude in its exposé of the unbelievable wealth and power of the Bush family, which permits them to spirit away bin Laden's oil-rich relatives from the United States after 9/11, without being questioned. *Roger & Me* frames it through the film's broad critique of capitalism as a system largely unburdened by a sense of responsibility for workers or for the community in which the corporation resides. (*Capitalism: A Love Story* takes this criticism up again.) In *Sicko,* Moore offers one exception to this rampant lack of responsibility, a repentant female medical insurance executive, Linda Peeno, who apologizes to Congress for denying treatment to people, including a patient she admits would have lived had she approved his request for "a necessary" operation. The reason she denied treatment? Her refusal saved the company a half million dollars, and she well knew that her climb to the top of the industry was dependent on denying patients coverage for life-sustaining treatments that were regarded as nothing more than "medical losses," that is, financial negatives for her corporate employers.

Moore's method of constructing socioeconomic boundaries reestablishes old-time lines of class played out around the issue of work, but do not address the conditions of work. Moore most frequently focuses on whether working-class people in the United States are allowed by multinational corporations to earn a secure living and to enjoy decent living conditions. His identification with the working class is anachronistic in rejecting any notion of a postmodern class identity based on consumption that might blur the boundaries of class difference.[32] As expressed in *Sicko* and *Capitalism: A Love Story,* consumption is a way to keep Americans in debt, bound to their jobs, and afraid of protesting inhumane conditions.

Moore's identification with the working class is displayed in *Roger & Me* as a nostalgic desire for a return to the past. The primary "lost object" of this nostalgia is Flint, in its mid-twentieth-century incarnation as a working-class utopia when militant union activism (recalled in *Roger & Me* through reiterated references to the sit-down strike of 1937) secured prosperity for blue-collar workers as well as for the corporation. Perhaps because nostalgic identification holds sway, in-depth analysis of class is lacking in Moore's films, especially across the categories of race and gender. This simplification could be a result of Moore's determination to entertain, but the result is that he falls back on familiar clichés in making his points.

As I have shown, by undermining conventional signifiers of masculine authority and power, Moore's on-screen masculine persona contributes to the viewer's empathetic identification with victims, many of whom are female. In fact, it might be argued that females are used primarily to represent the category of victim, whether they are highlighted in the women's gasps and screams in the sound mix accompanying shots of the Twin Towers coming down in *Fahrenheit 9/11,* in the shots of black women and their children being evicted from run-down rentals in *Roger & Me,* in *Bowling for Columbine* by the prayerful 911 call of the teacher who watches the life drain out of Kayla Rolland, or by the many women in *Sicko* who cry on-screen. They include those who are ill, those who lost loved ones to sickness, and even those who work for the health-care industry, such as Becky Malke, a woman who screens calls from insurance applicants and is fed up by the inhumanity of the industry for which she works.

Females are seen everywhere in Moore's films, as rich and poor, black and white, young and old, but women seem to function differently than men do in shaping the audience's intellectual understanding of the problem under analysis in his polemic. Most often and obviously they play the role of a victim or as a traumatized witness to a horror. This gendered pattern gains complexity with the story told by Lila Lipscomb in *Bowling for Columbine* and, in *Sicko,* with the testimony of Julie Pierce, who loses her husband to cancer. In the former, Lipscomb emerges as a relative anomaly in Moore's films, as the female who speaks for herself and traces a change in consciousness that leads from her "ignorance" and an unexamined belief in the Iraq war to a painful knowledge of the futility of her soldier son's death in combat. As with Lipscomb's appearance in *Fahrenheit 9/11,* in *Sicko* one of the film's most poignant and detailed stories of oppression comes from a white woman who describes the suffering of her interracial family at the hands of the health system. Although she worked for Humana hospital, Julie Pierce was unable to obtain a bone marrow transplant to treat the cancer of Tracey, her African American husband, who dies. Pierce defiantly points to racial and class disparities when she recounts accusing the Humana insurance review board of denying her spouse coverage of the treatment he needed because he was black, a treatment that she also angrily told

Moore's "solidarity strategy." Moore comforts Jimmie Hughes, principal of Theo J. Buell Elementary School, where Kayla Rolland was shot by a fellow six-year-old. Hughes has just turned away in grief. Copyright 2002 Alliance Atlantis Communications/United Artists.

them they would never deny the spouse of the chairman of Humana's board. Her passionate attempt to save her husband fails.

In moments such as in *Fahrenheit 9/11,* when he listens to Lipscomb read a letter written by her son before his death, Moore establishes himself as a different kind of American man, one who is more empathetic and feminine than conventionally restrained and stoically masculine. He becomes "feminine" in his ability to sympathize with female victims, to comfort them, and to share their pain, as he does not only with Lila Lipscomb but also, most notably, in his conversation in *Bowling for Columbine* with Jimmie Hughes, the African American principal of Buell Elementary, where Kayla Rolland was shot. When she is called upon by Moore to recount the events of the day of the shooting, Hughes is overcome with emotion and turns away from the camera. Moore cuts from an image of his comforting Ms. Hughes with a hand on her shoulder to a shot of Charlton Heston grinning broadly from behind a podium as he exhorts an auditorium full of NRA members. Although Moore's on-screen presence is more restrained in *Sicko,* he manages to convey—through vocal inflections and melancholy musical accompaniment—some of the same sense of feminized, empathetic masculinity in the episode in the film when, motivated by the dumping of poverty-stricken women patients on the streets by Los Angeles by hospitals, he asks: "Who are we? Is this what we've become? A nation that dumps its own citizens like so much garbage on the side of the curb because they can't pay their hospital bill?"

Although, as in this episode in *Sicko,* Moore 's films tend to gender the category of victim as female, he counters female examples of victimization, as in *Bowling for Columbine,* when he interviews a father who lost a son at Columbine High and subsequently joined a rally against the appearance of Charlton Heston and the NRA in Denver. In *Bowling for Columbine,* Moore throws in just enough images of women with guns—including a mother in the Michigan militia, stock footage of scantily clad women shooting automatic weapons, and shots of young girls in Virgin, Utah, learning to shoot—to help confound the fact that violence and masculinity are linked. (One can easily imagine what Moore would have done with photos of a gun-toting Sarah Palin had she appeared on the national scene in 2001.) As James Gilligan as remarked in *Violence: Reflections on a National Epidemic:* "Violence is primarily men's work; it is carried out more frequently by men; and it is about the maintenance of 'manhood.' "[33]

If, as Sally Robinson suggests, violence and power saturate the dominant mode of masculinity, then the relationship between guns and masculinity requires analysis.[34] Moore works across a broad spectrum of investigation to analyze American violence in *Bowling for Columbine,* but he refuses to acknowledge that gun violence (legal and illegal) is the domain of males who often use guns in aggressive acts that, whether consciously intended to do so or not, consolidate masculine identity in its dominant mode.[35] As Hilary Neroni discusses in her analysis of the Columbine High killings, violence creates and sustains the categories of the masculine and the feminine, and violence, as a signifier of masculinity, is often used, as it was by Dylan Klebold and Eric Harris, as a reaction to a loss of masculinity.[36] Committing violence makes men (or teenage boys) "ultra masculine" in assertions of aggression. Such assertions are symbolically equated with power, independence, individualism, and manly risk. In spite of this association, Moore is unwilling or unable to use his own evidence in *Bowling for Columbine* to suggest that violence is a signifier of masculinity, whether in gang cultures (which he doesn't address), or in survivalist groups (like the Michigan Militia, regardless of its "calendar women"), or in the highest government-sponsored organizations such as the strategic air defense program, both of which he does address.

The gendered alignment of gun possession, the necessary prelude to gun violence, is expressed by suspected terrorism coconspirator James Nichols, who is interviewed by Moore. Sitting in his modest Decker, Michigan, kitchen, Nichols proudly tells Moore: "I sleep with a .44 magnum under my pillow." Moore's scoffing response: "Come on, that's what everyone says," may be an attempt to prove his own immersion in male gun culture, but also suggests that he is egging Nichols on. He follows Nichols into the latter's bedroom to see the gun, but Nichols does not allow the camera to accompany them. Instead, subtitles describe the action and make intelligible what remains visually off-screen or heard in Moore's and Nichols's muffled voices. The subtitles indicate that Nichols puts his gun to his own head, and Moore pleads with him to put it down.

This disturbing moment with Nichols may divert us from asking: Who is "everyone" who Moore claims sleeps with a loaded gun under the pillow? It is unimaginable that "everyone" could include females. Joan Burbick analyzes gun shows and concludes that the ever-present displays of bumper stickers, clothing, and books at these male-dominated events constantly reiterate the shared sentiment in American gun culture that "judges, lawyers, and voters were giving women too much power, and the women were using that power to take guns away from their husbands, their boyfriends, and their constituents."[37] In keeping with Burbick's observation, Nichols complains to Moore that his ex-wife was the cause of his arrest as a conspirator in the Oklahoma City bombing. She told the feds, he says, "I'm a wild man, I've got a gun down every arm, every leg, in every corner of the house."

According to Burbick, 95 percent of hunters are white men, and this group remains among the most vocal segment of American gun culture and the NRA in defending the Second Amendment interpreted as the right to own guns.[38] Nichols's subsequent remark to Moore about his gun, "No one has a right to tell me I can't have it," is so childishly defiant that it might be attributed to the six-year-old killer of Kayla Rolland instead of a grown man. Nichols's comment reinforces the importance of guns as the fast-acting weapon of choice for defending, not only the American "way of life," but, more fundamentally, masculine identity. In this respect, it recalls the early cultivation of "gun" ownership as a masculine right displayed just after the film's credits, in footage from a 1950s television advertisement in which two young boys play with toy rifles. "Police officers" admire the toy guns for their realistic sounds.

Masculine pride in gun ownership is everywhere in the film, from the boys with toy rifles to homegrown radicals like Nichols to the mild-mannered bank clerk who tells Moore about his owning the same "straight shooter" of a rifle that Moore receives as a reward for opening a bank account at the North Country Bank and Trust. The pride of possessing something that so overtly speaks masculinity extends to Moore himself. In *Bowling for Columbine,* on exiting the bank, he triumphantly holds his just-acquired rifle over his head in a gesture that echoes Charlton Heston's famous speech at the 2000 annual meeting of the NRA when, upon receiving an antique rifle as a gift, he declared that the gun control lobby would succeed in getting his weapon only if they pried it out of his "cold dead hands."

The question of the complications that race and gender bring to violence in America is raised potentially by an extended sequence of the film that focuses on the shooting of Kayla Rolland, the six-year-old white girl old who was shot dead by a classmate, an African American boy, in the youngest school shooting in the country's history. As Moore tells the story, "No one knew why the little boy shot the little girl," but the *Flint Journal* reported that the boy argued with Kayla the day before he tucked the loaded .32 caliber handgun in his pants pocket and brought it to school.[39] The boy shot his classmate with a stolen handgun that his uncle had displayed to him. After the shooting, officials raided the uncle's domicile, a known crack house: numerous guns were found, including two shotguns.[40]

Never does Moore suggest a reason for this unusual killing except within the implied thesis that "if only" the shooter's mother, Tamarla Owens, had not been evicted and been allowed to stay at home rather than forced into a burdensome welfare-to-work system, the tragedy could have been avoided. Moore shows Tamarla in television news footage of her court appearance, but he does not talk to her to inquire why she left her two sons with her drug-dealing brother. (Presumably, she declined to speak with Moore on camera.) Instead, Moore points to the brutalities of a welfare system that forced Tamarla to spend three hours a day on a bus to get to two mall jobs where she made fudge and served drinks "to rich people." In this explanation of her situation, Moore suggests that working-class Americans all suffer under the economic domination of the white upper class. *Bowling for Columbine,* like *Roger & Me, Fahrenheit 9/11,* and *Sicko,* argues for the indifference or outright hostility of people in higher socioeconomic classes to poor people, especially poor black people like Tamarla Owens. That hostility is evidenced, Moore implies, in Michigan's welfare system. Confirmation of that hostility, one might argue, resurfaced in the 2006 gubernatorial election in Michigan, in which Dick DeVos, the Republican candidate, put the issue of welfare reform on the table. Former Amway CEO and multimillionaire DeVos ran television advertisements that focused on his desire to put a lifetime cap of four years for any individual to be eligible to collect welfare within the state.

As he focuses almost exclusively on the social system of welfare as responsible for the tragedy, Moore represses evidence that the boy shooter and his older brother were growing up in a seriously dysfunctional situation, surrounded by drugs and violence and perhaps also subjected to physical abuse by their mother.[41] While poverty goes a long way to explaining the child shooter's immersion in this dangerous world, Moore's telling of the story in *Bowling for Columbine* would be complicated even more by questions of masculine acculturation to violence and the child's identification with aggression. Before the shooting, the boy's father, who had been incarcerated for almost half his son's life, asked his son about previous incidents of fighting with classmates. "I hate them," the child told his father.[42] The child shooter's remarks suggest that he was a nascent version of the Columbine killers; that is, the shooting was his mimetic imitation of hate-filled violence intended as a reaction, as a "righting of wrongs" characteristic of dominant masculinity. The boy shooter was bound into the classic construct of "hypermasculinity" as a reactive formula against humiliation, shame, and identification with victims through an assertion of signifiers of masculine identity associated with violent acting out (as well as through decreased sensitivity and empathy).[43]

Instead of pursuing how violence functions as an assertion of masculine identity, even in the very young, *Bowling for Columbine* suggests that the shooter was just a normal child who just happened to find and bring a loaded gun to school. As is so often the case in his documentaries, Moore's view of the Buell Elementary shooting is supported by the testimony of men, including an African American man who took the same state-sponsored bus to work as Tamarla Owens and three articulate, middle-class white males, all Genesee county officials: the detective on the case, the county prosecutor, and the local sheriff. These "characters" all reinforce the idea that the system (of welfare) is to blame, not individuals or the family. Moore avoids grappling with the complicating presence of a chronically troubled male child by substituting a simplified view of a troubled system that exacerbates rather than solves social ills. The child shooter's normality is reinforced by Moore's consideration of the child's crayon drawing, a powerful signifier of innocence, made more poignant by its display on a wall in a Flint police station.[44]

The film also elides the issue of race in the Kayla Rolland shooting. Through a capsule history of the United States that imitates the animation style of *South Park, Bowling for Columbine* articulates the view that white violence in America rests on a baseline of paranoid fear directed at African Americans. Moore takes testimony from survivors of the Columbine High massacre that recounts how one of the killers singled out a black classmate to shoot. By way of contrast, Moore is silent about the racial element in the Kayla Rolland shooting. Never does he address either the rarity or pervasiveness of black-on-white shootings in general or among the working poor of Flint or anywhere else. Never does he suggest that working-class whites might be implicated in sustaining racist ideas and policies that push a black underclass further down to fuel racially charged reactions.

Because Moore elides complicating questions of race and gender and refuses to analyze how violence signifies masculinity, whether in film or on the world political stage, his examination of American violence in *Bowling for Columbine* breaks down into incoherence. As Sharrett and Luhr ask, is Charlton Heston's refusal to apologize for bringing the NRA to Flint after the Kayla Rolland killing *really* the problem?[45] Perhaps we are closer to the answer when an Oscoda, Michigan, teenager expresses frustration to Moore that he wasn't "number one" on his school's list of potential bombers. In this young man's response, the dominant values of masculine identity in America are transparent in the perverse connections between a sense of masculine empowerment and violence.

While Moore is interested in gun culture, the filmmaker moves the viewer away from a consideration of the link between masculinity and violence by providing tacit gender balance, a balance that he cultivates in all his films. However, *Sicko* implicitly raises the interesting question of whether women may possess a greater capacity of empathy and morality that could solve the American health-care problem created by elite, powerful men. Moore not only suggests this possibility through the presence of Linda Peeno, the conscience-stricken health insurance executive, but also through a brief (and ultimately qualified) tribute to Hillary Clinton, whom Moore has called "one hot feminist shit-kicking babe."[46] Clinton and Peeno are contrasted with men who dispassionately perpetuate an American health-care system that does not really care about the health of the American people. Among them is President Richard Nixon, heard in White House tapes as he conspires with John Erlichman to introduce managed care to America while knowing full well that it was intended to improve industry profits, not patient health. Unflattering court testimony shows Glen L. Hollinger, a self-satisfied California insurance claims reviewer who, unlike Peeno, his female counterpart, seems indifferent to the impact of the rubber-stamped refusals that he and his company churned out in response to patient requests for medical treatment. Congressional legislators, almost all men, are labeled (literally) by Moore with the sums of money they have taken

A woman with greater empathy and a stronger sense of morality regarding health care in *Sicko*. Dr. Linda Peeno, former medical reviewer at Humama, testifies before Congress in May 1996 on denying treatment to fatally ill health-care patients. Copyright 2007 Lions Gate.

from the health-care industry. Elite American men (usually white ones), Moore seems say, perpetuate a managed-care system that dupes, demeans, and kills people in a textbook illustration of the worst excesses of capitalism—an argument emphasized in *Capitalism: A Love Story*, where only two women appear to have some power: a female pilot testifying about the low salary she is paid, and Elizabeth Warren, President Obama's appointee for oversight of the bank bailouts.

By way of contrast, Hillary Clinton is introduced with a montage of flattering, even sexy pictures accompanied by Moore's admiring voice-over commentary. Moore then briefly details the former First Lady's attempt to move the country toward universal health care. Testifying before Congress, she is shown verbally sparring with conservative icon Dick Armey, who is obviously taken aback by her witty comparison of him with assisted suicide advocate Jack Kevorkian, aka "Dr. Death." In the end, Clinton is defeated by the financial might and political influence of a health-care industry that wants to retain the status quo and gets what it wants. In the wake of that defeat, Clinton is reduced to the role of a traditional First Lady: she is shown supervising the annual White House lawn Easter egg roll.

Clinton's status as a political heroine of unusual moxy (and sex appeal) is undercut, not by the revelation of the industry's defeat of her reformist efforts, but by Moore's acknowledgment that later, as a senatorial candidate, Clinton accepted large campaign contributions from the health insurance industry she once bravely battled on behalf of the American people. In this admission, *Sicko* suggests that she has become another one of the U.S. political elite—mainly but not exclusively men—whose advocacy for the status quo—or silence—as been bought. These men in power scheme for HMO profitability while hypocritically invoking the discourse of family: "No one loves his mother more than I do," declares former Representative Billy Tauzin repeatedly.

They are contrasted with all the women in the film, who not only represent their own victimization at the hands of the health industry, but also (like Pierce and Keyes and Smith), represent that of their children and husbands. American white men in power, insiders corrupted by capitalism and privilege, are distinguished by Moore, not only from the majority of women (of all colors and ethnic backgrounds) depicted in the film, but from foreign men, who are depicted as being more enlightened and socially committed to the common good than American men. This is especially the case in Moore's representation of the compassionate doctors of Canada, Cuba, France, and Great Britain. These professionals, often young and frequently of color, speak to Moore about their own systems of national health care that allow them live well as professionals but also give them the most important satisfaction of treating all their patients appropriately regardless of income.

CONCLUSION

The documentaries of Michael Moore bring vexing questions of national and local identity, as well as political reality and the force field of ideological fantasy, to the screen, in films that blend comedy and social tragedy, polemical argument and an emotionally loaded emphasis on victims. The representation of class, race, and gender in these films is inevitably related to the central presence of Michael Moore as the on-screen embodiment of straight, white, working-class masculinity. As I have argued, that masculinity is paradoxical in combining dominance associated with the traditional role of the always male Griersonian documentarian who defends the powerless with the characteristics of a naive, everyman figure representing an underclass unified across differences of race and gender by the commonality of their class subordination and systemic oppression.

The question of the sustainability of Moore's everyman persona was raised as early as 1998 by Janet Maslin in the *New York Times*,[47] but it is obvious that

Moore's on-screen efficacy as an undominating-dominating masculine presence has not yet been undone by the tremendous financial success of the filmmaker's books, speaking tours, and films. The latter have propelled him, quite publicly, into the lived circumstances of the upper class. Furthermore, and perhaps more important to the future of his film documentaries than the question of whether Moore will be able to sustain this persona, is the question of whether the filmmaker will also continue to structure his films around an American social landscape conceived almost exclusively in binary terms: two classes—rich and working class; two races—black and white; and two futures—complete comfort or a precarious existence that could be shattered at any moment by poverty, privation, or even death. This question speaks to whether Moore's films, including *Capitalism: A Love Story,* are capable of representing American history in more subtle terms, as well as whether they can convey an understanding of political institutions and social structures as more than a struggle of the haves and have-nots, the powerful and the powerless.

Considering the unprecedented success of his previous documentaries, one might ask, "Why should Moore worry about limitations in his films' approach to class, gender, and race?" Whether or not Moore moves beyond the position of the everyman "hero" who is featured as the voice of victims of a binary-ordered world has little influence on the ballyhoo surrounding his films, but it might well become the litmus test of Michael Moore's maturation as a filmmaker. Such a development speaks to the potential of his films to become more than commercially successful entertainment. Beyond the commerce and the controversy, they might enter that rarified circle of films associated with significant cultural change.

Notes

1. On the impact of Moore's films, see Anonymous (roundtable discussion), "The Political Documentary in America Today," *Cineaste* 30, no. 3 (Summer 2005): 29–37.

2. See the Michael Moore website, www.michaelmoore.com

3. See, for example, David T. Hardy and Jason Clarke, *Michael Moore Is a Big Fat Stupid White Man* (New York: ReganBooks, 2004). Ironically (or quite logically in commercial terms), this anti-Moore book was published under the same imprint as Moore's own best-selling *Stupid White Men* (New York: ReganBooks, 2001). For other anti-Moore commentary, see websites such as David Bossie's CitizensUnited, David T. Hardy's Mooreexposed.com, Jason Clarke's Moorelies.com; and www.michaelmoorehatesamerica.com. In *Sicko,* Moore claims that he saved one of these anti-Moore websites from closing down by anonymously paying for the treatments for the man's sick wife. Articles include Rick Marin, "The Truth about Michael Moore and *Roger & Me,*" *Washington*

Times, February 14, 1990; and Daniel Radosh, "Moore Is Less," *Salon,* June 6, 1997, www.salon.com. For a discussion of the many argument-centered criticisms as well as the bashing and berating responses made against Moore and his films, especially *Fahrenheit 9/11,* see Robert Brent Toplin, *Michael Moore's* Fahrenheit 9/11: *How One Film Divided a Nation* (Lawrence: University of Kansas Press, 2006), 52–70. On Moore's responses to "libelous" verbal accusations made against him, see Emily Schultz, *Michael Moore* (Toronto: ECW Press, 2005), 56–60.

4. Sergio Rizzo and Jeffrey P. Jones discuss Moore's prominence in his films at length in their essays in this volume.

5. Moore has been accused of being "too much at center stage throughout" *Bowling for Columbine* by Christopher Sharrett and William Luhr, "*Bowling for Columbine,*" *Cinéaste* 28, no. 2 (Spring 2003, reprinted in this volume): 34. Hardy and Clarke remark: "No matter what the subject of the book or movie, the main product is always Michael. Big Mike, always out front, the Michelin tire man of politics" (*Michael Moore Is a Big Fat Stupid White Man,* 149).

6. Diaz quoted in Anonymous (roundtable discussion), "The Political Documentary in America Today," *Cineaste* 30, no. 3 (Summer 2005): 34.

7. Ibid.

8. Linda Williams, "Mirrors without Memories: Truth, History, and the New Documentary," *Film Quarterly* 46, no. 3 (Spring 1993): 16.

9. Matthew Bernstein, "Documentaphobia and Mixed Modes: Michael Moore's *Roger & Me,*" in *Documenting the Documentary: Close Readings of Documentary Film and Video,* ed. Barry Keith Grant and Jeannette Sloniowski (Detroit: Wayne State University Press, 1998), 412.

10. Pauline Kael, "The Current Cinema: Melodrama/Cartoon/Mess," *New Yorker,* January 8, 1990, 92. On the "grating condescension" of Moore's films toward the working class as well as the critical controversy surrounding *Fahrenheit 9/11,* see Richard Porton, "Weapon of Mass Instruction: Michael Moore's *Fahrenheit 9/11,*" *Cinéaste* 29, no. 4 (Fall 2004): 3, 5. Harlan Jacobson was one of the first to question the veracity of the facts presented in *Roger & Me* in his interview with Moore, "Michael and Me," *Film Comment* 25, no. 6 (1989): 16–26. Jacobson later remarked on *Fahrenheit 9/11,* "It's one thing to have a strong political view, it's another to savage people using questionable tactics, and making fun of people while portraying yourself as a man of the proletariat." Quoted in Gary Strauss, "The Truth about Michael Moore," *USA Today,* June 21, 2004, 1D, http://www.usatoday.com/life/movies/news/2004-06-20-moore_x.htm.

See also Porton, "Weapon of Mass Instruction," 3, 5; Schultz, *Michael Moore,* 68–69.

11. On the distribution of Kael's review at GM, see C. Cohan and Gary Crowdus, "Reflections on *Roger & Me,* Michael Moore and His Critics," *Cinéaste* 17, no. 4 (1990): 25.

12. See Dan Georgakas and Barbara Saltz, "Michael and Us: An Interview with Michael Moore," *Cinéaste* 23, no. 2 (1998): 5. See also Spencer Rumsey, "The New York *Newsday* Interview with Michael Moore," *Newsday,* January 25, 1990, 65.

13. Georgakas and Saltz, "Michael and Us," 5–6.

14. One of the many complaints from the Right is that Moore fudges his working-class origins in Flint. They frequently point out that he actually grew up in Davison,

which Hardy and Clark characterized as a middle-class, overwhelmingly white suburb of Flint. See Hardy and Clarke, *Michael Moore Is a Big Fat Stupid White Man,* 17–19. Emily Schultz says that Hardy and Clarke confuse Davison with the much wealthier nearby town of Clarkston, Michigan (*Michael Moore,* 135).

15. Brian Winston, "The Tradition of the Victim in Griersonian Documentary," in *New Challenges for Documentary,* ed. Alan Rosenthal (Berkeley: University of California Press, 1988), 277. Matthew Bernstein calls attention to Moore's treatment of his subjects with humor "rather than with the paralyzing sentimentalism that Brian Winston locates in the Grierson movement's depictions of victims." See Bernstein, "Documentaphobia," 414.

16. For a similar take on Moore's persona addressing the filmmaker's "strategic personalization" and "non-professional relationship to his topic" in *Roger & Me,* see John Corner, *The Art of Record: A Critical Introduction to Documentary* (Manchester: Manchester University Press, 1996), 158–59.

17. Richard Schickel says of Moore in *Roger & Me:* "Far from being a hick, Moore is an experienced professional journalist who knows perfectly well that getting in to see the chairman of anything without an appointment is virtually impossible." See Schickel, "Imposing on Reality," *Time,* January 8, 1990, 77.

18. The American corporation's fear of bad publicity is also demonstrated in *Sicko:* after Moore gives notice on his website that he is looking for testimonials regarding the health care system, Moore explains in voice-over how one of the thousands of respondents, Doug Noe, took "matters into his own hands." He wrote his health care provider, Cigna, that he had told Moore the story of Cigna's refusal to provide Noe's small daughter, Annette, with cochlear ear implants for both ears. Noe asks a pointed question in his letter to Cigna: "Has your CEO ever been in a film before?" Moore recounts that Noe soon received a phone call informing him that Cigna was reversing its decision and would pay for the treatment for Annette.

19. Winston, "The Tradition of the Victim in Griersonian Documentary," 270, 276. The number of people who appear in Moore's films and subsequently sue the filmmaker because they feel aggrieved at the way they are portrayed raises questions of complicity and consent in relation to the subjects of documentary that Winston examines (278).

20. Sharrett and Luhr, "*Bowling for Columbine,*" 1.

21. See Richard Slotkin, *The Fatal Environment: The Mythology of the Frontier in the Age of Industrialization* (New York: Atheneum, 1985), 204; and Roderik Nash, *Wilderness and the American Mind* (New Haven: Yale University Press, 1967), 30–33.

22. Georgakas and Saltz, "Michael and Us," 5–6.

23. Anne Scott Beller, *Fat & Thin: A Natural History of Obesity* (New York: McGraw-Hill, 1977), 1–15.

24. For an analysis linking the political and media representations of masculinity in relation to the hard body in 1980s U.S. culture, see Susan Jeffords, *Hard Body: Hollywood Masculinity in the Reagan Era* (New York: Routledge, 1994).

25. Susan Jeffords, "Can Masculinity Be Terminated?" in *Screening the Male: Exploring Masculinities in Hollywood Cinema,* ed. Steven Cohan and Ina Rae Hark (New York: Routledge, 1993), 247, 259.

26. Corner, *The Art of Record,* 164–65.

27. Corner links Moore's interview tactics to those in earlier documentaries in the United States and Britain (*The Art of Record*, 165).

28. Sharrett and Luhr, "*Bowling for Columbine*," 1.

29. For an excellent analysis of the cinematic presentation of Heston's masculinity in epics of the 1950s, see Steven Cohan, "The Age of the Chest," in *Masked Men: Masculinity and the Movies in the Fifties* (Bloomington: Indiana University Press, 1997),164–200.

30. Through selective highlighting of words on the NRA website and glossing over the time frame, Moore makes it appear that the rally in Flint was held within a few days of Kayla Rolland's shooting when, in fact, it took place eight months later and was framed by the organization's attempt to get out the vote for the upcoming November election. See Emilie Raymond, *From My Cold, Dead Hands: Charlton Heston and American Politics* (Lexington: University Press of Kentucky, 2006), 315.

31. Emily Schultz identifies this person as Larry Stecco, a local lawyer who, Schultz claims, later sued Michael Moore for defamation in connection with how he was depicted in the film and won a four-figure settlement in Genesse County. Schultz, *Michael Moore*, 81–82.

32. On Hollywood's changing depiction of class in relation to consumer goods, see Steven J. Ross, *Working-Class Hollywood: Silent Film and the Shaping of Class in America* (Princeton, NJ: Princeton University Press, 1998), 175–82.

33. James Gilligan, *Violence: Reflections on a National Epidemic* (New York: Vintage Books, 1996), 16–17.

34. Sally Robinson, "Pedagogy of the Opaque: Teaching Masculinity Studies," *Masculinity Studies & Feminist Theory: New Directions*, ed. Judith Kegan Gardiner (New York: Columbia University Press, 2002), 150.

35. For one view of the complicated relationship between individual psychology and social construction behind acts of aggression, especially those characteristic of masculine violence, see Nancy J. Chodorow, "The Enemy Outside: Thoughts on the Psychodynamics of Extreme Violence with Special Attention to Men and Masculinity," in *Masculinity Studies & Feminist Theory: New Directions*, ed. Judith Kegan Gardiner (New York: Columbia University Press, 2002), 235–60.

36. Hilary Neroni, "The Men of Columbine: Violence and Masculinity in American Culture and Film," *Journal for the Psychoanalysis of Culture and Society* 5, no. 2 (Fall 2000): 259–60. On categories of masculinity and femininity, see also Robinson, "Pedagogy of the Opaque: Teaching Masculinity Studies," 150–53.

37. Joan Burbick, *Gun Show Nation: Gun Culture and American Democracy* (New York: New Press, 2006), 147–48.

38. Ibid., 68.

39. James L. Smith, Ken Palmer, Bryn Mickle, and Linda Angelo, "Boy Has Violent History: Young Suspect in Slaying Had Attacked Other Classmates, Father Says," *Flint Journal*, March 1, 2000, 1. See also Ken Palmer and Ron Fonger, "19-Year-Old Charged—What about Young Shooter? Violent Tendencies Detected, but Maybe Too Late," *Flint Journal*, March 3, 2000, 1.

40. Bryn Mickle and Ken Palmer, "Boy, Brother Leave Dilapidated Home," *Flint Journal*, March 2, 2000, 1.

41. "Boy Who Shot Kayla Awaiting Adoption with Brother at Whaley," *Flint Journal*,

February 29, 2004, 1. Kayla Rolland's family was equally, though differently, dysfunctional. Subsequent to her killing, her mother was accused of neglect and her stepfather of sexual child abuse, and both lost parental rights to the surviving children. See "Kayla's Mom Gives up Custody of 2, Pleads No Contest to Neglect Charges," *Flint Journal*, February 14, 2003, 1. See also "Kayla's Mom Loses Kids. Alleged Sex Abuse by Husband Puts Parental Rights in Jeopardy," *Flint Journal*, July 24, 2002, 1.

42. See also James L. Smith and Ken Palmer, "Father of Boy Has Spent Much of Son's Life in Prison," *Flint Journal*, March 3, 2000, 1.

43. Myriam Miedzian, *Boys Will Be Boys: Breaking the Link between Masculinity and Violence* (New York: Doubleday, 1991), 83–87.

44. On the political Right's take on the specifics of the Kayla Rolland shooting that Moore's film leaves out, see Andrew Collins, "Michael Moore: Part II," *Guardian*, November 11, 2002, http://film.guardian.co.uk/film/2002/nov/11/guardianinterviewsatbfis outhbank.

45. Sharrett and Luhr, "*Bowling for Columbine*," 10.

46. See the reference to this in Sergio Rizzo's essay in this volume.

47. Janet Maslin, "A Sly Lens on Corporate America," *New York Times*, April 10, 1998, sec. E, 1.

II. MOORE AND THE DOCUMENTARY TRADITION

Michael Moore and the Aesthetics and Politics of Contemporary Documentary Film

DOUGLAS KELLNER

I'm not trying to pretend that this is some sort of fair and balanced work of journalism.
—MICHAEL MOORE[1]

Despite the fact that Michael Moore is a high-profile critic of corporate capitalism, U.S. military policy, the U.S. health industry, the Bush administration, and the manifold injustices of U.S. society, he has been extremely successful in producing popular and award-winning documentaries, TV series, and best-selling books, as well as becoming a celebrity lecturer and media phenomenon.

What is the secret, then, of Moore's success? He is a populist artist who privileges his own voice and point of view, inserting himself as film narrator and often the subject of his films' action. Moore plays the crusading defender of the poor and oppressed, who stands up to and confronts the powers that be. He uses humor and compelling dramatic and narrative sequences to engage his audiences. He deals with issues of fundamental importance, and convinces his audience that the problems he presents are highly significant and concern the health of U.S. democracy. Moreover, despite the severity of the problems he portrays, the films and filmmaker often imply that the problems are subject to intervention, and that progressive social transformation is possible and necessary.

In this essay, I interrogate Moore's aesthetics and politics by providing critical readings of his three major documentary films, *Roger & Me* (1989), *Bowling for Columbine* (2002), and *Fahrenheit 9/11* (2004), with some concluding comments on *Sicko* (2007) and *Capitalism: A Love Story* (2009). I specify Moore's particular documentary strategies, aesthetics, and politics, and illuminate his work by contrasting it with that of documentary filmmaker Emile de Antonio, cinema verité directors, and other nonfiction filmmakers who used varied kinds of footage and complex editing to advance their interpretations of contemporary American politics.[2] I argue that many of Moore's critics fail to understand his partisan radical documentary tradition and his own sui generis mode of filmmaking. At stake is appraising the contributions and limitations of Michael Moore's political documentaries and what strategies work best for progressive documentary filmmaking.

MICHAEL MOORE, EMILE DE ANTONIO, AND THE POLITICS OF DOCUMENTARY FILM

Movies are lies that tell the truth.
—BERNARDO BERTOLUCCI

Among contemporary filmmakers, Michael Moore's role as outspokenly left-wing documentary provocateur is parallel in some ways to that of Emile de Antonio, although their work has major differences as well. Moore's first film *Roger & Me* appeared in 1989, the same year as de Antonio's *Mr. Hoover and I.* De Antonio (1919–1989) was one of the United States' greatest documentary filmmakers.[3] His works present a history of Cold War America from the McCarthy era through the Kennedy assassination, the Vietnam War, the Nixon era, and Reaganism. De Antonio's films made a significant impact on both the form of documentary cinema and the political practice of filmmaking. His politically committed and engaged cinema critiqued ruling-class figures, while sympathetically portraying oppositional political movements. De Antonio made use of archival footage, original interview material, and complex sound editing to create a montage or collage of images and sound to present his vision of the events of the era, such as the Vietnam War in *Year of the Pig* (1968) and his films on Nixon (1971), the Weather Underground (1976), or J. Edgar Hoover (1989).

In terms of style, both de Antonio and Moore use documentary montage to speak truth to power, juxtaposing statements by corporate and political figures with footage that refutes or ridicules them. Both Moore and de Antonio are masters of montage; both use interview material and documentary footage to assault dominant institutions and authority figures of U.S. society and to portray positively voices and forces of critique and rebellion.

De Antonio eschewed voice-of-God narration and even commentary, using the juxtaposition of materials from archives and interviews. As a filmmaker who used high-modernist aesthetics to create works expressing Marxist politics, de Antonio was highly innovative and experimental, meticulous in a distinct formalist structure where every image and sound resonates within a whole and combines a radical artistic and political vision with a highly original documentary style that varies significantly from film to film over his three-decade cinematic career.

By contrast, Moore inserts his personality into the center of his films and provides narrative commentary on the events. This Moore-centric strategy has, in part, made Moore's films and politics accessible and populist, which is not surprising, given that Moore is more rooted in popular entertainment than modernist aesthetics, and is apparently more interested in politics than art (although he too is a highly skilled creator of original and engaging documentary form, as well as purveyor of highly charged political content). Further, while de Antonio's classical modernism creates difficult works that require an active audience, Moore's more populist films attempt to make his message clear and comprehensible to mass audiences, using a unique documentary style that combines agit-prop cinema with his personal intervention and voice, combining the personal with pathos and humor, the political, and expository argumentation from a strongly critical point of view.

There is no evidence that de Antonio had a direct influence on Moore,[4] and, as noted, their differences are telling. Yet both de Antonio and Moore combine serious historical and political analysis with irony and humor. In terms of the broad scope of documentary history, both are left-wing partisans and eschew the ideal of so-called objectivity, admitting they are making committed and interventionist political films. Both sharply criticized cinema verité's aesthetic, which believed that documentary itself would reveal the truth if the filmmaker simply used the camera to capture events, without providing a narrative voice or point of view.[5] Against this aesthetic, de Antonio claimed that editing and choice of subject matter, image, or scene created a construct that contained a filmmaker's vision and politics and that pure objectivity is both impossible and undesirable. De Antonio spoke frequently of the "myth of objectivity," noting: "The very idea of *cinema verite* is repugnant to me. It is as if the filmmaker owned truth of some kind. I have never felt that I owned truth. I tried to be as truthful as I can but I know I am a man of deep-seated prejudices and many assumptions about the nature of society which colour all my thinking and feeling and the work that I do. For me there is no concept of objectivity. Objectivity is a myth."[6]

This myth of documentary objectivity came from a variety of sources, including a tradition of photography that saw it as a mode of reproducing reality;

journalism schools that reacted against the tradition of yellow and political journalism dominant in the United States in the nineteenth century; and documentary filmmakers who followed a realist aesthetic.[7] Moore appears to agree with de Antonio that objectivity is a spurious ideal, often making clear his biases, point of view, and politics,[8] although, as we shall see, critics frequently claim that Moore is not honest in his use of documentary montage and editing.

In the following discussion, I argue that Michael Moore's most popular films deploy three types of documentary strategy: personal witnessing, exploratory and confrontational quest dramas, and agit-prop political interventions. These categories, to be sure, are ideal types and to some extent overlap and characterize all of his work. Yet they highlight dimensions of Moore's documentary strategies that are useful to focus upon and raise questions about political documentary in the contemporary era and Michael Moore's films in particular.

ROGER & ME AND THE DOCUMENTARY OF PERSONAL WITNESSING: ISSUES OF CAPITALISM AND CLASS

It's not an NBC White Paper, *not an episode of* Nova. *To the guardians of documentary, I apologize that the picture is entertaining.*

—MICHAEL MOORE[9]

A proliferation of documentary films of personal witnessing emerged in the 1960s and 1970s as members of the civil rights, women's, gay and lesbian, and other social movements told their own personal stories to bear witness to injustices and explore social problems. Emile de Antonio's *Mr. Hoover and I,* his most overtly personal work, exemplifies this category, in which the personal becomes a vehicle for the political, as de Antonio uses his 10,000-page FBI file to contrast his life with that of J. Edgar Hoover and to bear personal witness against FBI domestic spying and wrong-doing.

Michael Moore's first documentary film, *Roger & Me,* bears witness to the hardships that the closing of the Flint, Michigan, auto plants caused for working-class people of the area. Moore's home movies inserted into the film, his narration concerning his father's employment in the Flint auto plant, and his documentary montage of the area's famous labor struggles and plant closing—all of these scenes bear witness to Moore's own personal participation in the history of the era and his empathy for the working-class people who have lost their jobs and seen their city decline. Like Emile de Antonio, Moore chooses resonant music and a sound track that is as rich and evocative as the visuals. Throughout the film, the sound track provides strong counterparts to the visual montage, and Moore's own voice bears witness to involvement in the events he is narrating.

Moore's central focus in *Roger & Me* is class and the impact of corporate relocation on the working class. The film presents illuminating contrasts between the rich and poor, the working class and the corporate elite, continually cutting from images of working-class devastation and despair in Flint, as General Motors closes down automobile factories, to upper-class prosperity and obliviousness to the plight of the workers and the poor.

The narrative hook for the film, expressed in the title *Roger & Me,* is Moore's quest to talk to Roger Smith, president of GM, and convince him that he should come to Flint to observe the consequences of his corporate restructuring that involves moving auto assembly to Mexico. The quest takes Moore to offices, clubs, elite restaurants, and hotels where Smith is allegedly to be found, interspersed with images of people in Flint thrown out of their houses, neighborhoods deteriorating, and dejected workers undergoing plant close-downs and losing their jobs.

Moore's personal involvement in the lives of the rich and the poor attests to and illustrates class differences and growing working-class oppression. As a longtime inhabitant of the area, Moore manages to get access to a rich panorama of local characters, ranging from poor blacks and laid-off workers to public officials and PR functionaries, and visiting celebrities to the area. The film establishes Moore as a major portrayer of Americana, an astute analyst of class and capitalism, an advocate for the poor and underclass, and someone personally involved in affirming the effects of class oppression.

Indeed, in retrospect, *Roger & Me* is a remarkable first film. When he began, Moore reportedly did not know anything about film production, with documentary filmmaker Kevin Rafferty serving as one of his cameramen and teaching Moore how to set up a shot. Rafferty himself made the successful and engaging *The Atomic Café* (1982) and an exposé of the white supremacist movement, *Blood in the Face* (1991), which Moore himself participated in making, obviously giving him a taste for documentary filmmaking.[10]

Moore's satirical and biting critical representations of the upper-class elite in Flint, enjoying life while misery explodes for the underclass, brilliantly capture the decadence, shallowness, and class privileges of the rich in the 1980s. Yet Moore's satire was so over the top that he was sued by one of the Flint elite that his film savaged, showing that Moore was willing to take personal witnessing and stinging satire to levels where he opened himself to litigation. In portraying the annual Flint Great Gatsby Ball, an annual charity event in which the Flint elite dressed up in Roaring Twenties' affluent styles, a local lawyer sued Moore for his presentation in the film. The episode portrayed showed unemployed blacks and workers standing as human statues, and cited a tuxedo-attired local attorney Larry Stecco making light of the unemployment, stressing that others were still working. When asked about the good aspects of Flint, Stecco answered, "Ballet, hockey. It's a great place to live."[11] He sued Moore for defamation under "false light invasion of privacy."

Moore proves equally effective at getting celebrities and public officials to hang themselves in front of the camera, presenting Flint native and *The Newlywed Game* host Bob Eubanks and portraying him in a bad light, telling a horribly anti-Semitic joke about Jewish women and AIDS. *Roger & Me* also skewers local politicians in Flint, attacking their efforts to bring a Sheraton Hotel, a convention center, and an AutoWorld theme park to town when obviously the city needed programs that would provide better housing, jobs, and human services to its working people and underclass. From a critical perspective, *Roger & Me* brilliantly puts on display the class privilege and racism and sexism of the upper classes and their lack of social conscience and humanity. Privileged public corporate and political figures deserve satire and critique, and the public deserves to see their unguarded and revealing moments.

Yet one aspect of Moore's critique in the film of political figures as unconcerned with Flint's troubles backfired loudly in the film community: the brief segment in which Ronald Reagan comes to Flint, has pizza with workers, and provides his usual upbeat patter, during which a cash register is stolen. Here critic Harlan Jacobson—in one of the first detailed interviews with Moore—took him to task for reordering the historical sequence of events, as Reagan actually came to campaign in Flint in the early 1980s, and the (later bankrupt) Sheraton and failed Convention Center and AutoWorld were begun in the mid-1980s. By contrast, Moore's narrative is focused on footage from around 1986 to the film's completion in the late 1980s. Yet it appears from Moore's sequencing that the Reagan visit and building campaign came after the layoffs that Moore is presenting.[12] Moore protested to Jacobson that he was making entertainment, condensing hours of footage to present Flint's tragic recent history, and that his story about Flint was largely accurate.[13] As Moore and de Antonio claim, all films are constructs, editing is highly subjective, and there are other criteria besides objectivity and accurate chronology to judge documentaries.

Since Jacobson's critique, there has been a cottage industry of Moore critics

Exploiting working-class characters? Moore interviews the "pets or meat" woman, Rhonda Britton, of Flint, Michigan, in *Roger & Me.* Copyright 1989 Warner Bros., Inc.

who have attacked Moore's editing sequencing and alleged distortions. In fact, Moore's films are of a unique genre, often departing from standard documentary conventions. Moore readily admits that he is doing polemics and satire, and, as the epigraph to this section indicates, presented his first film as entertainment. Yet, as we shall see, by the time of *Fahrenheit 9/11,* Moore would publish entire books documenting statements and claims made in his films and would use his website to attack his critics and defend his work.

In addition, *Roger & Me* provoked questions about whether Moore exploits the working-class characters and lower-echelon functionaries in his film. One example of this accusation focuses on his portrayal of the "pets or meat" rabbit lady, Rhonda Britton, which depicts a poor young woman struggling to pay her bills by raising rabbits that could be sold either as pets or meat.[14] Moore later returned to her in a short documentary showing her raising snakes and rats as well as rabbits, providing a poignant picture of how the struggle for survival in predatory capitalism drives people to engage in bizarre occupations—a theme that would later frequently reappear in his TV series.

Despite its controversial aspects, Moore's mode of personal witnessing and intervention in *Roger & Me* goes beyond the compilations in standard film documentaries, creating a highly condensed, fast-moving, and entertaining montage of sequences that express a sharp point of view in a well-constructed narrative about capitalism and class in the United States. This topic is seldom addressed in mainstream media, and rarely has a documentary on this topic provoked so much interest and discussion. Moore managed to take political documentary film out of the ghetto of a marginalized cinematic form and into mainstream film. His innovative and successful film, however, was highly controversial, winning acclaim and criticism from many corners and propelling Michael Moore into a life of public controversy.

Moreover, *Roger & Me* began the construction of a unique genre, the "Michael Moore film." Moore emerges from his first film as a storyteller, fabulist, satirist, and witness to the corporate downsizing and devastation of his beloved Flint, Michigan. But in retrospect he does not appear as a rigorous documentary filmmaker concerned about historical sequence, strict documentation of facts, or objectivity. Moore positions himself instead as an entertainer and provocateur who raises questions, attacks wrongs and wrongdoers, and speaks up for the oppressed and against the oppressors. Despite critiques of inaccuracies of historical sequences or "facts" in his films, much of what Moore says is true in the wider sense. Yet his practice strains certain conventions and traditions of progressive documentary filmmaking that uphold objectivity and historical accuracy as the norms, and his work elicited ferocious debate. As we shall see, by the time he made *Fahrenheit 9/11,* Moore would be more concerned about standard documentary conventions. Yet he would continue to develop his own unique, controversial, and hard-to-classify filmmaking in *Bowling for Columbine* and subsequent films.

BOWLING FOR COLUMBINE AND EXPLORATORY DOCUMENTARY MONTAGE: GUNS, U.S. HISTORY, THE MILITARY, AND VIOLENCE

> I have long admired the old filmmakers who used comedy and satire as a means to discuss or illuminate social conditions, whether it was Charlie Chaplin, Will Rogers, or even the Marx Brothers. I hope people will laugh at this movie harder than they've laughed at a movie in years—but that they will also find themselves choking back the tears.[15]

An exploratory documentary tradition uses film as a medium to probe social problems. A standard mode of the Left documentary tradition, exploratory films investigate social problems, such as in de Antonio's exploration of McCarthyism in *Point of Order,* his critique of the Warren Commission and investigation of the Kennedy assassination in *Rush to Judgment,* or his look at nuclear weapons production and a Christian pacifist anti-nuclear movement in *In the King of Prussia.*

After several bestselling books, two TV series and two additional feature films, Moore, by the time he made *Bowling for Columbine,* was a genuine American celebrity and he could use his strong persona to engage once again his audience in a quest narrative. Moore's voice is once again the narrative center of the film and it is more confident, self-assured, and insistent than in his earlier work. At the same time, *Bowling for Columbine* takes Moore's documentary aesthetic to new levels of complexity and controversy, eliciting both widespread praise and condemnation, as he explores connections among guns, militarism, and violence in American history and contemporary society, and investigates the question of why there has been so much violence in the United States.

Moore's hook was the April 1999 Columbine shooting where two white middle-class suburban teenage boys took an arsenal of guns and homemade bombs to school and slaughtered their classmates. The film opens with a clip from a NRA promotional film and cuts to Moore narrating, "April 20, 1999," another "morning in America," with footage of farmers, workers, milk deliveries, "the president bombed another country whose name we couldn't pronounce," and the shootings at Columbine High School, with "The Battle Hymn of the Republic" playing on the sound track.

Once again, Michael Moore uses a highly resonant sound track to highlight his themes, using ironical juxtaposition of music as a technique of social critique. As this opening sequence suggests, Moore's targets in *Bowling for Columbine* are much broader and more complex than in his previous work. Indeed, the real quest of the film is to understand America itself, in particular why the country has such an obsession with guns and so much violence. Again Moore establishes his personal history in relation to his topic with footage of him receiving his first gun as a youth, accompanied by "I was born in Michigan" on the sound track. We learn that at 15 Moore won an NRA marksman award and has been a lifelong hunter and rifle owner.

The following sequence introduces a fellow citizen who grew up in Michigan, Charlton Heston, who in movie scenes holds and shoots guns, and then emerges as NRA president. Moore has again developed a dialectical structure where he poses himself against a villain. In *Roger & Me,* Roger Smith incarnated corporate greed, insensitivity, and a privileged upper-class lifestyle immune to concern for the human suffering of GM employees and others in Flint devastated by the plant closings. Now, in *Bowling,* the Bad Guy is Charlton Heston, Moses himself, who represents the NRA with his attacks on all restrictions on gun ownership and use, and who appears at an NRA annual meeting after the Columbine shootings, despite requests from parents of the teenagers and the mayor of the city of Denver to stay home. Heston also represents a privileged white upper-class lifestyle; he champions guns and conservative views while living in a gated mansion above Beverly Hills.

While *Roger & Me* was in part a quest for Roger Smith, *Bowling for Columbine* is largely a quest to explore the question of guns and violence in the United States, so the confrontation with Charlton Heston is a secondary theme. Indeed, *Bowling for Columbine* has a much larger tapestry to weave, and it makes connections among U.S. history, culture, guns, the military, violence, and racism. A section on the Michigan Militia cuts to James Nichols, brother of Terry Nichols, who, along with Timothy McVeigh, was responsible for the 1995 Oklahoma City bombings. While the opening on the Michigan militia is lighthearted and followed by Chris Rock's comedy routine of imagining high-priced bullets as a better form of market-based gun control, the Nichols section goes into a darker side of U.S. conspiracy mavens and gun fanatics—particularly when Nichols shows Moore off-screen that he keeps a gun under his pillow.

The film continues to make "six degrees of separation" connections by moving to Oscoda, Michigan, home of the Strategic Air Command, where one of the Columbine shooters grew up, while his father worked for the military. Another scene focuses on Littleton, Colorado, and the Columbine shootings, and notes that Lockheed Martin, one of the United States' major military contractors, is located in the city and employed the father of one of the Columbine shooters. Further, by chance, one of the heaviest days of bombing took place in Kosovo on the day of the Columbine shootings, and the film shows President Bill Clinton announcing the Kosovo events and shortly thereafter addressing the Columbine shootings.

In addition to interviews and news footage that illustrate the connections, Moore constructs a sequence using "What a Wonderful World" as background in an ironical Brechtian fashion[16] against a panorama of U.S. military interventions ranging from complicity in the overthrow of democratically elected governments in Iran and Guatemala in the 1950s, to support for Osama bin Laden's group that was fighting the Soviets in Afghanistan in the 1980s and support for the Taliban in the 1990s—followed by the horrendous spectacle of 9/11, a matrix

Moore would explore in more depth in his following film, *Fahrenheit 9/11*. An animated cartoon "History of the United States," made in the style of *South Park*, suggests that—rather than just one or another isolated factor—the entirety of U.S. history and social organization is responsible for violence in the United States.

The film takes on the Columbine High School shooting and then more broadly violence in the United States, in part to put in question one-sided or reductive explanations of the shooting and more broadly violence in the United States. Moore goes through a litany of politicians and pundits who blame the Columbine shootings on heavy metal, the Internet, Hollywood and violent films, the breakup of the family, and Satan, including a rant by Senator Joseph Lieberman, who blames the shootings on youth culture and attacks rock singer Marilyn Manson. In a long interview sequence, Manson intelligently defends himself and makes the moralistic Lieberman come off a fool in comparison.

Bowling focuses compelling sequences exploring connections between the media and racism, while depicting in interview and montage sequences how African Americans are in fact victims of poverty and inner-city violence. Moore interviews University of Southern California sociologist Barry Glassner, author of *The Culture of Fear*, in Los Angeles's fabled black neighborhood, South Central. The two discuss how the media greatly exaggerate the violence in the United States, especially by scapegoating African Americans.

Moore subsequently devotes a long sequence to the story of the murder of a young white girl Kayla Rolland by a six-year-old black student at Buell High School. It turns out that the boy's mother was forced by welfare law to bus 60 miles from her Flint, Michigan, home to take two minimum-wage jobs in a mall; moreover, the young boy was left with a relative from whom the boy took the gun and shot the young girl. In a tense sequence, Moore confronts *American Bandstand* and TV impresario Dick Clark on how he feels about the mother of the boy working at one of his restaurants and whether he supports the law that requires welfare mothers to work at minimum-wage jobs and leave their children unsupervised. Clark coldly turns away and another American icon is deflated with the cameras of the iconoclastic Moore.

Other sections show how youth are scapegoated in the media and subjected to humiliating surveillance and school discipline and suspension in an attempt to blame youth for the maladies of U.S. society. Sequences of Moore interviewing teenagers from Columbine and other high schools show that he is highly sympathetic to youth, and he has gained a large audience of adoring young fans, bringing documentary film and radical politics to a group not usually exposed to such fare. Indeed, there is a youthful and rebellious aura to Michael Moore's work that makes him a spokesman for alienated youth, as well as oppressed racial and class members.

In addressing the media and fear, Moore suggests in *Bowling for Columbine* that one of the major effects of the media is to generate fear that ruling politicians can exploit. While Moore is making connections between U.S. history and military actions, guns, the media, and violence, he is not claiming to establish causal connections between these forces, but is suggesting that they interact in a complex social environment. Moore's film shows that it's not just one thing, but many that caused the Columbine shootings and violence in the United States. *Bowling for Columbine* thus provides a multidimensional view of violence, gun culture, and teen shootings. It is open and nonreductive and does not provide simplistic answers to the question, as its critics claim.

This openness is apparent in one revealing sequence, in which Moore interviews Tom Mauser, father of one of the Columbine shooting victims, about what causes the United States to have more violence and gun victims than other industrialized countries. Mauser passionately asks, "What is it?" The editing then cuts rapidly back and forth, with Moore and Mauser repeating the query multiple times, ending with Mauser saying, "I don't know." Neither is obviously able to answer the unanswerable question. While Moore cannot provide easy answers, his queries do ferret out responses like that of Charlton Heston, who in the film's penultimate interview with Moore blames violence on American history and then the country's "mixed ethnicity," suggesting a racist response that calls attention to how racially motivated violence in American history and contemporary fear-mongering in American politics and media have played a central role in American's love of guns.

Yet even this approach cannot provide a definitive answer to the questions Moore is asking. Instead, Moore has suggested connections among U.S. gun culture, history, the media, political organizations and policies, U.S. military interventions and the weapons industry, deteriorating families and living conditions, increasing divisions between the rich and the poor, and the alienation of segments of youth to suggest that this matrix of factors is likely to produce violence and will require systematic social change and transformation.

Yet Moore's complex sense of the factors that generate and sustain America's love affair with the gun is still open to criticism. One issue Moore fails to address is that of gender and violence in a country where over 90 percent of the violent crime is committed by males.[17] This oversight is symptomatic of the failure of progressive males to question gender more radically, and it may express Moore's own emotional attachment to guns that he connects, perhaps unconsciously, with his masculinity. Moore also does not make it clear that 25 times more black inner-city teens are murdered by gunfire. At the time the movie was made, "Of 10,801 gun homicides in the United States, 2,900 (a little more than one-fourth) involved whites; seven in 10 involved blacks and Latinos."[18] Further, as Moore's critics have pointed out, he exaggerates per capita gun violence and murder in the United States compared to other countries, and his editing dramatizes certain points at the expense of accurately portraying historical sequences of events. Moreover, the standard conservative attack is that "Michael Moore hates America" and presents a wholly negative view of the United States.[19]

This conservative critique misses the point of who Michael Moore is and what he is doing. Moore is presenting a new type of personal, exploratory quest for answers to social problems informed by satire and humor and the development of his own crusading character who exposes social wrongs and injustices, an investigation that also implies the need for intervention. Michael Moore's films run counter to the dominant ideology that idealizes the "American dream," and his work undercuts the idealized, fantasy representations of the United States shown in countless TV series, films, and the whole apparatus of advertising, as a beacon of affluence and prosperity, or as a highly functional system where (TV) cops get the bad guys and (TV) lawyers prosecute wrongdoers.

As part of this exploration, Moore also shows typical Americans who are overweight, undereducated, and not beautiful or glamorous as in standard entertainment industry models that dominate television and film. He puts on display the more freakish and bizarre aspects of Americana and the significant differences between a corrupt upper class, its political apparatus, midlevel functionaries and operatives, and the culture of class, racial, gender, and age oppression. Rarely before have so many common people, so many forgotten people, but also so many varied and interesting characters, appeared on the screen in a documentary filmmaker's panorama of individuals.

To outsiders, the United States is a very strange country with bizarre aspects to its economy, politics, culture, and everyday life, and Michael Moore puts the underside of American life on display. In this, he is similar to his fellow documentary filmmaker Errol Morris in his explorations of the margins of U.S. society in films like *Gates of Heaven* (1980), *Vernon, Florida* (1981), and *The Thin Blue Line* (1988), or to Ross McElwee, who uses a home-movie and personal quest format to depict quirky and more eccentric visions of Americans than are usual in U.S. film and television.[20]

Yet, in some ways, Moore is akin to Soviet filmmakers like Sergei Eisenstein and Dziga Vertov, who also fudged on facts or historical accuracy at times to communicate larger truths and to advocate specific political partisan positions (mentioning Moore in the same constellation with Eisenstein and Vertov speaks of his brilliance as a filmmaker, as well as his leftist partisanship). As noted, there are also similarities to the cinema of Emile de Antonio in the socially critical use of montage and commitment to radical politics. Like de Antonio, Moore would take on a sitting president and highly controversial war in his most widely discussed film to date, *Fahrenheit 9/11*.

FAHRENHEIT 9/11 AND AGIT-PROP: THE BUSH ADMINISTRATION, 9/11, AND IRAQ

> We like nonfiction and we live in fictitious times. We live in the time where we have fictitious election results that elect a fictitious president. We live in a time where we have a man sending us to war for fictitious reasons, whether it's the fictions of duct tape or the fictions of Orange Alerts.[21]

While there have been in Moore's films, as in the work of de Antonio, significant personal witnessing and exploration of social problems, there has always been an undercurrent of agit-prop, putting these filmmakers in the partisan tradition of left-wing documentary cineastes. In this section and the following, I will argue that the strong political motivations of Moore's films and his unique mode of filmmaking—one that combines politics with entertainment—cannot be readily captured by conventional cinematic categories and creates his own genre: a Michael Moore film.

Bowling for Columbine was the most successful documentary in history through 2002. While it received top honors at the Cannes Film Festival and Academy Awards, and was voted the top documentary of all time by the International Documentary Association (IDA), it also received fierce criticism. As the infamous quote cited above from the 2002 Academy Awards ceremony suggests, Moore was now identifying himself as a documentary filmmaker making nonfiction films in an era with a fictive president in a specious war undertaken for false reasons. In an era marked by one of the most mendacious presidents and administrations in U.S. history, which exploited the tragedy of 9/11 to push through an extreme right-wing agenda and immerse the United States in a highly unpopular war in Iraq, Moore felt it was important to provide an all-out assault on the Bush administration, including evoking the stolen election of 2000,[22] and George W. Bush's limitations and failures as president.

Fahrenheit 9/11 stands as Moore's most interventionist film, taking on the sitting president and his Iraq war during the 2004 election season. While *Roger & Me* bore witness to the assault on working-class jobs and lives in the Flint, Michigan, area and implicated General Motors in the deterioration of the socioeconomic situation, there was not really an effort to change these conditions. Likewise, *Bowling for Columbine* explored the social problem of guns, violence, and school shootings in the United States but came up with no answers or agenda to intervene and change this predicament; in fact, Moore seemed genuinely surprised and delighted when Walmart executives announced they would no longer sell 17-cent bullets, following Moore's visit to their Michigan headquarters with two surviving victims of the Columbine shootings, whose bodies still contained bullets.

It is clear, however, that Moore intended *Fahrenheit 9/11* to be an important and perhaps decisive influence on the highly contested 2004 presidential election campaign. In his foreword to *The Official Fahrenheit 9/11 Reader,* which contains the filmscript, reviews, and documentation of some of the controversial claims and segments in the film,[23] John Berger asserts that *Fahrenheit 9/11* "may be making a very small contribution toward the changing of world history. . . . What makes it an event is the fact that it is an effective and independent intervention into immediate world politics."[24] In his introduction to the same volume, Moore described the tumultuous response to the film, the thousands of e-mails that poured into his website, and claimed: "In an election year where the presidency could be decided by a few thousand votes, these comments were profound—and frightening to the Bush White House."[25] While the film was immensely popular, it also evoked fierce criticism, perhaps unparalleled in documentary history, unleashing the entire right-wing echo chamber and attack apparatus against Moore.[26]

In *Fahrenheit 9/11,* Moore continued to develop his own sui generis form of documentary film, serving as narrator and intervening occasionally in the action. While *Bowling for Columbine* examined a complex of issues centered around American guns and violence, *Fahrenheit 9/11* focused more intensely on the personality and politics of the Bush administration and in particular its exploitation of 9/11 to promote the invasion of Iraq. As in his earlier films, there was a centerpiece villain who was the target of Moore's scorn and critical animus, and it was the president of the United States. In taking on George W. Bush and the American presidency, Moore was going after his biggest target so far and the controversy over the film, as well as the fact that it became the largest grossing and arguably most influential documentary in history, provided an index of Moore's success in provoking his audience and promoting debate over issues of key importance.[27]

Playing on the title of Ray Bradbury's novel about book-burning, *Fahrenheit 451*, *Fahrenheit 9/11* refers to "the temperature at which truth burns." The first section of the film takes on George W. Bush, beginning with his stolen presidency after the controversial Florida election fiasco of 2000, and then going back through his prepresidential checkered career and failures in the oil industry; investigation by the securities exchange for insider stock trading; failure to fulfill his National Guard service; Bush family connections with the Saudis; his administration's neglect of warnings about terrorism prior to 9/11; and Bush's slacking off at his ranch and family vacation sites before 9/11.[28] Other segments document the Bush administration's response to the 9/11 attacks, how they and the media generated fear, and how the Bush administration manipulated the fearful climate to push through the USA Patriot Act, the Iraq war, and a right-wing agenda.

Just as Emile de Antonio used Nixon's own words and images to indict him in *Millhouse*,[29] so too does Moore present highly revealing images of Bush, such as his sitting aimlessly while *My Pet Goat* was read to a grade-school class for seven minutes after he was told that the nation was under terrorist attack on September 11, 2001. Bush is later shown making a statement to reporters on fighting terrorism and then seamlessly shifting to take a golf shot, telling the group to "watch my drive." Moore shows him clowning and smirking before announcing to the nation that he'd just attacked Iraq. These images of Bush were shocking because most audiences had not seen such critical, satirical, negative, or revealing images of him before—superficial, smug and smirkish, arrogant, and incompetent. After 9/11, criticism of the presidency was taboo and the mainstream media served as a propaganda machine for the Bush administration's "war on terror"—a point Moore makes with a collage of media clips.[30]

The right wing went on ferocious attack, screaming that Moore was making false claims about connections among the Bush and bin Laden family and other Saudis, about connections between oil companies, Bush administration officials and U.S. foreign policy, and that the film was a pack of lies.[31] While his critics generally had a reductive and positivist mind-set that claimed Moore was making specific dogmatic claims and arguments, in fact his vision is more dialectical, pointing to connections within a complex history among factors that interact in overdetermined and complicated ways. Moore did not make specific causal claims, but pointed to connections and raised questions. Just as

Bowling for Columbine posed questions that the film could not answer, so too does Moore inquire about the impact of the secretive relations among the Bush family, oil corporations, the Saudis, and U.S. foreign policy. Just as *Bowling for Columbine* questioned connections between guns, the military, media culture, and American history without making any reductive causal connections or arguments concerning the Columbine shootings, so too does *Fahrenheit 9/11* show connections among the Bush family, the oil industry, the Saudis, and recent events of U.S. history, which are left to the viewer to unravel and interpret.

Moreover, Moore was raising issues that had not been discussed in the mass and news media, such as U.S. support for bin Laden's Islamicist forces and Saddam Hussein in the 1980s, as well as relations between the Bush family and the Saudis and the failures of the Bush administration to address terrorism before 9/11 and its problematic policies in the aftermath. While admitting that the film was highly partisan, and again using his celebrity status to privilege his own voice as the narrator who tells the audience what is happening and to bear witness to the events depicted, Moore also published *The Official Fahrenheit 9/11 Reader* to document claims made in the film. He also frequently answered critics on his website.

Moore brilliantly demonstrates the contradictory directives of the Bush administration's manipulation of 9/11, in a montage with footage of Bush telling people to be happy, to travel, to go to Disneyland for a vacation, alternately interspersed with dark warnings from Cheney and Rumsfeld evoking fears of terrorism and a long brutal war. Congressman Jim McDermott (D.-Wash.) characterizes these mixed messages as "crazy making," for the American people are told to do two contradictory things at once.[32] Other contradictions Moore points out involve the Bush administration promoting fear of terrorism on the one hand and cutting back counterterrorist budgets on the other, allowing lighters and matches to be carried on planes but not a mother's breast milk, and extolling the heroism of young U.S. soldiers in Iraq while cutting back on veteran's benefits and health care.

The second half of the film focuses intently on the Bush administration's intervention into Iraq. Moore was criticized for showing an idyllic Iraq on the eve of the devastating U.S./U.K. assault on the country, but the sequence allowed a contrast between life before and after the invasion and provoked empathy for audiences to consider how they would respond to an attack on their country. Moreover, the Iraq segment anticipated revelations that the argument that the United States had gone to war to destroy Iraqi "weapons of mass destruction" was specious. The segment also presciently anticipated that the Iraq intervention would be a fiasco for the Iraqis and Americans, as it previewed Abu Ghraib debacle with images of U.S. soldiers sexually humiliating Iraqi prisoners.[33] In addition, *Fahrenheit 9/11* exposed the lies that were used to sell and justify the intervention, and the ways that U.S. troops would be brutalized and made to pay the costs of the war with life and limb.

While Moore was attacked for negative images of U.S. troops, the last half of the Iraq segment showed very sympathetic presentations of the U.S. military victims of the Iraqi war and made it clear that, in addition to Iraqis, it was poor and working-class young Americans who were traumatized, mutilated, and killed in Bush's failed Iraq intervention. Cutting to Flint, Michigan, to illustrate military recruitment in malls of working-class and African American youth for the Iraq war, a long sequence introduced Lila Lipscomb, a middle-aged woman who had risen from welfare mother to executive assistant at a jobs center. Lila tells of how her daughter and son had joined the military; her patriotism is demonstrated by showing the daily flag-raising at her house. Then it is revealed that her son was killed in Iraq, and the footage captures the aftermath for the mother and her extended family.

In one scene Lila showed Moore a multicolored and multicultural cross, and subsequent shots reveals that indeed her family is multiracial and rainbow colored. Again, Moore shows great sympathy for class and race victims of U.S. policies and takes their side against the powers that be.

After demonstrating the problematic ways that the Bush administration manipulated 9/11 and the horrific Iraq catastrophe, Moore cuts in the conclusion back to the villains of the piece—congressmen who urged the war and arch-villain George W. Bush. In one of his trademark confrontational episodes, Moore goes after congressmen who supported the war, asking them if they'd like to send their children to Iraq, highlighting again that it is the sons and daughters of the working class who are the fodder and victims of the elite.

Closing sections of *Fahrenheit 9/11* show a Halliburton ad touting its role in Iraq, revealing that the company, of which Dick Cheney was a former CEO, was garnering billions in no-bid contracts. Exposés of war profiting also depict businessmen at a conference on how to make money in Iraq, getting "a piece of the action." In an earlier scene, George W. Bush addresses a group of "the haves and the have-mores," telling them: "Some people call you the elite, while I call you my base!" Here Bush drolly revealed—albeit within the self-mocking humor characteristic of the traditional Alfred E. Smith memorial dinner held to raise money for Catholic charities at which Bush spoke—the antipopulist thrust of the Bush administration. The film ends with a flustered Bush trying to finish the old "Fool me once . . ." adage, finally blustering, "Fool me, can't get fooled again," and Michael Moore concludes, "For once, we agreed," as the film cuts to titles accompanied by Neil Young's "Rocking in the Free World."

Moore's film was thus an all-out assault on the Bush-Cheney administration, using satire and parody to mock the president and his administration, to raise questions concerning their connections to corporate elites, the military-industrial complex, and Middle East oil interests, and to demonstrate the horrific effects of the Iraq war on the American and Iraqi people. Moore's intervention was highly ambitious, and while it failed at its political intent, it has been recognized as one of the most popular, daring, and controversial documentary films of all time.

SICKO, CAPITALISM: A LOVE STORY, AND THE MICHAEL MOORE GENRE

My films are a work of journalism, but they're journalism of the op-ed page. . . . [My job] is not to present all sides. My job is to present my side.

—MICHAEL MOORE[34]

Broadly speaking, one can classify documentary/nonfiction films as either openly *partisan,* seeking to address a specific issue and offer a position, or claiming to be *nonpartisan,* seeking to gain the truth about a situation by minimizing biases, presuppositions, or a set agenda.[35] Thus within the documentary tradition, there are filmmakers who aspire to a norm of maximum objectivity, contrasted to those who insert themselves in a nonobjective partisan camp. The films of Michael Moore obviously fall in the latter camp—they are highly interventionist, asserting specific political positions, as well as attempting to inform and entertain.

In Moore's films, there is also more of an interaction between documentary and entertainment, fact and narrative, and archival/shot footage and creative editing than in nonpartisan documentaries. His films' entertainment value obviously accounts for their success, while many people identify with and applaud the Michael Moore character and love to see him confront the bad guys and uncover corporate or political wrongdoing. He is one of the few U.S. filmmakers to be consistently critical of corporate capitalism and to explore class differences and oppression in the United States. Thus, Moore's personal bearing witness to problems portrayed and presentation of these issues from his own point of view produces a much more subjective text that is found in a nonpartisan and "objectivist" documentary tradition.

Moreover, while one can quibble with facts and editing sequences in Moore's films, his cinema portrays larger truths neglected by other filmmakers and the media industry, such as the fact that corporate restructuring and downsizing has been creating great misery for the working class and devastating communities undermined by shutting down U.S. plants (as in *Roger & Me* and *The Big One*). Although one can argue about his editing sequencing and statistics in *Bowling for Columbine,* Moore raises important questions about the relations among guns, violence, the military, and culture in U.S. society, documents violence in U.S. history, and shows how the media generate fear that is exploited by right-wing politicians and those who scapegoat youth and media culture in connection with events like the Columbine shootings. Far from being simplistic or reductive, *Bowling for Columbine* presents a complex and multidimensional exploration of the problems of guns and violence in U.S. society and history.

In *Fahrenheit 9/11,* Moore raises questions about the Bush administration policies before and after 9/11, and especially right-wing support of oil companies and the military-industrial complex and the invasion of Iraq. Moore was also one of the first to raise questions about George W. Bush's competency, an issue that became mainstream after his inadequate response to Hurricane Katrina and the protracted, ongoing struggle in Iraq.[36]

Moore's *Sicko* builds upon his previous filmmaking. The film opens by Moore bearing witness to working and middle-class people who recount the suffering they experience because they do not have adequate health insurance. Moore sees inadequate health care as a major social problem in the United States and shows how the corporate health-medical complex, the insurance industry, and conservative politicians conspire to keep an inadequate system in place.

Moore then goes on a quest drama to discover if there are better health systems in other Western countries and visits Canada, England, and France, demonstrating that their national health services are highly popular and effective, without the bureaucratic red-tape and inequities that plague the U.S. system. In perhaps the film's most humorous extended episode, Moore goes to Guantánamo Bay, Cuba, suggesting prisoners there get better health care than average Americans. In a personal intervention, he takes into Cuba some nongovernmental emergency workers who voluntarily served at the 9/11 Ground

Zero site and who are not able to get adequate health care in the United States. He helps get them treatment from Cuban doctors.

Sicko is one of Moore's most radical films, attacking the presuppositions of an American, capitalist dog-eat-dog society where every individual is forced to secure health care on his or her own, and only the rich and fortunate are able to do so. Moore takes on the laissez-faire logic that the market should dictate the terms and availability of such crucial services, and shows how other countries operate their health systems on a completely different logic and assumptions. In extended sequences, Moore challenges the rationales for America's health systems by showing that Canadians, the British, the French, and Cubans have a completely different view of the world, one that believes that everyone should get adequate health care and that a society is more just and healthy that does so.

In *Capitalism: A Love Story* (2009), Moore takes on the capitalist system itself, excoriating a socio-economic system in which the top 1 percent owns 95 percent of the wealth and in which an unregulated economy is allowed to wreak havoc. Illustrating the flaws of laissez-faire capitalism, Moore focuses on the home mortgage and financial crises that exploded in public in Fall 2009. Interviewing people who were victimized by easy home loans that soon morphed into increased monthly mortgages that they could not pay, as well as interviewing individuals involved in the scandal, who were obviously motivated by greed, Moore shows the human consequences of an unregulated economic system.

Moore makes the argument that a system run by greed, competition, and profit-seeking above all will obviously ignore morality, social justice, and the negative impacts of an unregulated economy, and that stronger regulation, more progressive taxation (which Moore points out was the norm in the U.S. in the postwar period until the Reaganite era of the 1980s), and guaranteed rights to health care, education, and social welfare are minimal components of a just social system. To ground the latter argument in political history, Moore provides documentary footage of one of the last speeches of Franklin Roosevelt presenting an argument for a "second bill of rights" in his final State of the Union address, footage believed lost and which Moore's researchers unearthed in an archive in South Carolina.

Yet at the conclusion of the film Moore cannot without embarrassment proclaim that he is a socialist and part of his concluding argument contrasts the situation of his father and his own family as members of a working class community in which strong unions and reasonable salaries made it possible for working class families to achieve what was recognized as a middle class existence. Moore does not follow Marx in citing the endemic crisis tendencies in an unregulated capitalist economy, the injustice and horrors of exploitative industrial labor, or the argument central to the Marxist tradition of how capitalism inevitably leads to imperialism and war.

In *Capitalism: A Love Story,* Moore does, however, indicate what policies and which individuals were largely responsible for the deregulation of the economy and criticizes Obama for bringing in advocates of neo-liberalism, who were in part responsible for the economic failures of the era into his administration, including Treasury Secretary Timothy Geithner, who was part of the failed Wall Street regulatory apparatus and Larry Summers, a neo-liberal who was brought in as a top economic advisor. In interviews, Moore gives Obama the benefit of the doubt, and subtle pressure (perhaps with tongue in cheek) to follow his best progressive instincts, telling audiences that he hoped Obama had brought them on in the same way that some banks hire robbers to help them prevent future theft: "Maybe that's what Obama's doing—he hired the people who robbed all the money to help him get it back. That's the optimistic version."[37]

As with Moore's other films, *Sicko* and *Capitalism: A Love Story* are rich with detail and provide information, insights, and connections into relations between economic, political, and cultural forces often overlooked in an accessibly and often-entertaining format. Moore's critics fail to see that there is a long-standing and honorable partisan filmmaking tradition and that films can legitimately intervene into specific political contexts and hit specific targets without being "fair and balanced" (itself often, as with the Fox News Channel, an ideological construct).

Finally, as argued, Moore has developed a unique character in popular culture, himself, and a unique genre of filmmaking, the personal witnessing, questing, and agit-prop interventionist film that explores issues, takes strong critical points of view, and targets villains and evils in U.S. society.[38] He is as American as apple pie with his baseball caps, oversized body and ego, often disheveled appearance, and ability to continually redefine himself and come out on top. Moore exposes some of the seamier and more freakish aspects of American life, but also shows a whole panorama of American characters portrayed in the tradition of Diane Arbus, Errol Morris, and R. Crumb, who put on display marginalized individuals and voices and experiences not usually visible in an idealized U.S. media culture. As he does so, Moore embodies and presents in his films good decent common people, confused people overwhelmed by circumstances.

Michael Moore himself is a complex, larger-than-life character, embodying many opposites and many contradictions, as a number of admiring and critical biographies and the wealth of articles and news stories written about him demonstrate. Ultimately, Michael Moore is an American original, combining the crusading idealism of JFK liberalism with left-wing anticorporate populism, and the comic antics of the Yippies and the performance-oriented Left, still visible in the anticorporate globalization movement.[39] He is highly controversial, intensely polarizing, and extremely partisan. Yet his works raise important questions, make connections overlooked in conventional media, provoke discussion and inquiry, and rarely fail to entertain those willing to enter into Moore's cinematic universe.

Notes

1. Michael Moore in an article by Ron Hutcheson, *Knight-Ridder/Tribune Service*, June 23, 2004, quoted in Robert Brent Toplin, *Michael Moore's* Fahrenheit 9/11: *How One Film Divided a Nation* (Lawrence: University Press of Kansas, 2006), 80.

2. I am deploying a broad conception of documentary as nonfiction films concerned with depicting actual events, but the concept of documentary contains many different types of film, competing definitions, and a wealth of categories. As I will argue, Moore undercuts many traditional notions of documentary while drawing on documentary strategies in a partisan radical film tradition, ultimately producing his own genre of "Michael Moore film." For helpful comments on earlier drafts of this essay, I want to thank Rhonda Hammer; Jeff Share; Richard Kahn; Charles Reitz; and, especially, Matthew Bernstein, who provided many useful sources and editorial suggestions.

3. De Antonio's films include *Point of Order* (1963), a brilliantly edited montage of the Army/McCarthy hearings; *Rush to Judgment* (1964), a provocative documentary on the Kennedy assassination; *In the Year of the Pig* (1969), a major documentary on the Vietnam War; *America Is Hard to See* (1970), an excellent depiction of Eugene McCarthy's campaign for the presidency in 1968 that catches the political turmoil of the era; *Millhouse* (1971), a scathing documentary indictment of Richard Nixon that won de Antonio a place of honor as the only filmmaker on Nixon's infamous "enemies list"; *Painter's Painting* (1972), a set of interviews with the luminaries of the New York art scene; *Underground* (1976), a documentary about the Weather Underground Organization that reflects on the radical movements of the 1960s; *In the King of Prussia* (1982), which deals with the 1980 attempt by the Berrigan brothers and a group of Catholic activists, the Plowshare Eight, to call attention to nuclear madness by splashing blood on the cones of nuclear weapons in an assembly factory in The King of Prussia, Pennsylvania; and *Mr. Hoover and I* (1989), which tells Hoover's life story, utilizing his FBI files, which amounted to tens of thousands of pages of material culled from the Freedom of Information Act. On de Antonio, see the Introduction to Douglas Kellner and Dan Streible, eds., *Film, Art, and Politics: An Emile de Antonio Reader* (Minneapolis: University of Minnesota Press, 2000).

4. I am drawing on three books that provide overviews of Michael Moore's life and work, including the accessible introductory study by Emily Schultz, *Michael Moore: A Biography* (Toronto: ECW Press, 2005); Jesse Larner, *Moore & Us* (London, Sanctuary Publishers, 2005), which provides both critique and good political contextualization of Moore's biography and work; and a right-wing screed by David T. Hardy and Jason Clarke, *Michael Moore Is a Big Fat Stupid White Man* (New York: ReganBooks, 2004). In addition, I draw on a vast amount of film scholarship and Internet material on Moore, as well as his own books. In fact, Moore appears to be the best-documented and most controversial documentary filmmaker in history. Moore has reportedly said that Terrence Rafferty's *Atomic Café* is the only film that influenced him (see Schultz, *Michael Moore,* 64) and has never, so far as I know, discussed de Antonio's work; Rafferty himself was influenced by de Antonio and thanked him in the credits in *The Atomic Café* (see the discussion in text).

5. On cinema verité in the United States, see Stephen Mamber, *Cinema Verite in America: Studies in Uncontrolled Documentary* (Cambridge, MA: MIT Press, 1974).

6. See Emile Antonio, "Conversation with Bruce Jackson," http://www.sensesofcinema.com/contents/04/31/emile_de_antonio.html (accessed August 18, 2006).

7. On photography and mechanical reproduction in film and photography, see Walter Benjamin, "The Work of Art in the Age of Mechanical Reproduction," in *Illuminations,* edited and with an Introduction by Hannah Arendt, translated by Harry Zohn (New York: Schocken Books, 1969), 217–52. On the myth of objectivity in journalism, see Michael Schudson, *The Power of News* (Cambridge, MA: Harvard University Press, 1996).

8. Moore has said: "There's a myth of objectivity out there, whether it's a documentary or the *Philadelphia Inquirer.* We're subjective beings by nature. Even the decision of what to put in the paper, where to place it—it's all subjective." Quoted in Ken Lawrence, *The World according to Michael Moore* (Kansas City: Andrews McMeel Publishing, 2004), 98.

9. Michael Moore, in *Australian Financial Review,* May 4, 1990, quoted in Ken Lawrence, *The World according to Michael Moore* (Kansas City: Andrews McMeel Publishing, 2004), 110.

10. See Schultz, *Michael Moore,* 64.

11. On the Stecco story, see Schultz, *Michael Moore,* 81ff; and Larner, *Moore & Us,* 85.

12. See Harlan Jacobson, "Michael and Me," *Film Comment* 25, no. 6 (November–December 1989); this text is the mother lode of the anti–Michael Moore industry with the pathetic Larry Elder even taking the title for his "documentary" assault on Moore. For later critique of the sequencing of Moore's Flint narrative, see Schultz, *Michael Moore,* 61ff; Larner, *Moore & Us,* 66ff; and Hardy and Clarke, *Michael Moore Is a Big Fat Stupid White Man,* 17ff.

13. Jacobson, "Michael and Me."

14. For critique of Moore's depiction of some working-class people, see Pauline Kael, "Melodrama/Cartoon/Mess," *New Yorker,* January 8, 1990, 90–93.

15. Michael Moore, in *USA Today,* October 11, 2002, quoted in Lawrence, *The World according to Michael Moore,* 58.

16. On Brecht, see Douglas Kellner, "Brecht's Marxist Aesthetic," in *A Bertolt Brecht*

Reference Companion, ed. Siegfried Mews (Westport, CT: Greenwood Press, 1997), 281–95. Moore effectively uses Brechtian "separation of elements," ironically playing off soundtrack and music with image and narrative. Like Brecht, he also makes strongly political works. I have found no evidence in interviews with Moore or other material that would indicate, however, that he was directly influenced by Brecht.

17. See Jackson Katz, *The Macho Paradox* (Naperville, IL: Sourcebook, 2006). This point is also taken up by Gaylyn Studlar in this volume.

18. See Mike Males, "'Bowling for Columbine' Misframes Gun Quandary," November 6, 2002, http://home.earthlink.net/~mmales/bowling.htm.

19. See the anti-Moore films by Mike Wilson, *Michael Moore Hates America* (2004); and Larry Elder's *Michael & Me* (2004); and the attacks on Moore in Hardy and Clarke, *Michael Moore Is a Big Fat Stupid White Man.*

20. Morris has made eight highly acclaimed documentaries; see http://www.imdb.com/name/nm0001554/. McElwee's 12 documentaries include *Sherman's March* (1986), *Time Indefinite* (1994), and *Bright Leaves* (2003); see http://www.imdb.com/name/nm0568478/.

21. Michael Moore, at the 2002 Academy Awards ceremony, quoted in Lawrence, *The World according to Michael Moore,* 51.

22. For my take on the 2000 election and first nine months of the Bush presidency, see Douglas Kellner, *Grand Theft 2000: Media Spectacle and a Stolen Election* (Lanham, MD: Rowman and Littlefield, 2001). Toplin, *Michael Moore's* Fahrenheit 9/11, 91ff, provides a judicious and balanced appraisal of Moore's claims about the Bush presidency, conservative critiques, and counterarguments.

23. See Michael Moore, *The Official Fahrenheit 9/11 Reader* (New York: Simon and Schuster Paperbacks, 2004).

24. John Berger, "Foreword: The Work of a Patriot," in *The Official Fahrenheit 9/11 Reader,* by Michael Moore (New York: Simon and Schuster Paperbacks, 2004), ix.

25. Michael Moore, introduction to *The Official Fahrenheit 9/11 Reader* (New York: Simon and Schuster Paperbacks, 2004), xv.

26. See David Brock, *The Republican Noise Machine: Right-Wing Media and How It Corrupts Democracy* (New York: Crown, 2004). After his 2002 Oscar acceptance speech Moore stated: "For the next couple of months I could not walk down the street without some form of serious abuse. Threats of physical violence, people wanting to fight me, right in my face, 'F——YOU! You're a traitor!' People pulling over in their cars screaming. People spitting on the sidewalk. I finally stopped going out" (*Entertainment Weekly,* July 9, 2004, quoted in Lawrence, *The World according to Michael Moore,* 52).

27. Robert Brent Toplin even-handedly presents the conservative critique of the film and deals with criticisms in terms of the failure of many of his conservative critics to understand Moore's unique brand of filmmaking and the partisan reaction against his left-wing politics; see *Michael Moore's* Fahrenheit 9/11. Moore presents his own defense of the film and answers to his critics in *The Official Fahrenheit 9/11 Reader* (New York: Simon and Schuster Paperbacks, 2004) and on his website http://www.fahrenheit911.com/ library/book/index.php.

28. David Tetzlaff discusses *Fahrenheit 9/11*'s relation to the title of Ray Bradbury's *Fahrenheit 451* in his essay on Moore's film in this volume.

29. Moore could have paid homage to de Antonio and called his film *W: A White Comedy,* parallel to de Antonio's *Millhouse: A White Comedy* (Millhouse being an intentional misspelling of Nixon's middle name).

30. For my take on the 9/11 terror attacks and how the media promoted Bush administration policy thereafter, without raising serious questions or debate, see Douglas Kellner, *From 9/11 to Terror War: Dangers of the Bush Legacy* (Lanham, MD: Rowman and Littlefield, 2003); and *Media Spectacle and the Crisis of Democracy* (Boulder: Paradigm Press, 2005). See David Tetzlaff's discussion of *Fahrenheit 9/11*'s media critique in this volume.

31. See the attacks in Hardy and Clarke, *Michael Moore Is a Big Fat Stupid White Man,* which include Christopher Hitchens's demagogic and vicious assault on Moore and *Fahrenheit 9/11*. Two right-wing documentaries that take on the film include *Celsius 41.11* (2005) and *Fahrenhype 9/11* (2005). Toplin critically dissects the right-wing critique of Moore in chapter 3, "A Sinister Exercize," of *Michael Moore's* Fahrenheit 9/11.

32. Thanks to Rhonda Hammer for pointing out to me the use of paradoxical injunctions in Michael Moore's films. For discussion of how paradoxical injunctions, double binds, and the manipulation of fear can make people crazy, see Paul Watzlawick, Janet Beavin, and X Jackson, *Pragmatics of Human Communication* (New York: Norton, 1967).

33. These photos were the subject of Errol Morris's documentary *Standard Operating Procedure* (2008); for my interpretation of the photos and their effects, see Kellner, *Media Spectacle and the Crisis of Democracy.*

34. Michael Moore in Rene Rodriguez, "Controversial Moore Documentary Stirring up Passions for Both Sides," *Miami Herald,* June 24, 2004, quoted in Toplin, *Michael Moore's* Fahrenheit 9/11, 80.

35. Toplin, *Michael Moore's* Fahrenheit 9/11, makes a similar distinction and has a chapter on the partisan and engaged documentary tradition in which Moore's work should be situated and interpreted (71ff).

36. On Hurricane Katrina and the Bush presidency, see Douglas Kellner, "Hurricane Spectacles and the Crisis of the Bush Presidency," *Flow* 3, no. 3 (October 2005), http://jot.communication.utexas.edu/flow/?jot=view&id=1049; and Henry Giroux, *Stormy Weather: Katrina and the Politics of Disposability* (Boulder: Paradigm Press, 2006).

37. Michael Moore, cited in Alec MacGillis, "For 'Capitalism,' Moore Sells Short Politicians of All Denominations," *Washington Post,* September 16, 2009, at http://www.washingtonpost.com/wp-dyn/content/article/2009/09/15/AR2009091503314.html (accessed December 15, 2009).

38. Larissa MacFarquhar, "The Populist: Michael Moore Can Make You Cry," *New Yorker,* February 16 and February 23, 2004, 132–45.

39. MacFarquhar, "The Populist."

"Everything Is Personal": Michael Moore and the Documentary Essay

PAUL ARTHUR

Classification has been a persistent, surprisingly nonpartisan issue in the reception of Michael Moore's films. Nearly everyone, it seems, including the director himself, proposes a different descriptive category—sometimes tossing out multiple designations within the same discussion—for the kind of nonfiction work Moore has produced. From *Roger & Me* to *Fahrenheit 9/11*, and despite glaring dissimilarities among his four feature-length documentaries, a pronounced taxonomic confusion hovers over possible cinematic discourses to which the films adhere or, as frequently, from which they are said to triumphantly—or, depending on the commentator, scandalously—diverge. Far from a parlor exercise enacted for the benefit of fussy academics or inflamed media pundits, the problem of naming in this case goes directly to the heart of Moore's significance in contemporary culture while simultaneously illuminating American documentary's volatile public profile since 1990.

Although there have been multiple revisions in and around recent nonfiction cinema, a few basic facts will help situate Moore's films in a burgeoning arena long considered marginal at best.[1] For two decades prior to the release of *Roger & Me*, barely a handful of documentaries per year were shown theatrically in the United States. In 2005, more than 60 docs, or roughly 15 percent of total releases, had commercial runs. Due in part to a revolution in access and production expenses engendered by inexpensive digital video rigs and editing equipment, not only are more docs being made by more filmmakers than at any time in the past, nonfiction is decidedly more popular with general audiences. Of the 10 all-time nonfiction box-office successes, nine were made after 2001.[2] Taking into account relatively small shooting costs and, by industry standards, practically nonexistent advertising budgets granted the vast majority of docs, domestic ticket sales of $1 million is "boffo" business. During the 1990s, a total of three films surpassed this mark. Since 2001, an average of seven films per year have done so, and given a corresponding drop in receipts for foreign language pictures, documentaries now compete on an equal footing with both imports and so-called Amerindie narratives. Rentals and sales of documentary DVDs have followed suit.

A cyclical pattern of dissatisfaction with Hollywood's default escapism has, especially since 9/11 and the invasion of Iraq, magnified the appeal of fact-based entertainment. The rising popularity of reality TV, whose initial stirrings paralleled the explosion of nonfiction cinema in the early nineties, has bestowed a heightened appreciation for documentary idioms and modes of address. In a similar vein, the continuing market dominance of literary nonfiction—in particular, memoirs and self-help books—is paralleled by a growing propensity for first-person documentary narration. Not unexpectedly, enhanced exposure has resulted in unprecedented critical attention. A decade ago it was rare to find documentaries included in typical end-of-year roundups of favorite films; these days it is de rigeur for critics to cite at least one nonfiction achievement. A final measure of documentary's economic viability is a burgeoning institutional network encompassing specialized as well as inclusive film festivals. In 2004, for instance, nearly one-third of all feature submissions to the prestigious Sundance festival were nonfiction: from a host of independent distribution companies, Internet-based activist groups like MoveOn.org, and ever-expanding press coverage in mainstream venues as well as nonacademic film magazines.

Roger & Me did not simply arrive on the cusp of what now registers as a momentous transformation; rather, it acted as official harbinger and recurrent lightning rod for the movement's aesthetic initiatives and political controversies. Moreover, in a cultural domain normally oblivious to lures of authorship (how many knowledgeable viewers would recognize a photo of, say, Frederick Wiseman?), Moore has unquestionably emerged as the public face of contemporary nonfiction. Two primary, reciprocal factors informing this dubious honor are the ubiquity of Moore's image and the financial success of his various enterprises. Clearly, his best-selling books, intermittent TV series, and lecture tours have aided the promotion of his feature projects—and vice versa—whose popularity at the box-office in turn triggers demand for media appearances that generate fresh sources of funding.[3] Leaving aside the marketing of Eskimo Bars that briefly capitalized on Robert Flaherty's *Nanook of the North* (1922), documentary history offers no remotely comparable example of cultural synergy.[4] Hence Moore's movie career can be viewed as a categorical anomaly regardless of his films' contested generic status.

The critical debate surrounding *Roger* is by now overly familiar, if highly symptomatic. It would be tempting to conclude that claims for its lack of "balance" or "objectivity" as inconsistent with standard documentary practice reflect a historical blindness since rectified in the surge of theatrical nonfiction. Unfortunately, many of the same benighted, ideologically motivated distinctions between "documentary" and "fiction" or "propaganda" resurfaced with the release of *Fahrenheit 9/11*.[5] It makes no sense, at this late date, to rehash tired arguments concerning the legitimate boundaries of documentary discourse, its pretenses to truth or objectivity. What is worth noting, however, are the range of equivocations or linguistic displacements employed by commentators both pro and con. The locus classicus, as it were, of semantic hijinks is a notorious interview conducted by Harlan Jacobson. After attempting to deflect Jacobson's well-researched accusations of falsified chronology in *Roger,* the director—perhaps for the first but hardly the last time—rejects what he feels are overly restrictive labels: "It's not fiction, but what if we say it's a documentary told with a narrative style." In retrospect, this tack opened the floodgates for speculation about what to call his purportedly elusive style. A bit later Moore explains, "I think of it as a movie, an entertaining movie."[6] Whether or not he is being disingenuous, such statements form part of a broader pattern aiming to exempt the films from established tenets of documentary aesthetics or ethics—as D. H. Lawrence observed a century ago, these entities are deeply intertwined. As unleashed through his polished everyman persona, Moore disparages antiquated doc traditions, in particular canons of evidence and argumentation, while fostering loose comparisons with mass cultural products. "You're trying to hold me to a different standard," he tells Jacobson, "as if I were writing some kind of college essay"; and later, "I wasn't writing [a footnoted] article, I was making a movie."[7]

It is not evident, at least to me, how much film history Moore actually knows. An inveterate moviegoer in his twenties, with a couple of revealing exceptions he rarely acknowledges either documentary influences or other contemporary nonfiction directors (he is, however, unstinting in praise of Stanley Kubrick, a key inspiration for the fictional *Canadian Bacon*).[8] Instead, he frequently correlates his filmic method with alternative, nonmainstream journalism. As he put it in relation to *Fahrenheit,* "It's a work of journalism; it's the kind of journalism that journalists *should* be doing . . . it's an op-ed piece."[9] Given his background as a writer, grassroots newspaper editor, and head of a liberal magazine, it is certainly fitting for Moore to pose rough analogies between journalistic and filmic enunciation; indeed, as I will argue, his best-selling books and major films share themes, structural features, rhetorical strategies, and comic shticks. The point is that in an effort to avoid being tagged with an established generic designation—carrying certain obligations and viewer expectations—Moore resorts to either extradocumentary or extracinematic comparisons. So too do his supporters and bashers.

As several commentators have noted, one way of sidestepping shibboleths involving truth or objectivity is to describe the films as "comedies" rather than documentaries, a maneuver that segues with the director's own ideas about the value of democratic "entertainment."[10] Andrew Collins, writing in the *Guardian,* tries to counter criticism of Moore's subjective presence in *Fahrenheit* by inventing a tortured, and unnecessary, appellation: "author piece."[11] In another awkward stretch, Ed Halter humorously discovers in *Fahrenheit* "a new category of high-concept Hollywood product: the activist blockbuster."[12] Celebrated novelist John Berger, responding to attacks from the political Left as well as the Right, calls *Fahrenheit* "an event" rather than a mere movie, signifying "an effective and independent intervention into immediate world politics."[13] It is apparent that for many observers, Moore's movies—or some concatenation of textual elements and self-perpetuating media projections—are so unprecedented in public impact, sui generis as it were, that they require interpretive tools beyond the customary frameworks applied to documentary. Consequently, a resultant focus on naming can be addressed as integral to the films' wider compass of meaning.

Critics for whom the term *documentary* is not itself problematic nonetheless have conflicting opinions on where the films belong. Robert Brent Toplin, in a book devoted to public reactions to *Fahrenheit,* invokes the tradition of "committed documentary" (a term espoused by scholar Thomas Waugh) dating back to New Deal and militant labor docs. In other chapters, Toplin makes reference to "guerrilla theater" and "agit-prop" techniques.[14] His emphasis throughout is on the scrambling of fixed categorical distinctions. Adopting a taxonomic scheme proposed by theorist Bill Nichols, another commentator declares *Roger* a "hybrid" of "interactive" and "reflexive" modes,[15] an indication that no single category is adequate to the description of Moore's style. Adopting the exact same scheme, Matthew Bernstein calls the film a fusion of "expository" and "interactive" modes, going on to note *Roger's* strong resemblance to the presumably déclassé "illustrated lecture."[16] The notion of hybridization recurs in discussions of *Fahrenheit;* for instance, Richard Porton argues for a composite grouping that includes the essay film plus televisual practices such as rock videos, news magazines, and reality game shows.[17]

At the risk of simply adding to this onomastic free-for-all, I want to suggest a way of reconciling most, if not all, the preceding attributions while speaking to overarching dilemmas associated with Moore's work. Two textual features recognized by nearly every critic, often the crux of either approval or rebuke, are the director's first-person presence and a structural propensity for segmentation, digression, and clashing rhetorical tones. In other words, much of what is understood as the essence of Moore's approach centers on interrelated qualities of voice or discursive organization. Hence critics defend or excoriate his films' blatant subjectivity, the "me" that frames our intake of knowledge. By the same token, his quirky thematic trajectories are judged as either refreshingly open or self-indulgently messy. Setting aside issues raised by the interpenetration of films and public performances—Moore's slippery metatext—the assumption that his particular repertoire of audiovisual strategies is without precedent in nonfiction cinema, or at the least requires a fundamental revamping of critical terminology, is ill-founded. Taking a wider angle on film history, I would contend that *Columbine* and *Fahrenheit* fit comfortably within established critical paradigms for the documentary essay; *Roger* and *The Big One* have essayistic trappings yet lack an unequivocal commitment to this venerable and increasingly vital genre.

Although the epithet itself has yet to earn widespread critical acceptance,[18] the documentary essay was inaugurated in cutting-edge post–World War II European cinema as an extension of philosophical meditations on the Holocaust, on totalitarian social formations, and the legacy of colonialism. In other words, it began as an inherently politicized form capable of addressing abstract ideological concepts. A trio of French docs has achieved landmark status: Alan Resnais's *Night and Fog* (1955), Jean Rouch's *Les Maitres fous* (1955), and Chris Marker's *Letter from Siberia* (1958). New German Cinema artists Alexander Kluge and Werner Herzog, along with directing partners Jean-Marie Straub and Danielle Huillet, made occasional forays into essay territory in the 1960s. The genre took root as well among proponents of Latin American "Third Cinema," as evident in the work of the great Cuban collagist Santiago Alvarez and in Fernando Solanas's pioneering *Hour of the Furnaces* (1968).

From a trickle of dispersed titles in the sixties and seventies, the essay emerged as a full-fledged international movement during the 1980s, a period in intellectual thought stamped by the breakdown of master narratives. As I note elsewhere, contemporary essays, galvanized by the intersection of personal experience (or memory) and social history, have provided an ideal oppositional vehicle for women, for racial and sexual minorities, and, outside the sphere of Anglo-European moviemaking, for a robust nonfiction contingent in developing countries.[19] Globalization, the manifestations of postindustrial capital and the imprint of corporate power on mass media, constitute areas of thematic convergence for homegrown and non–First World artists. The relevance of this line of cinematic inquiry to Moore should be obvious.

A founding principle of the documentary essay is its challenging of conventional descriptive boundaries. In this sense the essay is a genre into which seemingly a-categorical docs frequently fit. Unlike adjacent genres such as the city symphony, celebrity portrait, or historical compilation, essays can't be identified strictly by subject matter, theme, or visual style (like the use of rapid montage to symbolize the hectic pace of modern cities).[20] Although not invariably heterogeneous in material, essays tend to use archival footage and found speech or music as historical evidence, as analytic taproot, or as editorial platform. Extant materials are typically blended with original scenes, interviews, and other present-tense images. Collage, then, is a common—although hardly inevitable—essay trait, in part a by-product of juggling different orders of representation: the "voice" of the filmmaker as imparted by spoken narration or intertitles, or as inscribed in functions of selection, camera work, editing, and sound; depictions of actual events, past or current; commentary by participants or talking-head authority figures. Essays are rarely unified in their address to the viewer, downplaying closure and internal consistency in favor of the fragmentary, the provisional, and the plurivocal. Voice-over commentary struggles against the immediate pull of an image, the sobriety of images is undercut by tacky music, successive shots or sequences are arranged as alternate views of the same verbal proposition, or augur outright contradiction. As is true of tense and level of enunciation, tone can shift from moment to moment—from pathos to humor, outrage to irony.

Even when an essay film is not overtly reflexive in calling attention to its own processes of production, the form tends to allegorize the building of spontaneous, or at least nonpredetermined, insights on a given topic, implying a journey in consciousness rather than a fixed itinerary. Of course this is a fiction, a rhetorical tool used to rationalize associative linkages and personal digressions. Nonetheless, in the absence of familiar devices like linear storytelling or the chronicling of a single character or event, narrative indeterminacy is a primary means of distinguishing essays from, say, social problem or cinema verité docs. Essays do not pretend to have all the answers or, for that matter, to ask every pertinent question but instead valorize quicksilver trains of thought understood to emanate from a central, subjective yet unstable source of knowledge. In contrast, political docs of the 1930s spoke in kind of a collective "we," while American verité of the sixties relied on a transparent "you," attempting—albeit unsuccessfully—to suppress indices of a controlling, subjective observer.

A decisive factor, then, in the attribution and explication of documentary essays is the manner in which subjectivity, the address of the "I," is deployed across the text. To be sure, not all first-person docs are essays. Morgan Spurlock's popular *Super Size Me* (2004), unmistakably under the sway of Moore's on-screen persona, has the structure of a diary and limits its thematic scope to physiological consequences of a fast-food diet rather than tackling the industry's economic ramifications. By the same token, not all essays are anchored by a diegetic, or even aural, directorial presence. For example, many of Harun Farocki's scintillating takes on postindustrial commodification of everyday life are devoid of spoken narration yet bear the filmmaker's indelible, deadpan formal approach. Alternatively, Guy Debord in *Society of the Spectacle* (1973) confines his authorial presence to a lengthy series of printed texts.

Columbine and *Fahrenheit* do not accede to the essay tradition simply because of Moore's foregrounded place in the action. Indeed, as we shall see, the degree of stability, or epistemological certainty, attached at times to his self-image paradoxically dilutes the potency of essayistic discourse.[21] Contrary to opinions of mainstream critics largely unschooled in documentary history, Moore's lively on-camera performances are hardly without filmic precedent. Earlier authorial appearances in documentary essays include Jon Jost in *Speaking Directly* (1974), Orson Welles in *Filming Othello* (1978), and Ralph Arlyck in *An Acquired Taste* (1981). By the late 1980s, this practice had gained increasing acceptance as prior restrictions on documentary expression were rapidly jettisoned. Of particular note are two theatrical releases, Ross McElwee's *Sherman's March* (1986) and Tony Bubba's *Lightning over Braddock: A Rustbowl Fantasy* (1988), both mobilizing first-person techniques—and in Buba's case, a thematic focus—with strong affinities to the persona and mode of address found in *Roger*. If we take into account an even wider sphere on nonessayistic first-person docs,[22] it should be evident that far from operating in an aesthetic vacuum, Moore parlayed an already legitimized documentary option into a flourishing, perhaps unduly influential media franchise.[23]

As the title intimates, *Roger* is not an essay. Driven by the clashing personalities of Moore and General Motors chairman Smith, it is site-specific—detouring only briefly from Flint to sample California liberal chic—and temporally compact, if chronologically challenged. The film's early autobiographical perspective, making fleeting reference to labor struggles of the 1930s while enumerating family ties to the local auto industry, quickly gives way to the structural gambit of securing a meeting with Smith (a device that, as critics realized, was doomed from the outset). Although *Roger* examines a problem that in a wider context limns the plight of manufacturing jobs in a postindustrial, multinational economy, it makes no sweeping indictment of profit-mad corporate ethics or government policies that sanction grievous damage to blue-collar communities. Instead, as he does in later projects, Moore imbues vividly drawn characters with abstract traits, dividing the world into easily digested binary oppositions: compassionate versus callous , salt-of-the-earth versus elitist, awkward versus media savvy.

There is little doubt on which side of divide the director—or more accurately, his crafted persona—falls. He makes acerbic observations on the generalized decline of skilled, unionized labor in America, a stance whose veracity has only deepened since 1989, yet builds his case around emotionally charged dramatic incidents such as the Christmastime eviction of a black family. As Larissa MacFarquhar puts it, "For Moore, everything is personal. He's not angry with capitalism, or even with companies; he's angry at Roger Smith. . . . He doesn't fight against war, he fights against Rumsfeld, Cheney, and Bush."[24] In subsequent films, although the structural interplay of person and idea, specific event and abstract principle, tilts slightly toward the general—hence in the direction of the essayistic—Moore's relationship to political discourse remains beholden to viewers' emotional responses to either sympathetic or villainous figures.[25]

Beyond the melding of personal experience and social history, *Roger* evinces a number of interesting family resemblances to the essay form. For example, Moore mobilizes diverse filmic materials for purposes of editorial comment as well as illustration of factual statements. Home movies, TV news clips, excerpts from studio-era Hollywood films, automotive TV commercials, newsreels, clips from industrial training films, and pop music—for instance, the satirical use of the Beach Boys' "Wouldn't It Be Nice"—produce not only humorous asides but decenter effects of a unified enunciative presence. Moore is clearly in control, yet the enacted "Me" speaks through an assortment of visual and aural registers, including montage and sound-image disjunctions—a rhetorical range encompassing glib irony, anger, and sincere empathy. On another front, qualms about *Roger's* manipulated chronology may be partially resolved by citing the essay's frequent recourse to *subjective* versions of events informed by personal memory or psychological impressions—rather than empirical depictions—of otherwise disparate incidents, for instance GM plant closings and civic initiatives to revitalize downtown Flint.[26]

Roger's stunning financial success (domestic box office alone totaled $6.7 million) spawned a made-for-TV short, *Pets or Meat: The Return to Flint,* less a sequel than an historical footnote. Here Moore details the subsequent fates of leading characters, giving special attention to "Bunny Lady" Rhonda Britton, whose initial portrayal proved a source of heated debate. Critics accused the director of demeaning humor aimed at working-class subjects, with a secondary tinge of sexism in scenes involving Britton and a waitress at a San Francisco café. Without explicitly responding to attackers, *Pets* is clearly intended to complicate his previous profiles of various Flint residents. In regard to Britton, it suggests a remedial fleshing out, as it were, of a woman for whom the killing and gutting of rabbits was read alternatively as a metaphor for the objectification of workers or as a positive sign of their resilience in the face of economic hardship.[27] From another angle, this minor addendum is noteworthy as the first in a substantial chain of interlocking media projects and as an essayistic acknowledgment that treatments of actuality are by nature unsettled, partial rather than closed discursive systems that can engender supplemental or even conflicting perspectives. As Moore has often maintained, "It's a movie, you know, you can't do everything."[28]

The Big One shares with *Pets* a provisional aura, an almost parasitic dependency on a prior text, in this case Moore's best-selling 1996 book, *Downsize This!* Staged as a casual diary of a reluctantly undertaken book tour, this feature-length road movie juxtaposes scenes of public speaking with observational footage of meetings with activist employees and the usual self-dramatizing confrontations with corporate authority. Just as the book follows up on labor themes raised by *Roger, The Big One* piggybacks on Moore's resistance to benighted policies of downsizing and outsourcing.

Of greater relevance to the essay aesthetic are two television series produced in the interim between *Roger* and *Columbine, TV Nation* and *The Awful Truth.* Like the later documentaries, individual programs are chopped into short seven- to ten-minute segments dealing with separate but occasionally interrelated topics. An unfortunate tendency to swaddle serious critique in increasingly strained comic stunts turns individual episodes into the equivalent of *Jackass* for lefties. Nonetheless, the series introduces a new target crucial to

Moore's fully realized film essays and to his subsequent writings: the ideological complicity of mass media in the agendas of conservative interest groups and the Bush administration. If nothing else, his scrutiny of deceptions perpetrated by nonfiction media—primarily TV news but also print journalism—around the packaging, and masking, of historical truths nudge *Columbine* and *Fahrenheit* into the essay camp. As a voice-over tagline to *The Awful Truth* intones, "In the beginning, there was a free press. Not really but it sounded good." Moore has referred to himself as a "subversive by default" due to the perfidy or plain incompetence of mainstream media.[29]

Blatant formal convergences spark the relationship between Moore's TV series and his punchy books. Both are short-form collections of (mostly) humorous sketches in which Moore tries out different voices and adduces surrogate authorial commentators. In *Dude, Where's My Country?* (2003), he addresses a letter to George Bush from God and conducts an imaginary interview with great-granddaughter "Anne Coulter Moore"; in episodes of *The Awful Truth,* he recruits cartoon stand-ins like "Crackers the Corporate Crime-Fighting Chicken" and "Joe Camel." The fabrication of lists is a staple of both mediums; a typical passage from *Dude* lays out "7 Questions for George of Arabia." Not unexpectedly, similar devices appear in *Columbine* and *Fahrenheit.* While Moore's background in short-form journalism and his subsequent immersion in TV's magazine format may not totally account for the pronounced segmentation in later documentaries, the imbrication of Moore's diverse media enterprises cannot be overstated. Isolated facts or associative links or comic bits migrate from written to cinematic contexts and back again.[30] In other words, regardless of any conscious stake in the documentary essay tradition, Moore has clearly adapted principles of exposition and address derived from established nonfiction literary genres.

Moore provides an intriguing reference to one American documentary landmark when he proclaimed *Hearts and Minds* "not only the best documentary I've ever seen—it may be the best film ever."[31] Although several critics have traced parallels with Emile de Antonio's provocative found footage collages,[32] Peter Davis's 1975 award-winning, commercially successful Vietnam War essay is arguably a more telling influence. Davis's key tactic in repudiating architects of the debacle in Southeast Asia is to abut statements by the likes of Walt Rostow and William Westmoreland to images and verbal testimony directly contradicting what was just said. In *Fahrenheit,* especially, Moore uses editing to counter official nonsense, as in a notorious montage of prewar peaceful Iraqis slapped against Bush's touting of the threat posed by Saddam Hussein. *Hearts and Minds* contains an elaborate football metaphor intended to embellish the causes of American military aggression, a folksy trope replayed in several guises in *Columbine.* The ironic insertion of shots from Hollywood movies such as *My Son John* and the caustic layering of music over image—for example, "Over There," a hymn to bravery, plays over shots of soldiers torching a Vietnamese village—is not unique to Davis's film but its unusual shifts from cheeky humor to trenchant analysis might well have struck a responsive chord in Moore.

Specific moments in *Fahrenheit,* such as talks with amputees in a military hospital, recall similar scenes in the earlier film. Equally important, Davis privileges what might be called "conversion narratives," stories related by former supporters of the war such as Daniel Ellsburg and veteran air force pilot Robert Muller that spell out reasons for their gradual opposition. Unlike de Antonio's complex historical treatment in *In the Year of the Pig* (1969), Davis aims for an emotional connection with politically moderate viewers by enlisting unassailable establishment figures as paragons of resistance, a device used to great advantage toward the end in *Fahrenheit* when Moore revisits a defiant Lila Lipscomb, the churchgoing, staunchly conservative mother of a marine killed in Karbala ("I thought I knew but I didn't know").

Descriptively elusive though it may be, a simple test for identifying the documentary essay is to ask what a given film is about, its overarching theme or idea. Just as the fate of Flint and its former factory workers, as administered by GM, is at the core of *Roger,* the irreducible quandary in *Columbine* is America's mania of handgun violence; in the final reckoning, the film is not *about* school shootings or the aftermath of 9/11 or the depredations of the NRA. Unlike *Roger,* and for that matter *Fahrenheit, Columbine* is not an attempt to intervene in an urgent political crisis. To be sure, not every sequence follows a logical path of inquiry toward a solution to questions posed by Moore. And "essay" is a descriptive classification rather than an honorific; it has no bearing on aesthetic value. Nonetheless, a partial review of how prerogatives of the essay function in *Columbine* will help to solidify the term's critical merits.

After a brief prelude consisting of a fake (found footage) NRA endorsement and lyrical invocation of the morning of the Columbine tragedy, Moore constructs the following scenic chain:

1. Moore visits a local bank offering free guns to new customers ("I'd spotted an ad in a Michigan paper").
2. Credits roll over archival shots of a bowling alley.
3. An old TV ad for realistic toy guns

4. Stills and home movies of Moore as a kid annotated by first-person voice-over reflections ("This was my first gun . . .")
5. Montage footage introduces Charlton Heston as an actor and gun enthusiast.
6. Interview with a state policeman about a humorous gun accident involving a dog, accompanied by illustrative/reenacted images
7. Moore gets his hair cut in a barber shop that also sells ammunition.
8. Excerpt of a comedy routine by Chris Rock in which he imagines the ramifications of setting ridiculously high prices for bullets.
9. Moore interviews members of a Michigan Militia outfit on a firing range and during nighttime maneuvers.
10. Moore visits James Nichols, brother of Oklahoma City bombing conspirator Terry Nichols, on his organic soybean farm ("James graduated high school the same year I did in the district next to mine").
11. Action shifts to Colorado, initiating Moore's inquiry into the contexts for the Columbine shootings.

Several stylistic tendencies are evident in this 20-minute section. The early pace is extremely fast—eight vignettes in less than 11 minutes—then slows down for scenes 9 and 10, each lasting approximately five minutes. *Columbine* and *Fahrenheit* both exhibit patterns of intense, multilayered activity—often reinforced by sound/image disjunctions—supplanted by less hectic interviews or thematic excurses. The tone in the opening section is relatively light but changes rapidly in scene 11 as Moore's attention turns to Columbine.

To a far greater extent than in *Roger,* montage is a fundamental tool of articulation, applicable to collisions of sound as well as image. Leaving aside the brief invocation of a national perspective, the first 10 scenes not only raise topics that echo across the body of the film—Heston; the unregulated sale of ammunition; connections between local shootings and international mayhem—but indicate the director's personal stake in nearly every character and event, generating a loose spiral from specific case to general circumstance. This mechanism serves two functions: it provides a jocular axis of viewer identification (who hasn't played with toy guns or joked about paramilitary nuts?) exploiting a prior familiarity with Moore's persona; and it sanctions a network of subjectivized associations bound simply by location or biographical synchrony or outright coincidence rather than by any exacting logic (the Oklahoma City bombing, for example, had little to do with problems of gun control). As is also true of *Fahrenheit, Columbine* tries to dispel the impression of hanging the-

Essay form in *Bowling for Columbine.* Moore cuts from a 1960s TV ad for Marx's "Sound-O-Power rifles" (military and western) to . . .

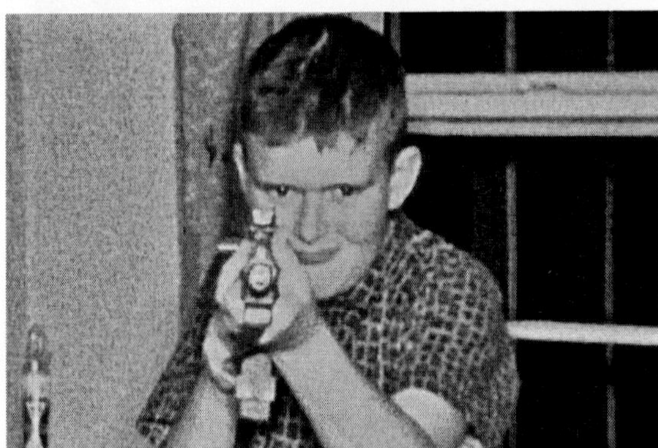

. . . home movies of Moore, here pointing a toy gun at the camera, as Moore speaks of his winning a National Rifle Association marksman's award. Both illustrations Copyright 2002 Alliance Atlantis Communications/United Artists.

matic threads through gestures of symbolic closure, first the return to Michigan to examine the aftermath of a horrifying grade school shooting, then an "impromptu" interrogation of gun advocate Heston.

In contrast to *Roger,* Moore inserts talking-head experts to speak on various aspects of gun violence as extensions of the director's own views. A criminology professor and a Michigan prosecutor are fairly standard documentary authorities, but the recruiting of cartoonist Matt Stone and singer Marilyn Manson—each connected, albeit indirectly, to the Columbine shootings—is a shrewd move both in terms of popular appeal and as essayistic fracturing of enunciative stability. Indeed, the animated history of American violence and fear of racial otherness, overseen by Stone's production crew, is in essence a film-within-a-film replete with a distinct rhetorical address and sporting ideas that appear nowhere else in *Columbine.* It is as if Moore had momentarily ceded the burdens of authorship to a kindred spirit. Nothing equivalent to this divisive interlude is evident in *Fahrenheit,* which otherwise maps a formal terrain quite similar to *Columbine's* episodic flow. In his uncompromising attack on the Bush presidency, the director reduces his own on-screen antics to a few minor sequences—reading the Patriot Act from an ice cream truck; soliciting members of Congress to send their children to Iraq—while exerting his unusually forceful voice-over presence.

That said, a noticeably more subtle, sophisticated approach to polemical editing suggests Moore's growing skill in manipulating film language. There are residual instances of sophomoric humor expressed through collage, as in the "Coalition of the Willing" roll call, which uses newsreel and fiction clips to poke fun at the clothing and customs of, mostly, people of color. But there is also a greater quantity of unsettling sound bridges, quick shards of speech or ambient sound either preceding or trailing an unrelated shot for purposes of puncturing the facades of officious spokespeople. A prime example of how deft editing can fashion a sinuous thread of argument occurs just past the halfway point in *Fahrenheit.* In a section dealing with Iraqi civilian bombing casualties, beginning with an unfortunately tendentious clump of gung-ho combat bragging, the following sequence is a virtual paradigm of essayistic construction:

1. Close-up of the soldier talking about how unprepared he was for seeing gruesome injuries: "It was like, shoot, what the hell do we do now?"
2. Brief black-and-white bomb-site shot of explosion on the ground below
3. Close-up of Donald Rumsfeld at a press conference describing the "care . . . and humanity" that goes into air force bombing missions (his voice is heard intermittently over shots 4 and 5).
4. Long shot of village houses being hit by a powerful explosion
5. Close-up of young boy's mutilated face being stitched up in a hospital
6. Black-and-white gun-site footage of two figures being mowed down by machine-gun fire
7. Rumsfeld reiterating his point about careful targeting practices
8. Medium shot of a distraught Iraqi woman facing the camera, grieving over a demolished village and cursing U.S. forces: "They have no conscience . . . God will destroy their houses."
9. Close-up of Britney Spears chewing gum, responding to an interview question: "Honestly, I think we should just trust our president."

The longest, most devastating shot in this skein is the black-clad Iraqi woman, likely culled from an Al Jazeera TV broadcast (a microphone with the network logo is briefly visible in the foregound). Her excruciating agony and rage occupies 50 seconds of an otherwise headlong 94-second sequence. The shock cut to Spears initially feels like a gratuitous slam, but there are other possible readings. In one sense she answers the question posed by the young, callow grunt in shot 1: "What the hell do we do now?" It is an answer Moore wants his audience to reject. Applause is heard at the very end of Spears's affirmation, bridging a transition into a prewar Bush warning a live audience about Saddam's weapons of mass destruction. Although I have isolated this group of shots from a longer integrated sequence, it is clear that what Moore is doing is moving from effect to cause, from graphic refutation of Bush administration lies to a representation of blind affirmation, itself a causal factor in the current mess in Iraq. That the source of affirmation is a young pop idol may make for easy laughs, but it also ties together the earlier faces of brash young soldiers and targets a constituency thought at the time to be of crucial importance in the upcoming election.

A final, unanticipated and decidedly extratextual measure of Moore's embrace of the essay form surfaced in the months following the release of *Fahrenheit.* Moore had insisted that his film was motivated by the need for a national conversation on Iraq and post-9/11 politics of fear, not just by a desire to smash George Bush's bid for reelection. It is indeed possible that, according to one critic, "no single work of speechmaking, writing, filmmaking or television sparked as much debate about the direction of U.S. domestic and foreign policy."[33] Regardless of the amount of mass media coverage and op-ed fulminating it received, *Fahrenheit* is unique in the annals of documentary—and in film history generally—for stimulating four separate feature-length filmic responses: Alan Peterson's *FahrenHYPE 9/11*, Kevin Knoblock's *Celsius 41.11*, Bruce Wilson's *Michael Moore Hates America* (all 2004), and Steven Greenstreet's *This Divided Nation* (2005). If one counts Larry Elder's provocatively titled but peripheral blast of shameless self-promotion, *Michael & Me* (2005), there have been five direct responses.

Taken together, this work seeks to accomplish several tasks: refuting factual representations or stated conclusions in *Fahrenheit;* defending the policies and ideological tenets of the Bush administration; and, in the first two films, taking jabs at Democratic candidate John Kerry. While the first two were directed by minor film-industry types, the latter two are efforts by first-time filmmakers for whom Moore's supersuccessful career serves as a transparent model. Both documentarians proffer versions of Moore's on-screen folksy address—Wilson even kicks off his response with a *Roger*-esque autobiographical sketch ("I was born into the heart of America")—and leaving aside their reactionary political views, both maintain a barely veiled ambition to use Moore's public appeal as leverage for potential future film projects. That is, they are industry "calling cards" in the guise of outraged personal rebuttals.

More germane to our purposes, all four films traffic in the formal idioms of the essay. They assert a wider thematic reach than the debunking of Moore's probity or status as "unbiased" documentarian—this ambit includes issues of free speech, national security, aesthetic distortion, and so on—and inadvertently suggest ways in which no account of historical events can be completely trustworthy or discursively stable. Moreover, these cinematic "op-ed" interventions wield the editorial tools of voice-over narration, mixed materiality, talking-head commentary, optical looping and slow motion, invidious music tracks, and creative montage to ends quite similar to those of their nemesis. To cite a blatant example, *Celsius 41.11* juxtaposes Moore with Adolf Hitler as twin practitioners of the "big lie," then adds a shot of Kerry as, presumably, a fellow dissembler. Had *Fahrenheit* premiered in a nonelection year it almost certainly would have faded without provoking such unprecedented filmic response. Nonetheless, the point I want to make is that the *form* adopted by the anti-Moore crowd assumes the cultural validity of essay techniques. From our present vantage, then, if Michael Moore has done nothing else, he has popularized a rather slippery genre whose legacy of heterodox, intellectually challenging discourse until recently was located only on the extreme periphery of nonfiction entertainment.

Notes

1. For an extended account of the recent cultural elevation of documentary forms, see my "Extreme Makeover: The Changing Face of Documentary," *Cineaste* 30, no.3 (Summer 2005): 18–23. In the same issue of *Cineaste,* Pat Aufderheide provides an informative take on the documentary in "The Changing Documentary Marketplace," 24–28.

2. Here as elsewhere I am referring to non-concert-related, non-sports-related docs; all box-office figures are taken from the invaluable website boxofficemojo.com.

3. The website IMDb.com lists literally dozens of TV spots on talk shows and other programs, nearly all of them broadcast in the last few years, or post–*Bowling for Columbine.*

4. Some might point to a film like Bruce Brown's *The Endless Summer* (1966) as a doc that generated product tie-ins such as T-shirts and an eventual sequel, *The Endless Summer 2,* yet I would argue that the Moore "franchise" is of a different order of magnitude and cultural significance.

5. Robert Brent Toplin makes copious references to critics wielding naive definitions of documentary in an effort to invalidate Moore's status as a nonfiction filmmaker; see

Michael Moore's Fahrenheit 9/11: *How One Film Divided a Nation* (Lawrence: University Press of Kansas, 2006), passim. Richard Porton parses the polemics over *Fahrenheit* from a slightly different perspective in "Weapon of Mass Instruction: Michael Moore's *Fahrenheit 9/11*," *Cineaste* 29, no. 4 (Fall 2004): 3–7.

6. Harlan Jacobson, "Michael and Me," *Film Comment* 25, no. 6 (November–December 1989): 23, 24, respectively.

7. Ibid., 23, 24, respectively. Elsewhere, under the banner of a vague populism, Moore advocates a creative method that abjures fealty to or even knowledge of documentary history: "I want filmmaking in the hands of people like us who know squat about filmmaking." Dan Georgakas and Barbara Saltz, "Michael and Us: An Interview with Michael Moore," *Cineaste* 23, no. 3 (1998): 5. In the same interview, he avers that "people who complain that I'm being too simplistic have usually spent too many years in school . . . and they have been thinking about things a little too much" (5). Among numerous similar barbs, one more will suffice: "Generally speaking, I don't like documentaries. I don't like PBS, [it's] boring." Quoted in Ken Lawrence, *The World according to Michael Moore* (Kansas City: Andrews McMeel Publishing, 2004), 104.

8. Moore's early fascination with movies is sketched by Emily Schultz in *Michael Moore* (Toronto: ECW Press, 2005), 18. I do not mean to imply that the director is personally ungenerous toward documentary colleagues. He famously urged fellow Academy Award nominees to join him on the podium for his 2003 acceptance speech, and the foundation he created with profits from *Roger & Me*, the Center for Alternative Media, has given money to important nonfiction projects such as *The Panama Deception* (1992).

9. Quoted in Lawrence, *The World according to Michael Moore*, 78. Once again, references to the proper role of a free press, often expressed in tandem with his repugnance for corporate media's complicity in government policy, are plentiful: "I wanted to make something that would be the kind of journalism I wish I could see when I turned on the news or picked up the paper." "The Ending Is up to You: Michael Moore Interviewed by Gavin Smith," *Film Comment* 40, no. 4 (July–August 2004): 3.

10. Christopher Sharrett and William Luhr discuss comedic attributions in "*Bowling for Columbine*," *Cineaste* 28, no. 2 (Spring 2003), reprinted in this volume.

11. Cited in Toplin, *Michael Moore's* Fahrenheit 9/11, 181.

12. Ed Halter, "The Big Ones," *Village Voice*, July 6, 2004, 78.

13. "The Beginning of History," *Guardian*, August 24, 2004, 6. In the same piece, Berger offers a persuasive rebuttal to charges that Moore makes "propaganda," arguing that the latter requires a permanent, state-endorsed network of communication able to stifle opposing views.

14. Toplin, *Michael Moore's* Fahrenheit 9/11, 71, 43, 120, respectively.

15. Miles Orvell, "Documentary Film and the Power of Interrogation: *American Dream* and *Roger & Me*," *Film Quarterly* 48, no. 2 (Winter 1994–95): 10–18, reprinted in this volume.

16. Matthew Bernstein, "Documentaphobia and Mixed Modes," in *Documenting the Documentary: Close Readings of Documentary Film and Video*, ed. Barry Keith Grant and Jeanette Sloniowski (Detroit: Wayne State University Press, 1998), 397–415.

17. Porton, "Weapon of Mass Instruction," 4.

18. While it is understandable for early documentary histories like Richard Meran Barsam's *Nonfiction Film* (New York: E. P. Dutton, 1973) and Erik Barnouw's *Documentary: A History of the Non-fiction Film* (New York: Oxford University Press, 1974) to ignore the essay, recent efforts such as Jack C. Ellis and Betsy A. MacLane's *A New History of Documentary Film* (New York: Continuum, 2005) have no excuse. More baffling still is the lack of a single entry on essays in the massive, three-volume *Encyclopedia of the Documentary Film,* ed. Ian Aitken (New York: Routledge, 2006). Unerringly perspicacious Kristin Thompson and David Bordwell cite the genre in their standard textbook, *Film History* (New York: McGraw-Hill, 1995), and it has appeared more frequently of late in newspaper and magazine critiques. Part of the problem stems from backward attitudes toward documentary as an undifferentiated genre rather than a mode of production, like Hollywood studio films or the avant-garde, with its own generic subset. An additional confusion is the fact that among major nonfiction directors, only Chris Marker and Harun Farocki have worked almost exclusively in the essay form. Several filmmakers, beginning with Sergei Eisenstein, have actively embraced the label, but many—including Farocki—dispute its explanatory value.

19. For specific examples, see my historicized sketch of the essay genre: "Essay Questions," *Film Comment* 39, no. 1 (January–February 2003): 58–63.

20. Michael Renov, the essay's best explicator, argues forcefully that such films elude the "law" of genre: see, for example, "*Lost Lost Lost:* Mekas as Essayist," *The Subject of Documentary* (Minneapolis: University of Minnesota Press, 2004), 70–73. I lean heavily on Renov's insights in what follows, but we disagree on the essay's status as a genre. For Philip Lopate, the problem of genre seems unresolved. He follows Renov in citing Adorno on the essay's "radical promise" of an "antisystematic, subjective, nonmethodic method" but goes on to treat the form as a stable collection of elements: "In Search of the Centaur: The Essay-Film," in *Beyond Document: Essays on Nonfiction Film,* ed. Charles Warren (Hanover, NH: Wesleyan University Press, 1996), 244. Other writers on documentary have utilized the term but fail to supply a definition or outline of historical-stylistic development.

21. The nature of the self inscribed in documentary essays has been a point of contention. Lopate, for instance, sees in the work of Marker, Ross McElwee, Ralph Arlyck, and others a unified authorial presence that goes against the grain of poststructuralism's insistence on fragmented, unstable subjecthood: "In Search of the Centaur," 252. Renov, on the other hand, valorizes the essay's grounding in dispersive, self-doubting narration: "*Lost, Lost, Lost,*" 70.

22. The broader issue of "personal" docs goes beyond the purview of this essay; it is, however, worth noting that numerous directors, from European auteurs like Jean Rouch, Jean-Luc Godard, Werner Herzog, and Wim Wenders to North Americans Michael Rubbo and Joel DeMott have constructed variations on the first-person voice. Among immediate precursors, Nick Broomfield in *Driving Me Crazy* (1986) exudes some of the same bumbling, constantly flabbergasted qualities perfected by Moore. I analyze a striking surge in first-person "therapeutic" practices in "Docu-Angst: *Tarnation,*" *Film Comment* 40, no. 5 (September–October 2004): 47–50.

23. A prime example of undue influence is the oft-repeated campaign taunt, "the Michael Moore wing of the Democratic Party."

24. Larissa MacFarquhar, "The Populist: Michael Moore Can Make You Cry," *New Yorker,* February 16 and February 23 , 2004, 140. Objections to Moore's reliance on allegorical character types is typical of attacks from the political Left; see, for example, Robert Jensen, "Stupid White Movie," counterpunch.org/jensen07052004.html. Ed Halter, on the other hand, turns Moore's proclivity into a political triumph: "[He] understands correctly that if popular, leftist positions are going to enter the medium of mass entertainment, proponents will have to speak in the writ-large language of the blockbuster" ("The Big Ones," 78). Halter's point is partially vitiated by the recent success of Al Gore's environmental lecture film *An Inconvenient Truth* (2006).

25. This is not to suggest that nonfiction explorations of character and essayistic discourse are mutually exclusive—far from it. What distinguishes Moore's approach from, say, Jean-Pierre Gorin's *Poto and Cabengo* (1981) or Ross McElwee's recent *Bright Leaves* (2003) is that the latter call attention to the very codes through which individuals are represented cinematically. That is, central figures in documentary essays are rarely transparent or offered at "face value."

26. Bernstein takes a similar position on chronology in "Documentaphobia and Mixed Modes," 405.

27. Orvell reviews the charges and defends Moore's handling of Britton in "Documentary Film and the Power of Interrogation," in this volume.

28. Jacobson, "Michael and Me," 22.

29. Quoted in Lawrence, *The World according to Michael Moore,* 93.

30. Among numerous examples, a brief segment on the Lockheed-Martin missile facility in *Columbine* is reprised and expanded in *Dude, Where's My Country?* A bogus endorsement from the Department of Homeland Security, mirroring the fake NRA imprimatur in *Columbine,* prefaces *Dude,* while elements of conspiracy mongering trumpeted in *Dude* are recast for inclusion in *Fahrenheit.*

31. Schultz, *Michael Moore,* 37.

32. See Toplin, *Michael Moore's* Fahrenheit 9/11, 76, and Douglas Kellner's essay in this volume.

33. Toplin, 9.

III. THE MAJOR FILMS

Documentary Film and the Power of Interrogation: *American Dream* and *Roger & Me*

MILES ORVELL

Nonfiction films rarely reach beyond a small, devoted congregation, but in recent years two works in particular have realized a mass audience—Barbara Kopple's Academy Award–winning *American Dream* (1991) and Michael Moore's widely celebrated and controversial film, *Roger & Me* (1989). That they have gained this wide audience speaks first of all to the fact that both films deal with the fate of the worker at the hands of the modem corporation, a subject that has been the focus of public concern for more than a decade, inflected most recently by the predicaments of postindustrialism: Given the new order of global capitalism, what power can labor unions claim against management? And what responsibility has management toward workers and their communities? Yet despite these similarities in subject matter—both films also happen to deal with plant closings in the beleaguered Midwest—the two could hardly be more different, stylistically and rhetorically.

Kopple works within the relatively traditional documentary forms that Bill Nichols calls expository and observational; *American Dream* conforms to our customary documentary expectations as viewers that we are comfortably in the hands of an all-seeing, all-sympathizing filmmaker, expectations that have been part of the documentary mode since its inception in the late nineteenth century. Exercising the authority of observation (an authority that is visible in ethnography, sociology, and psychiatric observation as well), the documentary filmmaker establishes an ethical norm that is implicit in the narrative and that we are asked to identify with: we are "for" the victims of oppression. But the ethics of this mode, and of Kopple's film in particular, are not quite this simple.

Stylistically altogether different from Kopple's film, Moore's *Roger & Me* eschews the tradition of observational documentary and opts instead for a more complex rhetoric, a hybridization of (again in Nichols's terms) the interactive and the reflexive modes.[1] Moore does not invent this mode—it has its precedents in several other projects dating at least from Kit Carson and Jim McBride's quasi-documentary, *David Holzman's Diary* (1968)—but he carries the form well beyond its predecessors to the level of significant social commentary. What is especially interesting about *American Dream* and *Roger & Me* is their concern, in quite different ways, with power, not only the power—or powerlessness—of the worker but the power of the filmmaker. For in describing the predicament of the worker, Kopple and Moore also portray, at times inadvertently, at other times explicitly, the situation of the filmmaker, and implicitly they invite our speculation on the authority and power of the documentary media.

Kopple's *American Dream* deals with the 1985 strike of the meatpackers union (Local P-9) at the Hormel plant in Austin, Minnesota, a strike that results from the workers' outrage at the accumulated cuts in Hormel's incentive programs, benefits, and hourly wages—from $10.69 an hour to $8.25. Eventually, Hormel offered to freeze wages at $10 per hour for three years (with new hires at $8), but the union rejects the offer by 93%, fueled in part by their knowledge that the company has reaped over $29 million in profits in 1984, the year the cuts began. While this seems like a relatively clear and morally solid position for the P-9 workers to occupy—they are claiming their right to a just wage against the seeming greed of the corporation—things get more and more complicated as Kopple's film unfolds.

Four principal figures emerge as the strike progresses, each with his own constituency and goals: the soft-spoken union president, Jim Guyette, who is determined to win at any cost; a union consultant hired by Guyette—Ray Rogers—who brings unrelenting optimism to the struggle; Lewie Anderson, the parent union's chief negotiator, who works against the local in wanting to rationalize wages across the whole union in order to maintain the industry's consistency and competitiveness (Hormel is already at the top end of the scale); and John Morrison, a leading dissident worker who criticizes the local union's leadership and sides with the national. Kopple traces the trajectory of the strike, from its optimistic beginnings to its depressing conclusion: Hormel shifts production to other plants, and their premier product, Spam—produced during this crisis by Hormel management—keeps rolling out of the factory. With armed escorts, scab workers enter the plants, including some of the disaffected union members who have reached the limit of their own endurance. Ultimately, the parent union cuts all benefits to the strikers (previously $40 a week), strips Guyette of his position, and negotiates a contract that fixes wages at $10.25, but only for those who cross the line. With no guarantee of job restoration to the strikers, only 20% of the workers are finally called back, and in the twenty-fifth week of the strike—400 replacements having been hired—no jobs remain.

What gives *American Dream* its power is the gradual unfolding of this defeat and the even-handedness with which Kopple serves as witness to what amounts to a tragic spectacle (as William Faulkner once defined it), in which the major union protagonists, all trying to do good in different ways, all fail. Union leader Guyette finds his confidence in labor's united power to be misplaced; the consultant likewise can't mobilize support to vanquish the intransigent managers, and he rides off into the setting sun like a failed Lone Ranger. Kopple's postscript tells us that the national negotiator (Lewie Anderson) is fired from his negotiating job, but he goes on (as if to resolve the dilemma he had himself habitually faced) to lead a reform movement against union concessions. Hormel is the real winner: following the strike's conclusion, Hormel leases half its plant to another company, a shadow company, that pays its workers $6 an hour. Nothing can stop the Spam.

Kopple's *American Dream* comprises many elements that are familiar in the tradition of the strike narrative—whether fiction or nonfiction. There is the small union, pitting its force against the giant corporation and the problem of keeping the ranks together; there is the ambiguous role of the outside organizer (personified by Rogers), and the question of whether he does more good than ill. There is the moral dilemma of the dissident, who might turn scab; and the problem of feeding a family during a prolonged strike. There is the use of local law enforcement officers—not to mention the National Guard—as tools of capital. More problematically, there is the distinction between what is legal and what is moral. Guyette claims the morality of rebellion when he invokes the history of the American Revolution (not itself "legal," as he points out) and the history of unionism. Against that position, sacred to the American Left, Kopple posits the seeming pragmatism (cloaking self-interest) of the American Right as voiced by a Hormel secretary who is kept from her job for one day because of the striker's blockade and declares, with angry simplicity: "I don't want to discuss moralities; is what the company is doing legal?" And in the end, there is the problem of what constitutes defeat, what victory. Do moral victories transcend matters of economic survival? Or is Anderson right when he asks, "What dignity is there when you don't have a job?"

All of this takes place within the framing irony of the nature of work in the Hormel plant: the opening shots of the film establish the brutal regime of meat slaughtering, and these images of violence recur at intervals, so that we may wonder whether Kopple has at times an even broader point to make about the dignity or indignity of this work in the first place. We are made to empathize with workers who are simply seeking an honest pay for an honest day's work, but that day's work happens to involve stunning, decapitating, dismembering, and disemboweling all these defenseless animals.

Despite its linkage to the main line of strike narratives, the overall tone of *American Dream* is markedly different from that tradition and different too from Kopple's own earlier *Harlan County, U.S.A.* (which also won an Academy Award for Best Feature Documentary, in 1976). And that difference sadly measures the distance labor has traveled in the last 15 years. The classic ending to the strike narrative—dating at least to the 1930s—represents the particular conflict as part of a longer march, an ongoing struggle that the worker is destined, even predestined, to win. Such was the structure of *Harlan County,* in which the 1974 coal miners' strike is placed within a historical chronicle that gives it an inevitable logic in an unabashedly progressive narrative: the miners, members of the United Mine Workers Union, stage a strike at Brookside (Kentucky) in which the moral courage of the miners—and their wives, who seem crucial to the energy and direction of the strike—is unwavering as they confront the legal violence of the corporation's gun thugs. As one old woman in *Harlan County*—a veteran of the 1930s—puts it: "If I get shot, they can't shoot the union out of me." In *Harlan County,* the workers have a unity among themselves that, despite minor rivalries, seems unshakable and will, we feel, gradually gain its victories over the greed and callous selfishness of the corporation.

There is no such "happy" ending in *American Dream:* the union is shattered, the corporation—with its higher obligations to shareholders—moves forward like a juggernaut, seeking the cheapest labor market, wherever that may be. Yet Kopple, the teller, seems not to have fully recognized the point of the tale itself. Certainly her remarks about the film have framed it in the conventional terms of the lost battle within a longer, ultimately winning war: "Maybe you don't win every battle but each one changes you and makes you smarter," Kopple replied to an interviewer's question about the purpose of the concluding information on life after the strike. It was "meant to be moving, to be reflective about past generations and struggles, and to convey hope for the future."[2] Such hope is hard to find in the film itself, however. The local union seems shattered, at least as a union, the victim of a corporation that, with "the law" on its side, would stop at nothing to win its point; the major union protagonists in the struggle scatter. Precisely the unity of the coal miners is what's missing at Hormel's P-9.

Instead, what we have in *American Dream* is unionism in the trickle-down Age of Reagan, when the corporation's obligations are to shareholders and their profits, regardless of the consequences to local economies and local communities. Under the set of incentives available to the contemporary corporation, that company profits most which most ruthlessly seeks the cheapest labor market, in whatever country. Against such odds, the Hormel workers can, at best, swallow hard and accept pay cuts that allow them to keep their jobs—all this in the face of extravagant corporate profits and executive salaries. At worst—and it was the worst for the great majority of the Hormel strikers—they can tough it out and eventually move out, to wherever. No wonder the sad but powerful drama of *American Dream* lies in the internecine war within the union ranks as they differently come to grips with this no-win situation. This is the knife-edge reality of the labor struggle in the 1980s, and it accounts for the power and impact the film has had as a spectacle of contemporary labor's plight.

Yet one aspect of *American Dream* that has gone virtually unnoticed is in some ways the film's most important point, though it is a point that Kopple, understandably, is loath to admit. In telling her story, Kopple has, one ultimately realizes, as little access to the corporate management as does the union. The powerlessness of the filmmaker is analogous to the powerlessness of the union. When an interviewer, after the film's release, asked Kopple whether she had had the same access to management as she'd had to labor, the filmmaker responded defensively, as if the objectivity of her picture were at stake: "We have an interview with Chuck Nyberg, Hormel's Executive Vice-President, and Richard Knowlton, the CEO. We also shot management press conferences and management interviews, but they always said the same thing." Of course they always said the same thing: they stonewalled Kopple's camera as they stonewalled the press and the union. But far from thinking she has been limited, Kopple boasts about her ability to get inside the factory: "They knew who I was, but I wasn't blocked. In fact, I was one of the few people who got in the plant to film. I couldn't believe it." And she adds, not seeing the full implications, "But there weren't a lot of labor/management negotiations because the company wouldn't talk to them. They wouldn't even be in the same room with them, so they had arbitrators going back and forth."[3] Precisely. In the Reagan-Bush era, communication between management and worker takes place ideally through an intermediary. And when, on rare occasions, they are forced into face-to-face talk, management has the right to say things to the worker that make a mockery of the "negotiating" table. Kopple records one such moment, when a corporate negotiator answers a member of a union negotiating team who has complained a little too long about certain issues: "If you want to come back, you keep your goddam mouth shut."

Kopple's camera is thus witness to what the filmmaker herself can hardly admit: that management controls the discourse and can exclude or limit her presence from the decision-making process as much as it can the worker's. In the face of this cinematic deficit, Kopple falls back tirelessly on interviews with the more accessible workers, mercilessly probing *their* feelings, scoring most triumphantly when she can capture an otherwise tough, proud worker broken down to tears by the spectacle of his own powerlessness—which is driven home by Kopple's interrogation. To a worker who is about to cross the picket line and go against his union, she asks, solicitously (and gratuitously), "Is that hard for you?" To a scab, out of work for six years, and about to report for work, she asks, "Is it hard to cross the picket line?" At times like these, her function resembles management itself, with its power to manipulate the worker's responses.

Of course Kopple wants to expose the emotional traumas of the workers so that we might more fully empathize with them, but she will do so at the expense of other values, such as the privacy of the subject. In talking about a sequence that had to be cut out of the final version because of its length, Kopple unwittingly reveals the filmmaker's ruthless delight in the medium's power to capture the authenticity of intimate emotion. She tells of sequences shot in Worthington, Minnesota (the site of an Armour plant), where a worker is shown feeling confident he can move to another job in another plant if need be, when suddenly his telephone rings. "A minute or two later he came out, looking very strange, and said, 'Cut.' *But we kept rolling as he sat down* and told his wife that he'd just been told they were selling all the Armour plants and that 'We won't be going anywhere,'" Kopple confesses [emphasis added]. "Both he and his wife burst into tears. He looked at her and said, 'What am I going to do? Meatpacking is all I know.' I shot *incredible* stuff in Worthington."[4]

Where management presents a shell too hard, too sophisticated, to penetrate, Kopple turns to the union, where she can work wonders, given her friendly status: "I had trouble sometimes with the international because they'd say, 'Union meetings are sacred. You can't be in there.' But I'm very persistent, so I'd give long speeches in front of all these packing-house guys as to why they should let me film their meetings. Some of them never got comfortable with it, and others sort of enjoyed it, or whatever."[5] On the question of whether or not her presence affected her subjects' behavior, adding "another dynamic to the events," Kopple straddles the issue, invoking in the end the mythology of documentary invisibility: "I guess it always does, but I think that for some of these meetings we were really insignificant and that they just forgot about us."[6] Such conclusions are comforting to the documentary filmmaker (or photographer, or sociological interviewer), but they fail to take account of the real intervention that the outsider's presence entails, however well intentioned she or he may be. As Heisenberg might have said, the results of such "objective" acts are indeterminate.

There is no question that Kopple has revealed in *American Dream* the condition of labor-management relations in this country in a way that we have not seen so clearly before. But for all its virtues, it is important to recognize that Kopple's documentary mode is, in rhetorical terms, squarely in the mainstream of the tradition, a function that has, from its beginnings in the work of photographer Jacob Riis, offered us the implicit spectacle of a sympathetic observer, empowered by the camera technologies of observation, picturing the powerless for the information (and often entertainment) of the more powerful. Kopple extends that tradition without essentially questioning it.

It is precisely the questioning of that tradition that Michael Moore accomplishes in his brilliantly conceived *Roger & Me*. Moore's film, his first, came out in the fall of 1989 and was met with both critical acclaim and—rare for a documentary—popular success. It seemed, in fact, a sure bet for the Academy Award, until an interview in *Film Comment* with Harlan Jacobson started its derailment by questioning Moore on what appeared to be certain factual misrepresentations.[7] Pauline Kael's subsequent *New Yorker* review raised similar questions and attacked more particularly the film's putative assumption of superiority toward its subjects, and the movie has been slightly, though I would argue unfairly, tainted ever since.[8] It's impossible now to discuss *Roger & Me* without taking into account some of these objections, but Moore's critics have, I think, asked the wrong questions of the film, failing to assess accurately its purpose. We should worry about whether Moore has violated the ethics of documentary—a question I want to come back to—but we must also observe the degree to which Moore successfully interrogates the whole premise of traditional documentary form that Kopple, incidentally, accepts.

The ostensible subject of *Roger & Me* is the plant closings of the 1980s by General Motors and their effect on the company town of Flint, Michigan. Like Kopple, Moore is sympathetic to the workers' predicament and to the whole plight of the city: throughout the film, recurring like a leitmotif, he shows us countless evictions being carried out by the local deputy sheriff—the door forced open, the victim's unavailing protests, household goods piled on the street curb, the search for a van or car. He shows us boarded-up stores on Main Street; unoccupied houses, vacant and dilapidated; a rat population in Flint that outnumbers the human population by 50,000. He interviews a former GM employee, temporarily deranged by the situation, shooting baskets outside a local mental health institution.

And to some extent Moore's story is the same as Kopple's: the worker is caught between a corporate management with nothing but profits on its mind and a national union leadership all too understanding of management's needs. At the final closing of the Flint truck assembly line, only four UAW members show up to demonstrate, as opposed to the thousands promised by the union earlier. One of Moore's workers puts the new situation of labor succinctly: "Why is the union getting weak? We're losing power. . . . Too many guys are friends with management." When Moore asks Owen Bieber (UAW president) whether a sit-down strike would do any good today in Flint—Flint was the site of the historic 44-day sit-down strike in 1936 out of which the UAW was born in 1937—he replies that the sit-down is not relevant today. "We have to accept reality that the plants are not going to remain open," he says.

What makes *Roger & Me* unusual—and what has left it open to criticism and misunderstanding—is its mix of motives, its hybridization of forms: it is part historical narrative, focusing on the fate of Flint, Michigan, following the GM plant closings, and dealing with the workers' plight (which invites our interest in the factual history of this "action"); but it is also part autobiography, beginning with childhood footage and first-person narration by the filmmaker. And it is Michael Moore himself who remains the central figure throughout the film, in the persona of the reporter in search of his story, the interviewer in search of his subject. Jacobson questions the factual inaccuracies in the film, and he is of course right to do so. Plant closings that actually took place over a decade or more seem to take place in a more condensed period of time, about two years. Still, none of these misrepresentations of chronology, and there are many others, makes any real difference to the central point of the film; no one disputes the fact of the plant closings and their effects. Moore has sacrificed historical accuracy in order to achieve the unity of satiric fiction. The exposition in *Roger & Me* is really its least important aspect: we are most struck by the filmmaker's presence as interviewer and as self-conscious maker of the film. These are the parts of the film that Pauline Kael objects to, especially what she takes to be Moore's targeting of the working class for his satire from a position of presumed moral superiority, all the time seeming to be sympathetic to them. This is a criticism that one might think twice about, since we naturally feel that if a work is making moral judgments, it must be better than what it judges. Kael is offended at the ridiculing tone of the movie, its depiction, for example, of people working in various elite establishments who are forced (by virtue of those jobs) to expel Moore from the premises as he searches for Roger Smith; they are made to seem flunkies, she says. But it's hard to see the point of her criticisms: if they are flunkies, they are simply doing their job. Meanwhile, the GM workers in the film are consistently treated without a trace of condescension: their comments are pithy, their anger is controlled. "What would you say to Roger Smith," Moore asks several GM workers at one point. "Roger Smith?" is the reply. "I'd tell him to retire." "He should be feeling guilty," says another. "I'm sick and tired of these damn fat cats."

Those whom Moore does ridicule (and there are indeed many) are simply given enough rope to hang themselves with. Unlike Kael, I don't feel sorry for Miss Michigan (and Miss America), 1988, when she says on camera, when asked how it feels to drive through Flint when so many workers have been fired from the auto plants—"I feel like a big supporter. . . ." What is all too obviously (and incongruously) on her mind is the upcoming beauty contest: "Pray for my victory in Atlantic City in two weeks." And I don't feel sorry for the woman on Social Security who cuddles one of her rabbits (she sells them for "Pets or Meat") and coos at it with demonic good humor: "What's gonna happen to him? He's gonna be eaten. He's gonna be the supper on our supper table." Moments later, the rabbit is clubbed and skinned.

Throughout, Moore views skeptically those possessing power, both the unfamous and the famous. Flint's famous son, Bob Eubanks (*The Newlywed Game*), is shown at a town fair doing a local version of the big show and, offstage but not off-camera, offers these jokes to Moore: "Why don't Jewish women get AIDS? Because they marry assholes, they don't screw 'em." Kopple's camera reveals the nature of powerlessness, but it conceals the awful silence of the powerful. Several ladies of the leisure class playing golf at the Flint country club offer Moore's deadpan camera the force of their bromidic wisdom when they say, "We have such a good welfare program here . . . they [the poor, the unemployed] just don't want to work." Again and again, Moore's deadpan camera observes the absurdities of Flint's upper-crust society, as in the "Great Gatsby Party"—for which the host hires several unemployed persons to pose as human statues. The new Gatsby's guests offer us further platitudes from the entrepreneur's toast book: "Get up in the morning and go do something. . . . Start yourself, get your own motor going!" How can one incriminate a filmmaker who exposes the extraordinary obtuseness of a society that holds a grand party to celebrate the opening of a new jail in Flint, including jailhouse pajamas, dancing to "Jailhouse Rock," and lockup for the night in a brand-new cell: "We're having a fantastic time here." Moore captures the culture of a new aristocracy whose pastorals beggar the imagination of conventional courtiers playing at shepherd and shepherdess. In short, one wonders why Kael should have found Moore—whose family has worked for General Motors or other automobile industries for generations—superior or hostile to the working class. His subject is power—its arrogance and stupidity—and his examples make the film as much an indictment of American society in general as a study of Flint's particular problems.

It is the admixture of Moore himself as a kind of comic persona in the film that has created the special virtues of *Roger & Me* and also its special problems. Seeing the traditional subject of the film (a plant closing and its effect on the community), the viewer expects "truth"; but much of what Moore delivers is not the "straight" truth of documentary but the oblique truth of satire.[9] And are not documentary and satire opposite modes, representing contrary motivations? We expect "truth" from documentary; we don't expect it in quite the same literal way from satire. "Documentary satire" is almost, then, an oxymoron, unless we are willing to admit it as a strikingly original hybrid—which is what I would argue is the case with *Roger & Me*. Once we view the film as "documentary satire," Kael's problems with it seem peevish.

What makes *Roger & Me* work is the unabashedly autobiographical nature of the film, its whimsical self-indulgence and seemingly absurd structure—the quest for an interview with Roger Smith, the chief executive of General Motors. At the center of *Roger & Me*, glowing with a kind of negative aura and repellent charisma, is Roger Smith, chairman of General Motors, whose refusal to be interviewed by Moore for his documentary makes him the defining "presence" of the film, all the more tantalizing for being absent virtually throughout. As

Moore tries literally to find his subject, he keeps approaching the goal only to be thrown unceremoniously off the field by Smith's various guards and gatekeepers. Moore's tracking effort is carefully documented on film: in the General Motors main headquarters, given the runaround by public relations staff, Moore fails to get into the elevators and off the ground floor; at the Grosse Point Yacht Club he is shown the door; he is ushered out by an officious manager at the Detroit Athletic Club. He can't even get to talk with the company's "spokesperson" on the last day of the Flint plant. Pointing his camera at her (inside the building) from his position outside, Moore records her line: "It's a very sad time," she says, simulating feeling. "A very private personal time." And when Moore presses her to speak (she is, after all, GM's "spokesperson"), she says, "You don't represent anybody. You're a private interest and I will not speak to you." "We're citizens of the community," Moore protests, to no avail. (The key word, *community,* seems almost an anachronism here.) The spokesperson signals to her police force to escort Moore, once more, from the private property of a publicly owned corporation. Moore does get an open mike during a GM stockholders' meeting, posing as a shareholder; but when Smith recognizes his man—evidently he has not been ignorant of Moore's persistent efforts—he quickly closes the meeting before the dazed filmmaker can utter a word. (Is he really dazed? It's hard to tell.) Moore's camera picks up the chit-chat immediately afterward: "I think he didn't know what the hell to do," Smith and his associate murmur to one another conspiratorially.

Moore does succeed, finally, in achieving a face-to-face confrontation with Roger Smith when he corners the executive, following the latter's unctuously avuncular Christmas speech at a General Motors party. It is the climax we think we've been waiting for, and it is, appropriately, an anticlimax, a reiteration of the film's point about the powerful and the powerless. "Will you come to Flint and see the evictions that are going on as a result of GM's plant closings?" Moore asks, like Percival who has at last found the Holy Grail. "I'm sure GM didn't evict them. I don't know anything about it," the Grail replies, and shuffles off disdainfully.

With this game of cat and mouse, Moore is making, implicitly, a powerful point about documentary form. Too easily, for a hundred years, creators of documentary (in various media) have made the powerless their subject. Arriving on the scene with still camera, movie camera, or tape recorder (that is, armed with the accoutrements of technologically advanced civilization), the documentarian has essentially not allowed his subject to choose whether or not to comply with his efforts. Often the efforts are presumed by the creator to be for the benefit of the subject, and sometimes the point is driven home to the subject in the form of money payment. Exposing the subject's "plight," the creator of the documentary feels virtuous and we, the viewers, likewise feel the glow of virtue, even if we do nothing, and say only that our "attitude" has changed. By pointing his camera at the unequal power and authority of those making the decisions, Moore turns the tables on the traditional documentary form: he himself, the man with the camera, becomes the "powerless" subject (and serves as an analogue to the powerless worker as well).[10] Showing us a Roger Smith who doesn't "have to" be subjected to Moore's camera, who is savvy enough to avoid it or powerful enough to wall himself off with guards and "spokespersons," Moore is making a devastating point about democracy and industrial policy: the powerful do not have to speak to "us"; they owe us nothing. Kopple is much more traditional in this respect, directing her inquiries to the victims only, asking the strikers, "How do you feel?" Moore is essentially not interested in how the worker "feels," or how "hard" it is to undergo this process; when he shows us "victimized" workers, he is not working to solicit our empathy; it is assumed. Instead, Moore acts as a satirist and critic, exposing the moral failures of the powerful by placing them before the camera's deadpan gaze, accompanied by Moore's own disarmingly ingenuous interlocutory style.

The closest Moore comes to Smith, in a way, is through his lobbyist, Tom Kay, who seems quite willing to talk with the filmmaker, although what he has to say may seem slightly biased: "I'm sure Roger Smith has as much social conscience as anyone in this country." (We learn in a satisfyingly ironic postscript that Kay ultimately loses his own job.) But actually Kay also supplies a point that the film does not attempt to refute—"GM has no obligation to Flint"—and it's a telling one, threatening in some ways Moore's whole premise: Why this heavy burden of guilt imposed on GM? In a free-market economy, where no incentives exist for industry to remain in a given locale, where in fact the incentives go the other way—to relocate in the cheapest labor market—we can see the point. (The greater good of the international consumer must, so the argument goes, outweigh the temporary losses of the individual worker and the community—or even the country.) So what if Flint now has the highest crime rate on the continent? GM is trying to compete profitably in a world market; that is its purpose, not to supply jobs to Flint workers. And it doesn't serve Flint if GM goes out of business altogether. If what is happening in Flint is symptomatic of what is happening all over America, the fault lies with forces that are much larger than General Motors, which functions within an economic system it did not create. Moore's neglect of the macroeconomic issue in his film may be a more serious problem finally than the worries about chronology, although to include it would have blunted his criticism of General Motors.

And yet, implicit in *Roger & Me* is an even larger social economic point: that the same high-handed evasiveness on the part of Smith and the GM management generally *is the whole problem* in the first place. American corporate management has never listened to the man or woman on the assembly line, has not wanted to acknowledge that they even have a human presence. Following the logic of Taylorism as defined by American industry ("a great art form," someone calls it at the Flint Gatsby party), the worker is a cipher, most valued when he most approaches an automaton. From such attitudes, quality control circles (and quality cars) do not come. And it has taken the example of the Japanese system, with its greater attention to what the worker on the line can contribute to the whole system, to teach American industry—slowly—something. Moreover, GM did in fact help create the larger forces, by lobbying for laws that promote its own corporate self-interest. And if we accept the legitimacy of GM, we accept as legitimate the destruction of our national economy in the name of "profit"; we accept the destruction of our communities in the name of creating private wealth.

Finally, where Moore goes far beyond Kopple is in creating an image of American life in the late twentieth century, in which the shift from an industrial to a postindustrial economy is fumbled miserably, with an awkwardness and absurdity that is both funny and pathetic: Flint tries desperately to survive the demise of its industrial base by re-creating itself as a tourist attraction, that is, by turning the production of consumer goods into a story about the production of consumer goods. But it doesn't work. Consumerism and artifice, the creation of an economy of the "simulacrum," as Baudrillard would put it, collapses in on itself. The rabbit is eaten for supper. The last car rolls off the assembly line. "I cannot come to Flint," says the corporate Pecksniff.

Kopple shows us that there are no easy victories, possibly no victories at all, for labor to celebrate at the end of the twentieth century. Moore shows us why: the corporate Father has turned out his sons and shut the door on their imploring voices. Bearing witness in their quite different ways, Kopple and Moore help us a little, at least, to understand such things or to clarify what we won't accept. Kopple's camera reveals the nature of powerlessness and gives it a voice, but it conceals the awful silence of the powerful. And that silence, absurd in its pomposity, infuriating in its Kafkaesque reticence, is exactly what Moore shows us. We have no power against it, except ridicule and irony.[11]

Notes

1. Bill Nichols, *Representing Reality: Issues and Concepts in Documentary* (Bloomington: Indiana University Press, 1991), 32–33.

2. Gary Crowdus and Richard Porton, "American Dream: An Interview with Barbara Kopple," *Cineaste* 18, no. 4 (1991): 38.

3. Crowdus and Porton, "American Dream," 38.

4. Ibid.

5. Ibid., 37.

6. Ibid.

7. Harlan Jacobson, "Michael and Me," *Film Comment* 25, no. 6 (November–December 1989): 16–26.

8. Pauline Kael, "The Current Cinema: Melodrama/Car-toon/Mess," *New Yorker*, January 8, 1990, 91.

9. The autobiographical form has been used before in a documentary film and also with great comic effect. See, for example, Ross McElwee's *Sherman's March* (1985), a film that begins as a documentary about Sherman and the South and soon develops into a quest for the filmmaker's soulmate. Another antecedent of Moore is Mike Rubbo's *Waiting for Fidel* (1974), which portrays the filmmaker's failed pursuit of his subject (after having been promised an interview).

10. I do not mean to argue that Moore is literally powerless. He is the filmmaker, creating a product with a clear point of view, guiding our judgment through the manipulation of his materials. Moore's power is a relative one: relative to Smith, in the situations depicted on film, it is nil; relative to Smith, in the movie theater, it is triumphant.

11. Unfortunately, the short sequel to *Roger and Me*, created in the wake of the film's success, is an embarrassing piece of self-congratulation on Moore's part, suggesting that Moore's compulsive self-revelation has not only a luminous side but a self-destructive component as well.

Bowling for Columbine: A Review

CHRISTOPHER SHARRETT AND WILLIAM LUHR

Leftist filmmakers working in nonnarrative formats aren't hard to find, but their films seldom receive mainstream distribution. Except for those by Michael Moore. He stands virtually alone, not as a filmmaker who interrogates social and corporate power, but as one able to place such films into the multiplexes of America.

Why? Two reasons come immediately to mind. The first is that his works—whether *Bowling for Columbine,* his first film, *Roger & Me* (1989), his various television shows (such as *TV Nation* or *The Awful Truth*), or his best-selling book *Stupid White Men*—are commonly classified not as sociopolitical criticism but as "comedy." Moore's comedy, however, serves a subversive agenda—a goofball wrapper encasing social critique. The second, related reason for his success in mainstream venues is his persona—a big, potbellied slob from the American heartland in a baseball cap who looks like he buys his clothes in Kmart and sleeps in them. During the 1960s and 1970s, Tom Smothers was perceived as having been able to push a leftist agenda on network television because, with his short hair, red sports coat, and aging choirboy appearance, he didn't look like a counterculture threat. Mainstream America saw him as one of "us," rather than one of "them." Moore, with his shambling demeanor, looks less like Leon Trotsky than one of the good ol' boys at the auto-body plant in his hometown of Flint, Michigan.

Moore places himself at the center of his work, which is almost as much about his persona as it is about the issues he engages. His films jubilate in the fish-out-of-water effect that his personal appearance radiates when shown shuffling through the corporate offices of General Motors, of Kmart, or Charlton Heston's L.A. mansion. He initially appears comically out of his element and unthreatening—a yokel without the common sense to suit up and wear a tie in such august surroundings. There is, however, a quick rebound effect. His apparent naïveté when dealing with officious corporate security personnel or the expensively dressed power elite garners him considerable spectator sympathy. Isn't he, after all, just a simple guy looking for answers to a few simple questions? Although he often uses "ambush" interview tactics, his persona makes him appear less aggressive and manipulative than, say, Geraldo Rivera in similar situations.

But is he? The reception of *Bowling for Columbine* has raised questions about the credibility of his persona and about his integrity as a documentary filmmaker that are not new. This "good ol' boy," who purportedly lives in a $1.9 million home in New York City, was accused over a decade ago of manipulating and even falsifying elements of *Roger & Me.* Comparable accusations have circulated about *Bowling for Columbine.* Although Moore attacks the statistical maneuvering of various groups in the film, the reliability of his own statistical assertions has been questioned. He has also been accused of various other distortions, such as doctoring the Willy Horton footage he uses in the film and of reenacting the footage showing a dog that inadvertently shot a man in deer camp when a rifle was placed on its back for a prank photograph.

Such carping also suggests an agenda on the part of certain reviewers, since Moore's humor makes transparent the "doctorings" or reenactments of which he is accused. One commentator notes that Moore doesn't alert the viewer to reenactments when he tests the laid-back Canadian lifestyle by opening several unlocked residential doors in Windsor, Ontario. Obviously Moore would have been insane not to get clearances from the residents, and reviewers yammering about such moments reveal either naïveté or stupidity. An idea implicit in complaints about Moore past and present is that he somehow violates the aspirations of "objective" documentary filmmaking (as if film history hasn't exposed this delusion decades ago), or that he fails to "tell both sides of the story," which would make his work about as compelling as network television. Such complaints reveal a conservative impulse having nothing to do with addressing Moore's real strengths and limitations.

Bowling for Columbine focuses on American gun violence, using the horrific 1999 shootings at Columbine High School in Littleton, Colorado, as its centerpiece and model of exploration. Moore puts numerous issues on the table as he takes the viewer through a first-person tour across the heartland, opting for a steady, at times annoying, ironic humor in his rapid-fire montage approach. This style is often merely suggestive, outlining for the viewer a sense of the illnesses within American society and of what is at stake, but doing so in too allusive a manner to foster substantive understanding. Moore's great talent is for uncovering the grotesque, almost incomprehensible features of American life, such as a bank that gives away guns as premiums to customers opening new accounts, or the fact that Eric Harris and Dylan Klebold, the two shooters who killed their classmates at Columbine High, went bowling on the morning of the atrocity. Moore visits the home of John Nichols, brother of Terry Nichols, convicted in the Oklahoma City bombing case. When Moore asks Nichols if his own ardent defense of gun rights would extend to allowing citizens to store weapons-grade plutonium, the unnerving Nichols, apparently wishing to appear to add a dollop of cautionary temperance to his agenda, replies, "There's a lot of nuts out there." This and other moments—including Moore's interview with camouflage-garbed survivalists—might have been little more than humorous diversions or cheap shots were it not for Moore's sympathetic interest in many of the people he encounters, and his efforts to merge his dramatis personae of the cult of weaponry with broader meditations on the nature of the American fascination with bloodletting.

On a number of occasions in *Columbine,* Moore steps back from a simple agenda of indictment to open up broader social issues. The indictment aspect at times seems confused and confusing. Although much of the film condemns the actions of the National Rifle Association, Moore does not theatrically burn but repeatedly brandishes his own NRA card, describing himself as a product of America's gun culture. In one of the film's central sequences, he mounts a highly theatrical ambush interview by bringing two seriously handicapped victims of the Columbine massacre to Kmart headquarters. Arguing that the bullets used by the Columbine killers were purchased at Kmart, they petition management to stop selling ammunition in their department stores. While the episode reveals the sliminess of the PR-supported corporate world, it takes an unexpected turn when Kmart's representative agrees to implement Moore's demands. Moore seems genuinely surprised and openly grateful. The sequence ends not on the expected note of "Evil Corporation swatting liberal yokel and handicapped victims away like flies," but with an unsettling progressive moment. Yet the moment actually addresses little of major importance, and one can't help but notice that Moore is too much at center stage throughout.

Part of Moore's complicated, at times disjointed, project is to suggest that violence is not caused by the kooks and weirdos who draw so much media at-

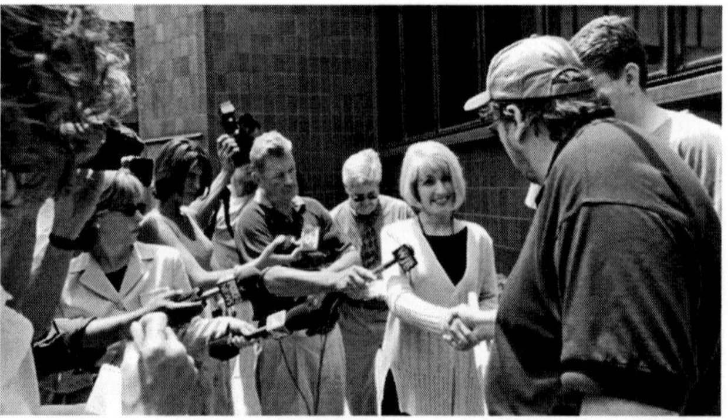

"An unsettling progressive moment." In *Bowling for Columbine,* Kmart announces it will not sell guns and ammunition of the type used in the Columbine shootings. Copyright 2002 Alliance Atlantis Communications/United Artists.

tention. He rejects the concept of Harris and Klebold as "monsters," the term commonly used in media descriptions; instead, he presents them as logical products of American life, no different from any kid at a video arcade, or any self-deluded military manufacturer. Moore builds a case for the cynical interconnectedness of ostensibly disparate elements within the corporate/political/ideological power structure and the disastrous social effects of those interwoven elements. He points out the presence in Littleton (not far from Columbine High School) of Lockheed Martin, and its role not only as a key defense contractor but also as a major sponsor of "workfare" alternatives to welfare that endanger the whole fabric of American society.

Attempting to connect the dots, Moore traces the gun murder, by another child, of a six-year-old left unattended by his mother in Flint, Michigan (whose economic destruction by General Motors was the subject of *Roger & Me*). On the day of the shooting, the boy's mother, a parolee, was bused miles into the suburbs, forced to fulfill her workfare obligations by tending a soda fountain at a shopping mall retro diner owned by rock impresario Dick Clark. In a moment rivaling Moore's offhand exposure of game show host Bob Eubanks as an anti-Semite in *Roger & Me,* Moore tries to interview Dick Clark outside his headquarters in Hollywood. Remaining within the dark confines of his van, the ever-cheerful whitebread promoter of rock and roll, when asked his views on the workfare horrors of which he takes advantage, tells the driver to slam the door in Moore's face.

This makes for dramatic footage but it again raises questions about Moore's tactics. It is, after all, an ambush interview. While it drives home its point about the complex network of corporate/governmental involvement, it also involves grandstanding by Moore. The issue is not discussed and explored as much as it is dramatically asserted. Furthermore, Moore's choice of a media figure such as Dick Clark to discuss workfare presages his choice of Charlton Heston to discuss the NRA. These confrontations seem to say more than they do. The Heston scene, which also contains more accusatory questions than substantive discussion, veils the fact that, in taking on an easy target like Heston, Moore has not interrogated anyone in the NRA lobby, the people with genuine political clout. But would they have been more illuminating than Heston, their ideology any different? Moore has always acknowledged his own nurturance by the mass media, and bringing in celebrities like Clark and Heston gives a more recognizable face to social crises than those of gray eminence corporate or government functionaries. Catching these celebrities off guard tends to render their public charm—and the policies in which they are complicit—suddenly very ugly.

Moore brings smog, corporate crime, racism, and other issues into play before finally associating American gun violence with simple hate and fear. In trying to debunk traditional shibboleths about the causes of violence, Moore tends to leave his own assertions only marginally explored. He raises questions he can't, and hardly tries, to answer. Using Canada's relatively low rate of gun murder as a locus of comparison, he questions traditional presumptions about U.S. violence. He notes that poverty can't be at the root of violence, since Canada has very high unemployment; neither can a violent pop culture (much of it an import from the United States); neither can a large number of gun fanatics; neither can the tensions of a multiracial society.

This provides a provocative opening up of *Bowling for Columbine*'s central issues while, at the same time, marking the point at which the film loses its focus. Moore makes tentative forays into cross-cultural explanation for the national differences in gun violence but his mode of exploration ultimately imperils the film's cohesion. On a trip to Windsor, Ontario, Moore concludes that the treatment of poverty and race are at issue. He places Canada's handling of social programs and generous welfare system head and shoulders above the United States (not a big discovery really, and a situation rapidly changing with the corporatization of Canada flowing from free-trade agreements). Rather than deal with social problems, the United States tries to stigmatize them, scapegoating the poor and minorities in news reports and "true-crime" shows about cops tracking down the raging underclass. The effect is to raise violence as an issue far beyond its actual reality. In support of this idea, Moore cites paranoid myths created by the mass media, ranging from poisoned Halloween candy to tweaked or unreported statistics about the actual (rather flat) level of violent crime in the last decade.

But if violence isn't so bad in America, what's the point of the film? From its early images of the realistic toy guns so popular in 1950s male juvenile culture, *Bowling for Columbine* argues that America is not only a nation obsessed with guns, but also one never hesitant to use them, especially against the racial Other. Moore makes great capital from the horrors of Columbine; the widespread gun culture; readily available weapons and ammunition; the insensitivity of the NRA; and the links among Lockheed Martin, the defense establishment, and other structures of social repression, but then seems to reverse direction and undercut all of it.

Moore discounts the notion of America as an endemically violent nation—after going through a checklist of U.S. aggression in the postwar period from the imposition of the shah of Iran in 1952 to the overthrow of Jacobo Arbenz to the Vietnam War, the 1972 coup in Chile, the Iran-Contra scandals, and the training of Osama bin Laden by the CIA. Yet Moore still counters notions of American exceptionalism, intercutting fleeting atrocity footage of Nazi Germany and imperialist Britain, France, and Japan to undercut notions that American violence has its foundations in its especially brutal conquest of its Wild West past. But comparing America to Europe may create a false debate.

Considering its very short history as the only major nation founded during the Enlightenment under principles of democratic compromise, U.S. history has been especially violent. Noam Chomsky has noted that the conservative European business press of the twentieth century was shocked at U.S. capitalism's savage assaults on workers. The Civil War, a conflict, as Shelby Foote notes, at the crossroad of our being, showed the murderous failure of democratic compromise, which may exist only as a facade to protect powerful financial interests, suggesting a basic hypocrisy regarding American notions of liberty and prosperity that may in the last several decades be coming home to roost for the white middle class. Acknowledging this demands that we reject a view of the Columbine shootings and other forms of juvenile violence as aberrant, which Moore clearly does. His refusal contains, however, a glaring omission long noted by scholars critical of media representations of Columbine: schoolyard shootings have been commonplace in inner-city minority communities for decades. As with the spread of narcotics, such crimes are frightful tragedies, it seems, only when the middle class is threatened.

Associating gun violence chiefly with hatred and paranoid fear of the racial Other tends to ignore the evidence of the political economy of violence that Moore rather haphazardly assembles. Racism isn't about racial paranoia alone. After all, racialist mythologies in America flowed from the need to dehumanize the people serving the stoop-labor economy of the agrarian slavocracy (African Americans), and the people in the way of mining, railroad, and cattle interests (Native Americans). Moore gives impressions of this dynamic, but not an ordered understanding.

At certain times Moore's compare/contrast editing sustains his insistence on humor; at other times it misfires. He deftly juxtaposes a speech by the smarmy, rabble-rousing Senator Joe Lieberman, the quintessential opportunist politician who loves to blame pop culture for the world's problems, with a chat with shock rocker Marilyn Manson, who, not surprisingly, is one of the more intelligent voices in the movie. But a long "cartoon history of America" is cute for only a bit, and almost stops the movie with its sense that Moore can't make a transition without a joke, and that these issues, which the film poses as overwhelmingly important, are regularly represented with a hip blitheness. The sound track for a montage of American atrocities is Louis Armstrong's version of "What a Wonderful World"—Moore's constant need for forced irony often feels adolescent.

Bowling for Columbine loses any attempt at sustained argument after its raising of the provocative comparison of American with Canadian violence. It builds to its climactic interview with aging film star and National Rifle Association front man Charlton Heston, whom we have earlier seen in file footage proudly uttering his mantra about not giving up his primeval flintlock rifle until it is taken "from my cold, dead hands." Some have argued that Moore bears down too brutally on the slightly enfeebled actor, who is, after all, courteous enough to allow the interview. It is a complex moment, filled with awkward tensions. While it provides the film with a dramatic conclusion, it also enables it to sidestep its central issues. Moore shows Heston his NRA card, then raises the question of the differences between the United States and Canada; Heston fumbles for a response. Moore then shifts gears and assaults Heston's insensitivity and the NRA's viciousness in staging rallies in towns such as Littleton while they are mourning children lost to gun murder. Heston walks away from the interview in a snit, losing himself in his L.A. estate. Moore leaves behind a photo of a child killed by a gun in a town where the NRA quickly flexed its considerable organizing muscle.

It is a curious ending. On one level it deflects the major concerns of the film because NRA insensitivity isn't really the issue, at least not the sole one. Moore himself repeatedly proclaims his NRA membership. The ending enables the film to drop its larger issues in favor of an awkward interview with Charlton Heston that implicates him in a social dynamic leading to a little girl's death. On another level, however, the image of the irate actor scurrying away as Moore props up the photo of the dead child of the American underclass against a pillar of Heston's palatial, gated home may be the best coda any recent film has enjoyed, a summary statement on life in a miserably polarized, heartless society.

Prelude to Moore: A Comparison of Rhetorical Techniques in Frank Capra's *Why We Fight* Series and Michael Moore's *Fahrenheit 9/11*

RICHARD R. NESS

"Audience reaction . . . was sharply divided. There was some applause at its conclusion and several walk-outs. That it is propaganda—although of the true sort—there can be no denying. The question it doesn't answer is whether propaganda—even as expertly documented as it is here—can be passed off as entertainment."[1] Although this sounds as though it could have been taken from a review of Michael Moore's controversial 2004 film *Fahrenheit 9/11*, it actually is from an article in the May 28, 1943, edition of the *Hollywood Reporter*, describing the premiere of Frank Capra's *Prelude to War*, the first entry in the War Department's seven-part Why We Fight series. An examination of Moore's film in relation to Capra's wartime series reveals not only that arguments generated by the release of *Fahrenheit 9/11* are just the latest manifestation of a long-standing debate about the relationship of propaganda and documentary, but that Moore employs a number of the same rhetorical techniques used in the Why We Fight films and other earlier persuasive nonfiction productions. Such comparisons indicate that, far from representing either the violation of documentary principles that Moore's detractors have contended or the innovative new direction in the genre his supporters have heralded, Moore's works are merely the latest extension of and variation on established documentary conventions.

Many critics of *Fahrenheit 9/11* contend that because of the film's clear propagandistic intent, it does not qualify as a documentary. Yet, Capra's *Prelude to War* won an Academy Award in the recently established "Documentary" category in 1942 (which it shared with three other war-related films) and is discussed in most basic texts on documentary, even though, as the *Hollywood Re-*

porter article indicates, it clearly was recognized even at the time of its release as propaganda.[2] Capra recalls in his autobiography that the film was even attacked by one senator who denounced the film as propaganda intended to guarantee a fourth term for Roosevelt and urged a government investigation of this and all government films.[3]

Typical of the attacks on Moore's film, many of which proliferated on the Internet even before the film's commercial release, is a review by Jurgen Fauth that questions whether the film is "overblown anti-American propaganda, or a must-see documentary," and a comment by the unnamed reviewer of lafilmcratic.com who calls the film "shameless propaganda" rather than a "true documentary" (although the reviewer fails to define what is meant by either concept).[4] Such attacks appear to assume, first, that propaganda and documentary are mutually exclusive concepts; second, that there is a single universally accepted definition of each term; and, third, that the term *propaganda* is inherently negative. Yet such an essentialist position ignores the history of the development of realist aesthetics in film. Writing as early as 1935, Paul Rotha, in his seminal study *Documentary Film,* observed that "running concurrently with the evolution of documentary, there has been an increasing tendency to realize and make use of the persuasive capacities of the medium" and added that "cinema pursuing the ends of propaganda and persuasion has been largely responsible for the documentary method."[5]

Disagreements about the nature and value of propaganda are evident even in Moore's own tie-in publication for the film. In his introduction to *The Official Fahrenheit 9/11 Reader,* John Berger, in defending the film, claims, "To denigrate this as propaganda is either naïve or perverse. . . . Propaganda invariably serves the long-term interests of some elite."[6] But in the same text Moore reprints a web article by Joel Bleifuss that states, "Yes, *Fahrenheit 9/11* is propaganda, in the same way the nightly news is, or the front page of your daily paper. It's just that Moore is more upfront with the point he is trying to make."[7] An even more positive acknowledgment of the value of propaganda is provided by Joe Saltzman in *Frank Capra and the Image of the Journalist in American Film.* Assessing the effectiveness of the Capra films, Saltzman, in a statement that could apply equally to Moore's work, dismisses as irrelevant the charges of manipulation of reality that have been brought against the filmmaker. As Saltzman concludes:

> Capra took all the tricks he had learned in producing Hollywood movies and turned them into brilliant propaganda. Whether it was a breathtaking montage

> of images and headlines or a particularly moving close-up of a baby bawling or the huge black letters on a newspaper's front page crying out for attention, the tools of cinema and propaganda have seldom been used more effectively. . . . It didn't matter whether the headlines were real or embellished or whether people listening to their radios were actually listening to the news. It all looked real and sounded real and gave added credibility to the narration and images.[8]

Basically, those critics who have attacked the film use the term *propaganda* in a negative context as a weapon to discredit its status as documentary, while those who support the film, if they invoke the word *propaganda* at all, afford it a more positive, or at least neutral, position. Or, as Harry Knowles, in his discussion of the film on his Ain't It Cool News website, succinctly states, "If you agree with the propaganda, is it propaganda?"[9]

Knowles's web critique of the film is one of the few to draw direct parallels between Capra and Moore, although other analyses of *Fahrenheit 9/11* have attempted to put the film in a larger context of the history of documentary. Louis Menand, in a *New Yorker* article entitled "Nanook and Me," provides a detailed overview of the documentary form to demonstrate Moore's connection to earlier works in the field and argues that "one thing that cannot be said about *Fahrenheit 9/11* is that it is an outlaw from the documentary tradition."[10] A Reuters report that appeared on the day Moore's film opened observes, "While some complain about Moore's lack of objectivity, others say the movie follows a tradition in documentary films that shun balance in favor of a strong point of view." The article acknowledges that the controversy over the film's propagandistic elements "is not new and that documentaries have long espoused causes and embraced artistic sensibilities," citing Capra's Why We Fight series as an example.[11] While not making direct references to the Capra series, Matthew Bernstein, in his detailed analysis of Moore's first film, *Roger & Me*, demonstrates that Moore draws heavily on two earlier modes of documentary production identified by Bill Nichols, the expository and interactive modes.[12] Both of these modes also are evident in *Fahrenheit 9/11*, although this time Moore downplays his own interactive role in the film in favor of a more expository approach that directly recalls the structure of the Capra series.

Before examining similarities of technique and structure in the Why We Fight series and *Fahrenheit 9/11*, it is useful to address some of the differences in these productions. The most obvious of these are differences in sponsorship, ideological orientation, and overall tone. At the risk of oversimplification, the intent of the government-sponsored Capra series was to encourage our involvement in one war, while the goal of Moore's independently produced film is to question our involvement in another. Capra's film is founded on a clearly delineated contrast between a free world, represented by the Allied forces, and a slave world, which is identified as the goal of the Axis powers, and Capra is quite clear about the nature of the enemy, establishing the leaders of the Axis powers as the villains of his piece. Although Moore shares Capra's concern for the people of the free world, he sees the biggest threat to them as coming not from the enemy they have been told to fight but rather from their own government, and Moore applies to George W. Bush and his administration some of the same attributes Capra uses to stigmatize Hitler, Mussolini, and Hirohito.

In the most extensive analysis that has been done on the Why We Fight films, Thomas William Bohn identifies the emphasis on the people of the free world as the "most dominant theme" and claims they are given "an almost mythical value and aura" that he links to the identification with the common man in Capra's earlier films.[13] This emphasis is apparent not only in the first and last films in the series that focus on U.S. involvement in the war, but also in the films focusing on other Allied countries, including *The Battle of Britain, The Battle of Russia,* and *The Battle of China,* all of which contain lengthy segments extolling the willingness of ordinary citizens to unite against a common enemy. In *The Battle of Britain,* for example, the narrator attributes Hitler's failure to his inability to understand that "in a democracy it is not the government that makes war . . . it is the people." When Allied leaders are shown, they often are depicted on the streets greeting people or surrounded by crowds of admirers, and there are constant references to the governments of free-world countries being in the control of the people. In the last film in the series, the narrator concludes, "The people were to rule. Not some of the people. Not the best people, or the worst. Not the rich people or the poor, but we the people. All the people." It is a statement that would not seem out of place in the finale of Moore's film. While Moore's concluding voice-over narration in *Fahrenheit 9/11* would seem to echo Capra's emphasis on the significance of the people in fighting wars, Moore contends that it is those who are most impoverished who are the first to come to the country's defense, and, unlike Capra, he criticizes the manipulation of these people by those in power and asks, "Will they ever trust us again?"

Although *Fahrenheit 9/11* shares with the Capra series an affinity for the average citizen, Moore identifies a clear rift in American society between the working class and the elite.[14] This diametric opposition has been a theme of Moore's work since *Roger & Me* (where it was effectively summed up in the succinct phrase "pets or meat") and is a prominent feature of the film *The Big One* and several segments of Moore's television programs. Although the concept is less overt in *Fahrenheit 9/11* than in these earlier works, it provides an undercurrent throughout the film, most notably in Moore's discussion of the privileged treatment afforded the Saudis who were major investors in U.S. business interests, in the sections of the film showing military recruitment efforts among the lower-class citizens of Flint, Michigan, and in the juxtaposition of Bush jokingly referring to a crowd of rich contributors as "the haves and the have-mores" with Moore's comments on the substantial cuts made to soldiers' salaries and benefits.

The opposition between the working and privileged classes is established early in the film when Moore implies that African American voters were disenfranchised in the last election. In keeping with his orientation toward class conflict, Moore comments on how much the American people pay for Bush's salary in contrast to the millions the Saudis have given to the Bush family, suggesting that Bush's constituency can expect less loyalty than those who have "outbid" them. Later he includes an interview with a soldier who indicates how little he is paid compared to what a Halliburton truck driver in Iraq earns. Playing up the threat represented by the administration to its own public, Moore introduces a montage of news reports about alleged terror threats by stating, "With the war in Afghanistan over and bin Laden forgotten, the 'war president' had a new target—the American people." Moore saves his most direct comments on class inequality and the value of the average citizen over bureaucratic institutions for his conclusion. Echoing the theme that runs throughout Capra's work, Moore states, "I've always been amazed that the very people forced to live in the worst parts of town, go to the worst schools, and who have it the hardest are always the first to step up to defend that very system. . . . They give up their lives so that we can be free."

Moore's sympathies with the working class echo the "common man" appeal of Capra's fictional works in the decade prior to World War II that Bohn regards as having influenced the approach Capra took to the Why We Fight series. This common man aspect of Moore's films is most evident in his own populist screen persona as the average guy trying to get answers from an indifferent bureaucracy. Although many critics noted that Moore inserted himself less into *Fahrenheit 9/11* than into his previous films, he remained a constant narrative presence, and by this point his film persona was well enough established that it was likely to be evoked by audiences even when Moore was not present on screen. Moore also provides "common man" surrogates through the use of average citizens who have been affected by the policies of the Bush administration, most notably Flint resident Lila Lipscomb and marine corporal Abdul Henderson.

Moore's own presence and style in *Fahrenheit 9/11* are indicative of the difference in tone from the Capra series. This difference is most immediately evident in the treatment of the voice-over narration in the films. Whereas Capra largely maintains a serious, informative (if at times dogmatic) tone reinforced by omniscient, unseen narrators, Moore often underscores his presentation of information with satiric commentary. Although, unlike Moore, the two principal unseen but omnipresent narrators in the Capra films, Walter Huston and Anthony Veiller, do not rely on a specific persona that would have been firmly fixed in the minds of their audience, Bohn comments on their use of a "colloquial-conversational style" throughout the series, in contrast to the literary or poetic style found in earlier expository documentaries such as the works of Pare Lorentz. Bohn notes that "a consistent attempt to couch ideas in ordinary language, including slang, is evident throughout the films" and provides a lengthy list of examples from the series, including constant references to "John Q. Public" in *Prelude to War.*[15] Bohn concludes that this style "spoke to the men on their own terms, in their own language. There was little of the deep-voiced narrator rolling off polysyllabic words. This was a narrator that talked the language of the G.I."[16] Moore's use of the colloquial style (what Pauline Kael disparagingly refers to as his "aw-shucks, cracker-barrel pastiche" approach)[17] may be intended to differentiate himself and his audience from the elitist class he opposes, but a condescending tone occasionally becomes evident in the film, as when, for the sake of an easy laugh, Moore incorporates footage intended only to demonstrate Bush's inarticulateness.

A direct connection between narrator and audience is encouraged at the outset of both *Fahrenheit 9/11* and *Prelude to War* by the use of a question (Moore asking, "Was it all just a dream?" and the first Capra film opening with the inquiry, "Why are we Americans on the march?"), suggesting that what follows will be a collective enquiry rather than simply an authoritarian commentary, and the device is employed throughout the films to reinforce this perception. The question technique is used extensively throughout *Fahrenheit 9/11*, as, for example, when a clip of Bush commenting that he isn't spending much time focusing on bin Laden is followed by Moore (in voice-over) asking, "Didn't spend much time on him? What kind of president was he?"; or when Moore concludes a segment in which he questions various members of Congress about not having family members in Iraq by asking, "Who could blame them? Who would want to give up their child? Would you?"

Another defining feature of the narration is the use of a punctuated style that relies on the deliberate pacing of short sentences or phrases. Capra often uses this for dramatic emphasis or to elicit an angry response, as when the narrator in *Prelude* observes, "The word of God and the word of the führer cannot be reconciled," then in a harsh voice shouts, "Then God must go!" as a rock shatters the stained-glass window of a church. Moore employs a similar style, but usually to provide a punch line to a lengthier setup or to emphasize a comedic point, as when he talks about Bush's ineffectiveness in his first several months in office and states, "With everything going wrong, he did what any of us would do. He went on vacation." Later, when introducing a segment on security measures on the Oregon coastline, Moore asks, "And, thanks to the budget cutbacks, the total number of State Police protecting it?" and then responds, "One. Part time. Meet Trooper Brooks." The effect of the narrative style in both Capra's and Moore's films is to provide a more intimate and casual interaction between narrator and audience that stands in contrast to the often formal and authoritarian voices of earlier expository documentaries.

Aside from a few person-on-the-street segments, which appear to have been taken from preexisting newsreels, Capra does not make use of the kind of direct-to-camera address found throughout Moore's work (a technique that was employed in documentaries as early as the 1935 British production *Housing Problems* and became increasingly common with the emergence of the cinema verité movement, as evidenced by, for example, the Maysles' films *Salesman* and *Grey Garden's.* But just as Moore employs Lila Lipscomb in the last part of the film to provide an even more direct appeal to the average audience member, the last film in Capra's series, *War Comes to America,* employs a similar shift in emphasis. In this film, as Bohn points out,

> Lloyd Nolan narrates a long passage describing the American people. The shift in narrator is an obvious attempt to achieve a "straight from the shoulder" approach. Previously, Huston is identified as a detached narrator, observing, but not participating. Nolan comes in with "Well, we are . . ." He is one of the people being described, one of the boys. The change is effective.[18]

In both cases, the intent of such narrative approaches is to make the audience feel like active participants in the events, rather than merely detached observers.

If the choice and style of narration provide the most direct indication of the more deliberately ironic tone of Moore's work, this difference also is apparent in other rhetorical devices employed in the film, and Bohn's identification of a number of constructive techniques and themes used in the Capra series provides a useful blueprint for examining how many of these elements also are employed in *Fahrenheit 9/11*. On a general level, the main constructive principle in the Capra films is to present information in the form of a history lesson that builds to a consideration of present conditions, an approach effectively employed in the earlier government-sponsored films of Lorentz, most notably *The Plow That Broke the Plains* and *The River*.[19] Moore also employs this device to some extent, though his scope and historical time-frame are somewhat more limited and mainly restricted to a reminder of events surrounding the 2000 election and a consideration of the history of investments by Saudis (including members of the bin Laden family) in such companies as Harken Energy and the Carlyle Group, for which George Bush Sr. and Jr. worked.

In terms of the visual dimension, the seven films in the Why We Fight series are compiled almost entirely from existing footage, most of which is taken from newsreels, government sources, and Axis propaganda films, but which also includes extensive use of material from fictional films.[20] Although Moore makes use in *Fahrenheit 9/11* of interviews and other material shot especially for his film, he relies more than in his previous works on preexisting footage. Whereas Capra takes existing enemy footage (particularly from Riefenstahl's work) and recontextualizes it to generate a response to the images different from what was originally intended, Moore's approach might be regarded as more a matter of *un*-contextualizing, since he often incorporates material that either was never intended to be seen or has been taken out of the context in which it initially was presented, and gives no background on the circumstances under which the material was generated. This is evident from the beginning of the film, in the shots that accompany the opening credits, which show Bush and other officials grooming themselves before making public appearances and were never intended to be aired.[21] Elsewhere, Moore makes use of still photos and footage of members of the Bush family meeting with prominent Saudi businessmen and officials, but does not provide any specific context for these images, allowing viewers to assume that these encounters all involved capitalistic dealings.

Much of the existing footage used by Moore or Capra involves quotations from prominent figures. Although Capra employs footage of speeches by leaders of the Axis powers, he clearly takes dramatic license with the translation at times, as in the sequence in *Prelude to War* in which he repeatedly employs the phrase "Stop thinking and follow me" over shots of the speeches being made by Hitler, Mussolini, and Hirohito. At other times, the narrator is careful to point out that he is presenting "an exact translation" of what is being said. In addition to making selective use of quotations in existing footage to support his positions, Moore is able to take somewhat more control than Capra over this aspect of his film by conducting his own interviews with politicians, officials, FBI agents, writers, relatives of 9/11 victims, soldiers, and civilians affected by the war in Iraq. Echoes of Capra's dramatic license are at times evident in Moore's work, though, as when he raises a series of questions that might be going through Bush's mind as he sits in a grade school classroom continuing to read to the children after being informed of the 9/11 attacks.

Capra's most dramatic use of quotations occurs in *Divide and Conquer*, in which Hitler's promises to neighboring European countries are juxtaposed against war and invasion footage detailing the violation of those promises. The concept of contrasting what officials say with what they do, employed as a strategy throughout the Capra films to emphasize the differences between the free and slave worlds, is used even more extensively by Moore in *Farhenheit 9/11*, as in all of his films. In one lengthy segment Moore compiles clips of various officials to show the mixed messages given about terrorist threats after 9/11 (such as cutting from Vice President Cheney warning that "terrorists are doing everything they can to gain even deadlier means of striking us" to Bush urging the American people, "Go down to Disney World in Florida"). At another point, Donald Rumsfeld's comments about the care and humanity shown when bombing targets are intercut with shots of Iraqi civilians whose homes have been hit and family members killed (which is then followed by a cut to Britney Spears at her most bimbo-esque declaring the need to support our president). The same strategy is used to juxtapose comments claiming Iraq is in possession of weapons of mass destruction with earlier statements claiming that Saddam Hussein does not possess any of these weapons, and to demonstrate the contradictory statements given by administration officials regarding the alleged connections between Al-Qaeda and Saddam. A comment by Moore that the title of a pre-9/11 security briefing may have been too vague is followed by Condoleezza Rice testifying during a congressional hearing that the title of the briefing was "Bin Laden Determined to Attack Inside the United States."[22]

The establishment of contrasts through the juxtaposition of contradictory quotes is indicative of an editing strategy that forms a major constructive element of both Capra's and Moore's films. Bohn notes that in addition to playing up the fundamental contrast between the free and slave worlds, Capra (particularly in the first and last films in the series) uses editing to emphasize the similarities that exist among the Axis countries. In keeping with the tone of his work, Moore relies on editing more for ironic contrast, as evidenced by a cut from Bush announcing that major combat operations have ended in Iraq to footage of the fighting escalating, or the cut from a crowd cheering Bush as he announces that the soldiers in Iraq will not have died in vain to a shot of Lila Lipscomb arriving on the mall in Washington, D.C., to protest the death of her son. The effects of these contrasts are not significantly different from those created when Capra cuts from Hitler declaring he wants peace to shots of German soldiers invading neighboring countries.

Another significant form of evidence Bohn identifies in the Capra films is the use of statistics, particularly with regard to the numbers of soldiers and weapons lost in major battles and budget figures demonstrating that while the United States was reducing its military strength Germany was increasing its power. Though Moore makes less extensive use of such direct quantitative evidence, like Capra the statistics he does include focus largely on casualties and government budget cuts. Specifically, Moore provides shots of budget reports showing the cuts made to terrorism funding for the FBI during the first year of the Bush administration, and provides statistics on the number of troops that will be retained in Iraq past their required tour of duty, as well as on the number of soldiers who were wounded during the first 13 months of the war (which are superimposed over footage of wounded soldiers in a military hospital). Again, however, while the basic technique is the same, the intent is different. Capra employs these statistics to demonstrate our lack of preparedness for war and the sacrifices other Allied countries already have made in the name of the "free world," while Moore provides statistical information to show the government's disregard for and indifference to its own military personnel.

Although not identified by Bohn, a device employed by both Capra and Moore to lend added credibility to the information being presented is the use of headlines and documents. The former provided a point of attack for Moore's detractors when it was discovered that a "headline" reading "Latest Florida recount shows Gore won election" that was presented as being taken from the December 19, 2001, edition of *The Pantagraph* in Bloomington, Illinois, actually had appeared over a letter to the editor in the December 5 issue and had been electronically altered in the film to make it look as though it accompanied a front page news story.

But here again precedent can be found in the Why We Fight series. Capra in his autobiography acknowledges,"Our only re-creations were newspaper headlines and, of course, the animated expository war maps."[23] As Saltzman discusses in detail, the first and last films in the series prominently emphasize the role of the media as an element of a free society. Saltzman provides a detailed description of the use of headlines in the series and notes that the films make use of "real and specially created newspaper headlines and stories to emphasize key points and add veracity to his war films."[24] In contrast, Moore again uses ironic juxtaposition to comment on the alleged independence of the press in American society by noting that we have an independent media that will tell us the truth, but following this claim with a montage of clips of various newscasters and reporters praising the war effort and adhering diligently and unquestioningly to the White House talking points about the success of the Iraqi operations.

Capra makes little use of direct documents, perhaps because of considerations of national security at the time the films were produced, although he does occasionally employ this evidence to show both the enemy preparation for war (such as the Tanaka plan) and the lack of preparation on the part of the United States (through the government's commitment to treaties that later were seen to work against us). Moore mainly uses documents to insinuate that official information was either manipulated or suppressed, as when he presents files allegedly showing Bush's altered service records, FBI reports detailing the training by Al-Qaeda operatives at flight schools in the United States, and papers reportedly showing that members of the bin Laden family and other prominent Saudis were allowed to fly out of the country immediately after the 9/11 attacks.

If the use of existing footage, quotations, statistics, documents, and headlines are intended to serve as factual cognitive evidence in the films, both Capra and Moore also resort to techniques that operate mainly on an affective level. Like Capra, Moore also incorporates material from fictional films. But in the Capra films this footage often either is used to visualize historical events (as in the footage from *Alexander Nevsky* and other Russian epics employed in the early scenes of *The Battle of Russia* or from the MGM production of *The Good Earth* in *The Battle of China*) or is incorporated into montages of newsreel footage without acknowledging its fictional origins (as in the use of shots from Hollywood gangster movies when detailing Mussolini's terror tactics in *Prelude to War*).

By contrast, Moore usually employs the technique mainly for comedic purposes, and relies on the audience's awareness of the incongruity of this footage to elicit a humorous response. For example, at one point he shows footage of a child being tucked into bed as he comments on Bush sleeping peacefully in a bed made with fine French linens on the night before 9/11. Later, when discussing members of the bin Laden family being allowed to leave the country af-

Capra used Hollywood gangster footage to portray one of the Italian fascists' political assassinations in 1943's *Prelude to War.*

ter the World Trade Center attacks, Moore asks what would have happened if Clinton had let members of Timothy McVeigh's family leave the country after the Oklahoma City bombing and briefly cuts in black-and-white footage of Puritans with torches from the 1960 British horror film *City of the Dead.* Moore also plays on the administration's own old-fashioned popular-culture-fueled attitudes, as demonstrated by his reworking of the opening credits of the *Bonanza* television series to show Bush and company riding into Afghanistan, or the clip of an old western showing a cowboy declaring, "Smoke 'em out" after a montage of sound bites of Bush making the same pronouncement at various press conference. At times, Moore even seems to be parodying the use of historical footage from fictional productions in the Capra films, particularly during a segment on the "Coalition of the Willing" that incorporates shots from an old Viking movie when mentioning Iceland and from the 1922 *Nosferatu* when referring to Romania.

Also functioning mainly on an affective level is another of the major devices

Moore uses a brief shot from 1960's *The City of the Dead* in *Fahrenheit 9/11* to answer a hypothetical question: what would have happened to President Bill Clinton if he had helped Timothy McVeigh's family to flee the United States after the Oklahoma City bombing? Copyright 2004 Lions Gate Films/IFC Films/Fellowship Adventure Group LLC.

identified by Bohn in the Capra films, the reliance on images of children. The Why We Fight series employs these images both to show the devastation of war and to contrast the treatment of children in the free and slave worlds (though apparently Capra and company failed to recognize the irony that to an objective outsider, a group of American children reciting the Pledge of Allegiance looks just as regimented as a classroom of German children singing the praises of the führer). Perhaps taking a cue from the effectiveness of scenes of dead and injured children in the Capra series, Moore limits his use of footage of children largely to the segments of his film dealing with the war in Iraq. In perhaps the most direct parallel to the Why We Fight series in Moore's film, he includes a sequence of shots of children at play in Iraq allegedly just before the bombing begins, which looks remarkably like the footage in Capra's films of children on a playground (taken from the 1939 documentary *The City*). Moore follows these shots with grim images of the aftermath of the bombing, including an Iraqi man holding his dead child as he screams at the camera and a shot of a child in a hospital getting his torn scalp stitched back together.

Another theme identified by Bohn in the Capra series is less evident in Moore's film. Capra puts a great deal of emphasis on religion throughout the series (even the *Battle of Russia* shows people in the Communist country gathering in churches to pray), particularly as an example of one of the freedoms that will be lost if the slave world is allowed to prevail. This is perhaps most directly conveyed in the striking shot in *Prelude to War* already alluded to in which a stained-glass window depicting Jesus Christ is shattered to reveal a poster of Hitler behind it. Surprisingly, given the connections of the Bush administration to the religious Right, Moore for the most part sidesteps this issue throughout his film, although at one point Lila Lipscomb discusses the multicolored cross she wears that she claims symbolizes God's love for all people.

Perhaps the most directly affective of the techniques used by both Capra and Moore is music. In addition to original background scoring, both directors make prominent use of preexisting music. Music scholar Warren Sherk notes, "Just as the war documentaries incorporated pre-existing footage, the music scores used preexisting music" but adds that "[Dimitri] Tiomkin went to great lengths to mold the music to support the drama using tempo, choice of key, texture, orchestration, and dynamics. A *mezzo forte* passage might be reworked *fortissimo* with octave doublings to match the onscreen action."[25] Sherk indicates that in *The Battle of Russia,* for example, Tiomkin composed only eight original cues, most of which were less than a minute long, and that the majority of the score was drawn from preexisting Russian music, including Shostakovich's Symphony no. 7, which Sherk describes as "a hymn of defiance against aggression," and the "Free World Hymn" based on the third movement of Tchaikovsky's Sixth Symphony for the film's conclusion.[26] This appropriation and application of contemporary symphonic works is evident throughout, as demonstrated by the use of a version of "Rhapsody in Blue" to accompany a montage of American life (taken from Van Dyke and Steiner's *The City*) in *War Comes to America.*

Again, whereas the Capra films employ preexisting music to encourage specific emotional responses (particularly through the use of recognizable patriotic songs, folk tunes, and hymns), Moore does so largely for ironic effect. Among the more obvious examples are "Vacation" by the Go-Gos to accompany shots of Bush on the golf course and his ranch, Eric Burdon's "We Gotta Get Out of This Place" when referring to members of the bin Laden family being flown out of the United States, R.E.M.'s "Shiny Happy People" during a montage of photos and footage of the members of the Bush family meeting with Saudis, an instrumental passage from Eric Clapton's "Cocaine" when showing records of Bush's absence from the National Guard, "The Theme from *The Greatest American Hero*" when Bush arrives on the aircraft carrier to declare "Mission Accomplished," and the apparently diegetic use of Bing Crosby singing "Santa Claus Is Coming to Town" during a Christmas Eve raid in Iraq.

Moore also augments the original score written for the film with other instrumental pieces, including the *Peter Gunn* theme when describing bin Laden and members of the Taliban escaping from the U.S. military, Elmer Bernstein's *Magnificent Seven* theme during the *Bonanza* parody (perhaps because Bernstein's score signifies "Western" even more than the actual *Bonanza* theme), and light music that sounds like the underscoring of a 1950s educational film during the segment on a peace group in Fresno that was infiltrated by a federal agent. The original background scoring for *Fahrenheit 9/11* by Jeff Gibbs and Bob Golden is both minimal and minimalist, adhering to a trend that has become a standard for documentaries since its establishment in the scores composed by Philip Glass for films of Errol Morris and Godfrey Reggio.

In its use of music, editing, imagery, and narration, the Why We Fight series is now regarded as a landmark example of persuasive filmmaking. Yet as Bohn indicates, research on the effectiveness of the films at the time they were shown to American troops was inconclusive. He notes that the films "had marked effects on the men's knowledge of factual material concerning events leading up to the war" but that "as a tool for changing opinions and attitudes they were less effective."[27] Bohn suggests that the latter outcome may have been due in part to the lack of effective opinion leaders, who might have been on hand to discuss the films. Bohn also states that the inconclusiveness of the studies on the effectiveness of the films may have been due to factors such as inadequate tools of research, and an emphasis on measuring attitude change rather than reinforcement. Although Bohn indicates that the films in the series generally received positive reactions from enlisted men to whom they were shown, Clayton R. Koppes and Gregory D. Black, in *Hollywood Goes to War,* claim that *Prelude to War* was not a success with the civilian population and conclude that the box office failure of the film most likely was due to the fact that by the time it was cleared for public showing in 1943 much of the information was already out of date and familiar to audiences.[28]

By contrast, *Fahrenheit 9/11* was a major box office success (to date it is the highest-grossing documentary in film history), although it did not succeed in its ostensible goal of getting the Bush administration out of office. Yet research may ultimately determine that, like the Capra films, *Fahrenheit 9/11*'s success had more to do with education and reinforcement than with specific attitude change.

While, as Paul Arthur notes, it may be difficult to determine if *Fahrenheit 9/11* "carried the [documentary] market on its coattails" or whether "Moore lucked into a situation already primed for financial breakthrough,"[29] it is clear that the film became the focal point for renewed interest in the commercial viability of the documentary form, and was at the forefront of a wave of often highly personal persuasive political productions (including a growing subgenre of films specifically concerned with responding to or refuting Moore's work). One of these, Eugene Jârecki's 2005 production *Why We Fight,* directly acknowledges the precedent set by the Capra films by appropriating not only the tone and many of the techniques but even the title of the series. Such works indicate that, six decades after the release of the Capra films, filmmakers are continuing to use many of the same techniques to address the questions raised in the series, even if it is clear they hope that audiences will arrive at different answers.

Notes

1. "Prelude to War," *Hollywood Reporter,* May 28, 1943, 3.

2. Although in the early 1930s the Academy Awards included a "Novelty" Short Subject category that allowed for nomination of nonfiction subjects, an actual Documentary category was not created until 1941 (and modified two years later to include divisions for both short subjects and features). During the first few years of the categories' existence the nominations were dominated by war-related entries. More recently the Documentary category became a subject of controversy when several prominent works in the field failed to receive nominations (including Moore's *Roger & Me*). The omission of the 1994 film *Hoop Dreams* from the Documentary category led to changes in the nominating process.

3. Frank Capra, *The Name above the Title: An Autobiography* (New York: Macmillan, 1971), 349. Capra's claim is supported by an article in the May 1, 1943, issue of *Motion Picture Herald,* which noted that a Senate judiciary committee was looking into U.S. information and propaganda services, including film production. The article quoted Senator Joseph C. O'Mahoney as stating that "Facts and opinion should be clearly differentiated in the motion pictures" and discussing "the problem of keeping fact apart from message, of using the Government's information services to inform the people rather than to 'sell' them on particular viewpoints" (13).

4. Jurgen Fauth, "Anti-American Propaganda or Must-See Documentary?" *World film.about.com,* http://worldfilm.about.com/od/documentaryfilms/fr/fahrenheit911.htm. "Fahrenheit 9/11," *LA Film Critic.com,* http://www.lafilmcritic.com/rev_latest.htm. It should be noted that such attacks are not limited to American commentators, as indicated by a *BBC News* website article, "Poles Call 9/11 Film 'Propaganda,'" *BBC News World Edition,* http://news.bbc.co.uk/2/hi/entertainment/3923385.stm (accessed March 12, 2005) that states that Polish film critic Gazeta Wyborcza has claimed the film is "too biased to be called a documentary" and compared it to the work of Nazi propaganda director Leni Riefenstahl.

5. Paul Rotha, *Documentary Film* (London: Faber and Faber, 1935), 92.

6. John Berger, "Foreword: 'The Work of a Patriot,'" in *The Official Fahrenheit 9/11 Reader*, by Michael Moore (New York: Simon and Schuster Paperbacks, 2004), x.

7. Joel Bleifuss, "Framing Michael Moore," in *The Official Fahrenheit 9/11 Reader*, by Michael Moore (New York: Simon and Schuster Paperbacks, 2004), 255.

8. Joe Saltzman, *Frank Capra and the Image of the Journalist in American Film* (Los Angeles: Norman Lear Center/Annenberg School for Communication, University of Southern California, 2002), 140.

9. Harry Knowles, "Fahrenheit 9/11 Review," Ain't It Cool News website, http://www .aintitcool.com/display.cgi?id=17835. Knowles's critique is one of the few that draws a direct connection between *Fahrenheit 9/11* and the Why We Fight series. Knowles has no problem directly acknowledging that both Moore's film and the Capra series are propaganda, but even he reinforces the incompatibility of the concept with documentary when he states that Capra's series was "terrible documentary and a farce of any concept of accurate journalism" but "it was great propaganda, though." Knowles contends that Moore's film is not quite as effective a piece of propaganda as the Capra series, but he observes that "Like Capra, Michael is looking to erase any sense of propriety from this administration."

10. Louis Menand, "Nanook and Me," *New Yorker*, August 9, 2004.

11. "Fahrenheit 9/11 Has a Point to Make," Reuters, http://www.msnbc.msn.com/id/5289413 (accessed March 12, 2005).

12. Matthew Bernstein, "Documentaphobia and Mixed Modes," in *Documenting the Documentary: Close Readings of Documentary Film and Video*, ed. Barry Keith Grant and Jeanette Sloniowski (Detroit: Wayne State University Press, 1998), 397–415.

13. Thomas William Bohn, *An Historical and Descriptive Analysis of the "Why We Fight" Series* (New York: Arno Press, 1977), 132.

14. It seems unlikely that the one connection to Capra's free world/slave world dichotomy in Moore's film, the use of Neil Young's song "Keep on Rockin' in the Free World" over the ending credits, is intended as a deliberate reference to the earlier work.

15. This was one of the few elements in the film to which critic James Agee objected, calling the repeated references embarrassing and claiming they underestimated the film's audience (*Agee on Film* [New York: Grosset and Dunlap, 1969], 41).

16. Bohn, *Historical and Descriptive Analysis of the "Why We Fight" Series*, 164–65.

17. Pauline Kael, *Movie Love* (New York: Plume, 1991), 242–45.

18. Bohn, *Historical and Descriptive Analysis of the "Why We Fight" Series*, 164–65.

19. Precedents for the history lesson approach employed by Capra can be found not just in earlier documentaries but even in general entertainment productions, such as the 1940 British morale booster *For Freedom*, which includes a lengthy newsreel sequence early in the film chronicling Hitler's rise to power and the unpreparedness of the Allied forces for war, using footage from *Triumph of the Will* and other sources.

20. The American Film Institute catalog entry for the last film in the series, *War Comes to America*, for example, claims that it incorporates footage from a number of Hollywood productions, including *Drums along the Mohawk, Confessions of a Nazi Spy, Saboteur, Washington Merry-Go-Round, The Roaring Twenties, A Yank in the RAF, The*

Pied Piper, The Story of Alexander Graham Bell, Crash Dive, The Big Parade, Union Pacific, and *High, Wide and Handsome.*

21. The footage of Bush being made up prior to announcing that the bombing of Iraq had begun did air on some public television stations when they cut to the White House feed earlier than was intended.

22. This latter example demonstrates a common strategy employed by Moore in his films, in which he appears to be defending or giving serious consideration to one of his opponents, only to undermine them. For example, after an interview subject in *Roger & Me* describes General Motors CEO Roger Smith as "a warm man" Moore asks, "Did I have Roger Smith judged all wrong simply because he was eliminating 30,000 jobs from my hometown?" and in *Bowling for Columbine* Moore regularly uses his own membership in the NRA as leverage to get gun owners to talk openly with him, usually in a way that is detrimental to them.

23. Capra, *The Name above the Title,* 341.

24. Saltzman, *Frank Capra and the Image of the Journalist in American Film,* 139.

25. Warren Sherk, "Dimitri Tiomkin and the Army Orientation and Information Films (1942–1945)," *Cue Sheet* 20, no. 4 (October 2005): 9.

26. Ibid., 16–18.

27. Bohn, *Historical and Descriptive Analysis of the "Why We Fight" Series,* 113.

28. Clayton R. Koppes and Gregory D. Black, *Hollywood Goes to War: How Politics, Profits, and Propaganda Shaped World War II Movies* (London: I. B. Tauris, 1987), 125.

29. Paul Arthur, "Extreme Makeover: The Changing Face of Documentary," *Cineaste* 30, no. 3 (Summer 2005): 19. Arthur adds, "Despite his unrivalled public imprint, Michael Moore merits neither the lion's share of credit or flagrant blame for the state of American documentary. His oeuvre, however, can and should be addressed as a lightning rod for much that is endemic to today's unsettled conditions." Also of note in the same issue of *Cineaste* is Pat Aufderheide's "The Changing Documentary Marketplace," which raises concerns about the ethical implications of economic developments in the field in recent years.

Truth and Rhetoric in Michael Moore's *Fahrenheit 9/11*

CHARLES MUSSER

It was wartime, and so the Seventy-fifth Academy Awards dispensed with the customary red carpet outside Hollywood's Kodak Theatre. Midway through the evening festivities Michael Moore strode to the stage—followed by all the other nominees in the Best Documentary category—and accepted his Oscar for *Bowling for Columbine* (2002). "On behalf of our producers Kathleen Glynn and Michael Donovan from Canada, I'd like to thank the Academy for this," he began. The bulk of his acceptance speech was not about that film, however, but addressed the ways in which principled documentary practice necessarily confronted the Rovian politics and Cheney-inflected conduct of the Bush administration—particularly the Iraq war, which had begun just five days earlier, on March 19, 2003.

> I have invited my fellow documentary nominees on the stage with us, and we would like to—they're here in solidarity with me because we like nonfiction.
>
> We like nonfiction and we live in fictitious times.
>
> We live in the time where we have fictitious election results that elect a fictitious president.
>
> We live in a time where we have a man sending us to war for fictitious reasons.
>
> Whether it's the fictition of duct tape or fictition of orange alerts we are against this war, Mr. Bush.[1]

His speech elicited a wide range of reactions from the audience inside the theater (and from those watching on TV): cheers, boos, and silent discomfort. The war was fresh, and many of those who thought it illegal or merely unwise hoped for a quick, relatively bloodless end. Were we not being told that ordinary Iraqis would greet us with flowers and hail us as liberators?

As time has passed, however, Moore's provocative statement has proved remarkably astute and correspondingly courageous. The principal reasons for the United States going to war—Saddam Hussein's possession of weapons of mass destruction, Saddam's ties with Al-Qaeda—turned out to be fictitious. Likewise election fraud in the United States—from the purging of voter rolls to the suspect counting of votes in 2000 and 2004—has been a recurrent and disturbing issue, which refuses to go away.[2] Underlying Moore's juxtaposition of nonfiction to fictions (or as he called them "fictitions"—a neologism worthy of Bush) was the association of nonfiction with truth, ethical integrity and documentary; and, correspondingly, of fiction with lies, dissembling, and falsehood. If his acceptance speech placed the filmmaker in the midst of controversy, it also placed him at the very center of the documentary tradition.

Whether the Veriscope (Latin for truth viewer) of 1897, Dziga Vertov's advocacy for *kino pravda* (film truth in Russian) of the 1920s, or Edgar Morin's 1960 call for a new *cinéma vérité* (French for truth cinema), the linking of truth claims to nonfiction has been a long-standing preoccupation of critics and practitioners. It is not surprising, therefore, that (1) at many points in his extensive body of public statements, Michael Moore has linked his documentary practice to the term *truth*, and (2) much of the controversy surrounding *Fahrenheit 9/11* would focus on its truthfulness. Moore's detractors have argued, for instance, that the filmmaker is actually a dangerous propagandist and rabble-rousing dissembler who stretches the truth, works with half-truths, and often simply lies. What then is the relationship of truth to fact on one hand and to rhetoric on the other when it comes to this landmark documentary? This essay seeks to take a dispassionate look at Michael Moore's film and evaluate it against the commentary of his critics, focusing in particular on the arguments in the 2004 anti-Moore documentary *FahrenHYPE 9/11*. To grasp what was at stake in this controversy, we should first consider briefly the history of the film's production, exhibition, and reception.

FAHRENHEIT 911: A BRIEF HISTORY

Roughly five days after accepting his Oscar and 10 days after the Iraq war had begun, Moore announced his next documentary project—entitled *Fahrenheit 911* (the slash in his title would be added later). "The primary thrust of the new film is what has happened to the country since Sept. 11, and how the Bush administration used this tragic event to push its agenda," Moore explained.[3] In announcing the project, Moore said he would complete *Fahrenheit 911* in time for the Cannes Film Festival (May 2004) and release it during the 2004 presidential election. Funding was supposed to come from another indie renegade: Mel Gibson's Icon Productions, which would make a fortune with *The Passion of the Christ*.[4] Moore and Gibson were both Catholics (Moore had gone to church before going to the Oscars), but the timing was not right: Gibson's movie would not be released until late February 2004. (Might political differences also have been a factor?) When this arrangement fell through, Bob and Harvey Weinstein at Miramax stepped in and bankrolled the project.[5]

The production of *Fahrenheit 9/11* called for a combination of original footage shot by Moore (of a Flint, Michigan, family that lost their son in the war, of Moore soliciting congressmen outside their offices, etc.) and stock footage. The latter included scenes of President Bush in a Sarasota schoolroom during the attacks on the World Trade Center. Moreover, Moore and his camera crews never went to Iraq. The scene of US soldiers breaking and entering an Iraqi household late at night was filmed by Micah Garen, who was in Iraq making a documentary about the pillaging of antiquities. Other material was purchased from the networks, including NBC News. Many such scenes—those of young American combat amputees at Walter Reed hospital, an Iraqi woman whose house had just been bombed and family members killed, and photographs of Abu Ghraib—echo scenes from the Vietnam war documentary *Hearts and Minds* (1974).[6] Commentators who argue that the antiwar movement around the Iraq war has been a pale version of the earlier Vietnam era need to reassess such conclusions based, in part, on Moore's precocious announcement—and timely delivery—of the film. Indeed, one aspect of political documentaries in the era of George "Dubya" Bush is the rapidity of the response as well as the close connection of many anti-Iraq war documentaries to U.S. elections.[7]

Fahrenheit 9/11, as we know, was the most commercially successful documentary of all times, grossing over $222 million worldwide.[8] Finished just 10 days before its May 17 premiere at the 2004 Cannes Film Festival, Moore's documentary received every imaginable accolade. At the afternoon screening, the film received "a 20-minute standing ovation that the festival's artistic director, Thierry Fremaux, said was the longest he had ever witnessed in Cannes."[9] *New York Times* reviewer A. O. Scott, hardly a Moore enthusiast, called it "the best film Mr. Moore has made so far, a powerful and passionate expression of outraged patriotism, leavened with humor and freighted with sorrow" and concluded that Moore "was arguably a great filmmaker."[10] The film went on to win the Palme d'Or—the festival's top award. At a moment when the United States was in the throes of anti-French sentiment for the country's refusal to join the "coalition of the willing" and send troops to Iraq, it is worth noting that four of the nine Cannes jurists were Americans—and only one was French. When jury president Quentin Tarantino announced the award, the choice "met with enthusiastic cheers from the audience in the Grand Theatre Lumière."[11]

Although Miramax had become the principal investor in the film and was poised to distribute it, the parent company (Walt Disney Company) blocked the effort, creating a high-profile scandal, which only fueled Moore's publicity machine. As the *New York Times* reported,

> "We advised both [Mr. Moore's] agent and Miramax in May of 2003 that the film would not be distributed by Miramax," said Zenia Mucha, a [Disney] company spokeswoman. "That decision stands." . . .
>
> Mr. Moore's agent, Ari Emanuel, said Michael D. Eisner, Disney's chief executive, asked him last spring to pull out of the deal with Miramax. Mr. Emanuel said Mr. Eisner expressed particular concern that it would endanger tax breaks Disney receives for its theme park, hotels and other ventures in Florida, where Mr. Bush's brother, Jeb, is governor.[12]

Mucha argued that "it's not in the interest of any major corporation to be dragged into a highly charged partisan political battle." To which Moore responded, "At some point the question has to be asked, 'Should this be happening in a free and open society where the monied interests essentially call the shots regarding the information that the public is allowed to see?' "[13]

The Weinsteins quickly bought the North American rights for *Fahrenheit 9/11* from Disney/Miramax and arranged theatrical distribution through a consortium involving Lions Gate and IFC Films.[14] On June 14, they hosted a star-studded sneak preview at New York's vast Ziegfeld Theater, which was attended by everyone from Al Franken and Tim Robbins to Yoko Ono and Martha Stewart. Roger Friedman of Murdock's Fox News Network was so moved by the experience that he declared, "It turns out to be a really brilliant piece of work, and a film that members of all political parties should see without fail."[15] *Fahrenheit 9/11* had its commercial debut on Wednesday, June 23 in two New York City theaters; in both instances, it broke house records.[16] The film had its "official" opening on the same day in Washington, D.C., a couple of miles from the Bush

White House. "With full Hollywood trappings—a red carpet, klieg lights and dozens of photographers—nearly 800 members of the capital's Democratic leadership turned out," reported John Files of the *New York Times.*[17]

Film critics generally greeted *Fahrenheit 9/11* with enthusiastic, powerful reviews. Kenneth Turan of the *Los Angeles Times* declared that "this landmark in American political filmmaking demands to be seen" and compared Moore to Émile Zola, "whose celebrated 19th century open letter [*J'Accuse*] assailed the French government for being a party to intolerable injustice." Like Zola, Moore had "launched an unapologetic attack, both savage and savvy, on an administration he feels has betrayed the best of America and done extensive damage in the world."[18] Desson Thomson of the *Washington Post* wrote,

> "FAHRENHEIT 9/11," is a guided missile aimed directly at the presidency of George W. Bush, just four months ahead of the national election.
>
> Its political purpose is unequivocal. But here's the part that matters: Its trajectory is guided with pinpoint accuracy. With an ironic narrative that takes us from the Florida debacle that decided the 2000 presidential election to the political nettling aftermath of war in Iraq, "Fahrenheit 9/11" sagely uses the public record, the facts and the president's goofiest statements and on-camera performances to score its points.[19]

Not all the reviews were in the arts sections. Paul Krugman devoted a *New York Times* op-ed column to the film, praising the documentary for what it revealed: "*Fahrenheit 9/11* performs an essential service. It would be a better movie if it didn't promote a few unproven conspiracy theories, but those theories aren't the reason why millions of people who aren't die-hard Bush-haters are flocking to see it. These people see the film to learn true stories they should have heard elsewhere, but didn't. Mr. Moore may not be considered respectable, but his film is a hit because the respectable media haven't been doing their job."[20] Or as Moore phrased the same idea: "[This] shows the American people haven't been given the whole story these last three years and they don't think they've been given the truth, so they've gone to the movies theaters to learn the truth and begin the important discussion that needs to take place in this country."[21]

RESPONSES FROM THE RIGHT

After Moore and the Weinsteins had successfully circumvented Disney's refusal to distribute *Fahrenheit 9/11*, right-wing operatives made efforts to limit its exhibition in the United States. The California-based Move America Forward—a nonprofit organization with close ties to the Republican Party—conducted an e-mail campaign in its effort to discourage theaters from playing *Fahrenheit 9/11*. Sal Russo, chief strategist for Move America Forward and a partner in the Republican-affiliated public relations firm Russo, Marsh & Rogers, had "asked Americans who find the film's intention of undermining the war on terrorism to be offensive and unpatriotic to contact movie theater operators and register their dissatisfaction with any theaters who [*sic*] push anti-war propaganda as family entertainment."[22] But as John Fithian, president of the National Association of Theatre Owners, remarked, "Any time any organization protests against a movie, they ensure that the movie will do better at the box office than it would have done otherwise. If they have any doubt about this, just ask Mel Gibson."[23] In the end, *Fahrenheit 9/11* boasted "the widest opening ever for a documentary."[24]

Efforts were also made to limit the kinds of people who could get into the movie theaters to see the *Fahrenheit 9/11*. The MPAA gave the film an "R" rating "for some violent and disturbing images, and for language."[25] This required all children under 17 to be accompanied to the film by a parent or guardian, making it more difficult for younger moviegoers to attend. Lions Gate appealed and sought a PG-13 rating, but without success. Moore protested, arguing, "Older teenagers are being sent to Iraq, some never to return. To say that teenagers shouldn't see this movie means that the truth should be kept from them. I encourage all teenagers to come see my movie, by any means necessary." The success of this restrictive strategy is unclear. My daughter Hannah, then 14 years old, went to see the film with her mother and stepfather—along with her two brothers who were then eight and 11.[26]

During its opening weekend *Fahrenheit 9/11* played 868 theaters and grossed a total of $23,920,637—averaging $27,558 per theater.

> "We sold out in Fayetteville, home of Fort Bragg," in North Carolina, Mr. Moore said on Sunday. "We sold out in Army-base towns. We set house records in some of these places. We set single-day records in a number of theaters. We got standing ovations in Greensboro, N.C."[27]

A happy Harvey Weinstein declared, "It's beyond anybody's expectations. I'd have to say the sky's the limit on this movie. Who knows what territory we're in."[28] Its first weekend broke the record for highest-earning documentary, set by

Bowling for Columbine, which boasted an accumulated domestic box office of $21.6 million.

As one might expect, Moore basked in the attention. On Independence Day, 2004, he wrote an open letter to his "friends":

> Where do I begin? This past week has knocked me for a loop. "Fahrenheit 9/11," the #1 movie in the country, the largest grossing documentary ever. My head is spinning. Didn't we just lose our distributor 8 weeks ago? Did Karl Rove really fail to stop this? Is Bush packing?[29]

In fact, the Republican Right was poised to counterattack, its political operatives doing whatever they could to undermine the film's credibility. As Moore reported,

> News editors told us that they were being "bombarded" with e-mails and calls from the White House (read: Karl Rove), trying to spin their way out of this mess by attacking it and attacking me. Bush spokesman Dan Bartlett had told the White House press corps that the movie was "outrageously false"—even though he said he hadn't seen the movie. He later told CNN that "this is a film that doesn't require us to actually view it to know that it's filled with factual inaccuracies." At least they're consistent. They never needed to see a single weapon of mass destruction before sending our kids off to die.[30]

The Bush political machine could also rely on anti-Moore authors, webmasters, and filmmakers, who were ready to spring into action and do the necessary work to discredit the film. (Most of them, at least, were eager to watch Moore's documentary.)

The anti-Moore political movement had started as a response to *Bowling for Columbine,* and its members had plenty of advance warning so they could prepare themselves to attack Moore's new effort in the approaching political season. These included Jim Kenefick, who started the website Watching Michael Moore's Every Move (www.moorewatch.com), in October 2002. Connecticut-based Kenefick, a former Republican turned independent, is into photography, movies, and guns. As is often the case, his blog's first postings "Michael Moore 'Fisked' to Death" and "Michael Moore: Truth-teller or Master Manipulator?" are archived on the website but linked to online articles that have since disappeared.[31] Another high-profile personality, David T. Hardy, had posted a critique of *Bowling for Columbine* and then started the short-lived website www.moorexposed.com. Jason Clarke started the website www.moore-lies.com in April 2003, "devoted to exposing the truth about America's pseudo-muckraker, filmmaker Michael Moore."[32] Hardy and Clarke then combined to cowrite *Michael Moore Is a Big Fat Stupid White Man,* which was published by the Murdock-owned HarperCollins in June 2004—just as *Fahrenheit 9/11* was entering the theaters. Other blogs and websites were devoted exclusively or primarily to attacking *Fahrenheit 9/11,* including Fahrenheit Fact, billed as "the truth about michael moore's 'Fahrenheit 9/11'" (www.fahrenheitfact.blogspot.com).

Two filmmakers were actively pursuing Michael Moore just as Moore pursued General Motors president Roger Smith in *Roger & Me* (1989): radio talk-show host and electronic journalist Larry Elder with *Michael and Me* and a young Midwestern slacker, Michael Wilson, with *Michael Moore Hates America.* Both began work in 2003, long before *Fahrenheit 9/11* was released: both sought to mime Moore's previous hit documentaries *Roger & Me* and *Bowling for Columbine* but to turn the tables so that he became the hunted personality and object of derision. Elder, part of a small band of conservative African American commentators, has been a strong advocate for the right to bear firearms and went after *Bowling for Columbine* on this issue. Wilson was more interested in critiquing Moore's filmmaking techniques and his persona. The aspiring filmmaker had been working on his documentary for at least a year when, in May 2004, he received crucial funding from "political donor Brian R. Cartmell, an internet entrepreneur, whose early career was associated with Internet pornography."[33] Cartmell enabled Wilson to finish his film. The poster for Wilson's film declares that Moore's "documentaries are full of venom and hatred, invented facts and inaccuracies, yet he's been rewarded with Hollywood's highest honor. But the truth is, *Michael Moore Hates America* and Mike Wilson is the guy to prove it."[34] Both films would debut at the American Renaissance Film Festival in September 2004.

Two other documentaries directly engaged Moore's *Fahrenheit 9/11:* Alan Peterson's *FahrenHYPE 9/11: Unraveling the Truth About Fahrenheit 9/11 & Michael Moore,* made with freelance politico Dick Morris and billed as "a documentary that tells the truth about a great nation," as well as Kevin Knoblock's *Celsius 41.11: The Temperature at Which the Brain . . . Begins to Die* (2004), which boasts the tagline: "The Truth behind the Lies of *Fahrenheit 9/11.*" Both were released in the weeks leading up to the election. *FahrenHYPE 9/11* went straight to DVD and was released on October 5, the same day as the DVD of *Fahrenheit*

9/11.[35] *Celsius 41.11* premiered at the conservative Liberty Film Festival in West Hollywood on October 1 and came out on DVD October 21.[36]

Celsius 41.11 does little to directly engage *Fahrenheit 9/11* and is an unapologetic purveyor of pro-Bush misinformation. It insists that not a single black voter was disenfranchised in Florida during the 2000 election. One of the documentary's heavily used experts, Mansoor Ijaz, poses as a Clinton official and Kerry friend, though he is actually a "foreign affairs and terrorism analyst" for Fox News.[37] Ijaz tells us that Saddam Hussein's government and Osama bin Laden shared intelligence and worked closely together, insisting on a relationship that even the Bush administration finally conceded was without merit. *Celsius 41.11* seeks to denigrate Moore primarily through out-of-context quotations that are periodically interjected on the screen in written form. The media equivalent of an Improvised Explosive Device (IED), this vicious little film briefly appeared in 116 theaters, two weeks before the election.[38]

FahrenHYPE 9/11, a more measured and direct engagement with Moore's documentary, uses well-established rhetorical structures of truth in defense of Bush and his administration. With the promotional line "You knew it was a lie . . . Now you know why," the film brought together a potent mix of Moore critics and neoconservatives. With Dick Morris "heading a search party for the truth,"[39] its on-screen commentators include David Hardy and Jason Clarke—authors of *Michael Moore Is a Big Fat Stupid White Man*. Writing credits were shared by Morris, his wife Eileen McGann, and Lee Troxler—who was in the Reagan administration and whose marketing company's clients included the Republican National Committee. Producers Michael R. Fox and Steve Haugen of Savage Productions were based in Salt Lake, where they catered to filmmakers seeking to reach a Mormon (LDS) audience. Ed Koch, Senator Zell Miller, Ann Coulter, and various other conservative commentators were prominently interviewed. Because *FahrenHYPE 9/11* presents itself as a serious critique of Moore's film and because it seeks to show that Moore's "truths" are lies and offers alternative truths in their stead, a comparison of *Fahrenheit* and *FahrenHYPE* can illuminate the methods and rhetorical strategies both employ.

STRUCTURES OF TRUTH-TELLING

Documentary practice in general has established a set of structures or tropes for presenting truth claims; these differ from the issues of correspondence between image and reality, which too often dominate discussions on this subject. First, in his efforts to offer more of 'the whole story," something closer to "the whole truth," Moore often shows what has been left out or forgotten; that is, he provides a more complete and therefore presumably more accurate picture. *Fahrenheit 9/11* is filled with tidbits that come as surprising revelations—or reminders since much of the information had appeared in newspapers but had been largely forgotten: Moore had gathered isolated facts/assessments and structured them into a narrative (but also a portrait) of the Bush administration's method of operating. For instance, during his first eight months of office, President George Bush was on vacation 42 percent of the time—ignoring memos from Richard Clarke among others as to the dangers Osama bin Laden posed to the United States.[40] The close ties between the Bush family and the Saudis, particularly the bin Laden family, are documented in excruciating detail. In particular Shafiq bin Laden, Osama bin Laden's half brother, and the president's father, George Herbert Walker Bush, were at a Carlyle Group meeting on the morning of September 11.

Another common trope of documentary truth has the filmmaker going beneath the surface of deceptive appearances. The title sequence of *Fahrenheit 9/11* intercuts key film credits with scenes of Bush, Donald Rumsfeld, Colin Powell, Dick Cheney, Paul Wolfowitz, and Condoleezza Rice preparing to go before the cameras—usually putting on makeup so they can "look good." Although some have considered these to be cheap shots or in bad taste, these images evoke the documentary tradition and its opposition to performance and masks. Moore and his credited associates promise to go beneath the Bush administration's PR image to get at what is hidden—the truth. Like Dziga Vertov, who wanted to reveal actors to be actors *playing* characters (and so expose the fictive nature of their performance), Moore wanted to show self-interested, unserious politicians putting on the false masks of statesmen. While these brief moments provide some comic relief, they symbolize what Moore would do throughout *Fahrenheit 9/11:* go behind the scenes to show us what the Bush government does not want us to see and so go under the public mask (the makeup) of Bush administration pronouncements. Bush was being made up and cracking jokes just as he was about to go on television to announce the onset of war. As Moore remarked, according to Frank Rich of the *New York Times,* "In your wildest dreams you couldn't imagine Franklin Roosevelt behaving this way 30 seconds before declaring war, with grave decisions and their consequences at stake."[41] What Moore does here, again and again, is to reveal what the Bush administration did its best to conceal—the essential modus operandi of his presidency. Bush's challenge to the growing insurgency to "Bring 'em on" is juxtaposed to Moore's exploration of the people who do the fighting and their families. *Fahrenheit 9/11* thus enacts a graphic used in Robert Greenwald's *Uncovered: The Truth About the Iraq War* (2003): pulling back the veil of patriotism as represented by the American flag, to show what has been hidden behind it.

A third documentary method of advancing truth claims is to show that previous accepted "truths" are not true but false (are lies) and so offer new truths in their stead. Moore, like Robert Greenwald in his *Uncovered: The Whole Truth About the Iraq War,* takes statements by top Bush officials—what might be considered provisional state truths ("truths" convincing enough to send us to war)—and juxtaposes them with scenes that suggest they are convenient lies. For instance, claims about the Iraq war are undermined by the reality on the ground. Secretary of Defense Rumsfeld's celebration of the U.S. military's "targeting capabilities" and "the humanity that goes into it" are placed against a woman screaming about the bombs that killed five members of her family and destroyed their home.[42] Likewise Bush's claim to military victory and the end of major combat operations is juxtaposed with the roll call of mounting U.S. casualties in the wake of his pronouncement. State truths asserted by the Bush administration are shown to be lies. All this is laced with a sense of irony, deadpan humor, and American pop music, which give the film energy and entertainment value.

A fourth technique is less often recognized and involves the simple reiteration of "facts" or events that have already been presented by "the other side": in Moore's case by the right-wing media or Bush operatives but more specifically by Bill Sammon, currently vice president of news for the Fox News Channel and author of *Fighting Back: The War on Terrorism—from Inside the Bush White House* (2002). Sammon wrote as someone who deeply admired Bush and his handling of the events on September 11 in particular. He also wrote at a time when Bush enjoyed wide popularity in the polls. His narrative played one way in 2002, but the same "facts" had a quite different valence when reiterated by Michael Moore two years later. While this will become more apparent in what follows, here is one example. Moore states, "On Sept. 10, 2001, Bush joined his brother in Florida where he slept the night in 'a bed made of fine French linens.'" His factual backups are two newspaper reports, one being "Tom Bayles, 'The Day Before Everything Changed, President Bush Touched Locals' Lives,' *Sarasota Herald-Tribune,* September 10, 2002." However, Moore may have originally garnered this tidbit from chapter 1 of *Fighting Back*: "On September 11, 2001, George W. Bush awoke in a bed . . . swaddled in the finest Frette linens and matching duvet" (9). Although Bayles states the linens were

French, Frette is the name of an Italian linen company. Either Bayles or Sammon may be "lying," but my point is that Moore and Sammon are in basic agreement about many more "facts" than one might suppose. This, one suspects, may have proved awkward for Sammon during the 2004 presidential elections.

Attacks on *Fahrenheit 9/11* often gloss over the fact that Moore's filmmaking is highly accomplished and his documentary is brilliantly constructed. Take the first section of *Fahrenheit 9/11,* which can be broken down into three sequences. The first, pretitle sequence, which starts with what appears to have been Al Gore's election night victory in 2000, moves fluidly back and forth in time as Moore traces the way Fox Network and Bush's first cousin John Ellis (behind the scenes) called the state of Florida for Dubya, giving him the election and the political maneuvering in the election's aftermath that culminated in the Supreme Court decision to support a Bush victory in Florida. The next subsection of this sequence begins with the election certification before Congress as black members of the House of Representatives object to the disenfranchisement of their constituents: their objections have no standing because not a single U.S. senator will joint their protest (upon Vice President Gore's request). Bush's Inauguration Day parade is disrupted, and his first months in office go badly. The president is shown going on vacation and retreating to his ranch for much of the summer. The first sequence thus ends with Dubya's arrival in Florida—greeted by his brother—on September 10, 2001. Many of the scenes are unfamiliar, and Moore weaves them together in a way that provides a highly personal yet omniscient view—often outraged, sometimes saddened, and frequently amused.

Following the second, credit sequence, the third sequence of *Fahrenheit 9/11* focuses on the morning of September 11 and begins with the attacks on the World Trade Center (which we hear rather than see), followed by scenes of others reacting to the unfolding carnage, and then glimpses of the immediate aftermath. After providing us with a visceral reencounter with these events, Moore cuts back in time to what the president was doing that morning—his visit to Emma E. Booker Elementary School in Sarasota and his decision to go ahead with his photo opportunity even though he knew the first plane had already hit the first tower of the World Trade Center. Shortly after entering the classroom, Bush is told that the second tower had also been hit. Moore ridicules Bush as he sits bewildered, reading the book *My Pet Goat* with the children, and waiting for direction from his aides: "Nearly seven minutes passed [after he was notified that a second plane went into the second World Trade Center tower] with nobody doing anything."[43] This is a damning juxtaposition—a powerful indictment of the president and his staff.

THE PROBLEM OF TIME (FIVE MINUTES—OR SEVEN?) AND ACTION

FahrenHYPE 9/11 challenges the accuracy of Moore's presentation of this historic moment. The opening, pretitle sequence of *FahrenHYPE 9/11* maintains that Moore got his facts wrong: in an on-camera interview, Bill Sammon, then senior White House correspondent for the *Washington Times*, claims to "have an uncut tape of the photo-op, which starts with President Bush walking into the room"—the second-grade classroom where Bush read *My Pet Goat* with the students. Since Sammon had made a transcription of much of the videotape that documented Bush's visit to the Booker Elementary School for his book *Fighting Back* (published October 7, 2002), he likely had special access.[44] Sammon asserts that this "uncut" tape shows that Bush "remained in the room for five minutes and not seven." Sammon then goes on to pronounce: "To me anyone who says it's seven minutes can't get the little details right; I'm suspect about them getting the big picture correct." In other words, Moore got his facts wrong and stretched the truth—and time—to suit his political goals. With filmmaker Peterson and Sammon raising the stakes around this moment in Moore's film, it is worth examining in detail.

In their five-minute rather than seven-minute argument, Alan Peterson and Bill Sammon are concerned about a specific kind of truth. To be sure it has to do with facts; but underlying this is a concern with an accurate correspondence between historical reality and what is shown—or more importantly what is *said*, since *FahrenHYPE 9/11*, like *Fahrenheit 9/11*, does not show this "unedited" tape. Ascertaining who is "lying" and who is "telling the truth" is complicated by language and available evidence. In regard to language: Among the many small points we might note is that "seven minutes" (Sammon) and "almost seven minutes" (Moore) are not quite the same thing. "Almost seven" is definitely less than seven and purposefully somewhat vague. Are six and a half minutes the same as "almost seven"? Is six minutes and 10 seconds?

Certainly another one of Moore's phrases open to variable interpretation is "nobody doing anything." At the very least, Bush's staff was seeking information about the attack. Perhaps then, "doing something" involves a subjective threshold of presidential action. Moore's casual (or more accurately, rhetorical) assertion comes under pressure when given sufficient scrutiny. The same kinds

The controversial Florida elementary schoolroom footage from *Fahrenheit 9/11* (2004) of President Bush reading *My Pet Goat* for seven minutes "with nobody doing anything." Moore added the clock time in the lower left corner.

of problems arise with Sammon's statement, though these issues seem more severe in *FahrenHYPE 9/11*. Peterson edits together two pieces of Sammon's interview (signaled in the following quote by a "//"), quite likely distorting his meaning. Sammon says, "I actually have an uncut tape of the photo-op which starts with the president walking into the room // and he remained in the room for five minutes, not seven." Although we do not know for sure to which tape Sammon is referring, there is a tape of five minutes and eight seconds that begins with Andrew Card telling the president the second tower of the World Trade Center had been hit and ends with him again whispering in Bush's ear, signaling the end of the photo-op session. Sammon's edited assertion seems to suggest that from the time Bush entered the schoolroom until he departed was only five minutes. Certainly given the tape that does exist, the president was in the room longer than five minutes—indeed almost certainly longer than seven. We might suspect that Peterson cut out a section of Sammon's interview, which would have started his time count from the moment Card whispered in his ear rather than *his* entrance into the schoolroom.

Although Peterson and Sammon collectively "misspoke," let us give them the benefit of the doubt. We will assume that Sammon and Moore started their metaphorical stopwatches with Card whispering into Bush's ear. On his web page, Moore offers a point-by-point defense of his narration. He backs up his statement, "Nearly seven minutes passed with nobody doing anything," with two newspaper items:

- "[H]e lingered in the room for another six minutes [after being informed of the second plane] . . . [At] 9:12, he abruptly retreated, speaking to Mr. Cheney and New York officials." David E. Sanger and Don Van Natta Jr., "After The Attacks: The Events; In Four Days, A National Crisis Changes Bush's Presidency," *The New York Times,* September 16, 2001.
- "Mr. Bush remained in the elementary school for nearly a half an hour after Andy Card whispered in his ear." Michael Kranish, "Bush: US To Hunt Down Attackers," *Boston Globe,* September 11, 2001.[45]

Certainly the "another six" of the *New York Times* is closer to Moore's "nearly seven" minutes than to Sammon's simple "five minutes." But perhaps neither Peterson nor Moore is exactly right, each slanting the timing to favor his agenda. Moreover, there is no guarantee that the *Times* article is precise.

What is worth noting, however, is that Moore chose to buttress his narration in the film with newspaper stories on his website rather than by using or citing these visual records, even though he had two different, partial video recordings of the event. His narration echoes and is supported by statements in "papers of record." Bush "lingered" and "remained"—nonactive characterizations of his behavior. That Moore focused on correspondence between his narration and the *written* record is revealing of his approach to filmmaking and probably reflects his experience as a journalist, best-selling author, and weekly magazine editor. It is also the kind of backup Moore needed so he could not be sued.

Enough of parsing words: what about the *visual* record of Bush in Sandra Kay Daniels' classroom? Would it not have been nice for Peterson to show all of Sammon's footage of the president, with a ticking clock burned into a corner of the image, as a kind of instant replay that could be analyzed and "deconstructed"? Don't we wish that videotape might do for Bush's confrontation with history in a Florida schoolroom as the Veriscope did for James J. Corbett's heavyweight championship fight with Bob Fitzsimmons over one hundred years earlier by offering a visual simulacrum of the event in question? Why didn't Peterson—or Moore—simply replay the unfolding events so that viewers can decide how Bush handled himself that morning?

The Memory Hole website, which has sought to gain full access to videotape of Bush in the classroom, reports:

> Until now, the only available footage had been a little film put together by Booker Elementary. . . . The problem is, there's a jump edit in the footage: From the time Card whispers to Bush until the end of the scene in the classroom, only 2 minutes and 10 seconds elapse.
>
> But this new, fuller footage shows Bush sitting for a full five minutes after he'd been told that "America is under attack."
>
> He declined to take action even longer than this, but unfortunately this footage ends before he leaves the classroom. Thanks to an amazing article by Allan Wood and Paul Thompson, we know what happened after the footage suddenly cuts off.[46]

The Memory Hole provides this video segment lasting five minutes and eight seconds as a downloadable QuickTime file (as well as a sequence of still images from the video). This footage begins with Bush seated as Card comes into the schoolroom to alert him that the second plane had hit the WTC and it ends with Bush still seated, after Card has reentered and is speaking to Bush for a second time. In a way the videotape might seem to show that the period of "nobody doing anything" is only five minutes since Card talking to the president a second time is "something." But Sammon did not repeat Moore's words—perhaps because he did not even want to suggest that the president was doing nothing even for five minutes, so he says Bush "remained in the room." But this uncut videotape shows that Bush was sitting in his chair for *at least* five minutes and doubtlessly "remained" somewhat longer—how much longer is unclear because the tape is cut at both ends. In short, If Card's act of whispering in President Bush's ear a second time—after five minutes have passed—in itself constitutes "something," then this is the kind of narrow, hair-splitting play with language that the Bush administration has often used when wanting to say something that seems to mean one thing but under further scrutiny can be said to mean something else.

In saying that "almost seven minutes passed with nobody doing anything," Moore doubtlessly meant "not responding to news of the attack in a more concrete and proactive way than Bush listening to Card." Here Moore's statement may actually understate the president's dawdling. According to Wood and Thompson in their article "An Interesting Day: President Bush's Movements and Actions on 9/11":

Nearly every news account fails to mention when Bush left the classroom after being told America was under attack. Three mention 9:12 a.m. [*New York Times,* 9/1/01 (B), *Telegraph,* 12/16/01, *Daily Mail,* 9/8/02]. Remaining in the classroom for approximately five to seven minutes is inexcusable, but the video of Bush in the classroom suggests he stayed longer than that. The video contains several edits and ends before Bush leaves the room, so it also doesn't tell us exactly how long he stayed. One newspaper suggested he remained "for eight or nine minutes"—sometime between 9:13 and 9:16, since Card's arrival is uncertain [*Tampa Tribune,* 9/1/02].

When Bush finally did leave, he didn't act like a man in a hurry. In fact, he was described as "openly stretching out the moment." [*Fighting Back: The War on Terrorism—From Inside the Bush White House,* by Bill Sammon, 10/02, p. 89]. When the lesson was over, Bush said to the children: "Hoo! These are great readers. Very impressive! Thank you all so much for showing me your reading skills. I bet they practice too. Don't you? Reading more than they watch TV? Anybody do that? Read more than you watch TV? [Hands go up] Oh that's great! Very good. Very important to practice! Thanks for having me. Very impressed." [Transcribed from Booker video, *Fighting Back: The War on Terrorism—From Inside the Bush White House,* by Bill Sammon, 10/02, 89–90]. Bush still continued to talk, advising the children to stay in school and be good citizens [*Tampa Tribune,* 9/1/02, *St. Petersburg Times,* 9/8/02 (B)]. One student asked Bush a question, and he gave a quick response on his education policy [*New York Post,* 9/12/02].

The only source to describe what happened next is *Fighting Back* by Bill Sammon. *Publishers Weekly* described Sammon's book as an "inside account of the Bush administration's reaction to 9-11 [and] a breathless, highly complimentary portrait of the president [showing] the great merit and unwavering moral vision of his inner circle." [*Publisher's Weekly,* 10/15/02] Sammon's conservative perspective makes his account of Bush's behavior at the end of the photo-op all the more surprising. Bush is described as smiling and chatting with the children "as if he didn't have a care in the world" and "in the most relaxed manner imaginable." White House aide Gordon Johndroe, then came in as he usually does at the end of press conferences, and said, "Thank you, press. If you could step out the door we came in, please." A reporter then asked, "Mr. President, are you aware of the reports of the plane crash in New York? Is there anything . . ." But Bush interrupted, and no doubt recalling his order, "DON'T SAY ANYTHING YET," Bush responded, "I'll talk about it later." But still the president did not leave. "He stepped forward and shook hands with [classroom teacher] Daniels, slipping his left hand behind her in another photo-op pose. He was taking his good old time. . . . Bush lingered until the press was gone" [*Fighting Back: The War on Terrorism—From Inside the Bush White House,* by Bill Sammon, 10/02, p. 90].[47]

Obviously, there is a deep irony here, since Sammon's interview in *FahrenHYPE 9/11* contradicted what he had previously written. Vehemently rejecting Moore's time line, he implicitly refutes his own account of the same events. Perhaps partially blinded by his deep admiration for Bush, Sammon had believed the president's leisurely pace was a laudatory instance of coolness under fire—a refusal to panic—until Moore offered a new interpretation of these events. Peterson (and Dick Morris) effectively called on Sammon to redeem himself, which he did in an obliging if ultimately self-flagelating manner. Interestingly, though it may simply be coincidence, *FahrenHYPE 9/11* does not identify Sammon (or any other interviewees in positions of authority) when he speaks, making it less likely that this flip-flop would be exposed.[48] Likewise, when Sammon evokes a five-minute piece of "uncut" video that was then unavailable (or so he thought), he could make claims about it that proved manifestly untrue when it became available. (It seems very likely that Sammon is referring to the school's five-minute, eight-second version that is also on the Memory Hole.)[49] No doubt in the heat of the presidential race, it was thought (or hoped) that no one would notice Sammon's inconsistency or locate the five-minute tape. And after November 2, no one would care.

Peterson and Sammon failed to show that Moore lied and so they failed to establish a new truth. But this failure may not have been as important to them as it might seem. In the companion book to *FahrenHYPE 9/11,* Kelton Rhoads remarks,

> How important are truthful or valid arguments in helping humans arrive at correct conclusions, anyway? The quality of an argument is largely irrelevant to humans. Professor James Stiff, a leading judgment researcher, found a wimpy correlation between quality evidence and attitude change. He found that humans don't pay much attention to argument validity—rather they pay attention to the argument's claim or conclusion, and how closely that claim or conclusion matches their prejudices. If a poorly argued message concludes with what a person already believes is true, he'll buy it.[50]

In pretending that they had caught Moore in a lie, Peterson and Sammon were, in fact, deceptive, and successfully deceptive in at least three ways. First, their attack on Moore was part of a systematic assault on *Fahrenheit 9/11* that encouraged people to devalue the film as inaccurate and biased, and so disregard it. In this respect the overall breadth of apparent outrage more than the actual substance or validity of their specific critique was important. Second, they were engaged in what Jane Gaines has called an act of "political mimesis." The filmmakers show their interviewees expressing moral outrage with such deep-seated conviction that viewers would not only believe their outrage but would emulate it.[51] In short, *FahrenHYPE 9/11* sought to flip the political logic of Moore's film and use *Fahrenheit 9/11* against Bush's political opponents. Third, the debate over "five versus almost seven minutes" functions as a red herring. It distracts viewers and critics from Moore's larger point about Bush's conduct while in office leading up to and including that moment. That is, Moore's real argument is that this brief moment is symptomatic of a much longer period when Bush did nothing. The president received intelligence reports before 9/11 but did not apparently read them, or if he did—he did not take them seriously. Bush was reading *My Pet Goat* instead (though the cover if not the book was upside down). All this is a metaphor for his administration's more serious failures to be vigilant.

Nonetheless, the truth value of Moore's representations may have their own limitations; and if Moore did not stretch the time line in his narration, he perhaps found visually creative ways to do something quite similar. A comparison of the Memory Hole video and *Fahrenheit 9/11* shows that Moore was often using different and better-quality footage. According to Salimah El-Amin, stock footage researcher on Moore's film:

> There was only one pool camera plus what the school had. This pool material was available at the news archive. . . . the cameraman decided not to run the camera for the entire event (which makes sense. You don't need 10 minutes of the president listening to school children reading *My Pet Goat*). So there are cuts in the material. I believe there is no complete, uninterrupted footage, due to a cameraman's choice not to record the entire event. But, most of it was there. We put that with the school's tape together to get pretty much the whole event.[52]

Carl Deal, archival producer for *Fahrenheit 9/11,* adds, "I have not seen one full uninterrupted take of the event, but do know that every minute was cumulatively documented."[53] This would suggest that they have (or had) the footage to back up Moore's assertion of "almost seven minutes." If so, why isn't it on Moore's website?

Although Michael Moore had a significant amount of footage with which to work, he still faced certain challenges on how to represent the event on screen. Here it is my turn to be somewhat speculative—even critical. That is, we might expect that the footage of Bush sitting in the classroom that was labeled 9:05, was taken at 9:05, and the footage labeled 9:07 was taken two minutes later—and so on. By dissolving from one scene of Bush sitting in his chair to the next, with simulated time codes—9:05, 9:07, 9:09, 9:11, and 9:12, Moore visualized his point—that time was passing with "nobody doing anything"—in a quite literal way. The literalness has additional implications, since we assume that we are seeing Bush's expressions and gestures in accurate correspondence to events. Instead, it appears that Moore manipulated the footage with slippages that intensified the gallows humor of the event. As Henri Bergson would have us recognize, the humor comes from the repetition of close-ups and medium close-ups of Bush sitting with *My Pet Goat.* Since neither camera was on the president the whole time, this required a certain "creative treatment of reality" (to invoke John Grierson). Moore did not seek to use videotape in this scene to provide a literal correspondence and precise image of what Bush was doing as the minutes progressed. Instead, he extracted this film from its already unstable temporal context and manipulated it to comically *illustrate* his narrational statement (rather than prove or demonstrate his point à la instant replay). The viewer is not getting the Veriscope, and perhaps not even *cinéma vérité.* The discourse of sobriety is in the narration, while the gallows humor is generated through the images. In this respect, although Sammon is incorrect, he points toward a construction of this scene that one might argue is overly clever or rhetorically fraught. The issue, however, is not in Moore's narration but with his mobilization of the image as illustration. It is not with fact but in his cinematic manipulation and rhetoric. Perhaps for this reason neither Peterson nor Moore has any interest is assembling a full videotape account (perhaps using split screen to show all the footage from the two cameras).

Bill Nichols characterizes documentary as a "discourse of sobriety."[54] Robert Greenwald's *Uncovered: The Whole Truth About the Iraq War* is a perfect substantiation of this conceptualization. Although Moore, like Greenwald, owes much of his success to taking on topics that are crucial to the body politic, he goes back and forth between sober discourse and biting, ironic humor—both in his images and his narration. Indeed, it is his special potent mix of sobriety and comedy that makes Michael Moore a household name. Showing Bush reading *My Pet Goat* while speculating that he should have been reading—and acting on—top-secret security reports with titles such as "Bin Laden

Determined to Strike Inside US"[55] is dark humor indeed. But in his "Factual Back-Up For Fahrenheit 9/11," Moore only provides "back-up" for his narration of sobriety—which is to say that (1) Moore's factual back up does not deal with those sections of narration that were said tongue in cheek (for instance when he speculates about what Bush was thinking while pretending to read *My Pet Goat*); and (2) Moore does not provide factual backup for his images, for instance by citing the day and place a scene was shot, listing its source, providing indications of internal cutting (as Errol Morris did with the transcript of *The Thin Blue Line)* and so forth.[56] In this, it should be emphasized that Moore is following the long-standing customs of documentary filmmaking.

PRESIDENTIAL BEHAVIOR IN THE CLASSROOM

Michael Moore and Alan Peterson also disagree in their interpretation of the president's behavior inside the Sarasota schoolroom. Moore sees a leader who was lost and over his head. Peterson counters in two ways. First, Sammon reads the videotape of Bush's expression—a subtle nod—as a way to note that he was an engaged and thinking leader who was communicating with his staff even as the photo-op was moving forward. Second, Peterson provides an interview with Gwen Tose-Rigell, the principal of Booker Elementary School in Sarasota who led the president into the classroom. Although she voted for Gore in 2000, Tose-Rigell (now Gwendolyn Rigell) quite forcefully maintains that Bush acted very presidential under the circumstances. She admires the way he conducted himself: his calm was reassuring to those people around him. The effect, certainly, is to challenge Moore on Bush's behavior even while the president was sitting.

Nonetheless, beyond this presumed calming effect (at that moment the second graders and their teacher had no idea that there was any reason to be uneasy), Bush's continued presence in the classroom may not have trumped other considerations. Most basically, if Bush was himself a target for terrorists, by staying with the children he was putting them at risk.[57] Nor should we discount his larger, more urgent responsibilities to the nation. Perhaps as someone whose own daughter was "at risk" that day, I am not entirely objective on this point. Then in her first week of middle school (grade 6), Hannah saw the World Trade Center attack from her classroom window; she had classmates whose parents were then working in the WTC (all of whom, it turned out, got out alive) and walked back to her mother's home over the Manhattan Bridge with people bleeding and covered with dust and soot. Many people might have benefited from presidential leadership that morning—as rumors spread that the president had gone into hiding. Tose-Regell may genuinely believe what she said about Bush; or her defense may have been a host's graciousness; or it may have been a somewhat pragmatic calculation of a Democratic, African American principal operating in a Republican state, where the president's brother was then its governor. Whatever the case, when a crisis hits, a president should be able to exit an event gracefully and virtually instantaneously.

FahrenHYPE offers an alternate interpretation of events so that Moore's characterization of Bush and his staff would not go unanswered. Its strategies of interpretation are reminiscent of those deployed by the attorneys defending the Los Angeles police officers who brutally beat Rodney King. George Holliday's graphic video footage of the beating was used as crucial visual evidence against them in the courtroom, where it seemed to present incontrovertible visual evidence that the officers had employed "assault by force likely to produce great bodily injury." And yet, by slowing down the motion and interpreting the policemen's actions as professionally appropriate responses to the threat posed by Rodney King, the lawyers for the three Los Angeles police officers won an acquittal.[58] Footage of Bush reading *My Pet Goat* was unfamiliar to most Americans—and therefore Moore's presentation was quite shocking. It did for that material what the television stations had done for the videotape of the police beating Rodney as he was lying on the pavement. In many respects, both presentations immediately established "media truths." Like the police officers' lawyers, Bush operatives needed to offer an alternate interpretation.

As average citizens, we did not know what to do immediately after the WTC was hit—other than to stare in disbelief at a television or computer screen of the burning buildings. Correspondingly, despite their access to top secret intelligence briefs, neither Bush nor his staff had taken the threat of terrorism seriously enough to even recognize what the attacks on the World Trade Center *might* be. He and his entourage were clueless, as even his defenders in effect admit. His behavior in the Sarasota schoolroom is not so significant in itself but rather for what it reveals about his administration's broader mind-set. Keeping the debate focused on whether it was five or seven minutes and the importance of a presidential nod narrows the focus on the president's behavior that day in ways that conceals more than it reveals. Certainly the issue of President Bush's ability to make rapid and appropriate responses in the face of this and other crises gained renewed relevance as a result of Hurricane Katrina.

Keeping the debate focused on the "was it five or seven minutes" topic also obscures some of Moore's adept use of cinematic rhetoric in this scene. As we have seen, Moore takes us rapidly through the seven minutes (more or less) of "nobody doing anything." However, the scene does not stop there. Rather, Moore dwells on Bush in the classroom, effectively going back in time when he was reading *My Pet Goat* with the children and essentially suspending the forward movement of time as Moore asks, "As Bush sat in that Florida classroom, was he wondering whether or not he should have shown up to work more often? Should he have held at least one meeting since taking office to discuss the threat of terrorism with his head of counter terrorism?" At this point Moore cuts away—first to Richard Clark waiting to testify, and then to memos and a statement by Condoleezza Rice about the briefing Bush and his administration failed to treat with due seriousness. Moore then *returns* to Bush in the Sarasota classroom as he intones, "As the minutes went by, George Bush continued to sit in the classroom. Was he thinking, 'I've been hanging out with the wrong crowd? Which one of them screwed me?' " The digressions and return to Bush reading *My Pet Goat,* followed by a digression for which we expect a return (which never comes)—repeats but then seems to stretch out the time Bush spent sitting, doing nothing "as the minutes went by." Although Moore now describes Bush as "sitting," he does not associate this with a specific amount of time. Moore stretches, if not the truth, then the impression of time passing (although from the moment Card whispers into Bush's ear to the end of the scene involves only two minutes of screen time). Certainly this is a remarkable display of rhetorical brilliance—of taking facts and image and restructuring them in a way that forcefully articulates Moore's assessment of Bush's conduct.

SOME OTHER QUIBBLES IN *FAHRENHYPE 9/11*

The remainder of *FahrenHYPE 9/11* continues its efforts to show us how Moore was more concerned with mocking and satirizing Bush than with a careful, "truthful" assessment. Moore's contention that Bush stole the election is, as one would expect, challenged: as is often the case in these debates, the proper outcome depends on the framework of the discussion. As Peterson points out, there were recounts that Bush won—and only a statewide recount, which Gore's campaign did not request, would have produced a Gore victory; but Peterson never considers the massive fraud that came from denying voting rights to many black Americans who were improperly removed from the voting rolls (because they were incorrectly and improperly identified as felons). Indeed, Peterson's search party for truth simply overlooks the protests by black congressmen, which Moore brought to our attention. To be sure, neither filmmaker goes into much depth on this subject, and neither makes any effort to investigate and substantiate its claims while giving credence (if only temporarily) to the other side—perhaps so far as Moore is concerned because other documentary filmmakers and investigative journalists had explored many of these issues (e.g., Danny Schechter's *Counting on Democracy* [2002], the Robert Greenwald production *Unprecedented* [2002], and books by Greg Palast and Mark Crispin Miller).[59]

Peterson's attacks against *Fahrenheit 9/11* are interesting and certainly useful for the questions they raise—perhaps more than for the conclusions they draw. For instance, Peterson and his interviewees argue that one lapse in *Fahrenheit 9/11* is particularly egregious: Moore took a letter to the editor, which was printed in a minor newspaper (*The Pantagraph*, published in Bloomington, Illinois); increased the font size of the headline ("Latest Florida Recount Shows Gore Won Election"); completely rearranged its layout; and made it appear to be a news article from the paper. In transposing it, Moore also somehow changed the date (December 5 became December 10)—and, it would seem, misspelled the title (in *FahrenHYPE 9/11, Pantagraph* is shown to become *Pantograph).*

Let's look at this more closely. In *FahrenHYPE 9/11*, Peterson created a pseudo-replica of Moore's *Pantagraph* graphic, but it was Peterson who misspelled the newspaper's name, not—as Peterson would have us believe—Moore.[60] Nonetheless, as Jason Clarke, blogger on the moorelies.com website and coauthor of *Michael Moore Is a Big, Fat, Stupid White Man*, points out, Moore "had attempted to take an opinion from a reader of the newspaper and pass it off as a legitimate news article." Clarke's coauthor, David T. Hardy, adds, "We are talking totally unscrupulous behavior here, I think." Adds Clarke as he shakes his head, "All for one second of footage in the film."[61] Peterson concludes this sequence with his own narration: "If you can make fun of people, why worry about anything else—like the truth." Truth here has to do with an accurate correspondence between what Moore shows on the screen and the actual newspaper item—something Peterson failed to achieve even as he condemns Moore!

Certainly this gap would seem to be an unfortunate moment for *Fahrenheit 9/11*. At the very least, it would appear to be shoddy documentary practice. Certainly there were newspaper articles from other sources that could have been used in its stead—so why did Moore do it? Undoubtedly one reason would be the pressures of the editing room (linked perhaps to the Cannes deadline?). The letter-cum-article is on the screen so briefly that viewers register few of its details, and it carries little weight in itself. Quite possibly this item started out as a placeholder in the film and worked well enough and was on the screen so briefly, that the postproduction staff just forgot about it and did not bother to consider that inaccuracies may have crept in. It may represent the dangers of depending on eager interns or the results of working too many late hours. Certainly, this does not excuse the mistakes, but Peterson and his group are excessive in their outrage. If nothing else, it demonstrates once again that Moore's emphasis is on his narration. His team focused on fact-checking his sobrietous discourse, not his images, which in this situation were deemed merely to illustrate what is said. If the letter to the editor had been part of the factual backup, for instance, someone might have at least picked up the wrong date.

Unlike Moore's repeated use of footage showing Bush reading *My Pet Goat,* this manipulation or recontextualization of a letter to the editor does not serve any rhetorical or aesthetic purpose. Moore may have wished to barrage viewers with the appearance of information, but the news item was never meant to provide evidence. Moore or his staff liked the headline. Shifting from two columns to a three-column format was perhaps designed to include all the text of the item in the frame. Increasing the font was meant to increase readability. All this was easily done—too easily done perhaps—in a digital age of computer graphics. They may not have even realized that these alterations subtly changed the status of the document. But wait . . . Let us step back for a moment and ask—which document? Although Peterson compares the shot in *Fahrenheit 9/11* to the hard copy of the newspaper, Moore probably never saw it in that format. His researchers almost certainly saw it on the Web, possibly the newspaper's website but more likely someone's blog—a blog that was probably dated December 10. The newspaper item had already been decontextualized—with distinctions between letter writers and correspondents already lost. Moreover, it is not clear that digital files of this kind have stable layouts. That is, Moore's team was faced with putting such files into a readable (or "filmable") format and quite likely had no idea of "the original" (in some sense an archaic concept in this context). The problem, then, is that of moving from a nineteenth- or twentieth-century medium involving hard type and newspaper clippings to twenty-first-century digital media and then back to late-nineteenth- and twentieth-century motion-picture formats.

Peterson's point is certainly interesting, but properly understood it reveals more about the new world of the Web, which poses all sorts of problems (including the disappearance of sites, which makes it difficult or impossible to verify quotations that were widely available just a year or so before).[62] More interesting perhaps is that Moore would never have used the *Pantagraph* as part of his "Factual Back-Up For Fahrenheit 9/11." In such cases he wants papers of established repute and international renown.

Peterson also considers Dubya's statement in *Fahrenheit 9/11:* "This is an impressive crowd, the haves and the have-mores. Some people call you the elite. I call you my base." *FahrenHYPE 9/11* reveals that it was delivered for laughs at the Al Smith Honorary Dinner and in keeping with a long-standing tradition in which both major presidential candidates speak in a humorous, purposely self-mocking manner. Certainly this contextualization is illuminating; but does it show, as Peterson has it, that "once again Michael Moore shows only half the story"? Moore may be guilty of a rather enjoyable "cheap shot"; and Peterson shows that one of Moore's fortes is his very ability to remove material from its full original context and let it stand on its own. In this instance, what is serious, Bush played for laughs; what Bush finds humorous, Moore reverses and makes telling and shocking—though the laughter does not entirely disappear. This has infuriated some, but it also provides new insights. In the end, Peterson's contextualization of Bush's jokes at the Al Smith dinner reminds us of something we already knew: Bush is most revealing of his true self when he uses it as raw materials for laughs. He is a jokester, and Freud has a lot to say about jokes.[63] (That Al Gore is also at the dinner and overhears the joke, as *FahrenHYPE 9/11* reveals, makes this moment that much richer.) But more generally, isn't Moore's use of this excerpt of a speech nothing more than what most documentary filmmakers do?

Again and again, *FahrenHYPE 9/11* offers a critique that turns on the issue of either Moore's failure to fully contextualize or his decision to recontextualize filmic material, particularly when he uses footage that others shot for their own, different purposes. For instance, Peterson includes an interview with trooper Andy Kenyon of the Oregon State Police. Kenyon is unhappy that his appearance in Moore's movie makes him look like he supports Moore's views—which he does not. He thought he was appearing in a documentary about the impact of budget cutbacks on state agencies; but when Moore saw the footage, he bought it and repositioned the material. Likewise, relatives of an American soldier who was killed in Iraqi express their resentment that Moore featured their brother/son in his film. But should Moore only include footage of people who agree with him? Whether they agree or disagree with him is not just beside the point—it is the point. Moore was almost certainly unfamiliar with their political viewpoints at the time he incorporated these scenes into his film. This is almost inevitable when buying file footage, and not investigating the beliefs of subjects therein is again standard documentary procedure.

One compelling observation that *FahrenHYPE 9/11* makes is this: partners in the Carlyle Group are not only Republicans such as George Herbert Walker Bush (41) but former Democratic officials as well. George Soros, who contributes heavily to Democratic campaigns, started the group with a $100 million investment. Moore does seem to give his conspiracy theory full throttle, but Peterson hardly gets the Bush family off the hook. His revelations may expose Moore's Democratic, electioneering bias on one hand, but they also point to the broader nature of a disturbing problem—perhaps helping to explain why Moore supported Ralph Nader in the 2000 election. If Moore shows the Bushes as having an uncomfortably intimate friendship with well-placed Saudis such as Prince Bandar (aka Bandar Bush), *FahrenHYPE 9/11* elaborates on the connection between the Saudi royal family and a series of American presidents going back to Franklin Roosevelt. Even if Moore provided spectators of *Fahrenheit 9/11* with strained conspiracy theories linking the Afghan oil pipeline to the U.S. invasion of that country, many learned to their amazement that Afghani president Hamid Karzai had been on the board of the Unocal oil company.

As Paul Krugman points out, Moore's conspiracy theories should not be viewed in isolation but in relation to those being advocated by Bush, Cheney, and their allies.[64] One important "truth," which the Bush administration was constantly asserting, involved ties between Iraq and Al-Qaeda, that is, between Saddam Hussein and Osama bin Laden. The basis for this conspiracy theory was so slight and suspect as to be almost comical—perhaps Mohammed Atta (one of the men who piloted a plane into the World Trade Center) met with a member of Saddam Husssein's intelligence service in Prague.[65] Three days before the invasion of Iraq, Vice President Cheney declared on *Meet the Press* that Saddam Hussein "has a long standing relationship with various terrorist organizations, including the Al Qaeda organization."[66] How do these supposed ties compare to the ties between Bush and bin Laden, for instance? In this regard, Moore turned the tables on the Bush administration. When announcing his plans to make the documentary, Moore explained, "It certainly does deal with the Bush and bin Laden ties. It asks a number of questions that I don't have the answers to yet, but which I intend to find out."[67] In fact the degrees of separation between the Bush and bin Laden families are far, far less than those between bin Laden and Saddam Hussein. The president's father was meeting with bin Laden's half-brother on 9/11. Cheney's evidence—somewhere between nonexistent and suspect—pales in comparison to what Moore was able to offer. Moore thus mischievously encourages us reassess these kinds of linkages. It is Bush's conspiracy theories—more than Moore's—that were unfounded.

As Keith Beattie has argued, "Truth claims reflect a tacit contractual agreement or bond of trust between documentary producers (whether an individual filmmaker or broadcasting institution) and an audience that the representation is based on the actual socio-historical world, not a fictional world imaginatively conceived."[68] *FahrenHYPE 9/11* and other anti-Moore documentaries seek to generate a litany of falsehoods and distortions that will weaken these bonds of trust between filmmaker and audience and make it so that voters will either not view the film or else immediately discount it.[69] Peterson and others seek to make Moore an unreliable narrator and unworthy protagonist of his own documentary. Certainly *Fahrenheit 9/11* is shaped by Moore's particular sense of outrage and comic deprecation, which inevitably includes techniques such as exaggeration, simplification, inversion, and contradiction. Moore does not keep these techniques a secret. After all, the advertisement on his website for *Fahrenheit 9/11* shows him strolling arm in arm with Bush on the grounds of the White House. Comedy itself can provide opportunities for truth telling that are usually different from, and even opposed to, the methods employed by discourses of sobriety. As Freud has remarked, comedy sometimes makes it possible to tell truths that cannot be said any other way. Moore shuttles back and forth between the two—Charlie Chaplin and Dziga Vertov reincarnated in a single body.[70] Certainly his film calls for an engaged, even skeptical, spectator who laughs or gasps at the unexpected juxtapositions and new connections—but finally goes to Moore's website to see what the filmmaker is ready to substantiate using more conventional journalistic standards.

FahrenHYPE 9/11 not only seeks to demonize Moore, it dismisses Moore's revelations as the rantings of a conspiracy theorist. *FahrenHYPE 9/11* belittles one of his film's basic arguments: that Bush wanted to go to war with Saddam Hussein. Founder of the Center for Security Policy and former Reagan assistant secretary of defense Frank Gaffney insists that any suggestion that President Bush "seized upon the pretext of 9/11 to have the war that he wanted to have is simply a fabrication." Gaffney rejects the very point that has been made so convincingly by intelligence experts in Robert Greenwald's *Uncovered: The War on Iraq*. Moreover a memo from a two-hour meeting between Bush and Tony Blair on January 31, 2003 (two months before the invasion of Iraq but made public years later) further supports this position. It reports that "Mr. Bush made it clear the US intended to invade whether or not there was a second UN resolution and even if UN inspectors found no evidence of a banned Iraqi weapons programme."[71] As Alice Lovejoy has remarked, *FahrenHYPE 9/11* attempts "to align 'truth' with the political right and more precisely, with President Bush."[72] *FahrenHYPE 9/11* claims to bring a rigor to bear on *Fahrenheit 9/11*, which it unfortunately fails to apply to its own undertaking. In the end the lies and unsubstantiated statements of figures such as Sammon and Gaffney (perhaps further distorted by the filmmaker) make Peterson's *FahrenHYPE 9/11* little more than a shill for Bush.

CONCLUSION

The Peterson-Morris film may have made some modest dents in Moore's truth claims, but it does not convince this spectator that either Moore's documentary is a set of lies for which *FahrenHYPE 9/11* provides a convincing alternative truth or that Peterson and Morris have revealed sufficient unacknowledged parts of the story so that they have undermined Moore's assessment of Bush and his administration. There is perhaps one small but noteworthy exception. Peterson includes a scene of President Bush speaking to the press on September 11, in the immediate aftermath of the morning's events. Here is another side of Bush—a leader who seems caring and engaged, who has responded to the events of that awful morning with some depth and humanity. Perhaps we should not forget that most Americans and indeed most of the world largely approved of his administration's early actions against Al-Qaeda and the Taliban in Afghanistan. It was in this period—when the Taliban were quickly overthrown, bin Laden seemed to face imminent capture or elimination, and Americans had not yet learned of the Bush administration's almost criminally lax pre-9/11 attitudes toward terrorism—that the president garnered the political standing that allowed for much that followed.

Along with moorelies.com and moorewatch.com, *FahrenHYPE 9/11* was part of a larger effort to obfuscate truth during the 2004 presidential season. It sought to do to Michael Moore what Swift Boat Veterans for Truth did to John Kerry. As a whole, these efforts were quite successful. Moore fought back quickly through his website www.michaelmoore.com, but both institutionally and personally most news and opinion makers kept a skeptical distance from Moore. When thinking about the issues his film addressed, they conceived of truth and objectivity as employing a simple correspondence theory when it came to the relationship between representation and reality. Whatever the problems of this approach when assessing traditional discourses of sobriety, to apply it to Moore's documentary methods involves a fundamental misrecognition or misunderstanding.

Moore came out of a 1980s documentary formation that claimed to understand that there could never be such a thing as objective—that is "true" or perfect—correspondences between representation and reality. At best, truth was relative and subjective—inevitably involving points of view and selection. Cinema verité filmmakers such as Ross McElwee, first with *Backyard* (1984) and then with *Sherman's March* (1986), and Nick Broomfield with *Driving Me Crazy* (1988) moved from behind the camera to in front of it, precisely for this reason—to make explicit the subjectivity of the filmmaker and to make it part of the film.[73] Moore appropriated and modified this approach in *Roger & Me* (1989). He emerged as part of a documentary formation that rejected simplistic notions of sobriety and objectivity. In order for audiences and students of the documentary to appreciate and understand Moore's method, we must not judge him within a paradigm that has often been seen as outmoded, using standards that had been under attack for decades and at some points dismissed. We must look beyond these notions or at least bracket them. Because *Fahrenheit 9/11* was made by a political satirist, viewers must distinguish between fact and rhetoric, between sobriety and comedy.

Viewers understandably look for and expect correspondences between Moore's documentary articulations and the historical world. Inevitably such correspondences will fall short, as they would for any other "creative treatment of reality" by any other filmmaker—certainly as they did for Peterson. As we have seen, powerful rhetorical and comedic engagements are likely to intensify this problem. Nonetheless, documentary film truth is not only (or even primarily) about such correspondences but is rather relational to other representations, other statements and understandings of the world. *Fahrenheit 9/11* was considered dangerous because the documentary challenged the Bush administration's self-description of itself (its competence, its trustworthiness) and exposed various "state truths" that were made possible by the attacks on the World Trade Center on September 11 and centered on the war in Iraq. Viewed outside the political season for which it was made and in the face of the continuing ordeal of the Iraq war and the unrealized promise of other governmental initiatives, viewed as it inevitably will be as a historical document, *Fahrenheit 9/11* seems destined to emerge as an audacious and courageous achievement that gains credibility and power much in the way that Moore's Academy Awards statement of 2003 has done in the years since.

Notes

This essay was written primarily during a fellowship at the Clark Art Institute in early 2006. It shares certain interests and even sensibilities with Robert Brent Toplin's *Michael Moore's Fahrenheit 9/11: How One Film Divided a Nation* (Lawrence: University Press of Kansas, 2006). Although our approaches are quite different (my essay is much more concerned with truth value), we are in complete agreement on at least one point: my essay and his book both begin with Michael Moore at the 75th Annual Academy Awards.

1. Transcriptions of Michael Moore's acceptance speech are readily available on the Internet. See, for instance, "Moore Fires Oscar Anti-war Salvo," *BBC News,* March 24, 2003, http://news.bbc.co.uk/2/hi/entertainment/2879857.stm (accessed July 27, 2008).

2. Mark Crispin Miller, *Fooled Again: How the Right Stole the 2004 Election & Why They'll Steal the Next One Too (Unless We Stop Them)* (New York: Basic Books, 2005); Mark Crispin Miller, ed., *Loser Take All: Election Fraud and the Subversion of Democracy* (Brooklyn: Ig Publisher, 2008).

3. Michael Fleming, "Dish," *Variety,* March 28, 2003, 1.

4. Ibid.

5. Jim Rutenberg, "Disney Is Blocking Distribution of Film That Criticizes Bush," *New York Times,* May 5, 2004, A1.

6. Shortly before *Hearts and Minds* was re-released in October 2004, Michael Moore declared, "If I were to pick the one film that inspired me to pick up a camera, it is *Hearts and Minds,* a film that remains every bit as relevant today. Required viewing for anyone who says, 'I am an American.'" http://www.rialtopictures.com/grisbi_xtras/hearts_links .html (accessed July 27, 2008).

7. Unlike *Fahrenheit 9/11* and other Iraq War documentaries, those made during the Vietnam War were not meant to influence electoral politics. Emile de Antonio's *In the Year of the Pig* (1968) was finished and copyrighted less than a week before the 1968 presidential election: it was not released until March of the following year.

8. "Fahrenheit 9/11," http://www.boxofficemojo.com/movies/?id=fahrenheit911 .htm (accessed March 25, 2007).

9. A. O. Scott, "History and Outrage in Films at Cannes," *New York Times,* May 18, 2004, E3.

10. Ibid.

11. A. O. Scott, "Moore's 'Fahrenheit 9/11' Wins Top Honors at Cannes," *New York Times,* May 23, 2004, 1–6.

12. Rutenberg, "Disney Is Blocking Distribution of Film That Criticizes Bush."

13. Ibid.

14. Dana Harris and David Rooney, "'9/11': The Moore the Merrier," *Daily Variety,* June 2, 2004, 1.

15. Roger Friedman, "'Fahrenheit 9/11' Gets Standing Ovation," June 15, 2004, http://www.foxnews.com/story/0,2933,122680,00.html (accessed March 27, 2007).

16. "'9/11' Fires up Gotham Wickets," *Daily Variety,* June 24, 2004, 1.

17. John Files, "The Like-Minded Line up for a 9/11 Film," *New York Times,* June 24, 2004, A20.

18. Kenneth Turan, "*Fahrenheit 9/11,*" *Los Angeles Times,* June 23, 2004,

http://www.calendarlive.com/movies/reviews/cl-et-turan23jun23,2,2756103.story?coll=cl-movies-top-right.

19. Desson Thomson, "'Fahrenheit 9/11' Turns up the Heat," *Washington Post,* June 25, 2004, WE33.

20. Paul Krugman, "Moore's Public Service," *New York Times,* July 2, 2004, A19.

21. "Box Office: North America," *Screen International,* July 30, 2004.

22. Move America Forward Press Release, June 17, 2004, www.moveamericaforward.org/index.php/MAF/FullNewsItem/zero_degrees_celsius/ (accessed March 24, 2007).

23. Nicole Sperling, "Group Puts Heat on 'Fahrenheit,'" *Hollywood Reporter,* June 17, 2004.

24. Gabriel Snyder, "MPAA Going 'R' Way on '9/11' Rating," *Daily Variety,* June 23, 2004, 1.

25. Ibid.

26. Hannah Grace Zeavin Musser to Charles Musser, e-mail correspondence, April 8, 2007.

27. Sharon Waxman, "The Political 'Fahrenheit' Sets Record at Box Office," *New York Times,* June 28, 2004, E1.

28. Ibid.

29. Michael Moore, "My First Wild Week with *Fahrenheit 9/11* . . . ," http://www.michaelmoore.com/words/message/index.php?messageDate=2004-07-04.

30. Ibid. Interestingly, these same sentiments—a vehement dismissal of the film without having seen it—were also expressed to me by a prominent neo-conservative professor at Yale University.

31. http://www.moorewatch.com/index.php/weblog/2002/10/. One was by David Brudnoy, who died in 2004.

32. www.hardylaw.net/Truth_About_Bowling.html and http://moorelies.com/about (accessed March 25, 2006).

33. "Michael Moore Hates America," www.sourcewatch.org/index.php?title=Michael_Moore_Hates_America (accessed March 25, 2007).

34. http://web.archive.org/web/20031011143301/www.michaelmoorehatesamerica.com/oneSheet.html (accessed April 13, 2007).

35. http://en.wikipedia.org/wiki/FahrenHYPE_9/11.

36. http://www.freerepublic.com/focus/f-news/1232884/posts (accessed March 26, 2007).

37. "Mansoor Ijaz," *Fox News,* September 5, 2003, http://www.foxnews.com/story/0,2933,46241,00.html (accessed March 16, 2006).

38. *Celsius 41.11* opened in 116 theaters on October 22, 2004, and played for three days, grossing $93,000, or $801 per screen. http://www.boxofficemojo.com/ movies/?id=celsius4111.htm (accessed March 14, 2006). *Michael Moore Hates America* played festivals and enjoyed extensive reviews but was not released on DVD until November 1, 2004.

39. http://www.fahrenhype911.com/ (accessed September 9, 2005).

40. Michael Moore, *The Official Fahrenheit 9/11 Reader* (New York: Simon and Schuster Paperbacks, 2004), 11, 138. See David Tetzlaff's essay on *Fahrenheit 9/11* in this

volume for a discussion of the film's revelations of events not reported, or not reported prominently, by American news media.

41. Frank Rich, "Michael Moore's Candid Camera," *New York Times*, May 23, 2004, AR.1.

42. Moore, *The Official Fahrenheit 9/11 Reader*, 76–77.

43. Ibid., 18–19.

44. Bill Sammon, *Fighting Back: The War on Terrorism from Inside the White House* (Washington, DC: Regnery, 2002).

45. "Factual Back-Up: Faherenhert 9/11" and "Film Footnotes: Fahrenheit 9/11," http://www.michaelmoore.com/books-films/facts/farehnheit_9/11. A rival "Viewer's Guide to Michael Moore's Film Fahrenheit 9/11," entitled "War, Lies, and Videotape: A Viewer's Guide to Fahrenheit 9/11," is on the Ethics and Public Policy Center website. "Its purpose is to help the viewer of the film sort through Moore's many varied claims; to separate fact from fiction and true from false impression; to provide context when the film fails to do so; and to weigh Moore's assertions, arguments, and narrative moves." http://www.eppc.org/publications/pubID.2189/pub_detail.asp. The Ethics and Public Policy Center (EPPC) "was established in 1976 to clarify and reinforce the bond between the Judeo-Christian moral tradition and the public debate over domestic and foreign policy issues." http://www.eppc.org/about/.

46. http://www.thememoryhole.org/911/bush-911.htm (accessed July 24, 2007).

47. Allen Wood and Paul Thompson, "An Interesting Day: President Bush's Movement and Actions on 9/11," *History Commons*, http://www.historycommons.org/essay.jsp?article=essayaninterestingday. Note that the citations are within the original article. According to its website, "The Center for Cooperative Research seeks to encourage grassroots participation and collaboration in the documentation of the public historical record using an open-content model." http://www.cooperativeresearch.org/aboutsite .jsp.

48. Moreover, while the DVD cover (and the back cover of the accompanying book) offer a picture of Sammon, his name is not given—in fact they would seem to imply he was Steven Emerson, who has also written about terrorism. Sammon's portrait is clearly identified in Lee Troxler, ed., *FahrenHYPE 9/11: Companion Book* (Michael & Me Lp, 2004), but Sammon's book *Fighting Back: The War on Terrorism* is not cited.

49. It is worth noting that an "independent" website, footnotetv.com, looks critically at *Fahrenheit 9/11* but does not challenge Moore on this point, noting, "As shown in *Fahrenheit 9/11*, Bush then waited five to seven minutes before leaving the classroom." However, its account of that morning otherwise differs significantly from Moore's film and also from the information on the Memory Hole website. See http://www.footnotetv.com/f911index.html and http://www.footnotetv.com/f911chap2-2.html.

50. Kelton Rhoads, "Propaganda Tactics and *Fahrenheit 9/11*," in Lee Troxler, ed., *FahrenHYPE 9/11: Companion Book* (Michael & Me Lp, 2004), 190.

51. Jane M. Gaines, "Political Mimesis," in *Collecting Visible Evidence*, ed. Jane Gaines and Michael Renov (Minneapolis: University of Minnesota Press, 1999), 90–93.

52. Salimah El-Amin to Charles Musser, e-mail correspondence, February 23, 2006.

53. Carl Deal to Salimah El-Amin, forwarded to Charles Musser, February 24, 2006. While the situation may not be quite as neat as Deal would seem to suggest (if every

minute was documented, was every second?), Moore seems on safe ground. It would be interesting to assemble all the footage from the pool and school cameras to see what was documented.

54. Bill Nichols, *Representing Reality* (Bloomington: University of Indiana Press, 1991), 3.

55. "Bin Ladin Determined to Strike Inside US," declassified April 10, 2004, http://www.cnn.com/2004/images/04/10/whitehouse.pdf (accessed April 1, 2007), cited in "Factual Back-up for Fahrenheit 9/11" (http://www.michaelmoore.com/books-films/facts/fahrenheit-9/11).

56. According to Carl Dean, "As a matter of course and professional courtesy to our sources, I generally don't disclose the exact origin of any archival footage without permission of the copyright holder." Dean to Salimah El-Amin, forwarded to Charles Musser, February 24, 2006.

57. An Arab camera crew tried to gain last minute access to the president that morning to interview him—with the quite possible intention of killing him instead. See http://www.cooperativeresearch.org/timeline/main/essayaninterestingday.html. The president was also the only one who could make the decision to shoot down civilian aircrafts that were aimed at other targets (the Pentagon, the White House, etc.).

58. Toby Miller, *Technologies of Truth: Cultural Citizenship and the Popular Media* (Minneapolis: University of Minnesota Press, 1998), 186–90; Robert Gooding-Williams, *Reading Rodney King/Reading Urban Uprising* (New York: Routledge, 1993).

59. Greg Palast, *The Best Democracy Money Can Buy* (London: Pluto Press, 2002), and Miller, *Fooled Again.*

60. One wonders why and how the "Pantagraph" newspaper became the "Pantograph." Was Peterson just playing with his audience, or did the same kind of inaccuracies creep into his documentary?

61. See also "Altering the Truth," moorewatch.com, August 12, 2004, in which "Lee" claims that "Once again, Michael Moore lies, distorts, and manipulates the facts, then hides behind his army of corporate lawyers, rather than simply admit his deceptions." http://www.moorewatch.com/index.php/weblog/C21/.

62. As of December 2009, moorewatch.com is still on the Web (having engaged both *Sicko* [2007] and *Capitalism: A Love Story* [2009] with its usual right-wing verve), but other sites have disappeared.

63. Sigmund Freud, *Jokes and Their Relation to the Unconscious* (London: Hogarth Press, 1960).

64. Paul Krugman, "Moore's Public Service," *New York Times,* July 2, 2004, A19.

65. "Fox News Spins 9/11 Commission Report," June 22, 2004, Fairness & Accuracy in Reporting, http://www.fair.org/index.php?page=1577 (accessed March 31, 2007). See also "Hayes, Limbaugh Falsely Cited 1998 Bin Laden Indictment as Proof That Clinton Administration Had 'Connected' Iraq, Al Qaeda," Media Matters for America, December 13, 2005, http://mediamatters.org/items/200512130004 (accessed March 25, 2007).

66. Frank Rich, "The Ides of March 2003," *New York Times,* March 18, 2007, "News of the Week in Review," 12. Former Vice President Cheney has continued to insist upon the connection that even the defense department, in a recent declassified document, has acknowledged not to be the case. R. Jeffrey Smith, "Hussein's Prewar Ties to Al-Qaeda Dis-

counted," Washingtonpost.com, April 6, 2007, http://www.washingtonpost.com/wp-dyn/content/article/2007/04/05/AR2007040502263.html?hpid=topnews (accessed April 7, 2007).

67. Fleming, "Dish."

68. Keith Beattie, *Documentary Screens: Non-Fiction Film and Television* (Houndsmills, England: Palgrave Macmillan, 2004), 11.

69. My informal survey of committed (and sometimes prominent) Bush supporters indicates that they had read about *Fahrenheit 9/11* but never seen it. It seems likely that some people would see *FahrenHYPE 9/11* but not the Moore film.

70. A similar point has been made by Miles Orvell: "Documentary Film and the Power of Interrogation," in *After the Machine: Visual Arts and the Erasing of Cultural Boundaries* (Jackson: University of Mississippi Press, 1995), 113–28, reprinted in this volume.

71. Richard Norton-Taylor, "Blair-Bush Deal before Iraq War Revealed in Secret Memo," *Guardian Unlimited*, February 3, 2006, http://politics.guardian.co.uk/iraq/story/0,,1700881,00.html (accessed February 15, 2006).

72. Alice Lovejoy, "Dueling Docs," *Film Comment* 41, no. 1 (January–February 2005): 69.

73. The place of subjectivity and of the filmmaker in his/her documentary has a long history. Although McElwee propelled this most recent shift, filmmakers such as Michael Rubio, Ed Pincus, and Amalie Rothschild provide important antecedents.

Dystopia Now: *Fahrenheit 9/11*'s Red Pill

DAVID TETZLAFF

It now seems that *Fahrenheit 9/11* will have the least staying power of Michael Moore's documentary films. While people still talk about *Bowling for Columbine* and even *Roger & Me*, it is almost as if *Fahrenheit 9/11* had never existed. Perhaps history has passed it by. The film's critiques of the Bush administration, so controversial when the film was released, now seem tame, or perhaps even taken for granted. Through Dubya's second term and beyond, mainstream news reports revealed a seemingly unending trail of torture photos, torture memos, mercenary murders, secret assassination programs, crony profiteering, and coverup after coverup. In truth, at this point, there's not much about the Iraq war, or G. W. Bush and his cronies, that *Fahrenheit 9/11* has left to tell us.

Yet I think the film deserves another look, and ought to be remembered, not for its specific critiques of this war—which everyone has talked about—but for the larger conceptual framework in which it offers them—which almost no one has talked about: its presentation of larger themes, or, if you will, its philosophy. To begin this looking afresh, let us first consider the title.

MICHAEL AND RAY: AND MARTEN AND JAN AND ANDREA . . .

Montag had done nothing. His hand had done it all, his hand, with a brain of its own . . .
—*FAHRENHEIT 451*, P. 37

In the early summer of 2004, a Swedish freelance journalist named Marten Blomkvist phoned Ray Bradbury, author of the classic science fiction novel

Fahrenheit 451,[1] to solicit his comments on Michael Moore's film, *Fahrenheit 9/11*. Bradbury apparently had little to say about the film itself, but offered some strong opinions about Mr. Moore. Blomkvist's interview with Bradbury was published in the Stockholm daily *Dagens Nyheter* on June 2.

The interview caught the attention of Jan Haugland, a Norwegian software developer who writes an English-language blog called *Secular Blasphemy* hosted by *Salon*. Though not a U.S.-style conservative by any means,[2] Haugland had strongly supported the invasion of Iraq, and had used his blog to attack critics of the war, whom he felt to be irrational and detached from reality. He had already compared Michael Moore's devotees to the "tin foil hat crowd." On the day Blomkvist's piece was published, Haugland wrote an entry about it in Secular Blasphemy: "Michael Moore stole the title to his fictitious documentary *Fahrenheit 9/11* from author Ray Bradbury, and the *Dagens Nyheter* interview showed Bradbury was 'mighty pissed off about it.'"[3] Haugland then offered his own translation of "the juicier bits of the interview."

> [BRADBURY:] "Michael Moore is a screwed asshole, that is what I think about that case. He stole my title and changed the numbers without ever asking me for permission.
>
> [BLOMKVIST:] Have you spoken to him?
>
> [BRADBURY:] He is a horrible human being. Horrible human!

The 'Michael Moore stole Ray Bradbury's title!' meme spread through the blogosphere like a virus.[4] Succeeding accounts are traceable back to *Secular Blasphemy* due to the idiosyncratic translation loop from English (Bradbury) to Swedish (Blomkvist) then back to English by a nonnative speaker of either (Haugland) resulting in the unusual locution, "Horrible human!"[5] One of the sites echoing the tale was the right-wing "news service" WorldNetDaily.com, which published a story on June 3 titled "Ray Bradbury rips Michael Moore" with the subhead "*Fahrenheit 451* author says filmmaker stole his title for Bush-bash."[6] While other conservative sites cited Haugland's blog and even congratulated him for providing ammunition against "FatBoy," the WorldNetDaily entry presents Haugland's version of Bradbury's remarks without background or citation, identifying them only as "an English translation of the story." The WorldNetDaily item was in turn used as the basis for an NBC-TV news item ("Bradbury Blasts Moore over 'Fahrenheit' Title") delivered to affiliates and appearing on local station's websites on June 7.[7] Thus did Haugland's translation of Bradbury's comments come to be cast as the official objective version.

On June 18, the Associated Press took up the story. No longer relying on Haugland's translation, the AP contacted Bradbury directly. Though the verbiage became more restrained, the 'peg' remained the same: "Ray Bradbury is demanding an apology from filmmaker Michael Moore for lifting the title from his classic science-fiction novel *Fahrenheit 451* without permission."[8] The Bradbury/Moore flap reached its zenith on June 28 with Bradbury's appearance on the MSNBC show *Hardball*.[9] Bradbury hewed tight to the theme that Moore "stole . . . my title." Interviewer Andrea Mitchell's softball questions failed to interrogate Bradbury's position, or to deviate from the 'Ray Bradbury thinks Michael Moore is an Asshole' frame first employed by Haugland.

I relate this seemingly trivial tale because it points to several key paths of inquiry for an attempt to understand *Fahrenheit 9/11*, and the ideological climate in which it was received. First, we have 'mainstream' journalism that exhibits a rigid pack mentality and an almost incomprehensibly narrow follow-the-leader framing. Why did none of the journalists point out, to us if not to Bradbury, that titles cannot be copyrighted? Why does no one involved in the whole chain of retold tales seem to know what a literary allusion is (or to note that Bradbury himself has used allusions in the titles of at least nine books)? Second, we have evidence that the mainstream journalists who love to challenge the rigor of Michael Moore's method and the legitimacy of his presentations may be living in glass houses. Why was NBC—now the primary target of Fox News / talk-radio attacks on 'liberal bias'—generating its 'objective' news from questionable translations made by Scandinavian bloggers recycled by ultra-right-wing websites? Third, we have the framing of a discursive agenda that shifts focus away from the film and its arguments and onto Michael Moore himself, and alleged flaws in his character and methods. Fourth, we see that Michael Moore so annoys both conservatives and the supposedly liberal media that neither group will pass up *any* opportunity to question his work, even if it means risking the exposure of a beloved author's embarrassing geriatric passage into egotistical codgerdom.

But what most concerns me is that, as far as I've been able to discern, this is the *only* discussion to reach the popular sphere that brings *Fahrenheit 9/11* and *Fahrenheit 451* together in any way, and then only to *deny* any connection between them other than linguistic plagiarism. But then, as we've already noted, *Fahrenheit 9/11* has been almost universally interpreted by media experts of all stripes as "a highly controversial political film that aimed its criticisms directly at the reputation of President George W. Bush and his administration."[10] From such a perspective, the film must be considered to stand or fall on the basis of the factual accuracy of its specific claims—many of which were under relentless attack not only in the blogosphere but in the best-selling book *Michael Moore Is A Big Fat Stupid White Man,* and a series of counter-documentaries including *FahrenHYPE 9/11, Michael Moore Hates America,* and *Celsius 41.11.*[11]

I want to argue that this interpretive framework—whether invoked against the film or in support of it—is missing a very important point. I suggest instead that we consider these hypotheses: The foibles of a particular leader and the folly of a particular war are merely *Fahrenheit 9/11*'s MacGuffins, holding our attention while deeper themes build underneath. The film is more about social control through the manipulation of imagery and information than it is about the Iraq war. It is more a cautionary tale about the construction of false consciousness in general than an attack on George W. Bush in particular. As such, the tradition it best fits, the genre whose conventions will best help us interpret it, is not the 'antiwar documentary' exemplified by *Hearts and Minds* or *No End in Sight,* but rather the 'dystopian narrative' exemplified by *1984, Brazil, The Matrix,* and, yes, *Fahrenheit 451.*[12]

Furthermore, I want to argue that the fact we have missed this aspect of the film, or that it has been repressed, matters. An inability to connect *Fahrenheit 9/11* to the discourse of dystopia harms our ability to truly understand and evaluate the policies undertaken in our names.

WHERE THERE'S SMOKE . . .

In again out again Finnigan, the Army called Pete yesterday. He'll be back next week. The Army said so. Quick war. Forty-eight hours, they said, and everyone home. That's what the Army said. Quick war.

—MRS. PHELPS IN *FAHRENHEIT 451,* P. 94

In *Dark Horizons: Science Fiction and the Dystopian Imagination,*[13] Raffaella Baccolini and Tom Moylan offer a review of the critical discourse on dystopia, out of which they draw a useful inventory of the typical features of dystopian narrative. I have borrowed some of their observations and added some of my own to explore ways in which *Fahrenheit 9/11* fits the genre.

The film opens with a surrealistic tilt-down shot, as fireworks and a celebration rise from the bottom of the frame into the night sky. Trancelike electronic music plays and Michael Moore asks in voice-over, "Was it all just a dream?" The answer, of course, is no, giving us what Baccolini and Moylan identify as the first formal strategy of dystopian literature: the real world remade on the order of a bad dream. "The text opens . . . within the nightmarish society. No dream or trip is taken to get to this place of everyday life. . . . the protagonist (and the reader) is always already *in* the world in question, unreflectively immersed in the society."[14]

Much dystopian narrative emphasizes the connection between protagonist and reader via the point of view of the narration. Orwell's *1984* stays within Winston's consciousness, as *Fahrenheit 451* does with Montag's. *Brazil* seldom strays from Sam's point of view, nor *The Matrix* from Neo's. *Fahrenheit 9/11* reconfigures this process of identification, as for most of the film the *viewer* is placed in the position of the protagonist. Only in the final segment is an on-screen protagonist introduced, in the person of Lila Lipscomb. However, before Lila appears, the film has already set forth a restricted narrative style, more akin to the dystopian examples just mentioned than to typical documentary. The film takes its viewers through the narrative as if it were unfolding in something like the present tense. Rather than looking back in the omniscience of hindsight as do *In the Year of the Pig,* or *The War at Home,* the film's mode of address positions the viewer in a state of relative innocence.[15] The deceptions unfold upon us as if we, too, were unaware. Although some critics have suggested the film takes a smug attitude, preaching to a self-congratulatory, already-enlightened-feeling choir, in fact it addresses us as average folk who have been hoodwinked by the system. We have a measure of culpability. Even though we may already know some of the film's revelations, the film asks us to re-experience them afresh. And so we watch *Fahrenheit 9/11,* not so much as our actually knowing selves, but as the more naive, disquieted-but-not-knowing-exactly-why, Montag-like selves we could imagine ourselves to be if we weren't lucky enough to have been reading *The Nation* or listening to *Democracy Now!* The film treats us as if we were new to the story, as Neo-selves.

The protagonists of dystopian tales are typically almost-normal members of otherwise stultified societies, who possess some small 'flaw' that prevents their total incorporation into false consciousness. The protagonist is outwardly average enough to suggest an everyman quality, and to allow us some small measure of hope, if not for utopia, then at least for the fall of dystopia, on the chance that whatever humanity beats inside the heart of Winston, Lowry, and Montag may yet awaken in enough of the citizenry to undermine the forces of authoritarianism. The process of awakening gains power in *Fahrenheit 9/11* because it occurs twice in the film. Lila's enlightenment repeats, with escalating personal horror, the sort of revelation the earlier parts of the film enacted for us. The two consciousnesses, hers and ours, eventually mesh in the end, as she stands in front of the White House, overflowing with grief and anger.

In the archetypal dystopian tale, the imperfect incorporation of the protagonist rarely sets that character's revolt in motion by itself. Something else must happen. Another character—Julia, Morpheus, Clarisse—must intervene, or the protagonist must witness something out of the ordinary by chance—Lowry gets involved in the Buttle/Tuttle mix-up, Montag sees the old woman burn herself amid her books, the spotlight falls at Truman's foot. The narrative function is the same: the interruption of routine leads the protagonists to discover the mechanisms of control, enables them to see the social puppeteer's strings. Of course, *Fahrenheit 9/11* has an intervening character: Michael Moore. He disturbs our routine not by introducing new ideas or emotions, as Clarisse does with Montag, but by sneaking us into Big Brother's editing room, and showing us the outtakes that have been removed in assembling the illusion that passes for our reality. He is Michael Morpheus to our Neo.

In classic dystopian fiction, up through *1984*, as Baccolini and Moylan put it: "The conflict of the text turns on the control of language."[16] That is, as opposed to rule by coercive force, the social order reproduces itself through "discursive power," and "language is a key weapon for the dystopian power structure." By the same token, a reappropriation of language is a crucial force in countering the dystopian regime. Orwell wrote *1984* in 1948, just before the broad dissemination of television began. Beginning with *Fahrenheit 451*, though, published in 1953, dystopian narrative has gradually shifted its depiction of the battleground from the realm of language to the realm of the image.

Language remains the medium of resistance in Bradbury's novel, in the form of memorized books, but it is no longer the medium of control. Montag's wife Mildred, the book's epitome of the brain-deadened masses, is addicted to pills and to her three-wall TV parlor, which the book ties together as functional equivalents—the exception being that while the drugs can be flushed from her stomach, no medicinal process is available to detox her mind. Language has been repressed in favor of the image in the name of order and contentment. The characters remain able to read, but words have been reduced to a purely functional and factual role (not unlike the factoids of *USA Today*). Books are banned not because they contain information, but because they contain ideas that arouse potentially troubling emotions.

As dystopian narrative moves from novels to films, the focus on images increases. By 1966, in Francois Truffaut's film adaptation of *Fahrenheit 451*, the narcotizing control mechanism is no longer mass culture in general, but television in particular, as the credit sequence makes clear. This dystopia is marked not by a restriction of literacy, but by its total absence. *All* forms of written language have been repressed, not just idea-filled books. Other than speech, communication is represented as occurring entirely through visual symbols. In *Brazil,* released in 1985, the imagistic power of the dystopic regime has left the realm of two dimensions and become embodied in the built environment, which includes not only architecture but also the transformation of the body via cosmetic surgery. By 1999, our most resonant dystopian narrative not only extends the notion of ubiquitous three-dimensional imagery into the concept of a totalizing virtual reality, it also explicitly rejects the power of language as resistance. Morpheus tells Neo: "No one can be told what the Matrix is. You have to see it for yourself."

It is control of the image that matters now.

NIGHTMARE VISION

By placing *Fahrenheit 9/11* at the end of this trajectory, we can open up new ways of interpreting the film. It is not primarily a film of factual explication, or of verbal argument, but of *seeing,* specifically seeing images that have heretofore been neglected or hidden. The most powerful sequences in the film—the administration officials clowning off-air, Bush in the classroom, Baghdad before the bombing, the humiliating raids and abuse of prisoners, the amputees—are all offered to us not just as *things we have not seen,* but things we *need* to see, to see for ourselves.

Correspondingly, the weakest moments in the film are the scenes that rely on more linguistic and argumentative form, including the ironic humor that has become Moore's trademark. The interview with the Oregon ranger, and especially the scene where Moore broadcasts the Patriot Act from an ice cream truck, seem forced and out of place within the larger context of the visual revelations that surround them, as they if they accidentally wandered in from some other sort of film.

Getting to see the unseen image, like discovering a copy of a banned book, poses inevitable questions: Why have I not seen this *before*? Why has this been kept from me? Though the focus may have shifted from words to images, or even to computer code, the dystopian narrative retains an emphasis on the apparatuses of sense-making as tools of power and means of resistance. Accordingly, in the final analysis, I suggest *Fahrenheit 9/11* is less about the Bush administration and the Iraq war than about the regimes of discourse, and especially of image, that support the right-wing power structure and its imperialist adventures. *Fahrenheit 9/11* draws direct attention to corporate media early in the film, as it frames the Florida vote as part of an election-fraud conspiracy centered around Fox News. Through the body of the film, the media critique is often more implicit than directly stated. But in case the 'you have to see it for yourself' strategy leaves anyone in doubt, the film concludes with Michael Moore reading a passage that makes direct connections between what we have seen during the film and Big Brotheresque media manipulation:

> George Orwell once wrote that it's not a matter of whether the war is not real or if it is. Victory is not possible. The war is not meant to be won. It is meant to be continuous. A hierarchical society is only possible on the basis of poverty and ignorance. This new version *is* the past, and no different past can ever have existed. In principle, the war effort is always planned to keep society on the brink of starvation. The war is waged by the ruling group against its own subjects, and its object is not the victory over either Eurasia or East Asia, but to keep the very structure of society intact.

This voice-over is accompanied by a montage that connects pieces of the quote to images drawn from previous scenes in the film. As Moore says "Victory is not possible" we see the "Mission Accomplished" sign on the USS *Abraham Lincoln.* The "hierarchical society" sentence is illustrated by footage of Bush receiving an ovation after his tux-and-tails speech to the "the haves and the have-mores." "This new version is the past": Bin Laden family business associate James Bath's name is inked out of Bush's National Guard records. "Keep society on the brink of starvation": tracking shot of boarded-up houses in Flint. "Against its own subjects": inner-city youths being targeted by military recruiters. "Eurasia": Osama bin Laden lies on a cot. "East Asia": Saddam Hussein dances foolishly. These shots are interspersed with bits of off-air footage of administration officials. In the film's title sequence, similar clips showed the pols preparing for their close-ups, suggesting that media appearances by politicians are mere staged performances, but here we see them taking off their mics and leaving the set.

Thus, the ending of *Fahrenheit 9/11* ties its images back to the words of the archetypal dystopian narrative, emphasizing the role of the media with the 'secret' off-air footage peeling back the PR curtain, and bolstering the film's resolution that "we won't get fooled again," by suggesting the Bushies can indeed have their microphones disconnected, their power to define and control 'reality' taken away.

FACTS, TRUTH, QUESTIONS

Cram [the people] full of noncombustible data, chock them so damn full of 'facts' they feel stuffed, but absolutely brilliant with information. Then they'll feel they're thinking, they'll get a sense of motion without moving. And they'll be happy.

—FIRE CHIEF BEATTY IN *FAHRENHEIT 451*, PP. 61–62

To me, the sorts of connections I've just made between *Fahrenheit 9/11* and the tradition of dystopian narrative alluded to by its title are so obvious that I am puzzled and disturbed by the fact that they seem to have played little or no role in how the film has been received by critics and scholars.[17]

If you look at the film solely as a fact-based critique of the 'War on Terror'—more akin to the traditions of investigative reporting than to the traditions of philosophical fiction—you not only miss the underlying media critique, but have to admit that the film has quite a few 'flaws,' as its right-wing critics have alleged. Yes, the film falsely implies that the bin Laden family was allowed to leave the United States while domestic flights were grounded.[18] Yes, the film falsely states that Iraq had never attacked or killed any American, when in fact a number of Americans living in Kuwait were casualties of the Iraqi invasion there. The list goes on. David Kopel provides a fairly comprehensive catalog of conservative complaints in his web article "Fifty-nine Deceits in *Fahrenheit 9/11*." The right-wing think tank Ethics and Public Policy Center, home of arch-conservative ex-U.S. senator Rick "man on dog" Santorum, builds on Kopel's pithy four-page file in presenting a 57-page "viewers' guide" to *Fahrenheit 9/11*, "War Lies and Videotape."[19]

Many of the critiques raised by Kopel, the EPPC, and *FahrenHYPE 9/11* are trivial, off-target, or overinflated. For example, the EPPC guide attempts to flip the evocation of Orwell in *Fahrenheit 9/11*'s closing narration back at the film, based on the fact that what Moore reads is not a contiguous direct quote from the novel:

> Orwell did not write this text. Moore wants us to think these lines come from Orwell's book *1984*, and indeed bits and pieces of this statement, in a different order, do appear that book. But the quotation Moore reads actually comes from a movie version of *1984*, and was not written by Orwell.
>
> But perhaps it is not a matter of whether the quote is not real, or if it is. Honesty is impossible. The film *Fahrenheit 9/11* is not meant to be real, but it is meant to be an overwhelming illusion, in the wake of which nothing is real. The anger it seeks to manufacture is only possible on the basis of deception and ignorance. The film produces a new version of the past and hopes that by insist-

ing it is the truth it might become the truth so thoroughly that no other version can ever have existed.[20]

Moore's narration *is* a condensation of several passages from *1984*, borrowed from the film version released in 1984, but it is hardly a misrepresentation of the novel.[21] However, the EPPC's paraphrase of Moore's ending is not presented as a parodic send-up. It does *exactly* what Moore's critics accuse him of doing: taking bits of information out of context and attempting to use them as a base for rhetorical overkill. It actually 'out-Michael-Moores' Michael Moore.

Nevertheless, even after the nitpicking and bombast are filtered away, Kopel and the EPPC have clearly documented a fair number of points at which the film's attacks on the Bush administration are thin at best, and play fast and loose with the facts. These 'distortions' can be seen as part of an overall tendency toward stridency and hyperbole on the part of the film, a rhetoric inappropriate to a serious discussion of vital issues. In such a view, Moore becomes the left-wing version of Ann Coulter, applying excess heat to the debate without shedding much light. Scholar Kenneth Nolley, approaching *Fahrenheit 9/11* from a position of political and philosophical liberalism, notes that the film employs an argument of guilt-by-association in connecting the Bush family to the Saudis that parallels the Bush administration's argument connecting Saddam Hussein with Al-Qaeda.[22] Nolley decries the tactic in both instances, and sensibly urges all sides in the policy debate to argue in a more rational and responsible manner.

Framing the film's discourse as an assemblage of facts allows, perhaps demands, exactly such a dispassionate, incrementalist approach. We can weigh each element of the critiques *in* the film, and *of* the film, decide which are valid and which are not, and wind up somewhere in the middle. However, as dystopian narrative, as *art,* this is exactly what *Fahrenheit 9/11* demands we *not* do. The concept of dystopia presents a radical philosophical argument, and *Fahrenheit 9/11* is a radical film. It reframes the old dichotomy of radical labor, 'which side are you on?' to 'Which reality do you want to be in?' Can you handle the possibility that most of what you think you know about the war is a lie? Do you want to trust the versions of events presented by the corporate media, or do you want to search for truth among the alternative, independent sources that normally fly under the radar? Do you take the Blue Pill, or the Red Pill? Just as there is no in-between in *The Matrix,* there is no in-between in the world of *Fahrenheit 9/11*. The realm of philosophy, of art, allows, perhaps even demands, that such radical propositions be contemplated. The irreducible binarism of *Fahrenheit 9/11* may look like a mirror reflection of the Right's rigid stance on moral values. Indeed, there may be formal similarities, but at the end of Bush-Cheney's guilt by associations and lines in the sand is a racist war and the violent deaths of hundreds of thousands. At the end of *Fahrenheit 9/11*'s insinuations and dichotomies is a resolution to Question Authority, to search for alternative sources and alternative interpretations, to be Montag.

At some point the interjection must come, "But it's a documentary. It has a responsibility to the truth that fiction doesn't have! It can't be *The Matrix*. It's real!"

Please.

The Matrix; Baudrillard, Philip K. Dick; what is reality; reality television? boundaries not blurred, but collapsed . . .

So why not flip the frame, and look at *Fahrenheit 9/11,* not as a factual form that deviates into fiction, but as a dystopian tale that deviates from genre tradition by generating itself from actualities? I think we can safely observe that the film dramatically upped the stakes of dystopia by placing it in the present tense. The connection to 'reality,' to *our* reality, to our *current* reality, makes the film's Blue Pill / Red Pill proposition all the more radical. The moral difference is profound: we are dealing not with the repression of fictional characters, but the life and death of real people. *Fahrenheit 9/11* places a measure of the blame for these deaths on *us.* When Moore asks, near the end of the film, "Will they ever trust us again?" the viewer is faced with the notion that 'we' who should be responsible—have allowed 'them' to die, because we have been deceived, perhaps allowed ourselves to be deceived. The implicit viewer of *Fahrenheit 9/11* is a full citizen, privileged to a degree, one who might be expected to do something, say something . . . That we have not done something, said something, raises the possibility that some of the very real blood of Lila Lipscomb's son is on *our* hands. *Fahrenheit 9/11* is not merely a cautionary tale, something that *might* happen in the future if we don't change our ways. No, the film asks us to contemplate that this *is* happening, right now.

Note that I have used the word *contemplate* more than once here. This is not a hedge, but an indication of a key distinction I think we need to observe. In assuming that, as 'documentary,' *Fahrenheit 9/11 is* an argument assembled out of a series of certifiable facts, most commentators would interpret the use of actualities as a warrant that the counternarrative it presents is 'the truth,' that the film asserts its Red Pill version of the Iraq war is what 'really' happened. I think this is a misreading of the film. (I must note here that I look at films through one of those intellectual traditions that discounts authorial intent in favor of examining the text itself, so I make no claims about what Michael Moore was *trying* to do. My argument is about what *the film does.*) I submit the thesis of *Fahrenheit 9/11* is 'hey, there's a plausible alternative to the official version of events you've been spoon-fed, and the fact you know basically nothing of this alternative proves you've been snookered.' Such a claim does not depend on the absolute veracity of the counterstory, only its *potential* validity, and its failure to get past the information gatekeepers.

Fahrenheit 9/11 compares dystopia to its other, not as a dichotomy of competing 'correct' answers, but one of easy answers versus a continuing series of questions. *Fahrenheit 9/11* does not aim to give us definitive truths. It aims to stir the pot.

THE BENEFITS OF THE MESSY

Such a limitation of goals ought to be inherent in every argument that calls for us to distrust media images but comes to us in the form of media images. Yet, somehow most media-borne media critiques manage to paper over the obvious contradiction, and avoid any reference to the self-reflexive conclusion that they themselves, being mediated, may not be entirely trustworthy, either. *Fahrenheit 9/11* is *way* too over the top to achieve this. It wears its enthusiastic exaggerations on its shirtsleeve, stretching facts so blatantly at so many points that it virtually assures that lists like Kopel's will be created and widely disseminated. Intentionally or not, the film undermines its own authority.

However, if we divide *Fahrenheit 9/11*'s rhetorical devices into the ones that stick, and the ones that peel away under the fact-checking of the conservatives, we find that the sequences most easily debunked are the weaker elements of the film anyway, some not even remotely necessary to the broad argument. What remains after the stuff that is factually suspect is tossed out, for the most part, are those elements based not on verbal assertion, but on "seeing it for yourself." The language may fall away, but the visions survive.

Even so, there are two instances in *Fahrenheit 9/11* where, for me anyway, the raw power of "seeing for yourself" exists in tension with elements that raise the possibility that the film is functioning as deceptive propaganda. I think these are the most interesting sequences in the film.

One is near the end where Lila's interaction with a protester in front of the White House is interrupted by a woman who breaks into the frame, turns to the camera and announces, "This is all staged!" On the one hand, this offers Lila the opportunity to assert the reality of her son's death in a powerful way in reply.

On the other hand, the interruption disturbs the emotional flow of the sequence and introduces the possibility that protests, and even documentary scenes *can* be staged. In a 'well-made documentary' the value of Lila's rebuttal would not be worth either the risk of allowing a suggestion of fakery to appear on screen, or interrupting the arc of Lila's narrative, much less both. There's plenty of powerful footage of Lila grieving that establishes the concreteness of her son's death without this exchange. The footage is also only semicoherent in the first place since the mic does not pick up what the protestor is saying well enough to make all of it intelligible. Most editors would avoid the possible deflections and cut the whole business. Yet it remains in *Fahrenheit 9/11*.

The other sequence is the montage of 'everyday life' in Baghdad before the U.S. attack. In his scatching critique of *Fahrenheit 9/11* in *Salon*, former lefty turned terror warrior Christopher Hitchens describes the scene as follows.

> In this peaceable kingdom, according to Moore's flabbergasting choice of film shots, children are flying little kites, shoppers are smiling in the sunshine, and the gentle rhythms of life are undisturbed. Then—wham! From the night sky come the terror weapons of American imperialism . . . I don't think Al Jazeera would, on a bad day, have transmitted anything so utterly propagandistic.[23]

Hitchens actually underreports the subtext of the sequence's editing. The kids flying kites, seen in long shot, are followed by a tighter shot of a cute Iraqi kid coming down a playground slide into close-up. But just as the child reaches the bottom and is about to land we cut to shot after shot of explosions going off in Baghdad under the U.S. bombardment. After this comes another shock cut, to the charred corpse of a small child being thrown into the back of a truck.

There is not even the slightest hint in this sequence that Iraqi citizens had been impoverished, tortured, and killed in horrifying numbers by the Hussein regime. When, like the good progressive I am, I dutifully attended *Fahrenheit 9/11* on opening day, I initially found myself thinking much the same thing as Hitchens when this sequence appeared. "This out-Eisensteins Eisenstein," I said to myself. Indeed, it would be hard to conceive a more propagandistic presentation. However, I did not draw the same conclusions about the effect of this part of the film as did Hitchens. He writes:

> I have myself written and presented about a dozen low-budget made-for-TV documentaries . . . and I also helped produce a slightly more polished one on Henry Kissinger that was shown in movie theaters.[24] So I know, thanks, before

Showing what no other media will show. Moore's "peaceable kingdom" of Iraq just prior to the bombing sequence in *Fahrenheit 9/11*. Copyright 2004 Lions Gate Films/IFC Films/Fellowship Adventure Group LLC.

> you tell me, that a documentary must have a "POV" or point of view and that it must also impose a narrative line. But if you leave out absolutely everything that might give your "narrative" a problem and throw in any old rubbish that might support it, and you don't even care that one bit of that rubbish flatly contradicts the next bit, and you give no chance to those who might differ, then *you have betrayed your craft.* If you flatter and fawn upon your potential audience, I might add, you are patronizing them and insulting them.

Hitchens, like Moore's Far Right critics, imagines the lefty audience who attends Michael Moore films to be a sheeplike herd who can be driven wherever Moore's devious methods desire, a brain-dead mass who sop up everything the films present at face value. (I happen to find *this* idea patronizing and insulting, not just because it assumes that lefties are political dupes but, more insultingly, that we can't tell a good movie from a bad one.) Hitchens suggests the proper way to make a political film is to clean out all the rubbish, and smooth out all the contradictions. Obviously, this guy hasn't read any film theory. So I'll agree with him that *Fahrenheit 9/11* has its full share of garbage and self-contradiction, but suggest that this may be a *good thing.*

Unlike the seemingly firm, real 'real world' Neo discovers in *The Matrix*, the Red Pill counter-reality in *Fahrenheit 9/11* is full of holes. It is, after all, a compilation film, pieced together out of footage détourned from mainstream media and footage captured by a wide variety of independent sources. Like the indymedia.com-type websites whose politics it reflects, it throws a lot of stuff together, including not only crucial revelations and valid insights but wild speculation, conspiracy theory, and didactic outrage. Formally, this multiplicity of different kinds of voice stands in contrast to the coherent and authoritative tone of establishment media. It also departs from Moore's earlier films, which establish his own singular voice (as ironic as that voice may be) as the controlling element of the presentation. It is no accident then that the film's critics have attacked it by focusing on Moore as an individual. To the extent the debate shifts to Moore, the wider alternative media movement that contributed to the film can be ignored. (Unfortunately, Moore sometimes seems to fall into this trap by talking about the film in personal terms.)

It is true that the different voices of *Fahrenheit 9/11* all criticize the war. But Hitchens completely misses the point when he argues that the film allows no space for differing perspectives. We might as well slam Morpheus for not giving the computer controlling the Matrix equal time. The point is that the differing perspective is already with us: It is the dominant media view of Iraq that had been pounded into all of our heads ad infinitum since the first Gulf War. This is why the EPPC's attempt to paint *Fahrenheit 9/11* as Orwellian is so ludicrous. Regimes of dystopian thought control depend on the constant repetition of the dominant vision and the systematic erasure of any contradictory points of view—burning the books containing any ideas that might trouble the masses. How would it have been possible for *Fahrenheit 9/11* to generate "an overwhelming illusion, in the wake of which nothing is real" in the midst of the Carlsons, Coulters, Hannitys, Hitchenses, Hillarys, Humes, Ingrahams, Krauthammers, Kristols, Liebermans, Limbaughs, and O'Reillys, not to mention Judith Miller and the countless other 'legitimate' journalists who pimped for the war? Fox News CEO Roger Ailes crows about his network's dominance in the ratings, and had the electronic news ticker wrapping around the exterior of the Fox offices altered to read "ATTENTION PROTESTERS: THE MICHAEL MOORE FAN CLUB MEETS THURSDAY AT A PHONE BOOTH AT SIXTH AVENUE AND 50TH STREET."[25] Yet are we to believe this same small minority of dissidents has ever been anywhere near achieving Big Brother–class power in redefining reality?

Journalist Ron Suskind wrote:

> I had a meeting with a senior adviser to Bush. He . . . said that guys like me were "in what we call the reality-based community," which he defined as people who

> "believe that solutions emerge from your judicious study of discernible reality." I nodded and murmured something about enlightenment principles and empiricism. He cut me off. "That's not the way the world really works anymore," he continued. "We're an empire now, and when we act, we create our own reality. And while you're studying that reality—judiciously, as you will—we'll act again, creating other new realities, which you can study too, and that's how things will sort out. We're history's actors . . . and you, all of you, will be left to just study what we do."[26]

How could *Fahrenheit 9/11* have hoped "that by insisting it is the truth it might become the truth so thoroughly that no other version can ever have existed" when not only was it up against the reality-making apparatus of the most powerful government on earth, but its discursive mode as much as begged Kopel and the EPPC to "bring it on?"

The convincing evidence that Saddam Hussein was a torturer and mass murderer is inescapable. If anything, *Fahrenheit 9/11* reminds us of it by ignoring it where we expect to find it, inducing a kind of Pavlovian response of fill in the blank. This is exactly why, like Hitchens, I was capable of recognizing the kids-and-bombs section of *Fahrenheit 9/11* as problematically propagandistic. My mind immediately created a dialog between what the scene showed and what I knew it did not show. The sequence disturbed me. Why would the film go so over the top? Yet the inner dialog continued, and as much as I realized *Fahrenheit 9/11* was leaving out the evil Iraq, I realized that our media images of evil Iraq had left out the images shown in *Fahrenheit 9/11,* that not everyone in Iraq is involved in torture or scamming the oil-for-aid program. I realized that it had never occurred to me that, like most modern cities, Baghdad has parks and playgrounds, and a middle class more concerned with the routines of everyday life than they are with the politics of their corrupt government—kinda like most people in the United States who went about their own affairs without paying that much attention to whatever schemes Bush, Cheney, and the gang were cooking up for their never-ending "war on terror." The images then, were both true and false simultaneously.

I don't know if Moore is a closet dialectician, or has just devolved via egotism into such a sloppy propagandist that he can't help undercutting himself, and I don't care. It really doesn't make any difference, because the film provokes us in ways that well-made documentaries do not, and provocation is what we need.

Which brings us back to *Fahrenheit 451*.

IF FOUR FIVE WAS NINE ONE

"Jesus God," said Montag. "Every hour so many damn things in the sky! How in the hell did those bombers get up there every single second of our lives! Why doesn't someone want to talk about it!"

—*FAHRENHEIT 451*, P. 73

Bradbury's novel doesn't have anything resembling a consistent ideology. It scatter-shoots political ideas all over the map, left and right. Its dystopic view of mass culture is deeply influenced by an elitist cultural conservatism—Ortega y Gasset even gets a passing mention. Beatty tells Montag that the people created their own stupefaction, by taking the easy path to pleasure and comfort. At other moments the outlook is more libertarian, and in the end Montag winds up in what appears to be an essentially socialistic commune when he joins the book people. This reads more like youthful confusion over the then-still-new fear of mass culture spawned by the spread of TV mixed with still-fresh memories of fascist rallies and the specter of advancing Stalinism, than it does like a clever literary strategy. But while the book may not have a politics (or have too many politics), it does have a philosophy, which centers exactly on the necessity of asking deep and troubling questions.

To explore *Fahrenheit 9/11*'s relationship not just to the dystopian tradition but to *Fahrenheit 451* in particular, I shall ask the reader to think about Moore's film, the aggressive stance it took, the multiple sources it drew upon, and the controversy it engendered in light of the following elements of the novel. I'll just report; you decide.

After Montag begins reading books, he starts telling his wife about his inner thoughts, his confusions, his doubt about being a fireman. She begs him to leave her alone. He replies: "We need not to be let alone. We need to be really bothered about something once in a while. How long is it since you were *really* bothered. About something important, about something real?" (52).

After Beatty lauds the positive social value of facts in keeping people happy, he notes that the firemen burn books to avoid having the ideas in the books—none of which agree with one another—cause conflicts in the readers' minds, leading to unhappiness. "Don't give them any slippery stuff like philosophy or sociology to tie things up with. That way lies melancholy. . . . We're the Happiness Boys. . . . We stand against the small tide of those who want to make everyone unhappy with conflicting theory and thought. We have our fingers in the dike" (61–62).

Many people only know *Fahrenheit 451* through Francois Truffaut's film adaptation. The film has several key differences from the book. The most interesting—given that it was made in 1966 at the height of U.S. escalation in Vietnam—is that the film leaves the question of 'what kinds of thought might disquiet the mind?' completely abstract, while in the novel one of the things the thinking characters think about and the numbed ones ignore is the continuing presence of vague, unending wars. In Bradbury's novel, as in *1984,* the equation becomes clear: totalitarianism, media control, restricted thought, war . . . all generate one another.[27]

Montag goes into a rant in front of his wife's friends, telling them that their husbands have been killed in wars, their deaths covered up as accidents. He berates the women for forgetting their lost men easily, moving on to new marriages, having abortions and disregarding the children they do have. He reads to them from Matthew Arnold's poem "Dover Beach." "Ah, love, let us be true to one another" since the world has "neither joy . . . nor light . . . nor help for pain," and we are "as on a darkling plain . . . where ignorant armies clash by night." This reduces the heretofore soulless Mrs. Phelps to tears.

Later after meeting the discarded English professor Faber, Montag wonders, "I made them unhappier than they have been in years, I think . . . Maybe they're right, maybe it's best not to face things, to run, have fun." Faber replies: "No, you mustn't. If there were no war, I'd say fine, *have* fun! But Montag, you mustn't go back to being just a fireman. All *isn't* well with the world" (103–4).

Montag speculates about the cause of the war: "Is it because we're having so much fun at home we've forgotten the world? Is it because we're so rich and the rest of the world's so poor and we just don't care if they are . . . Is that why we're hated so much?" (73–74).

After Montag has escaped from the city, the war suddenly moves into the foreground, in the form of a sudden, unexpected enemy attack through the air. Montag and the book-people see the city destroyed by a series of explosions:

> For another of those impossible instants, the city stood, rebuilt and unrecognizable, taller than it had ever hoped or strived to be, taller than man had built it, erected at last in grouts of shattered concrete and sparkles of torn metal into a mural hung like a reverse avalanche, a million colors, a million oddities, a door where a window should be, a top for a bottom, a side for a back, and then the city rolled over and fell dead (160).

Do I need to remark how eerily these passages, written in 1953, evoke more recent national history?

Granger, the leader of the book-people, leads the group back toward the ruins of the city. He likens mankind to the phoenix, who burns himself up, miraculously rises from his own ashes, and then burns himself again—over and over. But he asserts that humans have the power to stop the cycle if only they would use their memories:

> Even when we had the books on hand, a long time ago, we didn't use what we got out of them. We went right on insulting the dead. We went right on spitting in the graves of all the poor ones who die before us. We're going to meet a lot of lonely people in the next week and the next month and the next year. And when they ask us what we're doing, you can say, We're remembering. That's where we'll win out in the long run. And someday we'll remember so much that we'll build the biggest goddamn steamshovel in history and dig the biggest grave of all time and shove war in and cover it up (164).

Fahrenheit 9/11 asks us to choose our reality. That's what makes it radical. It also asks us to remember. That's what makes it dangerous. That is why the established authorities *must* treat the film as a show of facts that can be easily refuted, why its connections to artistic and philosophical tradition *must* be swept off the table, kept out of the discussion by definition.

That is why, as elections cycles come and go, long after George W. Bush has settled into the dustbin of history, we would do well to remember *Fahrenheit 9/11.*

Notes

1. Ray Bradbury, *Fahrenheit 451* (New York: Random House, 1953).

2. Though ardently pro-Israeli and pro-Iraq war, Haugland is also an atheist who has attacked creationism and the Jehovah's Witnesses with the same fervor with which he tweaked Mr. Moore, all in the name of rationalism.

3. Jan Haugland, January 2004. "Ray Bradbury: 'Michael Moore Is an Asshole,'" Secular Blasphemy, June 2, 2004, http://blogs.salon.com/0001561/2004/06/02.html.

4. A note on punctuation: in this essay, I use standard double quotation marks only to indicate actual quotes from specific sources. For the sort of concepts or generic phrases I wish to mark off from my direct 'authorial voice,' I use single quotation marks, as I have done here, to differentiate them from genuine sourced quotations.

5. Swedish blogger Paul O'Mahoney later translated this passage to "He is a dreadful man. A dreadful man" and rendered the phrase Haugland translated as "screwed asshole" as "stupid son-of-bitch." Stambord, *Stockholm Spectator Blog*, June 2, 2004, http://www.spectator.se/stambord/?p=24 (accessed March 8, 2005).

6. "Ray Bradbury Rips Michael Moore," http://www.worldnetdaily.com/news/article.asp?ARTICLE_ID=38776.

7. See, for example, "Bradbury Blasts Moore over 'Fahrenheit' Title," http://www.nbc6.net/entertainment/3390666/detail.html.

8. Paul Chavez, "Moore Film Title Angers Author Bradbury," Associated Press, June 18, 2004.

9. "*Fahrenheit 451* Author Wants Title Back," *Hardball,* June 28, 2004, http://www.msnbc.msn.com/id/5324876/.

10. Robert Brent Toplin, *Michael Moore's* Fahrenheit 9/11: *How One Film Divided a Nation* (Lawrence: University Press of Kansas, 2006), 3.

11. David T. Hardy and Jason Clark, *Michael Moore Is a Big Fat Stupid White Man* (New York: ReganBooks, 2004); *FahrenHYPE 9/11* (Alan Peterson); *Michael Moore Hates America* (Bruce Wilson); *Celsius 41.11* (Kevin Knoblock). See Charles Musser's essay in this volume for an extended discussion of the "truth claims" in *FahrenHYPE 9/11.*

12. *Hearts and Minds* (Peter Davis, 1974); *No End in Sight* (Charles Ferguson, 2007); George Orwell, *1984* (1949; repr., New York: Plume, 1983); *Brazil* (Terry Gilliam, 1985); *The Matrix* (Andy Wachowski and Larry Wachowski, 1999).

13. Raffaella Baccolini and Tom Moylan, eds., *Dark Horizons: Science Fiction and the Dystopian Imagination* (New York: Routledge, 2003).

14. Ibid., 5.

15. *In the Year of the Pig* (Emile de Antonio, 1969); *The War at Home* (Glenn Silber and Barry Alexander Brown, 1979).

16. Baccolini and Moylan, *Dark Horizons.*

17. Toplin devotes a short paragraph to the allusion to *Fahrenheit 451* in the title of *Fahrenheit 9/11,* which he takes as indicative of a media critique inherent in the film. However, he does not develop this notion in detail or take it beyond news coverage of the Iraq War. See Toplin, *Michael Moore's* Fahrenheit 9/11, 36.

18. *The 9/11 Commision Report,* 329–30, 556, 557.

19. Dave Kopel, "Fifty-Nine Deceits in *Fahrenheit 9/11,*" http://www.davekopel.com/Terror/Fiftysix-Deceits-in-Fahrenheit-911.htm; The Ethics And Public Policy Center, "War Lies and Videotape," November 5, 2004, http://www.eppc.org/publications/pubID.2199/pub_detail.asp.

20. The Ethics and Public Policy Center, "War Lies and Videotape."

21. The passage Moore reads is clearly borrowed from Michael Radford's film adaptation. However, this collection of "bits and pieces" is drawn almost entirely from the language of chapter 9, book 2, of *1984* (New York: Plume, 1983), where Winston reads Immanuel Goldstein's *The Theory and Practice of Oligarchal Collectivism.* "It does not matter whether the war is actually happening, and, since no decisive victory is possible, it does not matter whether the war is going well or badly. All that is needed is that a state of war should exist" is a direct quote from page 158). The phrase "a hierarchical society is only possible on the basis of poverty and ignorance" appears on page 157. "This new version *is* the past, and no different past can ever have existed" appears on page 176. On page 164, Orwell-as-Goldstein writes "The war is waged by each ruling group against its own subjects, and the object of the war is not to make or prevent conquests of territory, but to keep the structure of society intact." The wording of the phrase "In principle, the

war effort is always planned to keep society on the brink of starvation" appears to be Radford's. However, Orwell/Goldstein goes on at length on the connection between war, starvation, and poverty throughout the "War Is Peace" section of the chapter.

22. Kenneth Nolley, "*Fahrenheit 911:* Documentary, Truth-Telling and Politics" (paper presented at the War in Film, Television and History, Film and History Biennial, Dallas, TX, November 12, 2004).

23. Christopher Hitchens, "Unfairenheit 9/11: The Lies of Michael Moore," *Slate,* June 21, 2004.

24. The documentary *The Trials of Henry Kissinger* (Eugene Jarecki, 2002) is based on Hitchens's book of the same name (New York: Verso, 2001). Hitchens appears at length in the film as an interviewee but is not credited as a producer. The generally positive editorial review of the book on Amazon.com states, "Hitchens's fiery brief . . . is far from evenhanded." The generally positive review of the film on Amazon states, "This film is clearly biased against its target . . . additional viewings simultaneously deepen the film's conviction and reveal the weakness of its one-sided embrace of Hitchens."

25. Ken Auletta, "Vox Fox," *New Yorker,* May 26, 2003.

26. Ron Suskind, "Faith, Certainty, and the Presidency of George W. Bush," *New York Times Magazine,* October 17, 2004.

27. In another interesting shift, Truffaut's film makes Clarisse, the inquisitive neighbor who inspires Montag to begin asking questions, into a beautiful young woman (played by Julie Christie) to suggest the possibility of romance with Montag, and there is a happy ending, as Montag not only escapes to the land of the book-people but is reunited with Clarisse, who he discovers has been living there. In the novel, Clarisse is but a precocious teenager, disappears early on, and is presumed dead—no doubt a victim of the state for her subversive thoughts.

Sicko Movie Review

RICHARD PORTON

At this juncture, the challenge of reviewing a new Michael Moore film involves the conundrum of either being forced to assess the "controversy" that now inevitably surrounds every Moore project even before its formal release or maintaining a faux-naive stance concerning the attendant media onslaught and feigning neutrality. *Sicko,* Moore's latest piece of cinematic muckraking, is both a left-liberal provocation on the order of *Roger & Me, Bowling for Columbine,* and *Fahrenheit 9/11* and—somewhat surprisingly—a film that has won scattered kudos from a few isolated conservatives as well as a rave review from the Fox News Channel's film critic. (Bill O'Reilly and John Gibson were truer to form and assailed the film with impeccably reactionary fury.) After all, millions of Americans of all ideological stripes are frustrated by the machinations of health-care providers that routinely either make subscribers jump through hoops to attain basic services or deny care altogether.

Flying in the face of inveterate American individualism, Moore's emphasis on health care's systemic crisis fuels *Sicko*'s populism since it is very easy for most Americans to construct Big Health as a tangible villain. The film opens rather misleadingly with a famous clip of Moore's nemesis, George W. Bush, complaining, in a malapropism now part of Bush folklore, that "too many ob-gyns aren't able to practice their love with women across this country." Bush's garbled syntax is always—perhaps too predictably—good for a laugh. Yet, in a sweeping indictment of health-care malfeasance in which politicians of both parties played nefarious roles, Bush-bashing is beside the point. The film's first half offers something of a chamber of horrors laced with macabre humor. The focus is not on the indigent and uninsured but on Americans with health-insurance policies that often prove grossly inadequate. Consequently, hardworking middle-class Americans who have often been suspicious of Moore—the so-called Reagan Democrats—may now resist the right-wing whine that Moore "hates America," since *Sicko* speaks to one primary source of their everyday anguish.

While it's arguable that the mixture of pathos and humor Moore wrenches from a number of mini-case studies of the woefully underinsured becomes occasionally cloying and manipulative, the snarkiness that often suffuses the treatment of "ordinary people" in *Roger & Me* and *Bowling for Columbine* is exchanged for genuine empathy. A woman who recounts how her insurance company denied payment for her ambulance to the hospital after an automobile accident because she failed to obtain prior approval offers a succinct sketch of the Kafkaesque veneer of "managed care." Conservatives might cavil that a single-payer arrangement will create a huge impersonal bureaucracy. Moore's anecdotes refute this right-wing libertarian cliché by demonstrating how the chaos of private health care is much more impersonal and bureaucratic than the disparate forms of nationalized health insurance embraced by the rest of the industrialized world. For corporate health bureaucrats, the bottom line becomes a form of triage—a point driven home in a heart-wrenching vignette chronicling an insurance company's failure to approve a dying man's plea for a bone marrow treatment deemed "experimental."

Accusing Moore of narcissism at this late date might be merely stating the obvious. But Moore self-consciously employs his celebrity to amusingly illustrate how the insurance behemoths quaver at the very mention of his name. When Cigna decides that a little girl named Annette with a severe hearing disability deserves a cochlear implant for only one of her ears (attending to both ears is once again called "experimental," the apparent euphemism for callousness in the health-care industry), her father, Doug Noe, threatens to spill the beans on camera for Michael. With almost farcical swiftness, Cigna nervously agrees to pay for the second implant. In fact, one of *Sicko*'s signal strengths is its willingness to name names. Besides Cigna, Blue Cross Blue Shield, and Kaiser Permanente receive deserved thrashings.

Pulling the viewer's heartstrings in the service of a good cause is fine, but if Moore, despite his huge self-regard and occasional grandstanding, is essentially a documentary essayist (the director frequently compares his films to op-ed pieces), what is *Sicko*'s underlying thesis? Simply put, the documentary attempts to explain why Americans, perfectly content with government-run post offices and public libraries, have been brainwashed to believe that nationalized health care (or "socialized medicine," if you like) is akin to a communist conspiracy. Providing a popular gloss on scholarly works such as sociologist Paul Starr's *The Social Transformation of American Medicine* and sober journalistic exposes (Jonathan Cohn's *Sick* is the most prominent recent example), the lingering impact of Cold War rhetoric is viewed as the ultimate rationale for maintaining a basically irrational and inhumane health-care morass. The contrast with the unquestionably capitalist democracies of western Europe, long proud of their national health providers, is stark. But, as Starr points out, "The original European model began with the industrial working class and emphasized income maintenance," while "America developed an insurance system originally concerned with improving the access of middle-class patients to hospitals and of hospitals to middle-class patients." Of course, one of the implicit arguments of *Sicko* is that, by the eighties and nineties, the revamping of the New Deal under Reagan and Clinton threatened the interests of the middle class (their enthusiasm for Reaganism notwithstanding) as well of those of the working class and desperately poor.

In one of the film's most brilliant polemical strokes, the origin of our current malaise is traced to a conversation between John Erlichman and Richard Nixon, preserved for posterity thanks to the notorious Nixon tapes. Ehrlichman extols the Kaiser Permanente scheme for gearing "incentives" toward less medical care, and Nixon is charmed by Edgar Kaiser's profit-making venture. Equating the welfare state with Communist subversion has long been a conservative ideological linchpin, and Nixon's HMO Act of 1973 crystallizes *Sicko*'s argument by providing both a bridge to the past—post-1945 anticommunist hysteria is accounted for in a bleakly amusing recording of Ronald Reagan pontificating against national insurance during the fifties—and an exploration of our current crisis, which is encapsulated by Hillary Clinton's waffling and moral cowardice.

Moore once admitted in print that he had a palpable "crush" on Mrs. Clinton, and the jaundiced account of her sorry record with regard to saner health-care initiatives (supposedly resented by the film's producer, avid Hillary supporter Harvey Weinstein) results in one of *Sicko*'s more courageous sequences. In truth, Moore is much too kind in portraying Clinton as an initially altruistic crusader for health reform who only capitulated to the health-care lobby once her reformist schemes became the victim of Republican intransigence. Clinton in fact comes off as poised and witty in a famous exchange between the then First Lady and Representative Dick Armey, whom she blithely compares to Dr. Kevorkian. As Jonathan Cohn demonstrates, President Bush's "blind faith in private insurance for the elderly" is merely an embellishment of policies begun by Hillary's husband Bill. And her convoluted reform plan—too complicated to be properly understood by either her Democratic allies or Republican foes—in no way attempted to implement a single-payer system or anything approaching universal health care. Fortunately, Moore comes to realize that, despite Hillary's extremely superficial stab at taking on the health-care moguls, she eventually emerged as a tool of the very interests she once supposedly defied.

Sicko's second, more meandering half, while not without its rewards, is often frustratingly diffuse and, toward the film's conclusion, Moore reverts to his fondness for facile pranks that are often more glib than funny. Embarking on a picaresque journey to Canada, Great Britain, France, and Cuba in search of antidotes to our seemingly intractable health-care mess, his previous commendable restraint gives way to only intermittently effective shtick. An interview with former British Labour MP Tony Benn is by far the most effective interlude in Moore's "aw shucks" version of a road movie. Ironically enough, Benn's lucidity proves that, despite Moore's avowed contempt for traditional, allegedly "unentertaining" documentaries, a single talking head can often prove brilliantly effective. For Benn, a proud representative of "Old Labour," the social democratic commitment to universal health care "comes down to democracy." This is a key point in a film that presents the failure of American privatized health insurance as one of the main symptoms of an erosion in social solidarity and a major rupture in our government's social contract with its citizens.

Benn, the Labour stalwart, sets a definite standard for eloquence that Moore fails to meet in most of his folksy encounters with ordinary Britons, Frenchmen, and Canadians. Of course, Moore, employing a phony slack-jawed innocence, is being coyly and quite deliberately inarticulate. Be that as it may, his analysis of other, more exemplary health-care systems proves much less rigorous than his rage at American corporate capitalism. This is mostly attributable to Moore's refusal—doubtless justified by his preoccupation with remaining "entertaining"—to offer a nuanced account of the weaknesses, as well as of the strengths, of the European, and especially the Cuban, health bureaucracies.

Employing his carefully cultivated persona, the schlubby ordinary guy with the baseball cap and tortoiseshell glasses, Moore interviews a number of obliging doctors, patients, and homemakers. Although there is little doubt that France's health-care system is one of Europe's, and probably the world's, best, Moore's cutesy interview with a middle-class housewife, who takes the wonders of French medical care for granted and claims that "ze fish" is among her biggest expenses, does little to advance the argument. Tony Benn's enduring idealism notwithstanding, even casual tourists to Britain who chance on the odd article in the *Guardian* are aware that erosion in the standards of the National Health Service has been a hot topic among the Left since the regime of Margaret Thatcher and that similar debates have continued apace in the era of Tony Blair's New Labour. *Sicko* ignores these controversies and instead presents a totally rosy picture of the NHS. A chat with a suave, well-heeled NHS doctor could almost be lifted from a promotional film. Moore's characteristic praise for Canada has, needless to say, provided fodder for conservatives who love to issue apologias for America's ailing system by claiming that harried Canadians must wait months for certain diagnostic tests and elective surgery. These conservative qualms are hollow indeed given that the vast majority of Canadians would never exchange their single-payer system for an American-style private enterprise scheme in a million years—a point wittily made in an exchange with Moore's Canadian in-laws who express trepidation about even crossing the border for an afternoon and losing access to their generous benefits. But, in the name of intellectual honesty, it would not have eviscerated *Sicko*'s pro-Canadian stance to point out that reports of long waits for certain procedures are not entirely the products of American right-wing scare tactics.

Moore's decision to accompany ailing 9/11 rescue workers to Cuba is this documentary's closing gambit and a dubious polemical ploy indeed. It is certainly an amusing bit of comic bravura for our intrepid director to sail into Guantánamo Bay and ask the unresponsive authorities if they can provide our "heroes" with the same standard of health care apparently meted out to the prison's resident "evildoers." Traipsing on to Havana with the bedraggled workers irredeemably muddies the ideological waters. It is undeniably true that Cuban health care is frequently cited as among the best in the Third World, and we have no reason to doubt that the 9/11 contingent, denied vital treatment at home, received empathetic attention from a Havana doctor that Cannes audiences found "dreamy." On the other hand, it's also difficult to contest Christopher Hayes's assertion in *The Nation* that the Cuban adventure is "a major miscalculation and nearly squanders the first hour and a half of the film in which Moore so deftly guts arguments that socialized medicine represents the vanguard of Marxism." In addition, since Moore is a Gore supporter and far from a Stalinist, the rhetorical nod to a repressive regime in the final sequence, however ironically deployed, reflects a certain bad faith. One can in fact be considerably to the left of Michael Moore and still decry the persistence of social inequality (Party members reputedly receive much better health benefits than the average worker) in Castro's Cuba. With Moore, alas, it is always necessary to swallow some of his films' reflexive gimmickry and admire his generally good political instincts and intentions.

IV. BEYOND THE AMERICAN MULTIPLEX: MOORE IN THE MEDIA MARKETPLACE

Moore Muckracking: The Reinvention of TV Newsmagazines in the Age of Spin and Entertainment

JEFFREY P. JONES

What they have to deal with, with us, is not language or nudity or violence, it's ideas—and that's really dangerous.

—MICHAEL MOORE, ON NETWORK CENSORSHIP OF *TV NATION*

In the second season premier (July 28, 1995) of Michael Moore's satirical newsmagazine show *TV Nation,* Moore introduced viewers to Crackers, the Corporate Crime-Fighting Chicken. If certain social problems had mascots such as Smokey the Bear (forest fires), Woodsy Owl (pollution), and McGruff the Crime Dog (street crime), Moore and his producers believed America should also have a mascot to bring attention to the relatively underreported problem of corporate crime. With one of the show's writers dressed in a seven-foot chicken costume, Crackers seeks an explanation for how it was possible for First Boston Corporation to get a $50 million tax break from New York City by promising not to eliminate any jobs, and then laying off more than 100 employees 30 days later. Crackers begins his investigation by going to the corporate headquarters of First Boston, only to be escorted from the building by a security officer who tells Moore that Crackers is persona non grata (to which Moore retorts, "He'd be more like chicken non grata, wouldn't he?").

Crackers then heads to City Hall to get an explanation from New York Mayor Rudolph Giuliani. Unable to get an audience with the mayor, Crackers attempts to attend the mayor's weekly press conference. Though Crackers is barred entry, Moore attends and seeks an answer from the mayor in Crackers' stead. In an honest and serious tone, Moore asks the mayor, "When you gave them this tax break in January, and then a few weeks later, they turn around and lay off two hundred people, didn't you feel a little used? I mean, they must have been planning these job layoffs for some time." Giuliani dismisses Moore's inquiry by stating, "It's a very silly description of a very complex thing that is very important to this city." With that blow-off, Moore then asks the mayor, "Why won't you meet our Corporate Crime Chicken, Crackers, and discuss this?" Giuliani angrily snaps, "Because this isn't a joke, and you're presenting it that way." "Well," Moore responds, "this *isn't* a joke. That's our point."

Moore's critics have consistently pointed to such instances to demonstrate why he is either contemptuous, cruel, or a grandstander, or that his efforts result in little more than lame pranks, humiliation, or harassment.[1] Yet like the Yippies who shaped Moore's approach to political engagement and social satire, Moore appreciates the difference between the sophomoric and the subversive.[2] When corporations refuse to speak and when politicians only speak on their own terms, using a man in a chicken suit to call attention to important issues while also highlighting the means of obfuscation used by the powerful turns out to be an effective, if somewhat "illegitimate" means for advancing a political critique of the players involved and the system itself. By Moore's working-class thinking, a guy in a chicken suit seeking legitimate answers to corporate and government malfeasance is no more ludicrous than a guy in a business suit offering lame excuses for wasting tax dollars to benefit the rich. Plus it is funny. As Moore explains, "If you try to have a straight argument or discussion with [the big corporations], they'll have all their standard one-liners. So you kind of disarm them with their weakness—their inability to laugh or have a sense of humor. It's like the difference between judo and karate—there's no way you're going to win with a karate chop to the neck of corporate America."[3]

What such tactics highlight as well—perhaps more than anything else—is Moore's unruly approach to political discourse. Through his television programs and films, Moore consistently attacks the controlled (and controlling) nature of power in American life. Central to both political and corporate power is the control of political language and discourse—whether it is the scripted language of politicians and corporate spokespersons, the structured engagements between journalists and these elites (with unwritten rules governing who gets to talk about what subjects, in what ways, when, and in which places), or the accepted silences on matters of great social importance (such as class, racial, corporate, and political privileges). Moore wants to disrupt them all, bringing the silences to life and turning the controlled speech that dominates public life upside down. By making the silent speak, he reveals the areas of democratic discourse that are typically off-limits, as well as the lengths the powerful go to to keep them that way. By turning scripted engagements on their head, Moore has disturbed the familiar and the predictable. For many people, including viewers, such encounters can produce uncomfortable levels of social friction because the norms of social interaction have been violated. Yet in both instances, Moore has brought us, as viewers and citizens, exactly to the place where democratic discussion and deliberation should exist: a debate—however messy—over ideas, not in the controlled "publicity" that has taken its place in the public sphere.[4]

Unruly political discourse, however, is not the currency of news media, the primary arbiters of political life for most Americans. News is a manufactured commercial product derived from a series of accepted norms, routines, and conventions that are central to the construction of what is considered "news."[5] And although the journalists who participate in constructing this social reality can be watchdogs of power, they are just as capable of being conduits for the messages and meanings preferred and proffered by societal elites.[6] The public information officers, public relations experts, press agents, and company "spokespersons" typically at the center of Moore's filmic encounters are, by their title and functions, representative examples of the relationship between the press (a corporate enterprise also concerned with the bottom line) and the powerful. It is a controlled relationship, and one that rarely produces disorderly, undirected, or free and unfettered exchanges.[7]

In the summer of 1994, Michael Moore began to offer television viewers his own brand of news reporting that would operate outside the parameters of such controlled political discourse. First under the title *TV Nation* (on NBC, then Fox), and a few years later, *The Awful Truth* (on Bravo), Moore produced a television newsmagazine in the tradition of *60 Minutes, Dateline, 20/20,* and *Primetime.* When *TV Nation* first aired, NBC labeled the show an "investigative, comedic newsmagazine," while Moore preferred to describe it as "*60 Minutes* if it had a sense of humor and a subversive edge."[8] The show mimicked the generic conventions of the newsmagazine format, using investigative segments filed by correspondents, introductions of each by the host, and a repertoire of narrative approaches for framing each report. One difference between Moore's brand of newsmagazine and those produced by network news departments is the types of stories pursued. Moore covered topics that most news operations won't, or cover from a dominant or mainstream ideological perspective.[9] Moore's favorite topics (as repeated across all seasons of his shows) include corporate malfeasance, the corruption of the political system, racism, environmental pollution, gun violence, the prison industry, worker rights, the health-care system, and global conflict.

In covering these issues, the series was not content simply to highlight specific problems, but usually aimed its sights higher. "Even the better news magazine shows like *60 Minutes,*" Moore notes, "go after the one doctor who is defrauding the medical health system, but it's really rare that they'll go after the bigger fish and even rarer that they go after what is wrong systemically. The profit, the greed, they'll never approach that. We're unique on that level."[10] Moore's goals are to lead the viewer to see the assumptions of the system differently; to make these assumptions strange; to hold them up for scrutiny and criticism (or at least raise awareness); and, if successful, to lead people to get involved in advocating for change.[11]

The other primary difference between Moore's brand of newsmagazine and that of the networks is the use of humor to make his point. Like all newsmagazines, Moore's show employed a set of narrative techniques and reportorial conventions for presenting the story. For Moore, however, the fact that humor can be used as a weapon wielded by the weak against the powerful was central to each report. He argues, "Comedy and humour is a great way to discuss politics, not just because you can reach people who would otherwise be bored by it, but I also think it's a very effective tool and sometimes a weapon which people can use, especially when they don't have the money to fight the powers that be with the politicians in their back pocket."[12] Humor changes both the terms and the means of debate. The technique most often employed in his strategic use of humor is his on-screen persona as the hapless, everyday guy who simply seeks direct answers to his questions from politicians or heads of corporations. Yet his stories also exhibit several other narrative techniques quite unusual for traditional newsmagazines. These include staged encounters featuring costumed characters (such as Crackers), game shows or sporting contests, street theater, traveling road shows, and diplomatic conclaves (bringing enemies together, often to sing a children's song).

All of these means highlight the changed terms of debate, namely Moore's populist perspective on the differences between "us" (the common working people, including the assumed viewer) and "them" (the elite wrongdoers).[13] The ludicrousness of his scenarios often forces those he seeks to criticize into uncomfortable circumstances (or at times, so comfortable they incriminate themselves). As the "villains" seek to reestablish the appropriate terms of debate, they are highlighted as either ridiculous or agents of obfuscation. Perhaps this is an unfair tactic, as critics suggest, but what relevance does "fair" have when one chooses to play outside the rules of the game? Moore admits his tactics are unfair, but in his conception of unruly political discourse, the ends (true democratic discourse) justify the means. "Yes, we are unfair," Moore says. "We have feelings and opinions and a point of view, and we're going to be shameless about what we believe in. I think that's healthy again in a democracy. I think that's why people have tuned out to what's going on in the world these days. It is because it's all presented in such a bland way. Or people are always trying to sit on the fence. Or not make waves."[14] Moore can rationalize this by claiming his objects of investigation or ridicule are also not "playing fair," however he defines that term.

In short, Moore's approach to political discourse is a messy one, but one that nevertheless plays off the conventions of form (both journalistic and televisual) to achieve its ends. This essay first describes the structure and format of *TV Nation* and *The Awful Truth,* exploring the production aspects associated with such groundbreaking political humor on advertiser-supported television (network and cable). The analysis then turns to the various patterns of "reporting" that comprised the show, including the intertextual features that gave the programming its entertaining yet powerful critical perspective. The essay concludes by examining the importance of Moore's contribution to the nascent subgenre of political entertainment television (later honed to perfection by *The Daily Show,* but also programs such as *The Colbert Report, Politically Incorrect, The Chris Rock Show,* and *Da Ali G Show*). The newsmagazine format allowed for a critique of not only political and corporate power, but also the news media that have become ineffective agents of monitoring and critiquing that power, or as Moore says, "doing what the media should be doing."[15] Moore's play on form highlights the vacuousness of much news content, and his programs criticize—both implicitly and explicitly—the role of television news and entertainment in supporting the inequality endemic to America's corporate capitalist democracy.

TV NATION

On July 19, 1994, *TV Nation,* the satirical newsmagazine produced by Michael Moore and his wife, Kathleen Glynn, debuted on NBC. Executives from the network had approached Moore two years earlier after having seen Moore's breakout documentary film, *Roger & Me,* inquiring if Moore had any ideas for a television series. Moore reports that he believed his pitch to the executives would be the end of the idea, assuming the famously cautious television producers would find him either crazy or dangerous. Moore proposed that the newsmagazine program include a segment in which he would attend 20 different Catholic churches, confess the same sin, and see which would give him the harshest penance in a bit he called "the consumers guide to confessionals." Instead of kicking him out of the room, Warren Littlefield, the president of NBC Entertainment, told Moore, "that's the funniest idea I've ever heard."[16] The project was then green-lighted for Moore to shoot the pilot, and though successful with focus groups, the series would eventually require co-financing from BBC television (40 percent) to be shot and aired.[17] NBC decided to use the program as a summer replacement series, placing the program on the Tuesday night schedule at 8:00 p.m. (EST).

Each program was an hour in length, comprised of five eight-minute segments. As host, Moore would introduce each piece from Times Square. Although Moore would be featured in one or two of each week's segments, the show also employed numerous "correspondents" who would file reports as intrepid investigative journalists. These correspondents, almost all of whom had roots in comedy, included Janeane Garofolo (*The Larry Sanders Show*), Rusty Cundieff (*Fear of a Black Hat*), Merrill Markoe (*The Late Show with David Letterman*), Karen Duffy (*Dumb and Dumber*), Ben Hamper (author of *Rivethead*), Louis Theroux, Roy Sekoff, Jeff Stilson, and John Derevlany (as Crackers).

Each episode also included a *TV Nation* Poll that would air in the segment leading into the commercial break. Like other news organizations that *create* "news" by commissioning polls, Moore and crew decided to contract with its own polling agency in Flint, Michigan—Widgery & Associates—to conduct a more parodic take on the genre. Polls aired during that first episode, for instance, included the results such as "10 percent of the American public would pay $5 to see Senator Orrin Hatch (R-Utah) fight a big mean dog on Pay TV. Eighty-six percent of all viewers would root for the dog. One hundred percent of women viewers would root for the dog." A poll that aired during the second episode showed that "65 percent of American women believe there is 'a lot of difference' between a campaign contribution and a bribe. Only 35 percent of men see a difference."

Although Moore never explained the choice for the title, the opening montage and music suggest possible answers. As he did with *Roger & Me*, Moore deftly uses imagery and music from 1950s and 1960s television programming and advertising to refer to the dreamland of consumer leisure and pleasure that the new medium offered Americans (as well as ironically invoking a sense of nostalgia). The American Dream has always loomed large for Moore, particularly the myth as portrayed on television—a narcotic that corporations and politicians have used to promise the working class the commodity-based utopia to which their hard work would supposedly help them arrive.[18] The program opens with a montage of older news and advertising imagery, cutting back and forth between momentous historical news events and this consumer paradise. The pulsating music, written by the group tomandandy, sounds like *Leave It to Beaver* meets Metallica. The impression is a blending of consumption and nationhood. For Moore, America is a nation of television watchers. We love entertainment, and as John Hartley has put it, we are as much "citizens of media" as we are citizens of a nation-state.[19] Moore realizes that for the working class—to whom and for whom he believes he speaks[20]—to care enough about politics to watch it during prime time, it is almost necessary to blend entertainment and politics.

Yet this is not to say that Moore finds his audience stupid, or believes that they are only capable of consuming "information-lite." To the contrary, Moore contends that the audience is actually smart enough to get the cheekiness and irony that is his intent. "I end up trusting the intelligence of the audience," he says, "that they'll get it and they'll know where we're coming from. Too much of TV talks down to people and has very low expectations of the audience and I think that all contributes to the dumbing down of our society. I would rather expect something greater from the audience, and so we stick to our guns in terms of the kind of humor and the way that we want to present this material."[21] What it does show, however, is Moore's belief in the power of humor to attract and enlighten. Humor is used to "bring people into these issues, [and] make it funny so it won't be like PBS."[22] The viewers he is addressing, therefore, comprise a TV nation, and a newsmagazine show that presents politics in appealing and entertaining ways, he announces with the title, is what is being offered.

Segments in the first episode included Moore's decision to (supposedly) move the show's production to Mexico, taking advantage of the low wages guaranteed by the North American Free Trade Agreement. Other reports included a test to see if it was harder for a famous black actor (Yaphet Kotto) to catch a cab in New York than a convicted white felon; a visit to a prison built to improve the local economy, yet which housed no prisoners;[23] correspondents hunting for houses in the contaminated Love Canal; and Moore's visit to Moscow to find the missiles that were pointed at his hometown during the Cold War. Although the series covered such topics as relocating manufacturing operations to Mexico, corporate downsizing consultants, sabotage in the workplace, and corporate corruption in governmental contracts, the network owned by General Electric didn't, remarkably, censor a single segment during the show's summer run. As Moore later noted, "We actually had a pretty good relationship with NBC. I'm surprised we got away with some of the things we did."[24]

Although the series did respectable numbers, it did not prove to be the surprise hit that the network presumably hoped for (it was, after all, a summer replacement series). The premiere scored a 6.9 rating / 13 share, and ranked 54 in the Nielsen ratings.[25] Although the numbers decreased slightly as the summer progressed, industry trade magazines report that the show consistently won its time slot with the important 18- to 49-year-old demographic that advertisers covet. Nevertheless, the show was not picked up as a midseason replacement by the network. Moore and company did produce a year-end special (airing December 28, 1994) that parodied network news's tendency to summarize the year's big stories or make predictions of stories to watch in the coming year. For instance, because American troops were increasingly deployed around the world (Somalia, Haiti, Kuwait), the show surveyed people to see which country the United States should invade in 1995. Perhaps the most outrageous segment was called Corporate Aid, in which the show attempted to "help out" corporations that had received large fines from the government during 1994. Moore attempted to give a giant-sized $10,000 check to Pfizer (lying to the FDA) and the same amount in gold to United Parcel Service (OSHA violations). In the spirit of using concerts to raise money for worthwhile causes (such as Live Aid and Farm Aid), *TV Nation* put on a "Corp-Aid" concert staged on flatbed truck outside the New York Stock Exchange (with live music provided by the band Meat Puppets). The money raised was to help Exxon pay for fines related to the *Valdez* accident. The concert raised $275.64, which Moore then attempted to present to the chairman of Exxon at the company's headquarters in Dallas.[26]

With NBC not picking up the option, *TV Nation* moved to Fox, presumably with the promise of more money and greater creative freedom. Although the network is owned by conservative Rupert Murdoch, Fox had previously shown a willingness to air programming rich in social satire (such as *The Simpsons, In Living Color,* and *Married with Children*). With the move, the series kept its name and general format. The second season on Fox also turned out to be a summer replacement series only, airing a total of seven episodes. Besides the Crackers segment discussed above, the season premiere included *TV Nation* running its own candidate for president—Louie Bruno, a convicted felon; black correspondent Rusty Cundieff going to Mississippi to own six white slaves for a week (because the state had yet to ratify the Thirteenth Amendment to the U.S. Constitution outlawing slavery); "invading" a taxpayer-supported private beach in Greenwich, Connecticut; and accompanying a couple who own a business cleaning up violent crime scenes.

As it turned out, Fox showed that it was much more willing to censor certain programming ideas than NBC. As Moore reported at the time, "This show makes Fox executives extremely nervous. There's a daily phone call from them, and we're constantly fighting for what should be on the show. That means we're doing our job. If they didn't call, I'd think something was wrong, because it meant they felt safe and comfortable."[27] Although often meeting initial resistance, most of the show's controversial programming ideas were eventually approved, including "Love Night," where *TV Nation* visited various hate groups (featuring multiracial dancers outside an Nazi/Aryan/Klan encampment in Idaho singing, "Stop! In the Name of Love," and a gay men's chorus at the home of Senator Jesse Helms singing "What the World Needs Now is Love"), and "Cobb County," in which Moore visited Newt Gingrich's Georgia congressional district to see why this suburban county received the third highest level of federal funds when its congressman was the leading campaigner against "big government." Stories that were shot but never allowed on the air, however, included "Whatever Happened to Those S&L Crooks?" (following the fate of those responsible for the savings-and-loan scandal, including attending their "therapy sessions"); "Harassing Gays for Extra Credit" (where students earned extra credit in a Topeka, Kansas, school for participating in Reverend Fred Phelps's "God Hates Fags" campaigns); "Re-enacting the L.A. Uprising" (where Civil War reenactors simulated the Rodney King beating and riots); a report on those who advocate killing abortion doctors; and a segment on the search for small condoms (as Moore and Glynn note in explaining this segment, if condom sizes are only offered in regular and "EXTRA LARGE. MAGNUM. MAX," then "what about that other all-important size—*small*?").[28] All were deemed too controversial for the "family hour" of television, with the exception of the savings-and-loan piece (where no explanation was given for refusing to air it beyond it was "old news").[29]

In retrospect, what is remarkable about this short-lived series—with a total of 105 segments aired on 17 episodes over a 15-month period of time—is that it made it onto network television at all. Moore believes the reason the networks would allow a show that often explicitly critiqued the fundamental assumptions of the capitalist system is simple—money. Invoking Marx, he notes, "One of the beauties of capitalism is that they'll sell you the rope to hang themselves if they believe that they can make money [doing so]."[30] He recognizes that if *TV*

Nation had garnered strong ratings, the networks would most likely have continued to air his subversive programming. But with its airing during two summer schedules and in such an early evening time-slot, the show was never really given much of a chance to succeed. The show's ratings fell during its run on Fox, with viewership generating Nielsen ratings between 3.8 and 2.9.[31] Nevertheless, it was nominated twice for a prime-time Emmy, and actually won the award for "Outstanding Informational Series" for its 1994 season. The award was presented, ironically, on the night following the series' last episode on Fox.

THE AWFUL TRUTH

In April 1999, Moore returned to U.S. television, this time on the arts and culture cable channel Bravo. The program was produced by Canadian company Salter Street Films and financed by Channel 4 in Britain. The reformatted version of the newsmagazine was named *The Awful Truth,* and was reduced to 30 minutes in length (allowing for only two filmed segments in each show). During the first season, the show began with a new introduction that recast both Moore and the show as a socialist/communist savior of democratic thinking from domination and control by large media conglomerates. Talking over an animated graphic showing a cartoonish rendering of five CEOs of media corporations (Ted Turner, Rupert Murdoch, Bill Gates, Sumner Redstone, and Michael Eisner), the announcer intones, "In the beginning, there was a free press. Well, not really, but it sounded good. By the end of the millennium, five men controlled the world's media. Yet there was one man who operated outside their control (showing a shot of Michael Moore). He and his motley crew were known as the people's democratic republic of television. Their mission—to bring the people *The Awful Truth.*" Here again, Moore links citizenship to television, and the video montage that follows—showing a series of political and entertaining events—drives home the point further.

Unlike *TV Nation,* the first season of the show was shot in front of a live audience at the Illinois Institute of Technology in Chicago—presumably a "middle America" location where Moore's populist, working-class politics would be received warmly. Moore sets up each piece by engaging with the audience assembled in the auditorium, including cracking a few jokes. What results is part stand-up routine, part town hall meeting. Though highly edited, this town hall effect fits nicely with Moore's unruly approach to the type of political discourse he prefers. "I wanted the people at home," he explains, "to see that it's not just me and a couple of crazy people in Times Square that believe in these things.

It's like a big town meeting—1,000 people in the room and they're all hooting and hollering and mixing it up. I like that."[32] Yet despite the populist "we the people" approach, the combination stand-up routine and town hall meeting somehow sapped the filmed segments of their full humorous effect. The elements simply didn't go together very well, so the producers returned to Moore introducing each video segment from New York's Times Square for what became the show's final season in 2000.

The series retained correspondents Karen Duffy and Ben Hamper, while adding Jay Martel, Jerry Minor, Katie Roberts, and Gideon Evans (as the new Crackers). The opinion polls from *TV Nation* days were retained in season 1, and introduced simply as "tonight's Awful Truth." During season 2, however, the producers changed the formulation a bit by introducing "Lenny, The Awful Truth Bookie" (a real-life bookie who refused to give his last name, but admitted that he had been arrested three times) who would give odds for various predictions that the show's producers came up with. For instance, Lenny's "Odds that the winner of this year's election will lead the U.S. into 'A New Golden Age of Prosperity'" were 20 to 1, while the winner would lead the United States "straight to hell in a hand basket" was 40 to 1.

Also during the second season, each episode followed a particular theme between the segments. The theme for the second season premier, for instance, was "Advertiser Appreciation Night," in which the show ridiculed celebrity endorsements by having convicted felons endorse products such as American Express, Budweiser, and Microsoft Windows. The felons first identified themselves, including the crime they committed and time served, and then made their advertising pitch. Each segment (also filmed on the streets of New York) was used, ironically, as the show broke for a commercial break. The episode "Compassionate Conservatism Night" used a games motif (of the county fair variety) to pit rich Wall Street traders against each other in a sporting competition, using poor homeless people as the objects in each competitive event. The traders formed two teams—Team Dow versus Team Nasdaq—and then engaged in contests such as "Dunk the Homeless," "Pie the Poor," and "Working Poor Chicken Fight" (where we see if it really is possible to "balance our economy on the backs of the poor"). Although somewhat over the top in its polemics, the segments proved quite humorous nonetheless.

Over the course of the run on Bravo, *The Awful Truth* produced 24 episodes and landed an Emmy nomination in 1999 as Outstanding Non-fiction Series. Yet with the series appearing on a cable channel with limited carriage by cable companies, *The Awful Truth* did not have access to the potential eyeballs it did when its predecessor aired on network television.[33] Nevertheless, the series helped cement Moore's appeal as an irreverent, left-wing icon who was willing to take the fight to the enemy. His stature and fan base were allowed to grow further, of course, when the entire two seasons on Bravo were later released as a DVD box-set.

SATIRICAL REPORTER FORMULAS

Journalists are, of course, storytellers. Their job is to transform human experience into manageable, understandable, and memorable narratives that fit within the audience's cognitive and ideological frameworks. In television newsmagazines, this is no less the case. Richard Campbell's analysis of *60 Minutes,* for instance, demonstrates that the landmark television newsmagazine consistently employs a set of formulaic narratives built around three central metaphoric roles for its reporters: that of the "detective," "analyst," and "tourist."

> The detective, for instance, taps into our desires for truth, honesty, and intrigue. The analyst helps us come to terms with our inner self, with order, and with knowledge about experience. The tourist cherishes tradition, nature, and authenticity. These metaphorical transformations of the reporter offer us figures of and for modernity, carriers of ways of knowing and interpreting complexity.[34]

All of these roles create a mythic construction of Middle America, Campbell argues, a middle-class mythology that affirms "that individuals through adherence to Middle American values can triumph over institutions that deviate from central social norms."[35]

Michael Moore also employs a set of storytelling techniques designed to make sense of the world and impart meaning to Middle America. Yet Moore's Middle America is a different conception, one centered not on individualism and capitalist values, but the community of "have-nots" who are done in by the "haves" of capitalist society. Moore's vision is a populist one, a belief and rhetoric that date back to the founding of the United States.[36] The language of populism is one in which goodness is located in the common working people, who are hurt by exploitative, "self-serving and undemocratic" elites.[37] Indeed, Moore's stated intentions in his television programming are to show "complete and utter disrespect for people with money who hurt those that don't have money."[38] Therefore, when Moore examines corporate crime, corrupt politicians, wealthy elites, worker rights, and substandard health care for the working poor, he is operating from this populist perspective.

But Moore is more than simply a populist throwback of the late nineteenth century.[39] He is also a twenty-first-century progressive who opposes the death penalty and racism and believes in gay rights, gun control, campaign finance reform, and environmental protection. He is an unrepentant leftist, but as with his populist leanings, he knows how to wrap such progressive ideas in the language of common sense. His comic partisanship is obvious, but as Charles Schutz argues, humor can be used to mollify the separating tendencies of that partisanship, bringing the audience together over common things and common values.

> The comic partisan is once-removed from the immediate fray in that his claim is presented in the guise of humor. Thus, its overt aggressiveness is sublimated into a peaceful mode that pacifies the opponent while it covertly appeals to the audience on the grounds of commonly shared interests and values. The very nature of political humor as a communicative act requires its transcending of special interest in an issue and embracing a general interest of its audience. In the very act of challenging his opponent, then, the comic partisan by his humor declares for peace with him, calls upon the community of feeling, and reminds the audience of their moral commonality.[40]

While today Moore is often seen as a politically divisive or polarizing figure, the humor of his newsmagazine segments, paradoxically, almost always has this appeal to shared values and moral commonality. A display of racism by New York taxicab drivers, for instance, becomes an appeal for equality. Questioning the tactics of the gun lobby appeals to a desire for child safety. Criticism of special prosecutor Kenneth Starr and congressional Republicans appeals to a sense of propriety. The humiliation of a health maintenance organization and its representatives becomes an appeal for fairness for a dying man. And ridiculing the hatred displayed by citizens of warring nations comes across as an appeal for peace. Such appeals to common values ultimately rely on the commonsense thinking of viewing audiences—the way such end points are not seen as "political" or partisan, but rather, as worthwhile "truths" because they are simple, self-evident, accessible, and practical.[41] Again, for some viewers, Moore's tactics or persona might distract from the larger rhetorical project that leads to common values. But for others, these results are certainly more important than the means he uses to get there.

Part of the appeal for commonality is also located in the intertextual nature of Moore's televisual rhetoric. The narrative devices he uses are all too familiar to a nation of television watchers. A segment on corporate crime resembles a cop show by employing the appropriate music, voice-over, intonation, and dress of the genre. A piece on the death penalty adopts the style of NFL Films, pitting the states of Texas and Florida (and their governor brothers) against each other while employing the mise-en-scène of cheerleaders, a pro-death penalty pep rally, marching band music, a scoreboard, chalkboard, and color commentator. A report on the lack of gun control legislation in the wake of school shootings references a kid's show by employing children to embrace and sing a song with a costumed character—a big purple handgun named Pistol Pete. And an attempt to highlight class differences in America becomes a quiz show ("Beat the Rich") when Moore interrogates the residents of working-class Pittsburgh and upper-crust Manhattan on the cost of common consumer products, using on-screen graphics and bells and buzzers to keep score for the viewers at home. A TV Nation indeed!

As noted above, *60 Minutes* places the reporter at the center of each story by constructing the reporter as hero—the detective, analyst, or tourist who leads the viewer to the middle-class values that Campbell argues are central to the meaning of the program. Moore's storytelling formulas, however, are rarely centered on the reporters themselves (the prime exception, of course, being Moore, the show's only true star). More often than not, though, he and his writers and producers frame each story by using one of several types of performative scenarios. Across the 17 episodes of *TV Nation* and 24 episodes of *The Awful Truth,* a few repeated framing patterns emerge.

Beyond the technique of using other popular television genres to frame the story, the producers also relied heavily on the spectacle provided by street theater.[42] In "A Cheaper Way to Conduct a Witch Hunt," correspondent Jay Martel and a troop of hysterical women, all dressed in Puritan costumes straight out of *The Crucible,* enact a puritanical "witch hunt" on the streets of Washington, D.C., including outside the White House and on Capitol Hill. Moore accosts some Republican congressmen about their own sinful ways, while Martel paces the sidewalk reading aloud some of the more sexually graphic sections from the "Book of Starr" (*The Starr Report*). In "Funeral at an HMO," a sketch that previewed Moore's focus on America's failing health-care system in the film *Sicko* (2007), Moore conducts a funeral—with bagpipes, a casket, preacher, and hearse—outside the headquarters of health insurance provider Humana for a man who is likely to die (yet still alive) because he was denied a pancreas transplant thanks to a loophole in his insurance coverage. In "Presidential Mosh Pit," Moore promises Republican and Democratic presidential candidates that they will receive the endorsement of the show if they jump in a mobile mosh pit of rampaging youth. As Moore tells Senator Orrin Hatch, "This is the easiest endorsement you'll ever get. It doesn't require any favors, no backer meals, no dirty money; just 10 seconds in the pit with these kids."[43] And after an unarmed black man was shot 19 times by New York City police while pulling out his wallet, Moore goes to Harlem and sets up an "African-American Wallet Exchange" stand on the sidewalk. Reminding the pedestrians (with a bullhorn) about the dangers of being black and using a black wallet at night, he distributes day-glow orange wallets to people willing to exchange their black and brown ones—all while the police watch nervously nearby. In each of these scenes, it isn't the outcome (African Americans becoming safer) or even spectacle (presidential candidates debasing themselves by jumping in a mosh pit) that Moore is interested in. Rather, it is the ability that such public scenarios afford him to enunciate a political critique—in his own language and on his own terms—of the powers that be. The interest is in polemic, not dialogue, for the public square is rarely a place for deliberation and compromise.

A third formula involves the usage of costumed characters such as Crackers the Corporate Crime Fighting Chicken, who became a recurring character on the show. Beyond taking on First Boston Corporation in New York, Crackers also visited Detroit (newspaper strike), St. Louis (lead pollution), Philadelphia (banking overcharges), and Disney World (employment practices). The show also featured an unemployed Joe Camel looking for work; Thomas Jefferson heckling U.S. Congressman Lindsey Graham during an impeachment press conference; and Pistol Pete, a gun advocate. After noticing that the National Rifle Association had created a mascot named Eddie Eagle to teach kids what to do if they came across an unattended gun, *The Awful Truth* decided to create its own costumed character to appeal to children. After teaching children a pro-gun song, Pete goes to a gun show convention in Las Vegas (where he is warmly received), pays a visit to the National Rifle Association headquarters to ask a PR man to remove a gun slug from a piece of bloody meat, and goes to Congressman John Dingell's office in Washington to thank him for thwarting gun control legislation. When Pistol Pete and correspondent Jay Martel are removed from the Capitol by police, Martel concludes his report by noting, "Thanks to Pete, at least they can agree to one form of gun control. Sure, it only applies to big purple guns, but it's a start." The segment then ends with the following statistics flashed on the screen: "In the ten weeks since six-year-old Kayla Rolland

In Episode 8 of Season One, *The Awful Truth* (1998) follows a newly unemployed Joe Camel as he tries to collect unemployment and does odd jobs on the streets of Manhattan, while Moore plays the *Midnight Cowboy* theme song "Everybody's Talkin'" (Harry Nilsson) on the soundtrack.

was killed: Approximately 936 American children have been killed by guns. Nearly a million guns have been sold. Congress has not passed any gun control laws." This segment's connection to *Bowling for Columbine* (2002) is obvious; it's as if Moore tried out various techniques and foci (such as animated characters and the story of Kayla Rolland) on the show before expanding his treatment into a feature film.

A fourth popular formula for framing stories involved bringing enemies together. This usually took on one of two forms: invasion or détente. Invasion-framed stories typically involved Moore transporting one group of people (such as gays or blacks) into the space of other groups of people known for their hatred of the former. For instance, Moore constructs a "sodomobile" (a pink Winnebago) to take a group of gay and lesbian "Freedom Riders" on a tour of the 20 states with sodomy laws. The segment concludes in a square-off with the infamous "God Hates Fags" preacher from Topeka, Kansas—Reverend Fred Phelps—and his followers.[44] When Moore attempts détente, he brings together Pakistani and Indian citizens, for example, to demonstrate the ridiculousness of nuclear proliferation and dispel the conception that humans can actually survive a nuclear attack. To drive the point home, Moore teaches them a children's song ("Duck and Cover") from a Cold War cartoon used in America to teach kids preparedness for nuclear warfare.[45] In another episode, he brings together diplomatic representatives from Bosnia and Croatia to share a pizza (which they squabble over as if it were territory), ending the segment with them singing the song from Barney the Purple Dinosaur ("I love you. You love me. We're a happy family").

Finally, both *TV Nation* and *The Awful Truth* often hired a "specialist"—especially in the realm of politics—to assist in demonstrating some larger truth. In an attempt to show that politicians can be easily manipulated by lobbyists, the producers hired their own lobbyist to get a bill passed in Congress (which he achieves by obtaining a congressional proclamation for "TV Nation Day"). To further Moore's contention that politicians are "whores" for accepting special interest money, he hires a bona-fide pimp. To show the lack of alternative choices citizens have in selecting political candidates, the producers hired a convicted felon, Louie Bruno, to run for president. And simply to be funny, the show hired Yuri Svets, a former KGB agent, as their very own TV Nation Spy to investigate such issues as "who is actually buried in Nixon's grave" and finding the "heart and soul of the Democratic Party."

In sum, Moore realized that his programs would have to be comprised of much more than scenes of him chasing after corporate executives or politicians (his *Roger & Me* shtick) if he wished to keep an audience week after week. And whereas he was criticized for violating the unwritten rules of the documentary tradition through his work in film, working in television provided numerous avenues for creative freedom. First, he had a generous budget with which to interrogate a broad array of issues and topics, several of which would later be developed into feature films, including gun control (*Bowling for Columbine*), health care (*Sicko*), and corporate corruption and malfeasance (*Capitalism: A Love Story*). But with television's short form, he could visit topics quicker and easier than the years needed for a feature film on a single topic.[46] Second, Moore could make fun of the medium while simultaneously utilizing its strengths to make his points. Costumed characters already inhabit the world of television. Click the channel and the viewer will find other sporting contests and quiz shows nearby. News carries the story of warring nations and peoples everyday. Moore, therefore, uses the codes and conventions of television because they are familiar, but in the process, also highlights the manipulative nature of the codes themselves (such as the way ominous music is used to introduce certain" "bad people," but not others).

Third, a technique such as street theater combines the spectacle that is the currency of television with the openness of the street. Not only do such antics push the issue or point to an extreme, but they bring the burden of "publicness" to bear on those who might be targeted by the spectacle. When Moore enters a corporate office, the audience knows in advance that his questions won't be entertained or debated (signifying the larger social silences on the matter). The audience even anticipates the fact that those with power will drag him off the stage to shut him up. But with street theater, the process is inverted. Moore is on a public stage, and the silences of the businesses or politicians are no longer their power but their weakness. The laughter of the pedestrians participating in the witch hunt over "fornicators," for instance, thunders down Pennsylvania Avenue. The horror on the faces of Humana's employees as they leave work, not knowing whether they should walk through a funeral or stop and pay their respects, speaks volumes. And the look of disdain on the policemen's faces as Moore and the black citizens of New York express their own disgust and dismay is palpable.

Finally, the creative formulas Moore and his writers pursue show the limits of the traditional investigative model employed by newsmagazines. "Truth" is not always revealed by simply reporting "facts." As Moore noted, programs like *60 Minutes* will go after individual wrongdoers, but rarely examine the larger picture. But when *TV Nation* hosts a Corp-Aid concert on Wall Street, the program calls attention to the fact that numerous major corporations are constantly violating the law in a given year. The program adds it all up for viewers, not hoping that citizens will have read all the individual stories of corporate malfeasance buried in the business section of the newspaper and then be able to construct the larger meaning or "truth" of the matter. Moreover, traditional newsmagazines depend on the myth of objectivity to convince viewers that the stories they create are true. The use of humor to reveal alternative truths punctures that myth, and for some, that is the appeal of Moore's work. As one fan wrote about *TV Nation,* networks "usually follow a very well-established set of codes to maintain a false sense of objectivity. 'TV Nation' works by acknowledging that any statement made in a public forum implicitly carries a political position."[47]

NEWS AS POLITICAL ENTERTAINMENT: MOORE'S LEGACY

When *TV Nation* first aired, Moore seemed to recognize not only that his show was groundbreaking, but that there would be imitators to follow. In interviews at that time, one reporter noted that "Moore says it could be the first show of an as-yet-unnamed comedic genre; it's not a news-division show [for NBC], and even the entertainment division doesn't know whether to put it under drama or comedy."[48] Moore's prediction would, in many ways, prove correct. The genre of political entertainment television ("politainment") was just being born, with Bill Maher's *Politically Incorrect* on Comedy Central (1993–2002) and *Dennis Miller Live* on HBO (1994–2002) appearing at roughly the same time.[49]

But *TV Nation* and *The Awful Truth* weren't talk shows. Instead, these satirical yet serious takes on the newsmagazine genre directly employed the techniques of news reporting while simultaneously holding the industrial product known as "news" up for scrutiny. As one television critic put it at the time, "At last! News to amuse. If *TV Nation* exposes anything, it's the excesses and clichéd devices of those ubiquitous newsmags that take themselves so seriously."[50] Since that time, American audiences have witnessed numerous comedic programs that have either imitated Moore's style or taken a step further his usage of entertainment television to critique both news and politics. *The Daily Show with Jon Stewart* (1996–) is perhaps the best example of Moore's legacy on political entertainment television. Similar to Moore's employment of the television newsmagazine, *The Daily Show* simulates a newscast (with anchor and reporters) as its means for offering stinging critiques of both political life and the news media that report on it. The *Daily Show* is also indebted to Moore's newsmagazines when its "reporters" file reports from the field. Like Moore and his correspondents, they deftly use interviews to allow either bizarre people or politicians with bizarre ideas to incriminate themselves. They realize that by using the strategy of serious reporting in the right places, the satirical often presents itself without much need for further comedic treatment.[51] They also realize that there are many stories of political life that need telling, and are always on the lookout for stories that display deeper truths about the political world that structures public life. A satirical take on the news has been taken a step further with *The Colbert Report* (2005–), Comedy Central's send-up of the opinionated talking head programs that comprise much of the prime-time schedule of cable news channels (such as *The O'Reilly Factor* on Fox News).

Another program indebted to Moore is *Da Ali G Show*. British comedian

Sacha Baron Cohen embodies three character-personas—a British hip-hopper poseur, a gay Austrian punk-styled fashionista, and an anti-Semitic Kazakhstani reporter—all of whom pose as television personalities from these countries interviewing Americans. The humor most often arises because the interview subjects don't recognize that their interviewer is putting them on. The result is often a damning critique of dominant culture (and the bigotry and ignorance that supports it) through the lens of race, class, sexuality, and ethnicity. Like Moore's newsmagazines, the premise of an interview allows the subjects to incriminate themselves. And because the interviewer is unafraid to violate the unwritten rules of political and social discourse that usually structure such mediated engagements, humor results from watching these people (with almost every episode featuring a politician, bureaucrat, or political pundit) try to regain their footing within the mediated encounter.

And although programs such as *Dennis Miller Live, Politically Incorrect,* and *The Chris Rock Show* have less direct relationship to the stylistics or form that Moore created through his innovative work, they certainly benefited from Moore's critical success in showing that entertainment television had a rightful place in the broader critiques and analyses of the political world. Over a decade after Moore's programming appeared, critics now have a much harder time arguing that entertainment television "dumbs down" politics and distracts citizens from the serious business of politics.[52] Instead, political entertainment is often the best place on television for finding a true alternative to the increasingly timid news media in critiquing political life. In retrospect, Moore's no-holds-barred approach to politics and television entertainment helped to make it that way.

CONCLUSION

Moore's newsmagazines were more critical successes than ratings hits or revenue earners. Yet his foray into entertainment television proved that aggressive and subversive political critique can get aired on television (including network television) if it is packaged as entertainment. Audiences, in other words, will watch the programming *because* it is amusing and different, and social and political issues typically not covered by news agencies, therefore, can be brought to wider audiences via entertainment television. Nevertheless, with one network requiring funding from the BBC to get the show on the air, and the other more actively engaging in censoring the material, Moore demonstrated that certain ideas in a capitalist society are, as he notes in the epigraph, indeed "dangerous." Moore's programs offered a different means of thinking about such issues. By utilizing hegemonic thinking and turning it on its head, he showed that the powerful can be forced to justify their actions, and that citizens, emulating Moore and his correspondents, should refuse to accept the standard lines as adequate answers. The controlled nature of political and corporate speech and spin is challenged, and in its place, an unruly form of democratic discourse emerges. For some, the means of getting to this place might seem unfair. But in an age of spin and information management, such forms of political thought and discussion in a democracy are certainly something television could use Moore of.

Notes

1. See, for example, Tom Shales, "Michael Moore: Return of a Prank Amateur," *Washington Post,* July 21, 1995, sec. C, 1.

2. For reference to Moore's relationship to the Yippies, see Larissa MacFarquhar, "The Populist: Michael Moore Can Make You Cry," *New Yorker,* February 16 and February 23, 2004, 132–45.

3. Mike Higgins, "Guys and Dollars," *Independent* (London), March 3, 1999, 10.

4. Jurgen Habermas, *The Structural Transformation of the Public Sphere* (Cambridge, MA: MIT Press, 1991).

5. Mark Fishman, *Manufacturing the News* (Austin: University of Texas Press, 1988); Gaye Tuchman, *Making News: A Study in the Construction of Reality* (New York: Free Press, 1980).

6. John Hartley, *Understanding News* (London: Routledge, 1982).

7. Moore explains the prominent "use" of public relations people in his work: "I think it's very important that we talk to those PR people, because they're who those of you who work for the newspapers and the TV stations talk to and that's the face of the corporation. That's the person who spends their day feeding the BS line to the media, which then gets repeated as fact six hours later on the news. It's rare that the public gets to see how the PR machine works. . . . Most, if not all, of these PR people are former journalists. They now make three times the money in PR that they made as journalists. Long ago they went to journalism school because they wanted to tell the truth. They found out later that they could make a lot more money to not tell the truth." Kerrie Murphy, "Crimes and Misdemeanours," *Australian,* January 13, 2000, sec. T, 5.

8. Mike McDaniel, "Humor with a View," *Houston Chronicle,* July 19, 1994, Houston, 1; Chip Rowe, "A Funny, Subversive '60 Minutes,'" *American Journalism Review* 17 (July–August 1995): 13.

9. Whereas mainstream news media cover white-collar crime as isolated incidents of personal corruption, Moore is intent on showing how corporate corruption is endemic to the capitalist system, as well as how it is generally ignored, if not widely accepted.

10. Murphy, "Crimes and Misdemeanours," T5.

11. Moore and producer Kathleen Glynn believe the show invited participation, and they were buoyed by the relationship of their website to their show as a means of encouraging participation. As Glynn notes about that relationship during the airing of *The Awful Truth,* "It was a show that was designed to engage the viewer. You wouldn't want it on as a background noise in the house. The people who watched it got involved and wanted to see if there was anything else they could learn about or do." John Silberg, "Moore Is Merrier," *Variety,* February 26, 2001, S23. Elsewhere, Moore argued, "We're trying to ignite a spark in a part of the American public that's otherwise very discouraged right now. . . . The nightly news certainly doesn't do much to get people involved." Greg Quill, "Hilariously Subversive Moore Is Coming Back," *Toronto Star,* July 14, 1995, sec. B, 11.

12. Murphy, "Crimes and Misdemeanours," T5.

13. In the mid-1990s, populist thinking extended beyond the political field (such as Newt Gingrich and the Republican "Contract with America"). Numerous television programmers also employed the mantra of "Us" (the people/viewers) versus "Them" (liberal or conservative elites), including Rush Limbaugh, Roger Ailes (producer of the cable channel America's Talking), National Empowerment Television (a Republican cable channel), and Scott Carter (producer of *Politically Incorrect*). Indeed, when *TV Nation* went into production, Moore and Glynn report that they gave the following speech on the first day of shooting: "For one hour each week, we're going to give the average person like ourselves the chance to watch a show that is clearly on THEIR side." See Michael Moore and Kathleen Glynn, *Adventures in a TV Nation: The Stories behind America's Most Outrageous TV Show* (New York: HarperCollins, 1998), 12.

14. Alan Pergament, "Moore's 'TV Nation,' Still a True Original," *Buffalo News (New York),* July 19, 1995, sec. B, 12.

15. Ginny Holbert, "Moore Wit on the Way," *Chicago Sun-Times,* December 28, 1994, sec. 2, 39.

16. This recounting comes from Moore and Glynn, *Adventures in a TV Nation,* 1–5. This original pitch idea was finally shot and aired in the very last episode of *TV Nation* in 1995.

17. The show was always a hit in England, where it eventually made the British Film Institute's list "Top 100 Greatest British Television Programmes" of all time (ranked number 90).

18. Lizabeth Cohen, *A Consumers' Republic: The Politics of Mass Consumption in Postwar America* (New York: Vintage Books, 2003).

19. Hartley makes this point when he argues, "Audiences are understood as 'citizens of media' in the sense that it is through the symbolic, virtualized and mediated context of watching television . . . that publics participate in the democratic process on a day to day basis." John Hartley, *The Uses of Television* (London: Routledge, 1999), 206.

20. Moore says he speaks for the working class: "I want working-class people to know there's someone on TV who's thinking like they do, fighting for them. We can be a surrogate for that America." Quill, "Hilariously Subversive Moore Is Coming Back," B11.

21. Joshua Phillips, "Moore Where That Came From," *Newsweek,* October 19, 2000 (from Lexis-Nexis).

22. Patricia Brennan, "Michael Moore: At Large," *Washington Post,* July 17, 1994, sec. Y, 7.

23. Moore's interest in the prison-industrial complex was first exhibited in *Roger & Me,* where he showed scenes of a new, yet empty City of Flint jail being used for a party, where the guests dressed as guards and inmates.

24. Steve Persall, "Filmmaker Shares View on Ratings," *St. Petersburg Times (Florida),* January 27, 1995, sec. C, 10.

25. Each rating point represents 942,000 households. The share represents the percentage of television sets in use during that time slot.

26. Moore offered to write Roger Smith a check for some financial hardship in his short 1992 follow-up to *Roger & Me, Pets or Meat: The Return to Flint*

27. "The Insider," *Electronic Media,* August 28, 1995, Biography, 6.

28. Michael Moore, "What You Can't Get Away with on TV," *Nation,* November 18, 1996, 10; Moore and Glynn, *Adventures in a TV Nation,* 196.

29. Several of these episodes were later included in the two-volume videotape release of the program.

30. Alan Bash, "The Ironic Birth of a 'Nation' on NBC," *USA Today,* July 19, 1994, sec. D, 3.

31. The lower ratings than on NBC are also related to Fox still being a relatively new network at that time, a consistent fourth in the overall ratings race.

32. Higgins, "Guys and Dollars," 10.

33. In 1999, Bravo was received in 38 million households, yet its prime-time rating was .24, or approximately 66,000 households. During the second season, Moore seemed to realize that the show was really more of a British television program in its popularity and hence consistently made reference in his introductions to the British viewing audience.

34. Richard Campbell, "Securing the Middle Ground: Reporter Formulas in 60 Minutes," in *Television: The Critical View,* ed. H. Newcomb, 5th ed. (New York: Oxford University Press, 1994), 328.

35. Ibid., 327.

36. Michael Kazin, *The Populist Persuasion: An American History* (New York: Basic Books, 1995).

37. Ibid., 1.

38. Rob Owen, "'Truth' in Pittsburgh: Michael Moore Gives City Chance to Show Its Blue-Collar Stuff," *Pittsburgh Post-Gazette,* January 22, 1999, Arts & Entertainment, 36.

39. Some of the writers who worked on his television programs, however, dispute the notion that Moore is a champion of workers or labor. One profile of Moore in the popular press details several claims by former employees who contend that Moore's populist persona is a ruse, nothing more than a construction for entertainment purposes. See Larissa MacFarquhar, "The Populist: Michael Moore Can Make You Cry," *New Yorker,* February 16 and February 23, 2004.

40. Charles E. Schutz, *Political Humor: From Aristophanes to Sam Ervin* (Cranbury, NJ: Associated University Presses, 1977), 330.

41. Jeffrey P. Jones, *Entertaining Politics: New Political Television and Civic Culture* (Lanham, MD: Rowman and Littlefield, 2005), 132.

42. Again showing Moore's indebtedness to the Yippies' brand of political critique through public spectacle.

43. Only candidate Alan Keyes takes the show up on the offer. In bestowing the show's endorsement, Moore tells the viewers, "He may be a right-wing lunatic, but he's *our* right-wing lunatic. Alan Keyes—*The Awful Truth* candidate for President of the United States."

44. Other scenarios include "Love Night" (discussed earlier) and "Haulin' Communism," where Moore hires a bright red tractor-trailer rig with a hammer and sickle painted on its side to tour the southern United States for a Communist farewell tour (the truck cab is eventually firebombed in Alabama) .

45. "Duck and Cover" was also featured in *The Atomic Café* (1982), a documentary compilation film about America's ridiculous attempts to discuss and talk about surviving a nuclear attack, a film Moore has admitted to admiring greatly. One of the film's codirectors, Kevin Rafferty, was a cameraman on *Roger & Me.*

46. Industry reports say each episode cost from $350,000 to $550,000 at Fox.

47. The quote is from *TV Nation* fan Bob Boster, as reported in Rowe, "A Funny, Subversive '60 Minutes,'" 13.

48. Bash, "The Ironic Birth of a 'Nation' on NBC," 3D. In a separate interview, Moore boldly stated, "It's its own genre." Mike McDaniel, "Good News: 'TV Nation' Is Back," *Houston Chronicle,* December 28, 1994, Houston, 5

49. Elsewhere, I chart the rise of these forms of talk shows under the label "New Political Television." Both terms call attention to the new forms of television programming that appeared in the mid-1990s that offered politics as the central component and intent of their show (as opposed to the political jokes of stand-up comedian/talk show hosts like Jay Leno or the sporadically appearing political sketch comedy on *Saturday Night Live*). See Jones, *Entertaining Politics.*

50. Matt Roush, "Newsmag Nirvana, Moore or Less," *USA Today,* July 19, 1994, sec. D, 3.

51. A noticeable difference between Moore and *The Daily Show*'s model is how the latter goes out of its way to critique the idea of "objectivity" in reporting. *The Daily Show*'s segments feature the reporter making an idiot of him- or herself, getting obsessed with some detail or putting words in the subject's mouth. Moore and his correspondents rarely went that far.

52. Indeed, researchers at the National Annenberg Election Survey found that viewers of *The Daily Show* in 2004 possessed higher levels of campaign knowledge than viewers of network television news or newspaper readers. See http://www.annenbergpublicpolicycenter.org/naes/2004_03_late-night-knowledge-2_9-21_pr.pdf. While this small survey comprised of six questions only proves correlation, not causation (i.e., it is uncertain whether *The Daily Show* imparts this knowledge or whether the knowledge is obtained from other sources), it nevertheless suggests that viewers of political entertainment television aren't the "duped and distracted" masses that critics have traditionally made them out to be.

The British Take On Moore

RICHARD KILBORN

Lest readers should be misled by the title of this article into thinking that the Brits are setting up a national task force to combat the perfidious Michael Moore, let me quickly say that the essay sets itself quite different goals. The broad intention is to discuss the impact of Moore's work here in the United Kingdom. Is there something distinctive about the way his work has been received—and if so why? The fact that this article focuses on Michael Moore's reception in the United Kingdom is not to be interpreted as a wilful "turning a blind eye" to the rest of Europe. By and large, however, the response to Moore in the United Kingdom is paralleled to varying degrees in most other European countries. In Germany, for instance, his work has by and large been very warmly received.[1] Even the fact that his *Sicko* (2007) paints an overly rosy picture of health-care systems in this part of the world has not detracted from the generally high esteem in which Europeans hold him.

There can be no question, of course, that the British response to Moore's work—especially to *Fahrenheit 9/11* (2004)—was likely to have been partly determined by people's increasingly negative attitude to the United Kingdom's military involvement in Iraq. Many in the United Kingdom became increasingly concerned about what they saw as the government's dangerously close liaison with the U.S. administration over Iraq. This may explain why, in some UK reviews of *Fahrenheit 9/11*, Moore was taken to task for being so preoccupied in exposing the flaws of U.S. government foreign policy, that he fails to note the complicity of others (notably the UK government headed by Tony Blair) in the creation of an "alliance of the willing."[2]

Any attempt to assess the British response to the work of such a controversial figure as Moore will also have to be sensitive to a range of other issues, including the fact that much of his work has been tailored primarily for an American audience. Most UK critics have taken this into account when responding to Moore's work, particularly to *Fahrenheit 9/11*. Take, for example the following extract from a review published in the *Times:*

> Many of [Moore's] conclusions—war is hell, big business is dirty—feel disappointingly trite. Then again, Moore clearly composed this non-fiction blockbuster with US voters in mind, delivering a much-needed slap to domestic media bias. Tearjerking rage plays better in America than bitter irony, and *Fahrenheit 9/11* has unquestionably struck a chord across the Atlantic.[3]

The fact that Moore has been so openly and consistently critical of many aspects of American culture and society has also, of course, meant that he has encountered significant resistance on the part of many of his compatriots who are offended by what they see as his nest-besmirching activities. On the other hand the very fact that he has been a perennial thorn in the flesh of the American political establishment has endeared him to large numbers of viewers in the international film and TV audience.[4]

Given the high-octane political content of much of Moore's work, it is entirely predictable that the response to it has frequently been divided along political lines. Left-of-center observers have been broadly sympathetic to his work, while right-of-center commentators have often sought to cast him as a latter-day Satan and have railed against his alleged methodological improprieties. For many commentators, however, his work represents a significant and much needed contribution to political debate, particularly since, to the distant observer, there seems to be a relative absence of effective critical engagement in the U.S. mainstream media with a number of pressing sociopolitical issues.

For many critics in the United Kingdom the fact that Moore has been willing to take a determinedly alternative or oppositional stand against the conformist tide is one that has gained him considerable respect, even though there may still be some skepticism about certain aspects of his work. For the most part, however, he is generally included in that group of politically conscious film and program makers committed to producing work that challenged the neocon policies of the Bush administration. It is certainly no coincidence that here in the United Kingdom, Moore's work has sometimes been compared to that of John Pilger and Adam Curtis, both of whom have produced a series of highly regarded documentaries, such as Pilger's *Breaking the Silence: Truth and Lies in the War on Terror* (2003) and *Killing the Children of Iraq* (2000); Curtis's *The Mayfair Set* (1999) and *The Power of Nightmares* (2004). All these films, like those of Moore himself, offer provocative and insightful readings of contemporary political realities, as I discuss below.

Though it is tempting to pursue the issue of Moore's possible kinship with UK film and program makers, there is one area in which Moore has been conspicuously more successful than any of his European counterparts. He has, namely, succeeded—as no other contemporary documentary filmmaker—in harnessing the power of both old and new technologies—to dramatically extend his communicative outreach. Not only has he revealed consummate skill at exploiting all available traditional media (film, television, and the printed word), he has developed a highly successful website that has become a veritable hive of communicative activity (see Cary Elza's essay in this volume on Moore's website and its activities during the 2004 election). Any attempt to chart Moore's impact must acknowledge the crucial importance of this part of his work. In one sense all this website activity could be regarded as giving a more accurate "seismograph" of Moore's impact than more traditional measures of impact such as those that focus on the largely print-centered contributions of professional journalists and broadcasters.[5]

Moore's success at extending the outreach of his work is also reflected in his quite remarkable promotional ability. In spite of the occasional disrespectful comment about Moore demonstrating all the qualities of an American showman,[6] UK commentators have generally been in awe at his prodigious talent for (self-)promotion. At the same time they are also aware that there is a certain irony in the fact that—for someone who has launched regular attacks on the globalizing imperatives of modern capitalism—Moore has been remarkably adept at selling his wares in the international media marketplace. A further irony resides in the fact that no small number of those who sponsor, promote, and distribute his works are the very same people who are being targeted by his satirical broadsides.[7]

A NEW VOICE IN DOCUMENTARY?

While most UK observers have admired the way that Moore has promoted and publicized his work, there is much less agreement on what he has contributed to documentary. Within the last two decades there has been much talk of the supposed revival in documentary's fortunes, stimulated in part by the success of a number of feature-length, nonfiction films such as *When We Were Kings* (1996), *Touching the Void* (2003), and Moore's own film work. In Britain, however, there is a sense in which talk of a full-blown documentary renaissance should be treated with a degree of caution, since developments in UK-produced documentary have been significantly shaped and influenced by the world of broadcasting.[8] Changes in the way that television is organized tend therefore to have a much greater influence on the fortunes of documentary here than, say, in the United States, where another broadcasting model prevails. The radical changes in the structure of UK broadcasting in the last couple of decades have thus had a far-reaching impact on what is produced under the general label of "documentary."[9]

PUTTING A MARKER DOWN: *ROGER & ME*

It is against the background of a rapidly changing media environment and of the increasing pressure on traditional forms of documentary that one has to analyze the response to Moore in the United Kingdom. Some might even wish to draw a link between the warmth of the response to Moore's breakthrough film *Roger & Me* in the United Kingdom and the growing recognition that documentary, as traditionally conceived, would also have to change. From the British perspective, then, Moore was not only the proverbial "breath of fresh air"; he also demonstrated that documentary could be made accessible to much larger audiences than had previously been thought possible and that there were new ways of "doing documentary" that were refreshingly different from the practices developed by the old guard of documentarists.[10]

Moore was, however, not without his critics in the United Kingdom. Some were concerned about the methodological limitations of his work and his constant striving after crowd-pleasing effects. This, for instance, is the view taken by the critic of the prestigious *Sight & Sound* film magazine:

> Moore is not acting, I think, in bad faith. But he has, quite naturally, internalised that peculiarly American way of looking at the world which elevates the personal over the social, the individual over the systemic and the local over the universal. . . . By limiting himself to the death of one town by the actions of one company, easily personified by its chief executive officer, Moore has made a film which fails because it is ultimately harmless.[11]

This comparatively harsh judgement was not, however, shared by the majority of UK critics. Others were more inclined to explore the ways in which the film appeared to extend the range of documentary expression. John Corner, for instance, though accepting that the film was likely to remain controversial, was entirely persuaded by the film's invigorating potential, calling it an "extraordinary film which is likely to be regarded as a major landmark in contemporary documentary." For Corner the key to Moore's success was that *Roger & Me* (just like all of Moore's subsequent film work) was produced outside the straitjacketing confines of television, which tend to inhibit the more outspoken and invigorating types of factual/documentary work.[12] Corner's argument is that Moore's success at detaching himself from the documentary mainstream had provided a major new impulse for nonfiction work, one that could possibly have a revitalizing effect on what some thought to be a semimoribund genre.

Roger & Me did indeed pave the way for much that was to characterize factual and documentary programming in the United Kingdom during the 1990s. In particular it anticipated the progressive blurring of factual and fictional modes that became a defining feature of much of the work produced during this period. Thus it was that UK program makers—possibly encouraged by Moore's success with *Roger & Me*—began to develop an increasing number of new factual entertainment formats that spoke to contemporary audiences in a way that more traditional forms of documentary had failed to achieve.

UK program makers involved in the production of entertainment-oriented documentary/factual programming may seldom have had such an openly political agenda as Moore, but they were certainly following his lead in various attempts to extend the range of documentary's repertoire. Moore's essentially populist approach to filmmaking had meant that, naturally enough, he turned for some of his inspiration to Hollywood in order to produce work that was character-driven, rich in comedy, and full of dramatic incident. Likewise factual program makers in the United Kingdom sought to enhance the appeal of their work by resorting to similar popularizing styles and techniques. The result was that various types of docu-tainment—programs that focused on "real life" issues or concerns but that did not generally aspire to be much more than mildly diverting pieces of factually based entertainment—began to dominate the TV schedules.[13] Certainly, as the 1990s wore on, UK audiences began to respond ever more positively to these new forms of factual TV entertainment.

CONNECTING WITH THE NATION VIA TV

Though Moore has built his reputation principally on the basis of his highly promoted feature-length films, there are some in the United Kingdom who feel that his particular talents are more suited to television.[14] Moore may have scored a notable hit with *Roger & Me*, but he only became a household name in the United Kingdom when his series *Michael Moore's TV Nation* aired on UK television in 1994 (BBC 2).[15] Moore's later TV series, *The Awful Truth*, was aired by Channel 4 in the United Kingdom and by Bravo in the United States. With *Roger & Me* Moore had made a name for himself as a satirist of some note, so it is not difficult to see why television executives should have encouraged him to develop his own series built around his jovial, larger-than-life persona.

It was in the course of making *TV Nation* and later *The Awful Truth* that Moore honed many of the techniques that we have come to associate with his particular filmmaking style.[16] His principal aim in these shows was to attack, with all the satirical weapons he could muster, what he saw as the many iniquities and injustices wrought by the capitalist system in general and by representatives of corporate America in particular. What particularly appealed to UK critics and reviewers about *TV Nation* was the energy and resourcefulness that Moore displayed in putting together a program that had a genuinely satirical edge. As the TV critic of the right-wing tabloid the *Daily Mail* comments: "Michael Moore's *TV Nation* takes a sharper look at the pretensions and pomposities of the world than anything on this side of the Atlantic."[17] There was a measure of agreement among critics that what had contributed to the success of *TV Nation* was Moore's ability to combine political satire with "ethnographic" exposés of some of the quirkier aspects of American society. As Stuart Jeffries observes:

> Part of the reason for *TV Nation's* success is that it blends satire with reports which tap the strangeness of US society, like a high-class Eurotrash with a liberal political slant . . . but it is the satire which should make programme-makers here envious. British political satire is all but non-existent on our screens.[18]

What some critics neglected to mention in their generally positive response to *TV Nation* and later to *The Awful Truth* was that some of the qualities for which they reserve special praise are closely allied with the type of satirical humor that has at least some of its roots in the wider tradition of British comedy. Some of the stunts pulled in *TV Nation*, for instance, are very reminiscent of those staged in *Monty Python's Flying Circus*, while the delightful deflating of politicians' posturing pomposity reminds one of the 1960s TV satirical revue *That Was The Week That Was (TWTWTW)*.[19] What seems, then, to have endeared Moore especially to the British TV public in *TV Nation* is his capacity to reveal some of the realities behind the smokescreen of politicians' platitudes, while retaining a spirit of mischievousness and bonhomie.[20]

While Moore's principal target remained corporate America and those who represented its interests in the wider world, certain elements of Moore's critique will probably have had a particular resonance for a UK audience. Moore was clearly feeding the British public's appetite for satire at a time when British politics (especially as represented by the forces of New Labour) was becoming increasingly dominated by the news management attempts of specialist advisers and public relations officials. This may partly explain why Moore's work—with its biting critique of corporate and political elites and its well-aimed attacks on a largely compliant media—seemed to strike such a chord in the United Kingdom.

A GROWING SPHERE OF INFLUENCE?

Given the high international profile that Moore has attained, it should come as no surprise to learn that, both in the United Kingdom and elsewhere in Europe, a body of work has been produced in the last decade that allegedly bears traces of his particular brand of parodic and satirical humor. As far as UK media are concerned, two broad types of influence can be discerned. The first relates to his trademark modus operandi, that of producing a performance for the camera. The second concerns those cases where a certain stylistic or thematic indebtedness can be discerned.

In the case of Louis Theroux—a British TV presenter who has made a name for himself fronting programs that set out to expose celebrities for their fatuousness and politicians for their deviousness—there is an obvious and direct link with Moore. Moore actually helped launch Theroux's career when the latter joined the *TV Nation* program-making team. (Theroux achieved particular fame in the episode where he reported on attempts by the Klu Klux Klan to reposition itself as a civil rights movement for white people!) As a junior member of that team Theroux clearly learned a lot at the feet of the master and proceeded to borrow many of Moore's techniques in his subsequent television career, especially in the series *Louis Theroux's Weird Weekends* (BBC 1, 1998–2000) and *When Louis met . . .* (BBC 1, 2000–2002). Though Theroux's on-screen displays of deferential politeness are at some remove from Moore's all-American brashness, Theroux—like Moore—has also faced accusations that he maneuvers his subjects in a manner that is highly manipulative. At his best, however, and especially when his targets are celebrity personalities with grossly inflated egos, Theroux has succeeded in producing programs that provide some revealing insights into some of the more hilarious aspects of our celebrity-obsessed and publicity-seeking society. One of the best-remembered episodes of *When*

Louis met . . . for instance, featured the disgraced Tory MP Neil Hamilton and his celebrity-craving wife Christine. As if to illustrate the old adage that truth is always stranger than fiction, the episode was recorded at a time when the Hamiltons were the subject of a police investigation for alleged rape.

As already suggested, one of the possible explanations for the largely positive response to Moore's work in the United Kingdom is viewers' appreciation of his particular brand of sardonic humor. In a nation where special kudos are attached to being ironic, critics have traditionally had considerable admiration for those who use the tools of irony and satire to telling effect. Moore's satirical talents that came to the fore in *Roger & Me* and *The Awful Truth* have led to a series of attempts by UK critics to compare his working methods and accomplishments with those of successive generations of British satirists. Following the earlier success of *TWTWTW* and of programs such as *Not the Nine O'Clock News* (BBC, 1979–82) the 1990s arguably saw the dawning of a new era for British TV satire, one that seemed to place more emphasis on the performance ability of talented individuals. This was when Michael Moore made his first TV appearance in the United Kingdom. One might make the claim that Moore's particular brand of satire was especially well tuned to the spirit of the times and to the type of humor that was beginning to be popular. It is certainly no coincidence that several of the up-and-coming generation of UK satirical humorists, including Chris Morris and Mark Thomas, have been linked with the name of Moore. Not only have they homed in on the same satirical targets, there is even a similarity in terms of styles and modes of address. Let me therefore provide a little more detail of what these well-known UK performers have in common with Moore.

Chris Morris started his career with the radio series *The Day Today* (BBC Radio 4, 1994), a series that pointed a mocking finger at contemporary media practices. Morris eventually switched to television, where he became the lead presenter of *Brass Eye*, the Channel 4 series best remembered for its use of carefully prepared scams where celebrities and politicians are brilliantly but wickedly exposed.[21] In one especially memorable *Brass Eye* episode, for instance, Morris discusses with an unsuspecting Conservative MP the question of whether crime-prevention techniques developed by the American expert Bruce Wayne based in Gotham City might be effectively deployed in British inner cities. The trick that Morris used in his various "sting" operations was, just like Moore, to lull his subjects into a false sense of security by flattering them into believing that they would gain the much-needed oxygen of publicity by agreeing to participate in one of his over-the-top campaigns. The parallels with Moore are clear enough in that both men are concerned to expose the inanities of celebrity culture and the frailties of some of our public representatives. There is even a further parallel with Moore in that Morris too has become the subject of a sustained hate campaign when exception was taken to the alleged dubiousness of his methods.

In spite of these two performers being frequently bracketed together, one cannot claim that Morris is simply a British clone of Moore. The sense of crusading zeal that Moore displays is not there to anything like the same degree in Morris. As one critic put it:

> Morris sets up his prank to mock the mighty purely for satirical pleasure. The pointlessness is what makes them so delicious. But Moore likes to have a moral purpose, which can force him to walk a tightrope between being a hard cheese and being just cheesy.[22]

What also sets the two apart is that Morris, unlike Moore, has not been inclined to move into the political domain, believing that his particular brand of satire would be diminished if he did so. When challenged about this in an interview and asked why he thought that it was not possible to be satirical about the "war on terror," Morris commented that, while he felt that there were "mockable things about it [the war on terror]", there were for him too many risks involved in being able to base a whole show on this subject. As he pointedly suggests later in the interview, he didn't want to fall into the same trap as Michael Moore: "If you don't have the [comedy] element, you end in the position of someone like Michael Moore, building lame gags around some central thesis."[23]

The other British satirist to whom Moore is sometimes compared is Mark Thomas, best known for his TV series *The Mark Thomas Comedy Product* (Channel 4, 1996–98).[24] Like Moore, Thomas has developed a well-deserved reputation for exposing various types of institutional malpractice and capitalist exploitation. As with Moore, there is a strong "agit-prop" quality to Thomas's work that is rooted in his own strong left-wing convictions. He also reveals the same terrier-like capacity as Moore for following up a story and for holding individuals to account. He even stages similar sting operations to those practiced by Moore and his team. In one program, for instance, Thomas—masquerading as a member of a public relations company with a special remit to encourage dictatorships—succeeds in gaining access to an arms fair in Athens. Unlike Moore, however, Thomas has so far confined himself to the medium of television, a medium that has allowed him to make good use of the skills he developed as a stand-up performer in London comedy clubs.

QUESTIONABLE PRACTICE?

Given the prominence that Michael Moore has achieved and the controversy that some of his work has attracted, much attention has understandably been paid to the legitimacy of his methods and techniques. Particular interest has been focused in this respect on Moore's favored practice of posing as an apparently simple-minded ordinary guy, thereby encouraging the kind of unguarded, but often highly revealing responses on the part of those he approaches. This clearly can involve a degree of dissimulation on his part and the question arises as to whether the practice is ethically legitimate. Are subjects being cajoled and manipulated into making incriminating utterances? And furthermore, does the practice of "faux naïveté" inevitably lead to an undue privileging of the performance act itself with a corresponding loss of focus on what is actually being disclosed by the targeted individual?

In the case of television, faux naiveté can be one of several techniques employed by investigative reporters to get subjects to disclose more than they ordinarily might have been prepared to. Frequently the sought-after payoff is a dramatic confrontation between an unwilling interviewee and the intrepid seeker-after-truth. In the case of documentary, the practice of faux naiveté can be made to serve slightly different ends. It can—as the example of *Roger & Me* illustrates—become the major structuring principle for the whole narrative. This is also frequently the case in the work of the well-known British documentary filmmaker Nick Broomfield, to whom Moore is sometimes compared. Both Moore's and Broomfield's work is characterized by the regular appearance of the filmmaker in various guises, either that of faux naïf reporter or that of questing investigator. Both filmmakers might also claim that they are inviting a particularly knowing or considered response from their audience. They are seeking to encourage viewers to ponder the manner in which material for the film has been obtained and to consider the kind of relationship the filmmaker is trying to establish with their audience.

The fact that Moore and Broomfield put themselves in the frame so conspicuously also challenges the viewer into reconsidering the role of the filmmaker. The appearance of Moore as bumbling interviewer with scruffy beard and baseball cap or Broomfield as archetypally polite public-school boy constantly frustrated in his attempts to get an interview with the elusive key informant may at one level be seen as the simulation of professional ineptitude in order to activate a more sympathetic response from the subject. It can on the other hand be regarded as a useful means (especially in these media-savvy

The ethics of Moore's filmmaking: "Are subjects being cajoled and manipulated into making incriminating utterances?" Affluent women on a golf course in Flint being asked about the plant closings in *Roger & Me.* Copyright 1989 Warner Bros., Inc.

times) of getting viewers themselves to reflect on some of the processes by means of which the documentary in question has been constructed in order to secure a particular form of audience involvement.[25]

The problem for those who practice faux naiveté is that—like most other filmmaking techniques—it has its limitations and begins to lose its efficacy if overused. As one critic has observed: "The faux-naif thing has begun to annoy [even] me. Faux naiveté is a delicate craft that, when mishandled, can be very irritating. A lot of mishandling has been occurring of late, and so a backlash is brewing."[26] The nub of the critique—and it is one that has been leveled at Broomfield and Moore in almost equal measure—is that if you put yourself too prominently in the frame, you run the risk of appearing irritating and egotistical. With Broomfield's *The Leader, his Driver, and the Driver's Wife* (1991) the technique worked well, especially as the audience quickly recognized the target, TerreBlanche, the leader of the Afrikaner fascists, to be a monster. With some of

Broomfield's later work, however, the tactic becomes comparatively ineffectual, as too much attention is placed on the filmmaker's ongoing relationship with his subjects rather than on the attempt to provide new insights into the subject under discussion.

PROPHET? PROPAGANDIST? NEST-BESMIRCHER?

Having considered possible traces or echoes of Moore's style of filmmaking here in the United Kingdom, I want in the following section to explore what impact his work has had in the estimation of critics and reviewers. The first point to note is that, as a man publicly committed to exposing the crimes and shortcomings of the state in which he was nurtured, Moore has never had any problems, either at home of abroad, in attracting the attention of an audience. Nowadays his utterances have international, if not universal, resonance. Like the character of Truman Burbank in *The Truman Show* (1998), but much more knowingly, Michael Moore broadcasts to the world and the world harkens to his every word. As already suggested, much of this is due to his formidable talent for *self*-promotion, a talent that includes the gift of making it appear that he has been given a special mission to act as spokesperson for all those forced to bear the burden of real or imagined oppression.[27]

The one aspect of Moore's work on which most critics and commentators are agreed is that he has an unerring capacity for raising uncomfortable questions about the contemporary world. Moore's work has in recent years become decidedly more political, particularly where—as in the case of *Fahrenheit 9/11*—he was manifestly attempting to influence the outcome of a presidential election. One consequence of this has been that for many in Europe (both Old and New) Moore acquired the status of *the* voice of American opposition to the Bush administration, particularly with respect to what many see as the ill-judged decision to invade and occupy Iraq.

Not surprisingly, it is the critical response to *Fahrenheit 9/11* that provides the best opportunity for assessing the political impact of Moore's work. Most UK reviewers are concerned to weigh the political efficacy of this film, and some are of the opinion that the work draws attention to the gulf opening up between American foreign policy and that of most of the governments of continental Europe. Here, several reviewers pick up on what they see the politically inspired decision by a European jury to award the film the coveted Palme d'Or at the 2003 Cannes Film Festival. The film critic of the London *Guardian* offers the following analysis of this event:

> The festival hung a garland on Moore for his scathing denunciation of the president's dubious democratic credentials, the Bush family connections with the bin Ladens and the diversionary war on Iraq. *It was a spectacular rebuke to Republican and corporate America, a stunning Exocet of scorn launched from the epicentre of old Europe.* (Emphasis added.) [28]

The response of UK-based critics to *Fahrenheit 9/11* was, however, by no means unanimously positive. There was, for instance, a general consensus that the film was not as convincing as his earlier *Bowling for Columbine.* For many reviewers one of the principal reasons that the film failed to convince was that it did not fully accomplish the avowed task of a documentary: that of providing a reflective, well-argued account of events that allows viewers to draw their own conclusions from the available evidence. The other problem that UK critics had with *Fahrenheit 9/11* was that Moore was dealing with very current events. As other documentary film and program makers have discovered to their cost, the production of "instant histories" is a hazardous occupation at the best of times, especially when there was as much uncertainty about future developments as there is with events unfolding in the Middle East. As Stephen Dalton of the *Times* observed:

> *Fahrenheit 9/11* is unquestionably a bold and gripping work, but a lesser film than *Bowling for Columbine.* . . . *Fahrenheit 9/11* is at a disadvantage over *Bowling for Columbine* in that the events that are the subject of its critique are still unfolding. . . . The furor over US torture of Iraqi prisoners, for example, is far more shocking than anything Moore unearths. . . . *Fahrenheit 9/11* hits enough of its targets to qualify as an important and timely film. But it should have been a smart bomb, and it feels more like a blunt instrument.[29]

Not all critics, then, were persuaded that *Fahrenheit 9/11* actually delivered what it set out to achieve, though few went so far as Christopher Tookey in the *Daily Mail:* "There are some who think this film will make history, but really it just rewrites history in cartoon form."[30] Even those who were extremely hostile to the views being expressed by Moore were vehemently opposed to all attempts to muzzle him. As Philip Hensher wrote:

> I don't have a lot of time for Moore, whose films seem to me largely over-excited paranoid rants. But there is clearly a huge audience for his polemics, and it is monstrous that anyone should so blatantly attempt to silence him, simply because they disagree with what he says.[31]

In spite of all these condemnations of attempts to censor Moore, there were still a number of UK critics who felt that the problems that Moore had encountered in distributing the film were just another instance of him manipulating a situation to his own advantage. As the film critic of the *Observer* pithily remarked: "Politically, playing the censorship card was a masterstroke, proving that whatever else he may be, Moore is an accomplished spin-doctor."[32] Likewise the *Times* reviewer suggested that the spat over the distribution of *Fahrenheit 9/11* told us more about Moore's skills as a publicist than it did about any politically inspired attempt to silence him:

> How many times can a man be burnt at the stake? Michael Moore is so fond of portraying himself as a victim of corporate America that he is on his way to becoming the world's first recyclable martyr. . . . Moore's instinct for commandeering the news pages has paid off handsomely once again, as has his brand of populist leftwing politics.[33]

A MEASURE OF AGREEMENT

In attempting to evaluate the response of UK critics to Moore, one is constantly struck by the large measure of agreement about the purported strengths and weaknesses of his work. In the case of *Bowling for Columbine* and *Fahrenheit 9/11,* for instance, most UK reviewers lament the lack of a coherent structure and a well-developed argument in these films. Yet the same critics become almost euphoric in their praise of the energy and exuberance with which Moore presents his case. Philip French's review of *Bowling for Columbine* is typical in this respect:

> Moore's picture is about America's gun culture and tradition of violence but it is neither well argued nor highly responsible in any conventional sense. But it is extremely serious without being solemn, passionate in a deliberately laid-back fashion and both hilarious and chilling.[34]

A similar ambivalent response is to be found in many other reviews. Consider, for instance, this extract from the *Daily Telegraph* review of *Fahrenheit 9/11:*

> It's a grim film, containing all sorts of upsetting material, and whether or not one entirely believes Moore's allegations, manipulations and innuendoes, it creates a depressing sense that much of the decisive working of international pol-

> itics and business takes place—as ever—beyond the public's ken. Yet in the manner of much aggressive political satire, it enters an exhilarating arena outside that of normal democratic debate. Its mannerly exchange of facts and arguments breaks into a play zone of dangerous, intensely watchable, magnificently unfair entertainment, where matters of life and death collide with a grotesquely farcical vision of American politics.[35]

The response is representative of many of the responses of UK critics to *Fahrenheit 9/11* that praise Moore for being thought provoking and disturbing, but that criticize his work for being uneven and lacking in intellectual clarity.

What British critics like about Moore is that he represents a mode and style of filmmaking for which there is no equivalent in the United Kingdom. Thus, for all the problems they have with certain aspects of the work—especially his predilection for homing in on soft targets or some of his all-too-brazen acts of showmanship—the majority of critics are of the opinion that we would be the poorer without Moore's dramatic and entertaining forays into contemporary politics. Moore's approach may in some respects represent a flawed kind of filmmaking. He may also have to plead guilty on occasions to excessive manipulation to achieve some of his effects. Nevertheless, his films have undeniably succeeded in eliciting a strong audience response. It may even be the case that the very strength of this response may be partly explained by the great contrast between this unashamedly partisan and idiosyncratic form of filmmaking and the standard documentary fare to which UK audiences have become accustomed. As the *Guardian* critic observed when reviewing *Fahrenheit 9/11:*

> We've become very used to cool, fence-sitting documentaries without a voiceover or riskily overt editorial content: the kind of film-making that prides itself on guiding the bull elegantly through the china-shop leaving the crockery undamaged. Michael Moore's inflammatory polemic is very different. It's emotional and manipulative, brilliant and brazen.[36]

LEARNING FROM MOORE

If there is one thing on which all critics and observers are agreed about Michael Moore, it is that you can love him or you can hate him, but you cannot ignore him. For audiences at both home and abroad he has become the figure most closely identified with challenging and opposing the views of the political establishment. He has, moreover, done this in such a forceful and entertaining manner that he has succeeded in attracting the attention of a wide popular audience. Each new work that Moore produces and each new personal appearance acquires the status of media events. The Moore persona has, in short, become an established media brand. He himself has earned celebrity status both as professional "enfant terrible" and as activist communicator. Moore has thus—and the irony is not lost on him—acquired high commodity value.

As is hopefully evidenced by this present volume of essays, however, there have been a number of more serious attempts by cultural critics to engage with Moore's work. These seek not only to consider his work from a number of sociocultural perspectives, but also to assess its significance in the ongoing debate about the workings of documentary. This interest in Moore's work is by no means confined to the ranks of those who are professionally involved in reviewing and critiquing media products (journalists and academics), but includes the vast number of individuals who now participate in lively Internet debate about Moore and his work. One further result of the high profile that Moore has achieved is that his work has now begun to be featured on the syllabi of schools, colleges, and universities on both sides of the Atlantic.

What I would like to do in this final section, then, is to briefly explore a few of the ways in which Moore's work has been used in the United Kingdom within broadly defined media literacy projects. (I recognize that this is slightly broadening the idea of "reception," but I am persuaded that this approach may help to pinpoint an important aspect of the response to Moore.) The two areas of educational work I will focus on are (1) the attempt to understand more about the influence of media products in the shaping and reinforcement of sociocultural attitudes, and (2) the attempt to discover more about the workings of documentary, especially issues relating to the construction and dissemination of such work.

No one could fail to recognize that much of Moore's work reflects a deep dissatisfaction with corporate capitalism in all its many guises. It also contains an implicit critique of some aspects of American mass culture, though—as we have already noted—Moore cleverly makes use of popular media forms in fashioning this critique. UK media educators have therefore turned to Moore's work when looking for material to get students involved in a debate about the media's role in reflecting and representing the values that a particular society holds. Teachers in the United Kingdom, for instance, have discovered that *Bowling for Columbine* provides an ideal vehicle for launching this type of discussion. Writing in a leading educational journal, one secondary school teacher reports that he knows of no better text than *Bowling for Columbine* for stimulating debate on the topic of the representation of violence in the media and the possible links with violence in society. As the teacher in question enthusiastically exclaims: "If ever there was a documentary that cries out for use in schools it is the latest offering from maverick filmmaker Michael Moore."[37]

The other area where Moore has proved to be an invaluable educational aid relates to the hotly contested topic of the relationship of media and politics. One of Moore's objectives, as has been generally acknowledged, has been to point an accusing finger at the mainstream media and their inbuilt tendency to support the policies of the ruling elite. The question therefore arises about what responsibility these same media must bear for creating and reinforcing a climate of opinion where the views of establishment politicians—for instance the claim that a set of radical countermeasures is necessary to counter the threat of terrorism—have acquired the status of generally accepted truth. In the experience of many teachers of media studies, Moore's work can be used very productively as a launch pad to discuss issues relating to openly rhetorical documentaries and to how politics is represented in the mainstream media.

As far as media educationalists in the United Kingdom are concerned, getting students to respond to some of the above questions is arguably one of the most important tasks of the wider media studies "project," one of whose principal aims is to uncover the ideological work that the media perform. The two texts that, in recent years, have been most frequently used to provide an initial stimulus to the discussion of these issues are *Fahrenheit 9/11* and Adam Curtis's three-part documentary series *The Power of Nightmares* (BBC 2, 2004). The latter, which has also been screened in the United States but has not received wide network coverage there, provides a tightly argued analysis of how politicians in both East and West have systematically promoted a climate of fear and anxiety in order to help secure their respective power bases.[38] *Fahrenheit 9/11* and *The Power of Nightmares* offer media students a good point of entry into the debate about the impact that the media can have in shaping attitudes and reinforcing beliefs. At the same time, a comparison of Moore's and Curtis's filmmaking techniques facilitates an equally important discussion of the role and responsibilities of the filmmaker in raising awareness of these issues.[39]

If Moore's work can feed so productively into courses that aim to sharpen students' awareness of the media's role in attitude formation, the study of his work can be just as fruitful for the study of what—for want of a better word—we still insist on calling "documentary." It is no exaggeration to say that Moore's work is a veritable treasure trove for students wanting to discover more about how documentarists engage with the contemporary world. And as I can testify from personal experience, his work also provides an excellent starting point for the discussion of key issues relating to the production of both documentary and factual TV programming.

In recent years there has been an especially lively debate about the forms and functions of documentary; and Moore's work is often cited as exemplifying some of the problems confronted by contemporary documentarists. Here in the United Kingdom, one of the first to recognize the importance of including Moore's work in more general debates about documentary was John Corner, who used *Roger & Me* as a starting point for some more general reflections on the attempts by nonfiction filmmakers to represent reality. As already indicated earlier in this essay, Corner usefully alerts students to the potential shortcomings but also to the achievements of Moore's work. He is, above all, concerned to get students to question the legitimacy of various populist techniques practiced by Moore in *Roger & Me,* but at the same time is anxious to get students to appreciate the innovative qualities of this work, particularly when Moore's film is compared to more conventional documentary accounts of dying steel towns.[40]

If Corner was one of the first to use Moore's work to stimulate debate about the changing face of documentary, others have included it in programs of study that seek to heighten student awareness of key questions relating to producer-audience relations. Gill Branston and Roy Stafford, for instance, devote a whole chapter in one of the most widely used media studies textbooks in the United Kingdom (*The Media Student's Book)* to a discussion of the methods that Moore employs for securing and maintaining the attention of an audience. The authors adopt the bold pedagogic strategy of gathering together all the various objections that have been made to Moore's manipulative and attention-grabbing practices and then challenge the student to consider the validity of these objections. Many of these objections boil down to a consideration of how viewers are being positioned by the text and of the alleged "sleight-of-hand" methods by which Moore seeks to win over his audience. Are viewers, for instance, given sufficient contextualizing and explanatory material to reach an informed judgement on the rights and wrongs of a particular case? And following on from this question, what are some of the main ethical issues raised by Moore's work? Is he, for instance, occasionally guilty of holding up individuals to ridicule merely to achieve comedic or dramatic effect?[41]

Challenging students to give careful and critical consideration to the possible objections to Moore's work is also a good strategy for highlighting certain issues about documentary filmmaking practice, especially the question of the lengths to which film and program makers are prepared to go to win over an audience. In the United Kingdom there have been some major controversies—and also several major scandals—concerning the allegedly unethical behavior of some documentarists.[42] Moore may well have been frequently challenged about his propensity to set up and manipulate interviewees, but this is still a far cry from those more blatant instances of deceit that surfaced in Britain during the 1990s. (The most famous incident centered on a TV program *The Connection* [ITV, 1996], an hourlong, award-winning documentary that claimed to be a serious investigation into the smuggling of heroin from Colombia into the United Kingdom, but that was later revealed to have been largely faked.)[43]

In the wake of the scandals over alleged fakery and manipulation, there has been growing concern about the legitimacy of certain film- and program-making practices, especially as the increasing commercialization of broadcasting in the United Kingdom has resulted in ever greater pressure on film and program makers to deliver material against much tighter deadlines than hitherto. In the opinion of some critics, these developments—where decisions about programming and scheduling are now primarily driven by ratings—have also led to a significant decline in program quality and a noticeable reduction in the number of challenging documentaries. Others take the view that the complaints about a generally dumbed-down culture have to be set against other developments that have meant that individuals now have access, via diverse media platforms, to a larger pool of information and knowledge than at any point in human history. With these developments has come a heightened awareness of the means by which individual media seek to elicit and maintain the interest and involvement of their respective audiences. Individuals have, in other words, become increasingly media-savvy. According to those who take this view (and I count myself among them), audiences bring their own particular frames of reference to bear when they confront documentaries such as Moore's. Any idea that viewers will simply be bowled over by Moore's persuasive powers has therefore to be set against the likelihood that they will retain a due degree of scepticism about at least some of the ideas that Moore is attempting to get across.

British audiences of *Sicko,* for instance, cannot fail to have noticed that Moore's highly flattering account of the United Kingdom's National Health Service was not supported by a great deal of evidence. It may have even crossed their minds that the fulsome words of praise for the NHS provided by the young general practitioner whom Moore interviewed might not have reflected the experiences of thousands of other health service providers and users. Nevertheless, British viewers do seem prepared, for the most part, to accept the broader argument that Moore is putting forward about individual citizens' rights to receive the medical care they require at the point of need. As the film critic of *Time Out* wrote in his review of *Sicko* shortly after Moore's film had premiered in Cannes:

> Sicko offers more focus than Fahrenheit 9/11 and is a damning attack on the relationship between private health insurance and medical care in the United States. . . . There's not one combative interview in the film: all his witnesses are for the plaintiff. Unsurprisingly, Moore's analysis of the NHS feels simplistic from a British perspective, but he succeeds in eliciting a swell of national pride as he celebrates the post-war achievement of free health care for all in Britain . . . it's enough to make you forget MRSA [a so-called hospital superbug that affected a large number of hospitals in the United Kingdom], waiting times and health funding for two hours at least. . . . A better documentary-maker could craft a far more detailed and balanced work on this subject. Moore's style is unashamedly emotive and his argument unstintingly self-assured. Yet he succeeds in covering complex ideas with flair and comedy. Most pleasing is how Moore roots these different national approaches to healthcare in ideas about how lives should be lived and how governments should govern. . . . One thing's for sure: only Moore could make a film like this: one that has the potential to draw mainstream audiences into the cinema and convince them of his argument. For that, he can be forgiven his broad sweeps and bombast.[44]

Approaching Moore's work in the ways outlined above has also provided teachers and students with some additional benefits. It has furnished them with a corpus of material that has enabled them to critically engage with the whole phenomenon of factual entertainment. Nowadays in the UK, material located within the broad area of the "factual" spans a much wider range of programming than at any point in broadcasting history. In order to gain a place in the TV schedules, all factually based programming (including documentary) has to fulfill certain accessibility criteria. While some observers see this as signaling the end of documentary as we have traditionally known it, others see it as providing an opportunity for renewal and regeneration. The work of Michael Moore provides ammunition to those on both sides of this particular argument. The more pessimistically inclined see his contributions as proof of the slow decline of the "classic" documentary and the descent into a style of filmmaking that always puts striving after effects over the construction of a powerful and persuasive argument. Those who are more optimistically disposed and who do not think that "factual entertainment" indicates that the barbarians are already at the gate, look far more charitably on Moore's work. They regard his contributions as a brave though sometimes flawed attempt to produce work that combines strong popular appeal with the potential for reinvigorating political debate.

Notes

1. See in particular "The German Cult of Michael Moore," www.dw-world.de/english.

2. Peter Bradshaw, "Friday Review," *Guardian* (Part 2), July 9, 2004, 14. There was a special irony in this respect in that *Fahrenheit 9/11* was released at the very time (the first week of July 2004) when Tony Blair finally admitted that weapons of mass destruction would probably never be found in Iraq.

3. Stephen Dalton, "'Fahrenheit 9/11' Goes off the Boil," *Times,* Features, The Eye, October 16, 2004, 12.

4. Nowhere was this felt more intensely than after the screening of *Fahrenheit 9/11,* for which Moore received the coveted Palme d'Or, the first time that a documentary filmmaker had received the award since Jacques Cousteau's *The Silent World* (1956).

5. The website www.michaelmoore.com is a fine example of how a communicative activist such as Moore can remain in touch with a much larger group of sympathizers than those who are familiar with him through his books or his film and television work.

6. In November 2003, for instance, Michael Moore made a special appearance at the Old Vic in Bristol to promote his new book *Dude, Where's My Country?* (New York: Warner Books, 2003). Those who attended this event testified that it was quite a remarkable promotional performance on Moore's part.

7. Caroline Frost, "Michael Moore: Baseball-Capped Crusader," *BBC News in Depth,* March 29, 2002, http://news.bbc.co.uk/1/low/indepth/uk/200/newsmakers/1900832.stm.

8. This has arguably not only had a determining influence on the type of documentaries commissioned and aired, it has also shaped audience expectations as to what documentaries should deliver. Thus, for the average viewer in the United Kingdom the experience of watching a feature-length documentary in the cinema is still a relatively alien one. In other words, television is still considered to be the natural home for documentary. Older generations of UK viewers also look on documentary as a form of programming closely connected with the tradition of public service broadcasting. See John Corner, *The Art of Record: A Critical Introduction to Documentary* (Manchester: Manchester University Press, 1996), 9–30; Richard Kilborn and John Izod, *An Introduction to Television Documentary: Confronting Reality* (Manchester: Manchester University Press, 1997), 22–26; Paul Ward, *Documentary: The Margins of Reality* (London: Wallflower Press, 2005), 100–102.

9. John Corner and Alan Rosenthal, eds. *New Challenges for Documentary,* 2nd ed.

(Manchester: Manchester University Press, 2005), 2; Richard Kilborn, *Staging the Real: Factual TV Programming in the Age of Big Brother* (Manchester: Manchester University Press, 2003), 7–23.

10. The extent to which Moore's work represents a "significant shift in documentary filmmaking" has also been explored from an American perspective. See Paul Arthur, "Jargons of Authenticity (Three American Movements)," in *Theorizing Documentary,* ed. Michael Renov (New York: Routledge, 1993),126, and his essay in this volume; and also Matthew Bernstein, "Documentaphobia and Mixed Modes: Michael Moore's *Roger & Me,*" in *Documenting the Documentary: Close Readings of Documentary Film and Video,* ed. Barry Keith Grant and Jeannette Sloniowski (Detroit: Wayne State University Press, 1998), 411.

11. John Harkness, "'Roger & Me,'" *Sight & Sound* 59, no. 2 (Spring 1990): 131.

12. The Corner quotation is from page 156 of *The Art of Record.* As Corner (169) has noted: "*Roger* operates outside television's rules, its discourse is not anchored in the institutional proprieties of professional journalism and this contributes greatly to its appeal." See also Lynn Higgins, "Documentary in an Age of Terror," *South Central Review* 22, no. 2 (Summer 2005): 22. Jeffrey P. Jones discusses this aspect of Moore's TV work in his essay in this volume.

13. Kilborn, *Staging the Real,* 7–50.

14. Joe Joseph, "It's Easy to Be Brave while Toting a Camera," *Times,* March 4, 1999, http://www.theawfultruth.com/press/pressltimes3499.html.

15. A second series of *Michael Moore's TV Nation* was screened on BBC 2 in the autumn of 1995.

16. Dan Georgakas and Barbara Saltz, "Michael and Us: An Interview with Michael Moore," *Cinéaste* 23, no. 3 (1998): 4.

17. Peter Paterson, "Best-seller Is Brought to Book," *Daily Mail,* September 26, 1995, 31.

18. Stuart Jeffries, "An Honest Crook," *Guardian,* August 22, 1995, 10.

19. Moore concedes that his exposure as a younger man to the Monty Python shows was a factor in his own development. See Georgakas and Saltz, "Michael and Us," 6–7.

20. See Frost, "Michael Moore: Baseball-Capped Crusader."

21. Both *Brass Eye* and *The Awful Truth* were commissioned and aired by Channel 4, the UK channel that is required by its broadcasting remit to produce programming that is innovative and mold-breaking.

22. Joseph, "It's Easy to Be Brave while Toting a Camera."

23. Xan Brooks, "Chris Morris: The Movie," *Guardian Unlimited,* February 21, 2003, http://film.guardian.co.uk/print/0,,4609671-101730,00.html.

24. In later series of this show the word *Comedy* was dropped from the title, a move that some critics took to indicate the program maker's desire to emphasize the political properties of the show.

25. There are connections here with what documentary scholar Bill Nichols calls the "reflexive mode" of documentary. Nichols's central point is that in the reflexive mode it is the encounter between viewer and filmmaker that is emphasized, whereas in other forms of documentary the norm is to concentrate attention on the filmmaker's en-

counter with the world. See Nichols, *Representing Reality: Issues and Concepts in Documentary* (Bloomington: Indiana University Press, 1991), 57–60.

26. Jon Ronson, "The Egos Have Landed," *Sight & Sound* 12, no. 11 (November 2002): 21.

27. Nowhere was this better illustrated than in his acceptance speech at the 2003 Oscars for his award-winning film *Bowling for Columbine* when Moore breezily included *all* his fellow nominees in the same fighting camp, because, as he stated, "We like nonfiction and we live in fictitious times. We live in the time when we have fictitious election results that elect a fictitious president."

28. Peter Bradshaw, "Friday Review," *Guardian* (Part 2), July 9, 2004, 14.

29. Dalton, "'Fahrenheit 9/11' Goes off the Boil," 15.

30. The Christopher Tookey quotation is from his "Moore Means Less Truth," *Daily Mail,* July 9, 2004, 52. For critics denouncing attempted suppression of *Fahrenheit 9/11,* see Fiona Macgregor, "White House Scourge Moore Lifts Top Cannes Prize," *Scotland on Sunday,* May 23, 2005, 1; Sukhdev Sandhu, "Michael Moore Goes to War on Bush," *Daily Telegraph,* Features, The Arts, May 18, 2004, 18; and Philip Hensher, "Opinion," *Sunday Tribune,* May 9, 2004, 18.

31. Hensher, "Opinion," 18.

32. Mark Kermode,"Film of the Week: *Fahrenheit 9/11:* All Blunderbuss and Bile," *Observer,* Review pages, July 11, 2004.

33. Clive Davies, "Michael Moore: The World's First Recyclable Martyr," *Times,* Features, May 7, 2004, 24.

34. Philip French, "Oh Yeah: You and Whose Armoury? Film of the Week 2: *Bowling for Columbine,*" *Observer,* Review pages, November 17, 2002, 9.

35. Philip Horne, "'Fahrenheit 9/11,'" *Daily Telegraph,* Arts, October 16, 2004, 13.

36. Bradshaw, "Friday Review."

37. The teacher's quotation appears in Jerome Monahan, "The Way of the Gun," *Times Educational Supplement,* November 29, 2002, 6. For a useful and extended account of how *Bowling for Columbine* was used in an American Media Studies program see Anne Bader, "Media and Mass Culture: Moore Takes Aim in *Bowling for Columbine*" (paper presented at Webster University, October 12, 2002).

38. Victoria Segal, "'The Power of Nightmares': Baby It's Cold Outside," *Sunday Times,* Features, Culture, October 17, 2004, 72.

39. See Gill Branston and Roy Stafford, *The Media Student's Book,* 4th ed. (London: Routledge, 2006), 466–70.

40. Corner, *The Art of Record,* 155–70.

41. Branston and Stafford, *The Media Student's Book,* 466–70.

42. Kilborn, *Staging the Real,* 122–51.

43. This case is discussed at some length in Kilborn, *Staging the Real,* 131–36.

44. Dave Calhoun, "Cannes 2007—A Review of Michael Moore's 'Sicko,'" *Time Out* (London), May 21, 2007, http://www.timeout.com/film/news/1896. The medical term for "MRSA" is methicillin-resistant *Staphylococcus aureus.*

MoveOn, Michael Moore, and the Summer of '04: Marketing Online Political Activism

CARY ELZA

During the summer of 2004, tensions ran high in the United States as the nation prepared to elect a president. Democrat John Kerry faced incumbent George W. Bush, whose 2000 defeat of Al Gore involved the possible disenfranchisement of thousands of Florida voters. The Supreme Court voted along party lines against a recount of disputed Florida ballots, and the election went to Bush. This controversial election serves as the overture to Michael Moore's equally controversial documentary released in the summer of 2004, *Fahrenheit 9/11*. Over images of crowds cheering for Gore's victory-cum-defeat, Moore intones, "Was it all just a dream? Did the last four years not really happen . . . Or was it real?" Since what could be considered "real" in the news media was under substantial debate on election night 2000, as some networks called the election in favor of Gore, and others, Fox News in particular, called Florida for Bush, this event serves as a powerful opening to Moore's politically incendiary opus.

Fahrenheit 9/11, his 2004 entry in an ongoing crusade against conservative spin and corporate irresponsibility, was not just a film, however. The film served as the centerpiece of a massive media blitz, orchestrated on several fronts and with the aid (willing or not) of several different political organizations. The debate in print and television, lasting for several months, ranged from the civilized to the vitriolic, and, as many argue, ended up skewing conservative.[1] The film became an object around which discourse flourished, a moment of focused cultural attention that more or less kicked off the home stretch toward November 2. Moore's films have always incited controversy, but *Fahrenheit 9/11* coincided with an election in which the Internet played a greater

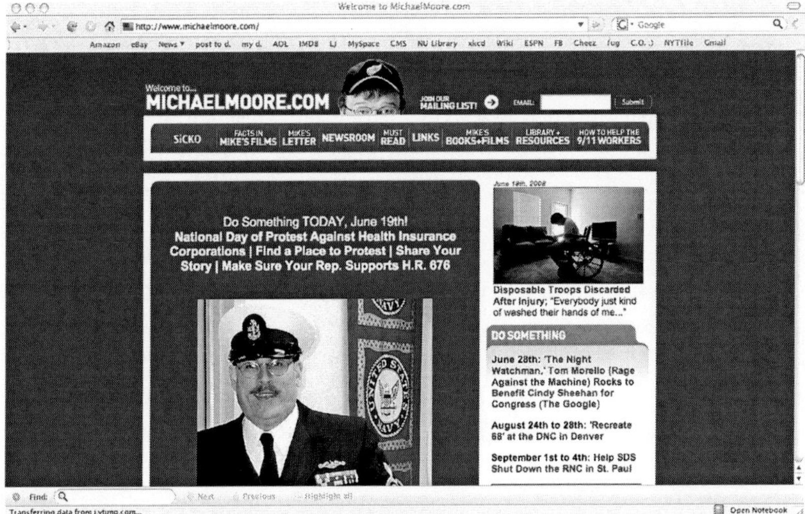

A screen capture of MichaelMoore.com's home page from June 19, 2008. Moore initially used the website in conjunction with MoveOn.org to campaign for John Kerry's 2004 presidential bid. Copyright 2008 MichaelMoore.com.

role than ever before. Michael Moore and his film became a touchstone for political action on the Internet, particularly for a younger demographic that had previously displayed little faith in their own ability to effect political change.

Starry-eyed optimism for the Internet's potential as a public sphere aside, the summer of 2004 saw a veritable explosion of Internet activism and community building, as organizations left and right geared up. Though candidates had used the Internet with some success during the 2000 election (John McCain, Republican senator from Arizona, was particularly savvy in his use of the Internet, especially to raise money), by the time the 2004 campaign season began, all major players took advantage of Internet polling, fund-raising, and information dissemination.[2] Democratic candidate Howard Dean, in particular, mobilized popular support online, even maintaining a blog while on the campaign trail. By spring 2004, advocacy groups that could be classified as 527s (not required to register as political committees, and named for a section of the tax code) were in the news because of the possibility of illegal campaign contributions.[3] One of the most visible of these groups was MoveOn.org, which graduated from its original status as a 527 to a two-part organization consisting of a political action committee (PAC), and a 501(c)(4) nonprofit called MoveOn Civic Action.

MoveOn was founded in 1998 by Joan Blades and Wes Boyd, a married couple disgusted with the unending circus surrounding President Bill Clinton's impeachment (hence the name—move on and get over it). Their first online petition was sent to 100 friends, but ultimately was signed by more than half a million people. As it became clear that the political web page was filling a social void on the Internet, Blades and Boyd, who had previously worked on a screen-saver featuring flying toasters and the online game *You Don't Know Jack*, expanded their activist operation and formed a political action committee. *Wired* reports that they "raised about $2.4 million online in 2000, which they contributed to the campaigns of 30 House and Senate candidates." By 2004, however, after a number of smaller political victories, MoveOn was powerful enough to raise $60 million for the presidential campaign, mostly from small donations. Some of MoveOn's moments in the sun included holding the first ever online Democratic primary in June 2003, and raising enough money to air an anti-Bush ad during the Super Bowl (CBS wouldn't broadcast the commercial, which depicted child labor, but the $2 million MoveOn raised was spent on airing it in swing states later in the spring).[4]

Central to MoveOn's success was its emphasis on power in numbers, in a peer-to-peer, user-friendly approach to political action. In what seemed like a counterintuitive move, MoveOn used the Internet to put personal contact back into politics. Adam Ruben, the MoveOn field director, noted in an interview, "'Politics used to be a face-to-face process. . . . Then advertising and TV and voice mail took over, and people stopped talking to their neighbors about political issues.' MoveOn found that making personal contact with a fellow American, even a total stranger, is far more effective than mass media campaigns, Ruben said: 'Face-to-face is still the most effective way to influence someone.'"[5]

When they said face-to-face, they meant it; part of the group's success came from encouraging members to meet each other in person, at parties hosted by other members. Around the time of *Fahrenheit 9/11*'s release, MoveOn placed great value, too, on its ActionForum software, which replaced a traditional online message board, and allowed members to vote on issues and decide which deserved the organization's attention. For users, this could seem both overwhelming (by the summer of 2006, for instance, the number of ActionForum comments was over 22,000) and liberating; although relevant issues were ultimately chosen by MoveOn staff, every member had input.[6] Of course, MoveOn also owed a huge part of its success to good ol' mass media campaigns. While a large percentage of MoveOn's actions relied on this sort of person-to-person contact, the organization also demonstrated masterful spinning skills, from organizing letter-to-the-editor campaigns to holding contests for original commercial creation—even something as simple as holding protests or vigils guaranteed to get on the news constitutes an example of mass-media manipulation. When the influence of the media comes from a large group of citizens instead of a small conspiratorial cadre, however, politicos take note: something different is happening, and it's happening because of the Internet.

Meanwhile, down the block but arguably in the same virtual neighborhood as MoveOn, a personal web page for polemicist documentarian Michael Moore was also bracing for a fight in the summer of 2004. By this time Moore was famous for his wildly liberal yet irreverently comic documentary and writing style, and was also no stranger to online politics. Moore had a long history of using the Web for activist purposes—searching Webarchive.org shows his site active since 1998, and according to an online article by Mark Glaser, the domain name itself was originally registered by a Moore fan in 1995 who voluntarily gave it up to Moore.[7] In February 2002, Moore, in the midst of a battle to get his book *Stupid White Men* published, posted a call for help on the website: "We don't have the money to do the site properly and have considered shutting it down (which we'd rather not do). For instance, I would love to post a daily journal from my book tour. How do you do that? But, if any of you know HTML and have a little time to spare to teach me or help me make this site a better site for people to use, then I would love to hear from you. Write me at mmflint@aol.com."[8] Moore's folksy tone here characterizes most, if not all, of his missives on the site, and accounts for part of his success. His carefully honed good-guy, friend-of-the-common-man persona and casual demeanor are well suited to a site that believes in the utopian promise of the Internet for community building and political action. On his site, just as in his films, Mike is everyone's buddy—as long as they're on his side.

When *Stupid White Men* was published, web design and hosting had been the project of Moore and his friend Ray Simon, author of *Mischief Marketing*. Shortly thereafter, his friendly solicitation for help was answered by a Montreal-based web design company called Plank Multimedia. His success with *Stupid White Men* probably had something to do with the need for heavy-duty professional web design—Plank's website boasts that between March 2002 and October 2004, the site's web traffic increased 2,600%. The site is also hosted by a Canadian company, Calgary-based Webcore.[9] I will discuss the site itself in greater depth later, but suffice it to say here that the site in 2004 combined two bloglike features, one written by Moore and one maintained by guest bloggers, news feeds in several different categories (Iraq war, coming elections, general interest), and a variety of links to activist organizations and movements. The site also served in 2004 to expand on *Fahrenheit 9/11* and allowed Moore to document fully and completely every moment of the film, acting as a giant, interactive works-cited page. Leading up to, during, and after the *Fahrenheit 9/11* fracas (which understandably blurred into the 2004 presidential campaign), Moore used the Web to mobilize his own army of supporters, to enflame and respond to his detractors, and to increase the reach of his controversial film by harnessing the power of the media on several fronts. Moore's online campaign ran parallel to and often coincided with MoveOn's. From pledges to see the film to virtual and real-world community gatherings, MoveOn and Moore made the Internet work for them.

This essay explores the online events of summer 2004, focusing primarily on MichaelMoore.com, but also on the part MoveOn played in the *Fahrenheit 9/11* brouhaha. By looking at archived pages of MichaelMoore.com and MoveOn.org, responses to MoveOn, Moore, and his film in the mainstream and independent press, and interviews with major players, I intend to unpack the meaning and social significance of *Fahrenheit 9/11*—not necessarily in terms of the film itself, but the online politics that surrounded it. As a turning point in the intersection of political action and Internet community-building, the event demonstrates the lasting impact 2004's online politics have had on subsequent elections, and the logic and rhetoric at work behind successful grassroots activism in a plugged-in society.

PUBLIC SPHERE OR REDACTIONAL SOCIETY?

New media scholars have repeatedly invoked the notion of the "public sphere" first described by philosopher and sociologist Jürgen Habermas in order to wax poetic about the democratic possibilities of the Internet. Other scholars have, of course, countered with arguments about the digital divide, about the impossibility of a technological utopia, about corporations' colonizing of the Web, and about the replication of issues of class and taste in online social atomization. But Habermas's idea has academic stamina, and any discussion of online activism should pay heed to his concept of citizenship. In *The Structural Transformation of the Public Sphere*, he writes: "The bourgeois public sphere may be conceived above all as the sphere of private people come together as a public; they soon claimed the public sphere regulated from above against the public authorities themselves, to engage them in a debate over the general rules governing relations in the basically privatized but publicly relevant sphere of commodity exchange and social labor." He goes on to suggest that "people's public use of their reason" forms the backbone of this rise in civic action, which he argues occurred in the seventeenth and eighteenth centuries, because of a variety of factors, not the least of which was the growth of capitalism, which widened the gaps between classes, and the rise of mass media, with its associated commodification of culture.[10] Habermas's concept has been roundly criticized for its exclusion of issues of, for instance, gender and race, but it remains a useful model for describing utopian visions of public discourse.

Whether or not Habermas's public sphere has the potential to be reborn in the twenty-first century, to rise on the Internet like a phoenix out of the ashes of corporate media empires, is certainly up for debate, but the concept of a free and open forum for political discussion undoubtedly drives online activism. Why expend so much effort otherwise? A truly fair and balanced future requires a bit of the aforementioned starry-eyed optimism. And much of this optimism comes from new media scholars. In their introduction to *Democracy and New Media,* Henry Jenkins and David Thorburn write:

> The current diversification of communication channels . . . is politically important because it expands the range of voices that can be heard in a national debate, ensuring that no one voice can speak with unquestioned authority. Networked computing operates according to principles fundamentally different from those of broadcast media: access, participation, reciprocity, and many-to-many rather than one-to-many communication.[11]

The Internet may not be a public sphere in the strictest sense, but it does fill some of the same functions: it operates (though certainly not entirely) beyond the control of the state, it enables debate with the state over relevant issues, and it is fueled by the power of people's own reason (ostensibly). But the idea that the people should be able to interact with authoritative figures and bodies would have pleased the founding fathers; other models for democratic political culture include the New England-based "town meeting." This process of give-and-take is not, however, restricted to purely political actions, such as voting. In fact, democratic political action and social change take place in many other arenas, including popular entertainment. John Hartley compares television to a "republic of letters," a concept bandied about in political theory for hundreds of years, but essentially "characterized by the interaction between authorial voices on the one hand, and a readership, often vast, on the other." He argues that television is just as republican as print has been in the past, and that the two media developed along very similar lines with regard to the relationship between author(s) and audience. Central to his thesis is the idea that "the platform of the medium—print, screen, or interactive—was less crucial for the purposes of citizenship than its speed, ubiquity, and the perceived trustworthiness of its information."[12] Furthermore, he argues, the Internet has developed along these same lines.

We still run into the problem, though, of MoveOn's now-defunct Action-Forum. While the mechanism for an electronic republic of letters appeared to be in place in the summer of 2004, what average Joe Citizen would have the time or inclination to read all 22,000 posts? Enter Hartley's useful figure of the redactor: "In any textual system undergoing massive expansion, a major priority is for someone to sort out order from chaos. This is what the redactor does." He continues:

> Redaction is a form of production not reduction of text (which is why the more familiar term "editing" is not adequate). Indeed, the present day could be characterized as a redactional society, indicating a time when there is too much instantly available information for anyone to see the world whole, thus resulting in a society that is characterized by its editorial practices, by how it uses the processes of corporate and governmental shaping of existing materials to make sense of the world. Individual authorship itself is increasingly redactional in mode. The most trusted and most visited sources of truth are not individuals but organizations, from CNN to the *Guardian Unlimited* Web site, depending on your preferences. It is redaction, not original writing (authorship) as such, that determines what is taken to be true, and what policies and beliefs should follow from that.[13]

I quote this passage at length because it shines particular light on Michael Moore and MoveOn. Few would dispute that Moore's filmic style tends toward the redactional—he recombines video clips, documents, found footage, and sound bites, many of which were discarded as valueless by the redactional mainstream press. By picking and choosing preexisting media material and giving it a new editorial slant, Moore's films conform nicely to Hartley's definition. This process also sounds a lot like postmodernism, but that's the point; in a information-saturated culture, a decoupage of other people's material can produce something new and singularly valuable.

On the Internet, though, Moore's role as redactor is just as apparent. MichaelMoore.com consists of a front page with several different sections, most of which were updated daily (and still are, as of this writing) by Moore's web team, headed by editor David Schankula. The "This Just In" and "The '06 Fix" windows contained news feeds with relevant information—the former including stories of injustice, the Iraq war, protests, and the like, and the latter restricted to campaign news for midterm elections. The "Bring Them Home Now" section kept a running tally of American soldiers wounded and killed in Iraq, and "More Soldiers' Letters" expanded on Moore's book of letters from the war. "Do Something" contained frequently updated news on protests and activism. "Must Read" was the site's guest blog, and "Mike's Letter" was Moore's commentary, which will be covered in greater depth below. The overall effect was of a liberal Democrat's (or independent's) news digest, combining on-topic news feeds with other, harder-to-find information related to activism. Although the news stories Moore's site featured did appear in the mainstream press, they typically counted as second- or third-tier news, and hence did not receive the prominent coverage Moore gave them. Stories like these function in much the same way that the chronicling of personal experiences, like grieving mother Lila Lipscomb's in *Fahrenheit 9/11,* does in his films: human interest stories are not only entertaining for the viewer or reader, but also shift the message of injustice away from the abstract and give it a face.

Similarly, MoveOn.org acted as a redacting organization, but in a slightly different manner. Not only could the site be considered a clearinghouse for important activist news, but at the time of *Fahrenheit 9/11*'s release, the aforementioned ActionForum software teemed with issues and begged for moderation. Not every issue was appropriate for MoveOn's wrath. MoveOn itself noted in ActionForum's FAQ that "MoveOn monitors the forum for input several times a day and uses the information to help set their agenda. Comments that are of immediate relevance are forwarded to the appropriate team member usually within hours." In this way, MoveOn redacted not only news stories from mainstream press, but also the thousands of comments of its own members (though not always successfully; see note 6). Their main page was less a compendium of news items than a listing of current campaigns being conducted by their political action committee and civic action division. But these campaigns represented the end product of a process of redaction that began with ActionForum, followed news leads and filtered through the MoveOn organization until it resulted in plans for activism. The *Pittsburgh Post-Gazette* noted in 2003, "The group chooses its issues carefully and tries to distill information about those issues to its members in a simple, common-sense way," and quoted Eli Pariser, one of MoveOn's campaign directors, as saying "the organization chooses issues 'that make sense to people outside the [Washington, D.C.] Beltway. We try to work on issues that are important to people, that we can make a difference on, and that people are already thinking about a bit.'"[14] During the summer of 2004, MoveOn singled out *Fahrenheit 9/11* as a worthy recipient of its considerable activist clout, and Pariser directed the charge.

A *FAHRENHEIT 9/11* TIME LINE

For both MoveOn.com and MichaelMoore.com, action and discourse took place around texts—news stories, films, commercials. Arguably, behind every movement toward political change is a text that alerted activists to the problem in the first place, whether it be a letter to the editor, an Associated Press article, or a politically charged film. Hartley quotes Joké Hermes' article "Cultural Citizenship and Popular Fiction" to further point out that community-based enjoyment or use of cultural texts constitutes a form of citizenship: "Citizenship also needs to be understood as intrinsically mediated practices" and "cannot be defined as the membership of one community only.... Individuals can be competent participants in different communities fully aware that codes or ideologies clash but not particularly concerned about this." In other words, citizenship can and should involve something as simple as gathering around a meaningful text, and producing reasoned discourse.[15] Different texts result in different discourses, and it is possible to participate in several at once, adapting one's voice and rhetoric to the rules of each community. MoveOn.org and MichaelMoore.com both singled out *Fahrenheit 9/11* as one of these texts—not particularly surprising for the latter, since Moore wrote and directed the movie. Thanks to its politically provocative subject matter, the film spawned dozens of subsidiary texts that generated discourse in their own right and ranged from letters to the editor and newspaper articles to online treatises.

As the figure at the center of the controversy, Michael Moore responded by stepping up his efforts to bring information to the public on the Internet, and repeatedly casting himself in the role of David, up against corporate Goliaths. Prior to the film's release, he regularly updated the "Mike's Letter" section of his website, keeping visitors informed about his battles with the Disney Corporation, which funded the film. Mike's address to his troops was a rallying point, a site of common purpose. Each letter dealt with topics relevant to the impending release of *Fahrenheit 9/11* and the Man trying to keep Moore and his film—

and by extension, the common man—down. The Man was first Mel Gibson's Icon Productions, which decided not to finance the film, then Disney, which under Michael Eisner refused to let boutique subsidiary Miramax distribute it. "Dear Friends," Moore writes in his blog on May 5, 2004,

> Yesterday I was told that Disney, the studio that owns Miramax, has officially decided to prohibit our producer, Miramax, from distributing my new film, "Fahrenheit 9/11." . . . The whole story behind this (and other attempts) to kill our movie will be told in more detail as the days and weeks go on. For nearly a year, this struggle has been a lesson in just how difficult it is in this country to create a piece of art that might upset those in charge (well, OK, sorry—it WILL upset them . . . big time. Did I mention it's a comedy?). All I can say is, thank God for Harvey Weinstein and Miramax who have stood by me during the entire production of this movie.

And on May 7: "Thank you for all the incredible letters of support as my film crew and I once again slog our way through the corporate media madhouse. Does it ever end? Are we ever going to get control of our 'free press' again? Can you wish upon a star?"[16] Although Moore did not maintain a message board in 2004, he did provide his e-mail address, and encouraged people to send comments.[17] The May 7 statement suggests that mail is read and considered, and also that visitors to his site did, in fact, rally around his May 5 letter, at least enough to express their support. In these posts, he repeatedly refers to "*our* movie," to the fight that "*we*" have to fight, implicitly including the reader in his struggles. Moore put his own experience at the center of his online publicity campaign, just as he and his image as fervent protector of the working man appear at the center of his films. His opposition to General Motors in *Roger & Me,* like the fight against the Bush administration in *Fahrenheit,* allows him to appear almost as a martyr, a heroic little guy struggling to hold institutions accountable for their transgressions. At the same time, his "we're all in this together" rhetoric calls attention to his populist goals. By placing himself first and foremost in his films and on his website, Moore encouraged viewers and users to associate themselves with the ideals of social justice he espouses, all while keeping them entertained with his snappy, down-home brand of sarcastic humor.

As Disney dealt with an outpouring of disgust from the public and, especially, the *New York Times* at its decision not to distribute the film, Disney finally relented and allowed the rights to be sold to Lions Gate Films and IFC

Films.[18] But more obstacles followed, of course. According to several articles on the film prior to its release, Howard Kaloogian's conservative activist group Move America Forward lobbied hard to keep the film out of theaters; the *Pittsburgh Post-Gazette* reports, "On the right, Move America Forward equated it to an al-Qaida training video and launched a campaign to keep it out of theaters. Fox News' Bill O'Reilly took it up a notch, comparing it to the propaganda of Joseph Goebbels" (harsh, but implicit in O'Reilly's statement was a previous MoveOn ad comparing Bush to Hitler).

Responding to all this, Moore wrote in his June 18 letter:

> A Republican PR firm has formed a fake grassroots front group called "Move America Forward" to harass and intimidate theater owners into not showing "Fahrenheit 9/11." . . . Please, contact your local theaters and let them know you want to see "Fahrenheit 9/11." Tell them that some people don't know that this is America and that we believe in freedom of speech and the importance of ALL voices being heard. (The members of MoveOn.org—an ACTUAL grassroots organization—have done a very cool thing. They are pledging to send a message to theater owners and are planning to attend a showing of the film on its opening weekend). I appreciate their efforts, but you don't have to be a member of MoveOn to help stop this effort to keep "Fahrenheit 9/11" from making it to screens across the country.[19]

Move America Forward played directly into Moore's need to maximize publicity during the week before the film's release, and in encouraging fans to come together against a common foe, he found one of the most effective ways to leverage support. The harder a time Goliath corporations gave him, the more his chosen role as David was secured. Such publicity-garnering practices, like the film itself, drew criticism from anti-Moore and conservative sites such as Moorewatch.com, which used *Fahrenheit 9/11*, Moore's web presence, and the associated media frenzy as a call to arms. Not unlike MoveOn's use of the film, right-leaning sites and pundits encouraged readers to band together against the liberal agenda, which both helped Moore's box-office sales and may have galvanized Bush supporters into taking advantage of the political possibilities of the emerging blogosphere.[20]

For MoveOn, the film was a highly visible rallying point that led to political action. In the weeks preceding the film's release, MoveOn members were contacted by e-mail and asked to pledge to see the film on opening night. A June 16, 2004, letter from Eli Pariser, director of MoveOn PAC, urged members to sign a pledge and recruit family and friends to see it as well. A week and a half later, on the day of the film's opening, Pariser updated members: "When *Fahrenheit 9/11* opened in New York on Wednesday, it broke box-office records. . . . And tonight, despite the right-wing campaigns to stop it, it will open at over 800 theaters across the country—totally unprecedented for a documentary. Well over one hundred thousand MoveOn members will be there over the course of the weekend, and we hope you can come, too." The relative success of the film—it was number one at the box office that weekend, and according to the *New York Times* was "the highest-grossing documentary of all time on its first weekend in release, taking in $21.8 million as it packed theaters across the country"—gave MoveOn the oomph it needed to harness members' support for the film and turn it into real action. Pariser's June 25 letter notes that the film's opening weekend "is just the beginning. On Monday night, tens of thousands of MoveOn members are gathering at house parties across the country in 'Turn Up the Heat,' a nation-wide virtual town meeting with Michael Moore. Together, we'll take the enormous momentum of *Fahrenheit 9/11* and channel it into strategic action to win back the White House."[21]

In addition to soliciting pledges to see the film, MoveOn orchestrated a letter-to-the-editor campaign that provided prewritten letters for members to send into their local newspapers.

Byron York writes in his book *The Vast Left Wing Conspiracy*, a chapter of which was excerpted for the *National Review Online*, that "scores of newspapers around the country printed the letters as if they had been written by the people who sent them. One letter, for example, found its way into the *Boston Globe*, the *Chicago Sun-Times*, the *Arizona Republic*, the *Fresno Bee*, and about a dozen other papers." A LexisNexis search confirms York's findings, and then some. One of these form letters, for example, stated: "Watching Michael Moore's new movie, 'Fahrenheit 9/11,' is a perfect way to practice some of our most important freedoms. When we watch and talk about the film, we exercise our freedom to be informed, to debate freely and to form our own opinions of the actions of our government."[22] This letter also appeared in the *Sacramento Bee*.

On top of this, MoveOn members volunteered to hand out flyers depicting Michael Moore and George W. Bush holding hands on the White House lawn, with copy that read, "You've seen the movie. You laughed. You cried. Now what are you going to do about it? For starters, we invite you to join Michael Moore for 'Turn Up the Heat: A National Town Meeting' this Monday evening, June 28th." "Turn Up the Heat," a joint Michael Moore-MoveOn project, was obviously the centerpiece of the activism surrounding the film. MoveOn encouraged members to sign up to host house parties during the weeks leading up to the film's release, and then posted information about local parties on their website. On the night of June 28, some 55,000 people gathered at 4,600 house parties to watch a live web broadcast from Moore and MoveOn that capitalized on the enthusiasm raised by the film, mobilizing thousands of members to help in registering new voters. "Turn Up the Heat" was especially interesting in its use of new technology to allow real-time interaction between Pariser, MoveOn founder Joan Blades, and Michael Moore on one end, and thousands of MoveOn members at house parties across the nation on the other. While Pariser, Blades, and Moore spoke over the Internet, Pariser encouraged participants to ask questions by typing them into dialogue boxes, then later in the broadcast asked members to volunteer to host phone bank parties to register voters. The specialized meeting software allowed participants to see a real-time U.S. map with colors representing the density of people volunteering to make phone calls. MoveOn reported that these phone bank parties managed to register over 14,000 new voters in battleground states.[23]

Near the end of the broadcast, Moore asked everyone to pledge to contribute to the cause of ousting Bush. As a parting remark, Moore congratulated attendees for taking action: "You did something historic, and now it's a roller coaster that they can't stop. And I'm glad all of us are on for the same ride here. Because all of us have just one vote, but all of us together, we are the majority." In a similarly laudatory manner, Pariser explained in an e-mail to members why MoveOn chose to throw its weight behind the film:

> We launched this campaign around *Fahrenheit 9/11* because to the media, the pundits, and the politicians in power, the movie's success will be seen as a cultural referendum on the Bush administration and the Iraq war. Together, we have an opportunity to knock this ball out of the park—to powerfully prove that when someone has the courage to publicly speak the truth, the American people will be right behind them.[24]

The numbers show that *Fahrenheit 9/11* was a popular film for certain Americans, and MoveOn ran a valuable campaign to channel the film's success into tangible results—registering voters. The film does not directly endorse John Kerry for president, but the message is clear. And while Moore had been using the Web for activist organization for some time, the partnership with MoveOn and the timeliness of the election allowed him to paint a vivid picture of what "taking action" might look like. Although the 2004 election went to Bush,

MoveOn considered its 2004 actions successful. To fully explain the importance of this event for democracy on the Internet, though, requires unpacking exactly why these efforts worked. By heaping praise on those who participated in the project, MoveOn and Michael Moore were fulfilling their end of the bargain—allowing members to feel like better people, and also like part of a community. These were, and are, vital components in the effectiveness of online activism, which also makes participation in the political process easy and entertaining.

BETTER LIVING ONLINE

MoveOn and Michael Moore praised true believers with good reason: taking part in political action, even online, is the mark of an informed citizen. Wyatt Galusky addresses the ways in which people, as citizens and users of the Internet, use the potentially politically empowering information given to them by watchdog sites. Rather than mindlessly absorbing all information available to them, "People need not, and indeed do not, take information at face value. They will critically engage the data and make more use of them as they see fit . . . access to more information, to the bevy of contradictions and contrary expert pronouncements on everything from diet to death, forces people to craft their own expertise for themselves." Galusky attributes this concept to Anthony Giddens's work on modernity and identity, and further argues that the user of "empowering" information online chooses *how* to incorporate a variety of information into his or her life, and essentially becomes his or her own expert. "The individual as expert, in this context, is an adjudicator between competing claims, cobbling together a hodgepodge of pronouncements on a variety of issues that he was told to be concerned about."

Since no visitor to an activist web page such as MoveOn.org or MichaelMoore.com can be reasonably expected to visit *only* that page, each user, surfing an indeterminate number of politically oriented sites, chooses whom to believe on a variety of issues, and then what to do about the knowledge she has gathered. And although Galusky is talking specifically about online environment groups (specifically Scorecard.org) that provide raw data to individuals and organizations and encourage them to use it for local activism, his point that the presentation of data, which "inserts a layer of analysis" and "constructs the potential visitor as citizen," is an important one.[25] Scorecard.org, an online database of local environmental statistics, and MoveOn.org or MichaelMoore.com are not the same animals. But each adds a layer of analysis to a collection of important facts, which are presented in an easy-to-understand format in order to maximize the user's ability to use that information for action in his or her own local area. Of course, this is in some ways a utopian vision of how citizens might use activist sites—it grants every user a power of reason or willingness to use it that he or she might not have—but people, generally speaking, are not automatons, and ought to be given the benefit of the doubt.

So here we have two somewhat different modes of making sense out of the cacophony of information online: on the one hand, we have the redactor, the singular authoritative figure or group that digests and interprets and rebroadcasts for the easy consumption of the user-viewer. On the other hand, we have the user-viewer taking those digests and choosing exactly how to use them. These models of information consumption are not mutually exclusive, though, and the one actually begets the other. By redacting in a way that speaks to the particular needs of a demographic—for the sake of argument, let's call this demographic "Americans between the ages of 18 and 34 who watch *The Daily Show*"—the redacting agent can be reasonably sure that the information it is providing will be absorbed by a particular audience who will react in the same way it usually reacts to popular culture. In other words, the redactor can reasonably predict how the audience will critically engage with the data it has presented in a certain way. For Internet activism, this means that if relevant information texts around which to rally, and so on, are offered up in a format and with a tone that appeals to users' desires to (*a*) feel improved in some way, whether educationally or morally, (*b*) be part of a community of like-minded peers, and (*c*) be entertained, then political action can be achieved.

Activism requires savvy marketing, and the ubiquity of such marketing also begs the question of how this relates to postmodern theory. To further complicate the figures of the redactor and the expert citizen, in his book *Simulacra and Simulation* Jean Baudrillard argues: "Today what we are experiencing is the absorption of all virtual modes of expression into that of advertising." By advertising, he means the removal of all real meaning and the reduction of every iota of culture into surface gloss, to put it simply:

> Propaganda becomes the marketing and merchandising of idea-forces, of political men and parties with their "trademark image." Propaganda approaches advertising as it would the vehicular model of the only great and veritable idea-force of this competing society: the commodity and the mark. This convergence defines a society—ours—in which there is no longer any difference between the economic and the political, because the same language reigns in both, from one end to the other.[26]

MoveOn and MichaelMoore.com are brands like anything else; simply by virtue of lending their redactional support to a cause or a text, they stamp that idea with a seal of approval.

What's more, as activist groups whose influence increases as more people participate, both also advertise for membership in a group that carries along with it a whole field of social associations. Cultural studies scholars differ on how to explain this—Bourdieu's concept of fields is especially useful—but even the casual observer would note that people tend to run in packs of their peers. People also tend to have a sense of what social group they would *like* to belong to, and this, too, is a result of cultural influences. As Baudrillard puts it, "Advertising is completely in unison with the social, whose historical necessity has found itself absorbed by the pure and simple *demand* for the social: a demand that the social function like a business, a group of services, a mode of living or of survival." Social groups advertise themselves like products or services, but this is not as corrupt as it sounds. If everything is advertising, then social groups or movements must adapt to the language of the culture at large. Baudrillard again: "It is not by chance that advertising, after having, for a long time, carried by an implicit ultimatum of an economic kind, fundamentally saying and repeating incessantly 'I buy, I consume, I take pleasure,' today repeats in other forms, 'I vote, I participate, I am present, I am concerned.'"[27] If advertising itself speaks to us in a language that suggests we take social action and form our identities through the choice of products, then it stands to reason that social activism, which speaks in those same terms, could be viewed as a product in itself. This is Baudrillard's argument—that there is no difference between the product as product and the social movement as product. This may sound bleak, but it's not, if you consider that advertising is coming at us from a million different directions, not just one Big Brother source. Baudrillard certainly wouldn't be this optimistic, but predicting the loss of all meaning only takes you so far. People do produce meaning, but they do it by mobilizing forms and images familiar to them—the language of media.

So if anything and everything is filtered through media, nay, through *advertisements,* what's an online activist to do? How does one translate the awareness-raising and expert-making function of the redactor, itself merely a culled-together group of media sounds and images, into something "real" enough to change the world around us (or our perception of the world, if you want to go there)? The key, of course, is to find something—an idea, an image—that appeals to a particular segment of the population, and market it in such a way that guarantees it will reach the right people. *State Net California Journal* quotes media analyst Douglas Rushkoff on the success of MoveOn: "'The reason it replicated is not because they're so brilliant, but because it struck a chord with a whole lot of Americans. . . . A great viral idea won't spread unless there's already a cultural space for it. They named it and it spread. They made politics cool because the Internet is cool.'" And the Internet is especially "cool" for younger Americans. Jenkins and Thorburn write that the Pew Research Center reported that for the 2000 election, "Fifty percent of Internet users under the age of thirty said the Net had affected their vote, a finding that suggests a generational shift in political culture."[28]

Given the widely accepted notion that younger Americans are more likely to go online for information, MoveOn and MichaelMoore.com could be reasonably sure they were addressing a Gen-X or younger audience. And part of what characterizes younger demographics' use of the Web is the tendency to create an alternate identity online. For the MySpace generation, the persona one creates online is tantamount to an idealized version of self.[29] Even cynical, media-saturated Gen X, Y, and Zers want to feel like they are the best people they can be. Much academic discourse on new media has centered around people's use of the Internet (and gaming) to reimagine identity online. The *New York Times* quotes media expert Sherry Turkle's take on the matter: "'I think what people are doing on the Internet now,' she said, 'has deep psychological meaning in terms of how they're using identities to express problems and potentially solve them in what is a relatively consequence-free zone.'"[30] An Internet user's decision to participate in a political movement is not the same thing as creating an eight-foot-tall avatar of a wizard, or posting glamour shots and suggestive language on MySpace, of course. But all three stand as examples of using the Web to improve self-image. Online activism speaks to users' need to maintain an idealized self, because it provides an easy and fun way to be socially conscious and politically responsible, while appealing to the citizen's desire to become an expert, to make his or her own sense of the world in an authoritative manner.

MoveOn.org and MichaelMoore.com facilitate the maintenance of an online ideal self several ways: by emphasizing the importance of "doing one's part," by constantly praising members and fans, and by offering a sense of community. Both MoveOn.org and MichaelMoore.com use a technique of direct address to the reader-user. In virtually all of Moore's "Mike's letters" on his website, he addresses the letter "Dear Friends," and uses *you* frequently. MoveOn, too, uses personal language that speaks to the user. "Well over one hundred thousand MoveOn members will be there over the course of the week-

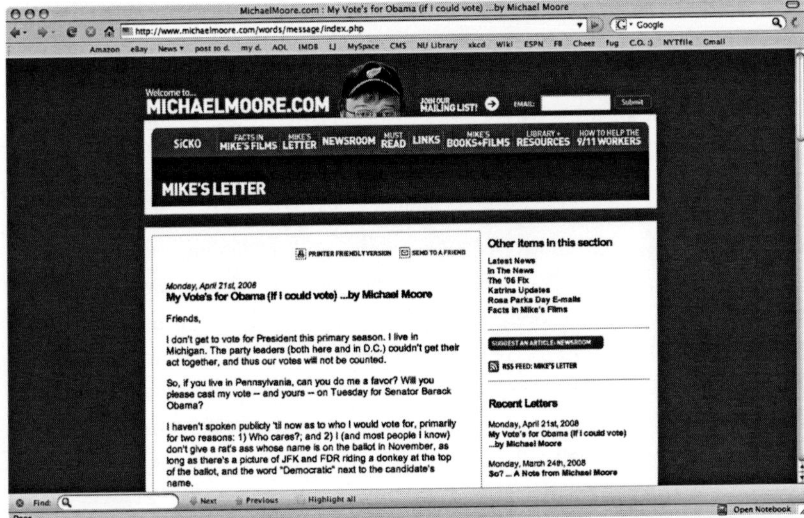

One of the most personal features of MichaelMoore.com, where Moore addresses his fans directly. This screen capture from April 2008 expresses his support for Barack Obama during the spring primary season. Copyright 2008 MichaelMoore.Com.

end, and we hope you can come, too," reads Pariser's letter to MoveOn members on the eve of *Fahrenheit 9/11*'s release. The illusion of a personalized message, delivered regularly into an e-mail inbox, goes a long way toward making a member feel valued. MoveOn and Michael Moore rely on this system of regular e-mail newsletters to keep potential activists informed. The soliciting of pledges, too, allows the user to "make a difference" simply by engaging in a virtual conversation. For instance, MichaelMoore.com's post "Turn Up the Heat" list of action items read like a to-do list: "1. I Will Register 10 People to Vote This Summer . . . 2. I Will Spend One Weekend In October In a Swing State . . . 3. I Will Adopt 5 Nonvoters I Know and Take Them to the Polls . . . 4. I Will Take-Off Work or School on Election Day and Volunteer to Get Out the Vote."[31] Even some of MichaelMoore.com's window titles suggest direct address—"Do Something!"

During the "Turn Up the Heat" broadcast, both Moore and Pariser kept their remarks optimistic and laudatory, in effect rewarding participants for their intelligence and social consciousness. Letters from Moore and MoveOn usually include such praise—telling people they've made the right choice is a vital component of building a strong community. The us-versus-them rhetoric Moore and MoveOn have used should be obvious by now—comments like "Some people still don't want you to see my movie" and "Right-wing groups who call Moore a 'domestic enemy' are using censorship and intimidation tactics to try to get it pulled from theaters" trade in stock techniques for rallying political support. Figuring your side as the underdog, as the good guy, goes a long way toward encouraging people to participate. Moore's persona as a spokesman for the common man also extends to how he figures himself in his films, as I mentioned, and as Sergio Rizzo explores in far more depth in this volume. The way in which Moore manipulated the media fervor over *Fahrenheit* mirrors the fight against big corporations or institutions that each of his films features. Despite his own success, Moore has carefully maintained his friend-of-the-people image, through his physical appearance in his films and in public appearances (baseball caps, jeans, shaggy hair, and corpulence), and, importantly, through his sense of humor; this is a persona constructed as the antithesis of the Republican Party. In his September 20 letter, Moore described Republicans thusly: "It's never over for them until the last ballot is shredded. They are never finished—they just keep moving forward like sharks that never sleep, always pushing, pulling, kicking, blocking, lying. They are relentless and that is why we secretly admire them—they just simply never, ever give up." To "Turn Up the Heat" partygoers, he stressed the organization skills of the Republican Party and the need to beat them at their own game, because: "Our side? We never see the crack of dawn unless we've been up all night."[32] This sort of rhetoric, which translates to: we're way cooler and younger than the Republicans, certainly served Barack Obama well during the 2008 presidential campaign too; Obama's tendency to show up at rallies with no jacket or tie, his sleeves rolled up, seemed less affected and more the result of his staying up all night working (or social networking online). In contrast, John McCain's attempts to reach out to a younger demographic often seemed a bit forced, as when he appeared on *Saturday Night Live* just before the election in November 2008, joking about a strategy called the "Sad Grandpa" to guilt the nation's youth into choosing him over the much younger Obama.

Opposition to the power elite characterizes youth in general, too—looking to Bourdieu's description of struggles within fields or even Raymond Williams' concept of emergent cultural elements makes this reliance on contrariness clear. The very act of instigating change contains a challenge to the orthodoxy, and this is usually the realm of youth. And while Moore's version of community tends toward the abstract, he knows exactly to whom he's talking—Americans between the ages of 18 and 34 who watch *The Daily Show.* Moore parlayed his success with *Fahrenheit 9/11* into a series of sort of comedy show / town hall meetings called "The Slacker Uprising Tour" in October 2004, which he filmed and then distributed for free online in fall 2008 from his website. The use of town hall meetings hearkens back to Habermas's bourgeois public sphere and related models of political interaction; the town hall format itself, of course, was and is a traditional American method of local government. At dozens of college campuses in swing states, Moore encouraged young adults to band together and become politically active. He also blogged about it: "I loved this audience tonight. They were so anxious to take their state back. The level of their commitment was infectious, especially for me, as I really didn't want to leave and spoke for way too long. 3,000 people wanted to get into a place that seated 1,700. So they had a lottery for the seats and the rest watched it outside on a Jumbotron."[33] Moore knows his audience, and his tendency to quote statistics works—the more popular he appears, the more popular he (and his political cause) becomes.

MoveOn, by necessity, also foregrounds the importance of community whenever possible. The *Fahrenheit 9/11* plan centered around packing theaters across the country on the film's opening weekend. One of Pariser's letters read, "Today, we're asking MoveOn members to pledge to see the film on the opening night—Friday, June 25th. (If you can't make it on Friday, pledging to go on Saturday or Sunday is fine, too). It'll be fun, of course—you'll be watching the movie with lots of other MoveOn members." The next updated this to include a visual signifier of membership in the group—"if you do go, don't forget to wear blue—our way of helping MoveOn members identify each other."[34] Like Moore, MoveOn also stressed the size of their community. Screen captures from the "Turn Up the Heat" event show that even as members participated in a nationwide meeting, real-time photos provided visual representation of the thousands of parties taking place. A color-coded key in the corner indicated population concentrations and percentages of participants willing to host phone parties to get out the vote, which simultaneously congratulated members for their commitment and nudged others toward joining the group and pitching in.

THE SLACKER'S GUIDE TO POLITICAL CHANGE

MoveOn was not exaggerating its numbers during "Turn Up the Heat"; at the time of this writing (summer 2008), the organization boasted 3.2 million members. *Wired* reports that MoveOn's use of peer-to-peer linkage online brought activism into the present: "How does a large collection of citizens influence a great national campaign without succumbing to a fatal dependence on a small cadre of professionals? Geek activists naturally expect a good part of the answer to come from technology. The people are rational and can be empowered. They just need better tools." But why take such pains to speak to younger demographics in a format and language most fitting for them—they're statistically less likely to vote! *Adweek* brought this to their readers' attention: "On the bright side for Bush, one-third of those who had seen the film, and one-fifth of those who expected to see it, are between the ages of 18 and 29, a group with historically low voter-turnout levels." *U.S. News & World Report* did as well, quoting the director of the Pew Research Center, Andrew Kohut: "Fahrenheit stands to have the most sway with young voters, Kohut says, but young people vote in comparatively small numbers, and, according to an e-mail sent last week by the film's distributors, almost 60 percent of Fahrenheit's audience is over 35." Ah, but the other 40 percent is under 35. The wildly lucrative 18–34 demographic, the holy grail of advertisers, are the up-and-comers with disposable income and are often considered tastemakers of the mainstream population—at least the mainstream population represented on popular television. If convinced to go vote, they represent a not-insignificant chunk of the population. They are statistically more likely to use the Internet regularly, and according to the last election results, they are more likely to vote Democrat. After the 2004 election, the *San Francisco Chronicle* reported that "Fifty-two percent of the under-30 population turned out to vote Tuesday, up from 42 percent in 2000. Fifty-four percent of young voters preferred Democrat John Kerry, making it the only age group that chose him over President Bush, who received 44 percent of their support. In 2000, young voters preferred Democrat Al Gore to Bush by 48 to 46 percent." Likewise, Moore noted in his November 5, 2004, letter, "The only age group in which the majority voted for Kerry was young adults (Kerry: 54%, Bush: 44%), proving once again that your parents are always wrong and you should never listen to them." Moore then packed his November 7 letter, "The Kids are Alright," with statistics indicating that more people under the age of 30 voted in the 2004 election than ever before, and a majority of them voted Democrat. He attributed some of the voter turnout to veteran MTV campaigns "Rock the Vote" and "Choose or Lose," writing, "From the beginning, I believed that young adults and 'slackers' would rise up in this election. As we began our slacker tour in Syracuse's football stadium on September 20, we could tell that this election would be like no other. It was no longer uncool to talk politics like it was five or ten years ago. Now, you were considered a loser if you didn't know what was going on in the world."[35] Moore's observation about the coolness factor of political action gets to the crux of why Internet activism works. In post-millennial America, by manipulating the media, you change the world. If people's perception of what goes on around them changes, then what goes on, essentially, changes. In a democratic society, perception equals policy. By making activism seem accessible and enjoyable, MoveOn and Michael Moore in effect made it so.

The proliferation of information is overwhelming for anyone. But for younger Americans, whose comfort level with a redactional society probably exceeds that of their parents, going online for research and identity formation is a fact of life. Part of becoming an "expert," according to Galusky's definition, is making decisions based on which version of the "truth" to believe. Once a user makes these choices, however, he or she finds the digest versions of activist literature with the right spin—the redactors with the relevant collections of information. MoveOn.org and MichaelMoore.com acted as one-stop shops for the time-pressed political consumer. Living in a redactional society means that even if every bit of news you read has been filtered by various media outlets several times, you are still able to consider yourself an expert on a given issue by choosing which outlet to believe. No original research required—just point and click. As Galusky puts it, "Most generally, easy access can imply that substantive sociopolitical change can occur with a few clicks of the mouse."[36]

The online petition, a form of activism that MoveOn helped to make popular, allows anyone to create a petition with very little forethought.[37] Signing one is even easier—usually all a site's visitor has to do is enter his or her name and e-mail address and hit Enter. Pledges to see *Fahrenheit 9/11* functioned like a petition, since MoveOn was able to use statistics generated by its pledge drive software in statements to the media. Even if only half of those who pledged to see the film actually did, the effect for MoveOn's presence in the mainstream media was the same. And as I mentioned above, during *Fahrenheit 9/11*'s media blitz, MoveOn made sending local letters to the editor as easy as choosing a template, adding your name, and entering a zip code. MoveOn also provides this service for letters to congressmen and the president, and it has proven effective in convincing thousands of members to make their voices heard. When making your voice heard is this fast and simple, it follows logically that more people—more people accustomed to conducting business and social activities on the Internet, that is—would be willing to do it.

MoveOn also mastered the art of viral marketing, which makes sense, given the fact that the organization itself was built on a viral communiqué years ago. On the pledge page for *Fahrenheit 9/11,* MoveOn encouraged members to send the film's trailer to friends; a trailer is entertaining in itself, and as a forwarded e-mail would be less obnoxious than, say, an angry polemic demanding the recipient of the e-mail see the movie. Finally, MoveOn.org repeatedly used the technique of having members host parties as a way of making political action both painless and enjoyable. "Turn Up the Heat" was a success because, as I stated above, people enjoy feeling like part of a community, but also because for most people, going to a party and watching an online broadcast does not feel like work. For MichaelMoore.com, ease of use translates to maintaining a sense of awareness. On the site's "Do Something" section, which the site's staff continues to update, there seems to be an endless array of chances to make a difference. Apart from the fact that the barrage of opportunities makes it very easy to procrastinate, the user might feel (through direct address and efforts toward being a self-made expert) that simply knowing what's going on is half the battle. Moore's site suggested that the success of *Fahrenheit 9/11* amounted to a political victory. By telling his fans that seeing the film counted as a political act, he made being an activist easy—both MoveOn and Michael Moore insisted that being an informed citizen could be as simple as going to the movie theater.

In a *New York Times* article about branding one's own identity, Rob Walker writes, "It is often said that this generation of teenagers and 20-somethings is the most savvy one ever in its ability to critique and understand commercial persuasion, and it is probably true—just as it was true when the same thing was said of Generation X and of the baby boomers before that. . . . But understanding or 'seeing through' the branded world is not the same thing as rejecting it."[38] It just means that a company, or a social group, must use different techniques for capturing and keeping the attention of the most jaded generation—which is a generation that will be affected by what happens in politics today far more than their parents will be.

MichaelMoore.com and MoveOn offer models of political activism in the age of the Internet that weave together direct address, redaction, and users' desire to idealize themselves, be entertained, and build community. In Moore's case the politics are served with a hefty dollop of sardonic humor, and his tone walks the razor's edge between hope and futility. Paul Andrews in the *Seattle Times* writes, "Perhaps MoveOn's prime contribution has been to show an alternative path to political action—beyond the voice mail, TV ads and junk mail that have numbed many to the electoral process. Even if the Internet winds up simply being a conduit to the ultimate political persuasion—person-to-person contact—it will have served a pivotal role in transforming democracy."[39] MoveOn and MichaelMoore.com have encouraged people into banding together for change; it's fun, and it's easy, and it allows one to think of oneself in idealized terms. On the Internet, which Turkle calls a "consequence-free zone," many of us are used to trying on different identities, seeing what fits. But participating in MoveOn has real consequences, and MichaelMoore.com is a gateway for that participation, which strives to instill in its users a sense of being a part of a movement that's cooler-than-thou, that laughs at despair to keep from crying. This ironic detachment, in today's social context, isn't detachment at all—it's a coping mechanism that allows would-be activists to feel like experts, to stay in the know, even though hiding one's head in the sand might be a more appealing option. Redactors who speak to young audiences in this mode of jovial disbelief have captured the *tone* of the consequence-free zone without actually relinquishing the consequences.

The June 2007 premiere of *Sicko* only proves the staying power of the kind of Internet activism MoveOn and www.MichaelMoore.com developed around *Fahrenheit 9/11*. MoveOn used the film as a rallying point when they asked members to pledge to see it opening weekend and hand out flyers: "After the movie, we'll ask presidential candidates to promise not to take campaign money from any of the industry's PACs, lobbyists, or executives. And to turn up the heat, we'll pass out fliers to movie-goers encouraging them to call up their favorite candidate." Although Moore and MoveOn were less closely allied for *Sicko*'s release, Moore too asked viewers to use the film as a jumping-off point for further political action; in a missive to his site and mailing list, he praised those who were "using the movie to do something" and even compiled a handy set of links to activist groups and Congress members' addresses.[40]

With the conclusion of the Bush years and the ubiquity of Barack Obama's rhetoric of "change," youth-oriented online marketing and community in politics only promise to become more complex and nuanced. As the 2008 campaign season approached, though, Moore's choice to remain coy with regard to his choice of candidate during much of the long Democratic primary season indicated his familiarity with the changing role of the Internet redactor—while many argue that Moore's highly visible polemics in the 2004 election season helped convince political moderates to skew Republican. 2008 brought a more subdued Moore, at least prior to Obama's victory. Instead of 2004's almost-daily update of facts in *Fahrenheit 9/11* and campaign issues, Moore's April 2008 letter posted on his site drips with disappointment and weariness. Moore writes: "I'm almost at the point where I don't care if the Democrats don't have a backbone or a kneebone or a thought in their dizzy little heads. Just as long as their name ain't 'Bush' and the word 'Republican' is not beside theirs on the ballot, then that's good enough for me. . . . I, like the majority of Americans, have been pummeled senseless for 8 long years."[41]

As MoveOn continues to employ many of the same techniques for political action as in 2004 (with a few hiccups here and there—Pariser has been condemned for, among other things, his vitriolic denunciation of General Petraeus and the June 2008 anti-John McCain "Not Alex" ad), Moore's comments suggest an aesthetic of exhaustion—the idea that anything's got to be better than what we have now. This might suggest to the more cynical among us that the bloom's off the rose of online activism, but I would argue that Obama's emphasis on reaching younger (and hipper) voters with his message of progress merely assimilated the elements of online activism and community-building that MoveOn and Moore deployed four years before—as of mid-June, 2008, Obama had more than one million Facebook friends, and listed his favorite movies as *Godfather I* and *II* and *One Flew Over the Cuckoo's Nest*, and his interests as "basketball, writing, and loafing w/ kids."[42] By the time the election rolled around in November, his media campaign had taken advantage of everything from a central website, My.BarackObama.com, to Facebook and MySpace sites, text alerts, and even an app for the iPhone. This extensive use of social networking tools, which leveraged the latent political activism in hundreds of thousands of younger Americans, stood in marked contrast to McCain's more traditional campaign tactics. Obama's skill in creating a popular public image over various media platforms, including a successful online profile (arguably an act of redaction in itself), effectively convinced a majority of Americans of his presidential potential. Although his popularity with mainstream America has dropped since his election, Obama has continued to use the power of Internet communication to keep younger demographics interested in policy decisions, and committed to the idea that online community activism can create real social change.

Notes

1. Thanks to John Coffey for conversations that helped give shape to some of the ideas presented here. For a comprehensive discussion of reviews and print debates over *Fahrenheit 9/11*, see Robert Brent Toplin, *Michael Moore's* Fahrenheit 9/11: *How One Film Divided a Nation* (Lawrence: University Press of Kansas, 2006).

2. For more on the campaigns of 2000, see Elaine Ciulla Kamarck, "Political Campaigning on the Internet: Business as Usual?" in *Governance.com: Democracy in the In-*

formation Age, ed. Elaine Ciulla Kamarck and Joseph S. Nye, Jr. (Washington, DC: Brookings Institution Press, 2002). For a detailed and engaging account of McCain's 2000 campaign, see David Foster Wallace, "Up, Simba: Seven Days on the Trail of an Anticandidate," in *Consider the Lobster and Other Essays* (New York: Little, Brown, 2006).

3. Carl Hulse and Sheryl Gay Stolberg, "G.O.P. Is Taking Aim at Advocacy Groups," *New York Times,* March 31, 2004, A12.

4. Kim Zetter, "MoveOn Moves Up in the World," *Wired,* July 2004, http://www.wired.com/news/politics/1,64340-0.html (accessed July 21, 2006); Paul Andrews, "MoveOn.org Moves into Neighborhood," *Seattle Times,* April 11, 2005, C1; Gary Wolf, "Weapons of Mass Mobilization," *Wired,* September 2004, http://www.wired.com/wired/archive/12.09/moveon.html (accessed July 21, 2006).

5. Andrews, "MoveOn.org Moves into Neighborhood," C1.

6. "ActionForum," MoveOn.org, http://www.actionforum.com/forum/?forum_id=266 (accessed July 27, 2006). The ActionForum was ultimately taken down in September 2006, after the site was accused of fostering anti-Semitic sentiment. The issue with open forum software, here as with Moore's site, is the relative uncontrollability of user behavior. Anti-MoveOn and anti-Moore sites such as Moorewatch.com pointed to the hypocrisy in allowing such antisocial commenters to continue posting, but keeping them quiet proved too much of a challenge: in September 2006, Eli Pariser released a statement (http://www.moveon.org/content/pac/pdfs/statement_090206.pdf) citing MoveOn's attempts to curtail negativity, and whether for this reason or others, the site was put on hiatus in October 2006 and hasn't seen the light of day since. Recent (2008) visits to MoveOn.com suggest that most of the community-building action has moved to networking sites such as Facebook (as have more traditional sci-fi/TV/comics-related fandoms, which tend to favor LiveJournal), which allow for the creation of more specific interest groups and also the locking of posts to keep out intruders. The question of how problematic that might be extends beyond the scope of this paper but might be worth considering as networking sites play a larger role in the political process.

7. Mark Glaser, "MichaelMoore.com: Lightning Rod for Political Debate, Action," *USC Annenberg Online Journalism Review,* June 30, 2004, http://ojr.org/ojr/glaser/1088543500.php (accessed June 20, 2006).

8. Michael Moore, "It Was Headed to the Shredder, and Now They Say It's a Bestseller. Go Figure," MichaelMoore.com, February 13, 2002, http://www.michaelmoore.com/words/message/index.php?messageDate=2002-02-13 (accessed October 29, 2006).

9. Ray Simon passed away in August 2002. For more on his contribution to MichaelMoore.com, see http://www.mischiefmarketing.com/. Statistics come from *Plank Multimedia Portfolio,* http://www.plankdesign.com/site/portfolio/feature.php?client=michaelmoore (accessed October 29, 2006). Moore briefly came under fire for outsourcing his Web service to Canada, but it makes a certain amount of sense—though Moore himself is not Canadian, by keeping his site off American servers he both avoids the possible censorship of U.S.-based media and exudes a sort of counterculture Vietnam-era vibe.

10. Jürgen Habermas, *The Structural Transformation of the Public Sphere: An Inquiry into a Category of Bourgeois Society,* trans. Thomas Burger (Cambridge, MA: MIT Press, 1989), 27.

11. Henry Jenkins and David Thorburn, "The Digital Revolution, the Informed Citizen, and the Culture of Democracy," in *Democracy and New Media,* ed. Henry Jenkins and David Thorburn (Cambridge, MA: MIT Press, 2004), http://web.mit.edu/transition/subs/demointro.html (accessed July 16, 2006).

12. John Hartley, "From Republic of Letters to Television Republic? Citizen Readers in the Era of Broadcast Television," in *Television after TV: Essays on a Medium in Transition,* ed. Lynn Spigel and Jan Olsson (Durham, NC: Duke University Press, 2004), 388, 391.

13. Ibid., 402.

14. "ActionForum Frequently Asked Questions," MoveOn.org, http://www.actionforum.com/general/faq.html (accessed July 24, 2006); Karen MacPherson, "Grass-roots Politics Turns to Internet," *Pittsburgh Post-Gazette,* June 29, 2003, A14.

15. Joké Hermes, "Cultural Citizenship and Popular Fiction," in *The Media in Question: Popular Culture and Public Interests,* ed. Kees Brants, Joké Hermes, and Liesbet van Zoonen (London: Sage, 1998), 160, quoted in Hartley, "From Republic of Letters to Television Republic?" 409. For another interesting approach to the concept of citizenship as overlapping groups, see Michael Warner, *Publics and Counterpublics* (New York: Zone Books, 2005).

16. Michael Moore, "Disney Has Blocked the Distribution of My New Film," MichaelMoore.com, May 5, 2004, http://www.michaelmoore.com/words/message/index.php?messageDate=2004-05-04 (accessed July 24, 2006); Michael Moore, "When You Wish upon a Star?" MichaelMoore.com, May 7, 2004, http://www.michaelmoore.com/words/message/index.php?messageDate=2004-05-07 (accessed July 24, 2006).

17. Looking at archived pages of MichaelMoore.com indicates that Moore did, in fact, maintain a forum up until December 2002, at which point technical difficulties led his Web team to remove it. This site, http://www.michaelmoore.com/dogeatdogfilms/guestbook.html, went up in August 2004 but was taken down again in October, citing posts being "out of control."

18. Jim Rutenberg and Laura M. Holson, "Disney Takes Heat on Blocking Bush Film," *New York Times,* May 6, 2004, A30; "Disney's Craven Behavior," *New York Times,* May 6, 2004, A34.

19. Scott Mervis, "What's Everyone So Fired Up About?" *Pittsburgh Post-Gazette,* June 25, 2004, W23; Michael Moore, "Some People Still Don't Want You to See My Movie," MichaelMoore.com, June 18, 2004, http://www.michaelmoore.com/words/message/index.php?messageDate=2004-06-18 (accessed July 24, 2006).

20. While a full discussion of the conservative movement against Michael Moore and its possible association with reiterating the evils of liberalism just in time for the 2004 election is beyond the scope of this paper, it's worth noting at least in brief that many of these same techniques for political activism on the Web were also adopted and used by conservative groups online. This doesn't lessen the contribution of MoveOn or MichaelMoore.com, though, for in my opinion, the strategies used by these two sites were novel at the time. Vitriolic message boards, both liberal-leaning and conservative, have been a part of the Web for a while, but MoveOn and MichaelMoore.com relied upon specific characteristics of the Internet in order to draw more effective correlations between community online and community action in the "real" world.

21. Eli Pariser, "Stop the Censorship of Fahrenheit 9/11," MoveOn.org, June 14, 2004, http://www.moveon.org/pac/news/f911.html (accessed July 8, 2006); Eli Pariser, "'Fahrenheit 9/11' Opens Tonight: Parties and More," MoveOn.org, June 25, 2004, http://www.moveon.org/pac/news/f911-tonight.html (accessed July 8, 2006); Sharon Waxman, "The Political 'Fahrenheit' Sets Record at Box Office," *New York Times*, June 28, 2004.

22. Byron York, "Going Viral," *National Review Online*, April 7, 2005, http://www.nationalreview.com/york/york200504070810.asp (accessed July 24, 2006); Sharon Murnane, letter to the editor, *San Diego Union-Tribune*, July 1, 2004, B11.

23. "Michael Moore Wants to Know: Are You Ready to Turn up the Heat on George W. Bush?" MoveOn.org, June 25, 2004, http://cdn.moveon.org/pac/media/moveonf911flyer.pdf (accessed July 25, 2006); "Turn up the Heat Town Meeting a Massive Success!" MoveOn.org, http://political.moveon.org/f911/mappics.html (accessed July 25, 2006); "2004 MoveOn PAC Action Archives," MoveOn.org, http://political.moveon.org/archive/ (accessed July 25, 2006).

24. Michael Moore, "Mike's Action Guide," MichaelMoore.com, http://web.archive.org/web/20041102054645/http://www.michaelmoore.com/takeaction/vote/pledge.php (accessed July 27, 2006); Moore, "Turn up the Heat: A National Town Meeting," June 28, 2004, audio at "2004 MoveOn PAC Action Archives," MoveOn.org, http://political.moveon.org/archive/ (accessed July 25, 2006); Pariser, "'Fahrenheit 9/11' Opens Tonight."

25. Wyatt Galusky, "Identifying with Information: Citizen Empowerment, the Internet, and the Environmental Anti-Toxins Movement," in *Cyberactivism: Online Activism in Theory and Practice*, ed. Martha McCaughey and Michael D. Ayers (New York: Routledge, 2003), 196, 190. See also Anthony Giddens, *Modernity and Self-Identity: Self and Society in the Late Modern Age* (Stanford, CA: Stanford University Press, 1992).

26. Jean Baudrillard, *Simulacra and Simulation*, trans. Sheila Faria Glaser (Ann Arbor: University of Michigan Press, 1994), 87, 88.

27. See Pierre Bourdieu, *The Field of Cultural Production*, ed. Randal Johnson (New York: Columbia University Press, 1993); Baudrillard, *Simulacra and Simulation*, 90, 91.

28. Pamela Burdman, "MoveOn.org," *State Net California Journal* 35, no. 8 (August 1, 2004): 46; Jenkins and Thorburn, "The Digital Revolution, the Informed Citizen, and the Culture of Democracy."

29. For more on MySpace, including the requisite Dangers of New Technology rhetoric, see Janet Kornblum, "Teens Hang out at MySpace," *USA Today*, January 9, 2006, D1; James Verini, "Will Success Spoil MySpace?" *Vanity Fair*, March 2006.

30. Benedict Carey, "The Secret Lives of Just about Everybody," *New York Times*, January 11, 2005, F1.

31. Pariser, "'Fahrenheit 9/11' Opens Tonight"; Moore, "Mike's Action Guide."

32. Moore, "Some People Still Don't Want You to See My Movie"; "Help Make *Fahrenheit 9/11* a Huge Hit," MoveOn.org, http://political.moveon.org/f911/ (accessed July 8, 2006); Michael Moore, "Put away Your Hankies," MichaelMoore.com, September 20, 2004, http://www.michaelmoore.com/words/message/index.php?messageDate=2004-09-20 (accessed July 28, 2006); Moore, "Turn up the Heat."

33. See Raymond Williams, *Marxism and Literature* (New York: Oxford University

Press, 1977); Michael Moore, "Conway, Arkansas . . . ," MichaelMoore.com, October 3, 2004, http://web.archive.org/web/20041011094735/http://www.michaelmoore.com/words/blog/ (accessed July 27, 2006).

34. Pariser, "Stop the Censorship of Fahrenheit 9/11"; Pariser, "'Fahrenheit 9/11' Opens Tonight."

35. Wolf, "Weapons of Mass Mobilization"; Costas Panagopoulos, "Don't Believe the Hype," *Adweek,* July 19, 2004; Dan Gilgoff and Michael Tobin, "Moore or Less," *U.S. News & World Report,* July 12, 2004, 38; Joe Garofoli, "Next Challenge Is Keeping Young Voters Interested," *San Francisco Chronicle,* November 7, 2004, http://www.sfgate.com/cgi-bin/article.cgi?file=/chronicle/archive/2004/11/07/MNG5F9NFFP1.DTL (accessed July 10, 2006); Michael Moore, "17 Reasons Not to Slit Your Wrists," MichaelMoore.com, November 5, 2004, http://www.michaelmoore.com/words/message/index.php?messageDate=2004-11-05 (accessed July 26, 2006); Michael Moore, "The Kids Are Alright," MichaelMoore.com, November 7, 2004, http://www.michaelmoore.com/words/message/index.php?messageDate=2004-11-07 (accessed July 26, 2006).

36. Galusky, "Identifying with Information," 193.

37. See http://www.thepetitionsite.com.

38. Rob Walker, "The Brand Underground," *New York Times Magazine,* July 30, 2006, 29.

39. Andrews, "MoveOn.org Moves into Neighborhood," C1.

40. "See *Sicko* This Weekend," MoveOn.org e-mail to mailing list, June 28, 2007; Michael Moore, "See the Movie, Start the Revolution," MichaelMoore.com, July 26, 2007, http://www.michaelmoore.com/words/message/index.php?messageDate=2007-07-26 (accessed June 23, 2008).

41. Michael Moore, "My Vote's for Obama (If I Could Vote)," MichaelMoore.com, April 21, 2008, http://www.michaelmoore.com/words/message/index.php?messageDate=2008-04-21 (accessed June 20, 2008).

42. Barack Obama, http://www.facebook.com/barackobama (accessed June 20, 2008).

Contributors

Paul Arthur was Professor of English and Film Studies at Montclair State University until his death in March 2008. He was a regular contributor to *Film Comment* and *Cineaste,* and was coeditor of *Millenium Film Journal.* He published *A Line of Sight: American Avant-garde Film since 1965* in 2005.

Matthew H. Bernstein is Professor of Film Studies at Emory University. He is the author of *Walter Wanger, Hollywood Independent* (1994, 2000) and *Screening a Lynching: The Leo Frank Case on Film and TV* (2009), editor of *Controlling Hollywood: Censorship and Regulation in the Studio Era* (1999), and coeditor (with Gaylyn Studlar) of *Visions of the East: Orientalism in Film* (1997) and *John Ford Made Westerns: Filming the Legend in the Sound Era* (2001).

Cary Elza is a Ph.D. candidate in the Screen Cultures Program in the Radio-TV-Film department at Northwestern University. She has published essays on the Internet marketing of *Smallville* and *The X-Files* and literature, and is currently working on her dissertation, which examines female boundary-crossing figures in TV and filmic representations of imaginary worlds, from *Alice in Wonderland* to *The Wizard of Oz.*

Jeffrey P. Jones is Associate Professor of Communication and Theatre Arts at Old Dominion University in Norfolk, Virginia. He is the author of *Entertaining Politics: Satiric Television and Political Engagement,* 2nd ed. (2009) and coeditor of *The Essential HBO Reader* (2008) and *Satire TV: Politics and Comedy in the Post-Network Era* (NYU Press, 2009).

Douglas Kellner is George Kneller Chair in the Philosophy of Education at UCLA and is the author of many books on social theory, politics, history, and culture, including *Camera Politica: The Politics and Ideology of Contemporary Hollywood Film,* coauthored with Michael Ryan (1990) and *Emile de Antonio: A Reader*, co-edited with Dan Streible (2000). Other works include *Critical Theory, Marxism, and Modernity* (1989); *Jean Baudrillard: From Marxism to Postmodernism and Beyond* (1990); works in cultural studies such as *Media Culture* (1995) and *Media Spectacle* (2003); a trilogy of books on postmodern theory with Steve Best; and a trilogy of books on the media and the Bush administration. Kellner's *Guys and Guns Amok: Domestic Terrorism and School Shootings from the Oklahoma City Bombings to the Virginia Tech Massacre* won the 2008 AESA award as the best book on education. Forthcoming in 2010 is Kellner's *Cinema Wars: Hollywood Film and Politics in the Bush/Cheney Era.*

Richard Kilborn is Senior Lecturer in the Department of Film, Media, & Journalism at the University of Stirling (Scotland). He has also taught at the University of Munich and has been a visiting professor at Northwestern University. His main research interests have been in film and television documentary and in television drama. He has just published a new book, *Taking the Long View: A Study of Longitudinal Documentary* (2010).

William Luhr is Professor of Film Studies and English at Saint Peter's College in Jersey City, New Jersey, and is the author of *Raymond Chandler and Film* (1982), *World Cinema since 1945* (1987), and coauthor (with Peter Lehman) of *Thinking about Movies: Watching, Questioning, Enjoying* (2008), as well as editor of *The Coen Brothers'* Fargo (2003) and coeditor (with Krin Gabbard) of *Screening Genders* (2008).

Charles Musser is Professor of Film Studies and American Studies at Yale University, where he regularly teaches courses in documentary. He is the author of many books, including the multi-award-winning *The Emergence of Cinema: The American Screen to 1907* (1990), *Before the Nickelodeon: Edwin S. Porter and the Edison Manufacturing Company* (1991), and coeditor (with Jane Gaines and Pearl Bowser) of *Oscar Micheaux and His Circle: African-American Filmmaking and Race Cinema of the Silent Era* (2001). He is currently working on a book entitled *Truth and Documentary in the Age of George W. Bush.*

Richard R. Ness is the author of *From Headline Hunter to Superman: A Journalism Filmography* (1997) and *Alan Rudolph: Romance and a Crazed World* (1996). His articles and reviews have appeared in *Cinema Journal, Quarterly Review of Film and Video,* the *Hitchcock Annual,* and the anthology *Print the Legend: Cinema and Jour-*

nalism, published by *Cahiers du cinema*. He teaches film and media studies courses at Western Illinois University.

Miles Orvell is Professor of English and American Studies at Temple University, and is the author of *The Real Thing: Imitation and Authenticity in American Culture, 1880–1940* (1990), *After the Machine: Visual Arts and the Erasing of Cultural Boundaries* (1995), and *American Photography* (2003). He is co-editor recently of *Public Space and the Ideology of Place in American Culture* (2009) and is completing a book, *Main Street in the American Mind*. Orvell serves as Editor in Chief of the *Encyclopedia of American Studies Online*.

Richard Porton has taught cinema studies at the College of Staten Island (CUNY). He serves on the editorial board of *Cineaste*, writes for many publications, and is the author of *Film and the Anarchist Imagination* (1999) and editor of *Dekalog 3: On Film Festivals* (2009).

Sergio Rizzo is an Assistant Professor of English at Morehouse College, where he teaches courses in writing, literary theory, and world literature. He writes on literature and popular culture, and his work has appeared in publications such as *Journal of Modern Literature, Convergence, M/C: Media Culture*, and *Film Quarterly*.

Christopher Sharrett is Professor of Communication and Film Studies at Seton Hall University. He is the author of *Crisis Cinema: The Apocalyptic Idea in Postmodern Narrative Cinema* (1993) and *The Rifleman* (2003) and editor of *Mythologies of Violence in Postmodern Media* (1999). His work has appeared in *Cineaste, Film International, Senses of Cinema, Cinema Journal, Postscript, Framework, Kinoeye*, and numerous critical authologies.

Gaylyn Studlar is David May Distinguished Professor of the Humanities at Washington University in St. Louis, where she directs the Program in Film and Media Studies. She is the author of *This Mad Masquerade: Stardom and Masculinity in the Jazz Age* (1996) and *In the Realm of Pleasure: Von Sternberg, Dietrich, and the Masochistic Aesthetic* (1988, 1993), and she is currently completing *Precious Charms: The Juvenation of Female Stardom in Classical Hollywood Cinema*. She has coedited the anthologies *John Made Westerns: Film the Legend in the Sound Era* (2001), *Visions of the East: Orientalism in Film* (1997), *Reflections in a Male Eye: John Huston and the American Experience* (1993), and *Titanic: Anatomy of a Blockbuster* (1999). She is also the author of numerous publications on gender and sexuality in cinema.

David Tetzlaff has made some documentary films, has old-fashioned left-wing politics, and is extraordinarily fond of ironic humor. He hails from the upper Midwest, is overweight, wears glasses, and dresses in a casual if not slovenly manner. Nevertheless, he claims complete objectivity in his analysis of the films of Michael Moore. And he does not wear a baseball cap.

Index

Abu Ghraib, 96, 169
Academy Awards, 42, 92, 133, 167
  and Best Documentary (for *Bowling for Columbine*), 3, 167
  and Moore's 2003 speech, 102, 196
AC Spark Plug factory, 21, 31, 36
Adventures in a TV Nation (1998), 5
Adweek, 298
Afghanistan, war in, 153
agit-prop, and cinema, 81, 82, 92, 108
AIG, 22
Ailes, Roger, 216
Ain't It Cool News Web site, 151. *See also* Knowles, Harry
Alda, Alda, 4
Alfred E. Smith memorial dinner, 96
Al Jazeera, 118, 214
Allen, Woody, 39
Al-Qaeda, 157, 159, 168, 193, 195, 211, 288
Altman, Robert, 28
Alvarez, Santiago, 109
ambush interview, 60, 143, 145
American Bandstand (1952–), 89
American Dream (1991), 11, 127–31, 133, 236
American Revolution, 129
Amerindie films, 106. *See also independent films*
An Acquired Taste (1981), 111
Anderson, Lewie (featured in *American Dream*), 128–30
Andrews, Paul (former *Seattle Times* columnist), 300
anti-Moore campaigns, 168, 173, 174, 194, 288
AP. *See* Associated Press
Arbus, Diane, 100
Ari Emanuel, 170
Arizona Republic, 289
Arlyck, Ralph (filmmaker), 111
Armey, Dick, 70, 225
Armour plant, 132
Armstrong, Louis, 147
Arnold, Matthew, 219
Arthur, Paul, 34, 163
Associated Press, 204, 286
Atomic Café, The (1982), 93
Atta, Mohammed, 193
authorship
  auteur, 27, 28, 29, 30, 35, 36
  auteur of commerce, 30
  auteur-star, 35, 38, 40–43
  commercial auteur, 16, 30, 32, 36, 43
Awful Truth, The (1999–2000), 5, 113, 114, 141, 233, 235, 240, 241, 244–47, 249, 260, 262
  airing in UK of, 260
  Emmy nomination of, 241
  first season of, 240
  format of, 240
  polemics and humor in, 241
  storytelling techniques in, 244
  themes of shows, 241
  use of specialists in, 247
Axis powers, 152, 156
Axis propaganda films, 156

Baccolini, Raffaella (author), 207. See *Dark Horizons: Science Fiction and the Dystopian Imagination*
Backyard (1984), 196
Baldwin, Tammy (congresswoman), 41
Battle of Britain, The (1943), 152
Battle of China, The (1944),144, 152
Battle of Russia, The (1943), 152, 159, 161, 162

Baudrillard, Jean, 212, 292, 293
and economy of the "simulacrum," 139
Bayles, Tom (reporter, *Sarasota Herald-Tribune*), 177, 178
BBC, 250, 260–62, 271
and co-financing of *TV Nation*, 236
Beach Boys, 112
Beattie, Keith, 194
Benn, Tony (former British Labour MP), 226
Berger, John, 93, 108, 150
Bergman, Ingmar, 39
Bergson, Henri, 186
Bertolucci, Bernardo, 80
Best Documentary Academy Award (for *Bowling for Columbine*), 3, 167
Bieber, Owen (UAW president), 134
Big One, The (1997), 4, 20, 22, 35, 98, 109, 113, 152
Big Picture: The New Logic of Money and Power in Hollywood, The (2005), 42
bin Laden, Osama, 13, 88, 94, 95, 146, 153, 154, 156, 163, 176, 186, 193–95, 209
bin Laden family, 159, 162, 210, 267
Black, Gregory D. (co-author, *Hollywood Goes to War*), 163
Blair, Tony, 194, 227, 255
Bleifuss, Joel, 150
Blitzer, Wolf, 44
Blomkvist, Marten (Swedish journalist), 202, 203
Blood in the Face (1991), 83
Bloomfield, Nick, 15
Blue Cross Blue Shield, 224
Blue Pill, 211, 212
Bohn, Thomas William, 152–58, 161, 163
Bonanza (1959–1973), 17, 160, 163
Booker Elementary School, 178, 179, 182, 187
Boston Globe, 181, 289
Bourdieu, Pierre, 293, 296
Bowling for Columbine (2002), 3, 4, 5, 10, 11,12, 14, 15, 17, 19, 20, 22, 27, 35, 37, 51, 52, 54, 55, 59, 60, 62–65, 67–69, 86–90, 92, 93, 95, 98, 109, 111, 113–16, 118, 120, 141–47, 167, 173, 174, 202, 223, 224, 246, 247, 267, 268, 270
and Best Documentary, 3, 167
and Rolland, Kayla, 35, 54, 59, 60, 63, 64, 66–69, 89, 245, 246
Bradbury, Ray, 94, 202–4, 218, 219
Branston, Gill (author). See *Media Student's Book, The*
Brass Eye (British satirical TV show), 262. *See* Morris, Chris
Bravo channel, 233, 240–42, 260
Brazil (1985), 13, 205, 206, 208
Breaking the Silence: Truth and Lies in the War on Terror (2003), 257. *See* Pilger, John
British TV satire, 262
Britton, Rhonda ("pets or meat lady" in *Roger & Me*), 85, 113
Brookside, Kentucky, 130
Broomfield, Nick, 196, 264–66
and similarities to Moore, 264
Bruce, Lenny, 33
Bubba, Tony, 111
Buell Elementary School (in *Bowling for Columbine*), 64, 68
Bunny Lady. *See* Britton, Rhonda
Burbick, Joan (gun show analyst), 66
Bush, Jeb, 170, 177
Bush, President George Herbert Walker, 156, 176
Bush, President George W., 6, 13, 27, 41, 44, 45, 58, 61, 93, 94, 96, 98, 119, 152, 153, 154, 155–57, 159, 160, 162, 169, 171, 176, 177, 178, 179, 180, 192, 194, 195, 202, 205, 216, 220, 225, 278, 301, 302
on September 11, 2001, 180–83, 186–88, 191
Bush (President George W.) administration, 6, 12–14, 17, 19, 20, 79, 92–98, 114, 119, 153, 158, 160, 162, 163, 169, 175–77, 182, 183, 189, 193, 195, 202, 204, 208, 211, 256, 266, 287, 290
and antipopulist thrust, 97
and challenge to, 196
and White House, 93, 183
Bush family and the Saudis, 176, 193
Bush family connections, 267

cable television, 29
Caine, Rick, 17
Campbell, Richard (journalism professor), 242, 244
Canadian Bacon (1995), 4, 20, 22, 107
Candy, John, 4
Cannes Film Festival, 3, 18, 42, 43, 92, 169, 170, 190, 227, 266, 274
Palme d'Or, 3, 42, 170, 266, 275

Capitalism: A Love Story (2009), 5, 6, 10, 11, 17, 20–22, 27, 45, 52, 62, 70, 72, 99, 100, 247
capitalism, growth of, 283
Capra, Frank, 12, 149, 150, 154
  and effectiveness of, 150
  and emphasis on religion, 161
  vs. Moore, 156, 158, 162
  series, 151, 152, 156, 161, 163, 164
  and techniques and themes used in, 156
  and use of Riefenstahl's work, 156
  Why We Fight films
Card, Andrew, 180, 181, 182, 189
Carlyle Group, 156, 176, 193
Carson, Kit, 128
Cartmell, Brian R. (Internet entrepreneur & Moore backer), 174
CBS, 14, 58, 280
Celsius 41.11 (2004), 51, 119, 120, 174, 175, 205
  Moore vs. Adolf Hitler, 120
Chaplin, Charlie, 28, 33, 86, 194
Cheney, Vice President Dick, 95–97, 112, 157, 167, 176, 181, 193, 194, 212, 217
Chicago Sun-Times, 289
Chilean coup of 1972, 146
Chomsky, Noam, 146
Choose or Lose (2004 MTV campaign), 298
Chris Rock Show, The (1997), 235, 250
Cigna Insurance, 22, 224
Cinéaste, 52
cinéma vérité, 81, 111, 155, 168
  and directors, 80
  and filmmakers, 196
Citibank, 22
City, The (1939), 161, 162
City of the Dead (1960), 160, 161
Civil War, 146
Clark, Dick (TV show *American Bandstand* host), 60, 89, 144, 145
Clarke, Jason (founder www.moorelies.com), 174, 175, 190. See also *Michael Moore Is a Big Fat Stupid White Man*
Clarke, Richard (counterterrorism coordinator under President, George W. Bush), 176, 189
Clinton, Hillary, 19, 38, 51, 69, 70
  and health care, 225
Clinton, President Bill, 14, 88, 160, 161, 280
  and revamping the New Deal, 225
CNN, 44, 173, 284
coalition of the willing, 118, 160, 170, 255.
Cohen, Sacha Baron, 250
Cohn, Jonathan (journalist and author of *Sick*), 225
Colbert Report, The (2005–), 58, 235, 249
Cold War, 80, 225, 237, 247
Colin, Powell, 176
Collins, Andrew (writer for *Guardian*), 108
Columbine High School, 55, 60, 68, 87, 89, 142–44
Columbine shootings, 35, 87–90, 93, 95, 98, 116, 117, 144, 146
Connection, The (faked documentary TV program in UK), 273
conservative commentators, 39, 175
conservatives, political, 53
conspiracy theories, 193, 194, 216
conversion narratives, 115
Coppola, Francis Ford, 30
Corner, John, 259, 272
corporate restructuring, 98
Corporation, The (2003), 5
Corrigan, Timothy, 29, 30, 36, 42, 45, 49, 50
Coulter, Ann, 114, 175, 211
Counting on Democracy (2002), 190
Crackers, the Corporate Crime-Fighting Chicken (character in Moore's *TV Nation*), 231, 232, 234, 236, 238, 245
Crispin Miller, Mark, 190
Crowdus, Gary, 39
Crumb, R., 100
Culture of Fear, The (2000 book by Barry Glassner), 89
Curtis, Adam (British filmmaker), 256, 271

Da Ali G Show (2000; 2003–2004), 235, 249
Daily Mail (UK newspaper), 183, 260
Daily Show with Jon Stewart, The (1996–), 5, 14, 15, 58, 235, 249, 297
Dalton, Stephen (columnist, *Times* of London), 267
Daniels, Sandra Kay (teacher in Booker Elementary School), 181, 183
Dark Horizons: Science Fiction and the Dystopian Imagination (2003), 205. *See also* Baccolini, Raffaella (author)
Dateline (1984, 1998, 1999), 233
David Holzman's Diary (1968), 128

Davis, Peter, 114. See also *Hearts and Minds*
Day Today, The (British satirical radio series), 262. *See also* Morris, Chris
dead peasant life insurance, 21
Dean, Howard (2004 Democratic candidate), 279
de Antonio, Emile, 10, 15, 79–82, 84, 87, 92, 94, 114, 115
  compared to Moore, 10
  as left-wing partisan, 81
Debord, Guy, 111
decentralized control, 29
Democracy and New Media (2004), 283
Dennis Miller Live (1994–2002), 249, 250
DePalma, Brian, 39
Detroit Athletic Club, 137
DeVos, Dick (2006 Michigan Republican gubernatorial candidate and former Amway CEO), 67
Diaz, Philippe, 52
Dick, Philip K., 212
digital divide, 282
Dingel, John (former congressman), 245
disenfranchisement of blacks, 178
Disney Corporation, 7, 18, 42, 43, 157, 170, 171, 245, 286, 287
Disneyland, and Bush advice, 95
Disney/Miramax, 18, 170
distribution methods, 30
Divide and Conquer (1943), 151, 157
documentary, 5, 6–9, 22, 27, 52, 53, 86, 108, 168, 258
  as discourse of sobriety (Bill Nichols), 186, 196
  essay form of, 11, 18, 86, 109–15, 224
  and ethical issues in, 127, 142, 168, 273
  history of, 10, 93, 94, 119, 163, 169
  hybridization of, 134
  Michael Moore's influence on, 6,7, 259
  Michael Moore's relationship to, 8, 92, 105, 107–14, 116, 187, 196, 205, 206, 247, 257, 259, 271, 272
  modes (Bill Nichols), 11
    expository, 127, 151
    interactive modes, 108, 128, 151, 154, 155
    observational, 127, 128
    reflexive mode, 128
  and objectivity, 10, 82, 98, 142, 196
  point of view in, 9, 10, 215
  powerlessness of subjects (victims) in, 10, 18, 19, 55, 137–39
  and propaganda, 8,12–13, 107, 149–51,
  and radical partisan filmmaking, 80, 92, 97, 217, 219, 243, 269
  recent changes in, 105, 106, 257, 272
  and satire, 11, 136
  traditions (conventions) of, 2, 10, 15 (in U.K.), 80, 85, 86, 107, 110, 115,117, 127, 113, 134, 137, 151, 162–163, 175–78, 187, 192, 193, 196, 247, 265, 267, 269, 272, 274
  and truth, 13, 136, 168, 175–78, 185, 194, 197, 212
Documentary Film (Paul Rotha, 1968), 150
documentary television, 258, 259, 264, 274. *See also* newsmagazines
Donovan, Michael, 167
Dover Beach (1867), 219
Downsize This! (1996), 4, 38, 113
downsizing, corporate, 98
Dr. Death. *See* Kevorkian, Jack
Driving Me Crazy (1988), 196
Dude, Where's My Country (2003), 5, 114
Durant, W. C., 33
DVDs, 29, 106
Dyer, Richard, 36, 38, 39
dystopian narrative, 18, 205–8, 210, 211
  archetypal, 205, 207
  and everyman characters, 206
  and *Fahrenheit 9/11*, 13, 18, 205–7, 208–9, 211–13, 223, 227, 231
  and role of the media, 209
  and thought control, 216

Eisenstein, Sergei, 92
Eisner, Michael, 42, 170, 240, 287
El-Amin, Salimah (researcher for Moore), 185
Elder, Larry (show host and electronic journalist), 119, 174. See also *Michael and Me*
Ellsburg, Daniel, 115
Elza, Cary, 15, 18, 257
Emanuel, Ari, 42
Emmy Awards and nominations, for *TV Nation*, 240
Encyclopedia Brittanica, 21
Enron: The Smartest Guys in the Room (2005), 8, 85
EPPC. *See* Ethics and Public Policy Center
Epstein, Edward Jay (author, *Big Picture: The*

New Logic of Money and Power in Hollywood, The), 42, 43
Erlichman, John, 69
Eskimo Bars, 107
Ethics and Public Policy Center, 210
Eubanks, Bob (host, *The Newlywed Game*), 84, 135, 144

Facebook friends of Obama, 302
Fahrenheit 451, 13, 203–7, 217, 218
 as dystopian narrative, 207, 218
Fahrenheit 9/11, 3–14, 16–20, 27, 29, 36, 40–44, 51, 52, 54, 60, 62–64, 79, 85, 86, 89, 92–96, 98, 105, 107, 109, 111, 114–16, 118–20, 149–54, 156, 157, 163, 167–69, 171–81, 183, 185, 187, 189–96, 202–17, 223, 255, 256, 266–68, 271, 274, 278, 280, 282, 285–89, 290, 295, 297, 299–301
 as about social control, 13
 as antiwar documentary, 205
 and attacks on, 178
 and domestic box office, 172
 as dystopian narrative, 13, 202–20
 and *Factual Back-up for* (written by Moore), 192
 and "Fifty-nine Deceits" in (Web article by David Kopel), 210
 and importance of images, 208
 and Lipscomb, Lila, 9, 13, 36, 54, 60, 63, 64, 96, 115, 154, 155, 158, 162, 206, 212, 213, 285
 and MoveOn.Org house parties, 290
 and opening weekend online campaign, 289
 and opening weekend virtual town meeting, 289
 and origin of title, 202–4
 and political action, 300
 and proposed thesis of, 213
 as provocation, 217
 and reception in UK, 269
 and relationship to *Fahrenheit 451*, 218
 and stretching facts, 213
 and systematic assault on, 185
FahrenHYPE 9/11: Unraveling the Truth About Fahrenheit 9/11 & Michael Moore (2004), 13, 51, 168, 174, 175, 179, 180, 184, 185, 188–90, 192–95, 205
 and alignment with political right, 195
Farocki, Haroun, 111
fast-food industry, 8
Faulkner, William, 129
Fauth, Jurgen (film reviewer), 150
FBI, 82, 157–59
FDR. *See* Roosevelt, President Franklin D.
Fellini, Federico, 21
Ferguson, Charles, 8
Fight Back: The War on Terrorism—from Inside the Bush White House (2002), 177, 179, 183, 184
Film Comment, 40, 133
Filming Othello (1978), 111
First Boston Corporation $50 million tax break, 231
Fithian, John (president, National Association of Theatre Owners), 172
Flaherty, Robert, 107
Flint, Michigan, 9, 30, 32, 33, 54, 82, 85, 86, 89, 93, 96, 112, 113, 134–37, 141, 144, 153, 169, 236
 sit-down strike of 1936, 31
Flint Beecher School District. *See also* Rolland, Kayla
Flint City Council, 31
Flint Journal, 67, 75, 76
Flint Voice, 5, 31, 34
Fonda, Jane, 39
Foote, Shelby (historian), 146
found footage, 12, 21, 114, 115, 284
Fox, Michael R., 175. *See* Savage Productions
Fox Network, 3, 43, 204, 209, 216, 233, 238–40, 249
Fox News, 3, 100, 170, 175, 178, 209, 216, 223, 239, 278, 288
Franken, Al, 45, 170
free-market economy, 138
Fremaux, Thierry (Cannes film festival director), 169
French, Philip, 268
French New Wave, 29, 109, 171, 226
Fresno Bee, 289
Freud, Sigmund, 192, 194

Gaffney, Frank (assistant secretary of defense under Reagan), 194, 195
Gaines, Jane, 185
Galusky, Wyatt, 291, 299
Garen, Micah (filmmaker), 169
Gates of Heaven (1980), 91

Geithner, Timothy, 100
gender, issue of in violence in America, 67, 69
General Electric, 238
General Motors, 6, 8, 16, 22, 31–35, 53, 83, 93, 112, 134, 136, 137, 139, 142, 144, 174, 287
  CEO Roger Smith, 7
  Flint, MI sit-down strike of 1936, 31
  founder. *See* Durant, W. C.
  and layoffs, 58
Gibney, Alex, 8
Gibson, John (Fox News), 223
Gibson, Mel, 169, 287
Giddens, Anthony, 291
Gilligan, James (author of *Violence: Reflections on a National Epidemic*), 65, 75
Gingrich, Newt, 239
Giuliani, Mayor Rudolph, 231, 232
Glaser, Mark (online writer on Internet issues), 281
Glassner, Barry (California sociologist), 89
global capitalism, 127
Glynn, Kathleen, 5, 167, 235
GM. *See* General Motors
Godard, Jean-Luc, 39, 40, 42
Good Earth, The (1937), 159
Gore, Vice President Al, 158, 178, 187, 189, 190, 192, 227, 278, 298
grassroots activism, 282
Greatest Story Ever Sold, The (2007), 20
Great Gatsby Ball (in Flint, MI), 61, 84, 136, 139
Greenstreet, Steven, 119
Greenwald, Robert (filmmaker, *Uncovered: The Whole Truth About the Iraq War*), 13, 177, 186, 190, 194
Grey Gardens (1975), 155
Grierson, John, 18, 55, 56, 186
Grosse Point Yacht Club, 137
Ground Zero, 18, 99
Grub Street, 33
GSMPA Medical Group, 61
Guantánamo Bay, 17, 18, 52, 55, 98, 227
Guardian (UK newspaper), 108, 226, 266, 269, 284
guerrilla theater, 108
Gulf War, 216
gun culture, 52, 66, 69, 90, 143, 146, 268
gun violence, 10, 12, 20, 60, 65, 91, 117, 142, 145, 147, 234
Gupta, Dr. Sanjay, 44
Guyette, Jim (meatpackers union president), 128, 129

Habermas, Jurgen, 282–83, 297
  and the public sphere, 282
Halliburton, 96, 153
Halter, Ed (critic and curator in NYC), 108
Hamilton, Neil (disgraced Tory MP), 262
Hamper, Ben (author), 33, 34. See also *Rivethead: Tales from the Assembly Line*
Hardball, 204
Hardy, David T. (attorney), 173, 175, 190. See also *Michael Moore Is a Big Fat Stupid White Man*
Harken Energy, 156
Harlan County, U.S.A. (1976), 130
Harris, Eric (Columbine High killer), 65, 143, 144
Hartley, John (media authority), 237, 283, 284, 286
Hatch, Senator Orin, 236, 245
Haugland, Jan (writer of English-language blog, Secular Blasphemy), 203, 204
health care, 3, 4, 8, 9, 14, 17–20, 38, 44, 45, 52, 54, 55, 60, 61, 63, 69–71, 79, 95, 98, 99, 223–27, 234, 243, 244, 247, 255, 273, 274
  universal, 226
Hearts and Minds (1975), 114, 169, 197, 206
Helms, Senator Jesse, 239
Henderson, Abdul, 154
Hensher, Philip (British broadcaster and reviewer), 267
Hermman, Bernard, 21
Herzog, Werner, 109
Heston, Charlton, 12, 22, 26, 35, 44, 59, 60, 64, 65, 67, 69, 87, 88, 90, 116, 117, 142, 145, 147, 148
Hitchcock, Alfred, 21, 39
Hitchens, Christopher ("terror warrior"), 214–17
Hitler, Adolf (vs. Moore in *Celsius 41.11*), 120
HMOs, 71, 225
Hochschild, Adam, 32, 33
Hollinger, Glen L. (California insurance claims reviewer), 69
Hollywood, 27, 30, 31, 33, 34, 39, 40, 42, 54, 57, 89, 106, 108, 112, 115, 144, 150, 159, 160, 167, 171, 174
Hollywood Goes to War (1979), 163

Hollywood Reporter, 149
Hoover, J. Edgar, 80, 82
Hormel meatpacking plant, 128, 130, 131
Horton, Willy, 142
Hour of the Furnaces (1968), 109
House of Representatives, 178
Housing Problems (1935), 155
Huffington Post, 16
Hughes, Jimmie (principal). *See* Buell Elementary School
Huillet, Danielle, 109
Humana (health insurance provider), 63, 64, 244, 248
Hurricane Katrina, 20, 188
Hussein, Saddam, 95, 114, 119, 168, 175, 193, 194, 209, 211, 217
Huston, Walter, 154

Icon Productions, 169, 287
IFC Films, 161, 170, 215, 287
Il Bidone (1955), 21
Inconvenient Truth, An (2006), 7
In Living Color (TV show), 238
interactive and reflexive modes (Bill Nichols), 108. *See also* documentary modes
International Documentary Association (IDA), 92
Internet, 9, 15, 16, 29, 30, 89, 106, 150, 174, 279, 280, 281, 282, 285, 286, 290, 291, 293, 294, 298–301
  and activism and/or propaganda, 279, 292, 293, 299
  and community building and political action, 281
  and information consumption, 292
  and mass-media campaigns, 280
  and media, 283, 284
  and online politics, 282
  and polling, 279
  and public sphere, 283
  and redaction, 284–85, 293, 300, 301, 302
  and role in 2004 election, 278
  and social networking, 302
  and transformative role, 16
  and viral marketing, 299
interview tactics, ambush, 142
In the King of Prussia (1982), 87
In the Year of the Pig (1968), 80, 115, 205
investigative journalism, 15, 58
Iran-Contra scandals, 146
Iraq, invasion of, 106
Iraqi detainees, 43
Iraq war, 8, 12, 13, 20, 44, 54, 58, 63, 92–94, 96, 97,158, 159, 161, 163, 167–69, 171, 177, 196, 202, 205, 208, 212, 255, 267, 282, 285, 290
  and documentaries critical of, 8
  and post-9/11 politics of fear, 119
Isthmus Engineering, 22

J'Accuse (Émile Zola's letter), 171. *See also* Zola, Émile
Jacobo Arbenz (Guatemalan president overthrown in 1954), 146
Jacobson, Harlan, 84, 107, 133, 134, 140
Jarecki, Eugene, 8, 164, 222
Jay Leno Show, The, 6
Jeffords, Susan, 57
Jeffries, Stuart (British TV critic), 260, 276
Jesus Christ, 21, 162
JFK liberalism, 101
Johndroe, Gordon, 183
Jost, Jon, 111

Kael, Pauline, 27, 53, 133, 135, 136, 154
Kaiser Permanente, 224, 225
Karzai, Hamid, 193
Katrina, Hurricane, 20, 104
Kay, Tom (General Motors spokesman), 22, 36, 138
Kenfick, Jim (developer of www.moorewatch.com), 173
Kennedy, Ted, 51
Kennedy assassination, 80, 87, 101
Kenyon, Andy (Oregon State Police trooper), 192
Kerry, John, 119, 195, 278, 290, 298
  and Swift Boat Veterans for Truth, 195
Kevorkian, Jack, 70, 225
Keyes, Dawnelle (featured in *Sicko*), 60
Killing the Children of Iraq (2000), 257. *See* Pilger, John
King, Barry, 38
King, Larry, 20, 45
kino pravda ("film truth"), 168
Kissinger, Henry, 214
Klawans, Stuart, 37

Klebold, Dylan (Columbine High killer), 65, 143, 144
Kluge, Alexander, 30, 45, 109
Kmart, 12, 22, 55–57, 141–44
Knight, Phil, 36, 44
Knoblock, Kevin, 119, 174
Knowles, Harry, 151
Knowlton, Richard (Hormel CEO), 131
Kodak Theatre, 167
Kohut, Andrew (director, Pew Research Center), 298
Kopel, David, 210, 211, 213, 217
Koppes, Clayton R. (co-author, *Hollywood Goes to War*), 163
Kopple, Barbara, 11, 12, 127–35, 138, 139
Kotto, Yaphet (actor), 237
Krugman, Paul, 171, 193
Kubrick, Stanley, 107

Labash, Matt, 37, 39, 48
la camera stylo, 28
Larry King Live (1985), 6
Late Night with Conan O'Brien (1993–2009), 5
Late Show with David Letterman, The (1993–), 5
Laurel and Hardy, 33
Lawrence, D. H., 107
Leader, his Driver, and the Driver's Wife, The (1991), 265. *See* Broomfield, Nick
left-wing partisans, 81
left-wing politics, 28, 30, 32, 38, 108, 129, 268
Lehane, Chris, 29, 46
Les Maitres fous (1955), 109
"Letter from Flint, Michigan," 35
Letter from Siberia (1958), 109
Liberty Film Festival, 175
Lieberman, Senator Joseph, 89, 147
Lightning over Braddock (1988), 111
Limbaugh, Rush, 29, 38, 45
Lions Gate, 70, 161, 170, 215, 287
Lipscomb, Lila, 9, 13, 36, 54, 60, 63, 64, 96, 115, 154, 155, 158, 162, 206, 212, 213, 285
Littlefield, Warren (former NBC president), 236
Littleton, Colorado, 88, 142, 144
Lockheed Martin, 88, 144, 146
Lone Ranger, 129
Lorentz, Pare, 154, 156
Los Angeles Times, 171, 198
Louis Theroux's Weird Weekends (1998–2000), 261
Love Canal, 237
Lovejoy, Alice, 195, 201
lower-class victims, 10
Luhr, William, 12, 56, 58, 69

MacFarquhar, Larissa, 40, 112
Mad About You (1992–1999), 5
Maher, Bill, 6, 249
mainstream media, 14, 16, 44, 86, 94, 114, 215, 256, 271
Malke, Becky (whistle-blower featured in *Sicko*), 19, 63
managed-care system, 70
Manson, Marilyn, 89, 117, 147
Mansoor Ijaz, 175
Manufacturing Dissent (2007), 17
Marker, Chris, 109
Mark Thomas Comedy Product, The (satirical British TV show, 1996–1998), 263. *See also* Thomas, Mark
Married with Children (1987–1997), 238
Marx Brothers, 33, 86
masculine identity, 55, 57–60, 63–66, 68, 69, 72
masculinity and violence, 69
Maslin, Janet, 71
mass media
  and Internet, 283, 284
  and politics, 114, 271
  and shaping sociocultural attitudes, 270
Matrix, The (1999), 13, 205, 206, 208, 211, 212, 215, 216
Mattson, Kevin, 39
Mauser, Tom (father of Columbine victim), 90
Mayfair Set, The (1999), 257. *See* Curtis, Adam
Maysles Brothers' films, 155
McBride, Jim, 128
McCain, John, 28, 45, 279, 296, 302
McCarthy era, 80, 87
McDermott, Congressman Jim, 95
McElwee, Ross, 11, 28, 91, 111, 196
McVeigh, Timothy, 88, 160
Media Student's Book, The (UK media studies book), 272
Melnyk, Debbie, 17
Memory Hole Web site, 182, 184, 185

Menand, Louis, 151
Michael and Me (2005), 119, 174. *See also* Elder, Larry
MichaelMoore.com, 45, 279, 282, 285, 286, 291, 293–95, 299–301
Michael Moore Hates America (2004), 51, 119, 174, 205
Michael Moore Is a Big Fat Stupid White Man (2004), 174, 175, 190, 205
Michigan Militia, 65, 88, 116
Michigan Voice, 5, 31, 32
Mike's Election Guide (2008), 5
Millhouse (1971), 94
Miramax, 7, 42, 43, 169, 170, 287
Mitchell, Andrea, and interview with Moore, 204
Montag (*Fahrenheit 451*), 13, 202, 206, 207, 212, 218, 219
Monty Python's Flying Circus (British TV show 1969–1974), and similarities to Moore's *TV Nation*, 15, 260
Moore, Michael
  Academy Award speech by, 167–68
  Academy Award won by, 3
  and American politics, 3, 20, 23, 29, 31, 37, 43–45, 95, 243, 256, 278–79
  as book author, 3, 5
  box office performance of films of, 3, 4–5, 27, 93–94, 113
  as celebrity icon, 5, 6, 8, 9, 36–42, 52, 79, 100–101, 266, 270
  class and critques of capitalism in the work of, 9, 10, 26, 32–34, 37, 53–61, 67–68, 83, 86, 91, 97, 98, 99, 100, 139, 153
  and conservative critics, 6, 28, 31, 51, 52, 91, 93, 94–96, 120, 168, 171–75, 177–78, 179–81, 184–85, 187–88, 189–93, 194–96, 210
  and documentary films, 8, 10, 11, 79, 82, 85, 91, 105, 106, 107, 133–34, 137–38, 175–78
  as dystopian filmmaker, 13, 18
  as film auteur-star, 8, 27–45
  and film critics. *See* Jacobson, Harlan; Kael, Pauline; Scott, A. O.; Turan, Kenneth
  films of (See also *The Big One; Bowling for Columbine; Canadian Bacon; Capitalism: A Love Story; Fahrenheit 9/11; Pets or Meat: The Return to Flint; Sicko; Slacker Uprising*
    agit prop political inventions in, 92–97
    compared with Nick Bloomfield's films, 264
    compared with British documentarians, 256, 271
    compared with Frank Capra's *Why We Fight* films, 12–13, 156, 158, 162
    compared with Emile de Antonio's films, 10, 80–82
    as documentaries, 10–11, 105, 109
    as documentary essays, 10–11, 21, 109, 244
    exploratory and confrontational quests in, 86–92
    as a genre, 86, 92
    personal witnessing in, 82–86
    style in, 10–11, 13, 21, 28, 41, 53, 80, 81, 87, 88, 93, 109, 110, 113, 120, 155, 157, 158, 160, 162–163, 194, 244–46
  gender in work of, 9, 10, 32, 38, 53, 56–58, 60–61, 63–70, 90
  as humorist/satirist, 3, 4, 5, 6, 10, 12, 14–15, 21, 22, 25–26, 33, 34, 52, 83–84, 85, 86, 97, 135–136, 232, 237, 264–65
  impact on film history of, 7, 23
  impact on media studies of, 15, 270–71, 274
  influence on documentary film of, 6, 7, 259
  influence on television of, 15, 255, 258, 261, 262, 263, 266, 271
  international popularity of, 5
  Internet presence of, 15–17, 35, 281
  irony in the work of, 6, 10
  as journalist/muckraker, 5, 15, 28, 31–34, 52, 58
  as left-wing filmmaker, 80, 92, 97, 100
  and liberal critics, 53–54
  persona of, 4, 5, 9, 28, 30–32, 33–45, 52–54, 55–57, 60, 63, 71–72, 107, 111, 134, 141, 142, 153, 226, 234, 243, 264, 296, *See also* Flint, Michigan
  as political activist, 5, 39–41, 81, 211, 243, 299
  as populist, 4, 8, 12, 14, 79, 81, 243, 259, 296
  quest narrative in, 83, 87, 88
  race in the work of, 9, 10, 58, 61–69, 89
  reception in the UK of, 15, 243 255, 258, 261, 262, 263, 266
  as redactor, 284, 285
  social solidarity in the work of, 9, 34, 36, 54, 59
  "solidarity strategy" (Studlar) in, 9, 54–55

Moore, Michael (*continued*)
as target of American conservatives, 6, 28, 38, 39
TV shows of, 5, 14–15, 113–114, 233, 234, 244. See also *TV Nation* and *The Awful Truth.*
use of documentary modes in, 11, 105, 108, 109, 110, 128, 134
moorelies.com, 174, 190, 195. *See also* Clarke, Jason
Moore's books, 5, 22, 114
Adventures in a TV Nation, 5
Downsize This!, 4, 38, 113
Dude, Where's My Country, 5, 114
Mike's Election Guide, 5
Official Fahrenheit 9/11 Reader, The, 35, 93, 95, 150
Stupid White Men, 5, 38, 48, 72, 141, 281
Morin, Edgar, 168
Morris, Chris (UK satirical humorist), 15, 262
and comparison with Moore, 263
Morris, Dick, 184. See *FahrenHYPE 9/11*
Morris, Errol, 8, 28, 91, 100, 163, 187, 195
Morrison, John (featured in *American Dream*), 128
Mother Jones, 5, 9, 32, 33, 57
Move America Forward, 172, 198
and lobbying against *Fahrenheit 9/11,* 288
MoveOn Civic Action, 280
MoveOn.org, 15, 16, 18, 106, 279–86, 288, 289, 290, 291, 293, 294, 295, 296, 297, 298, 299, 300, 302
and Moore, 282, 296, 301
and political action, 302
and success of, 293, 294
Moylan, Tom (author), 207. See *Dark Horizons: Science Fiction and the Dystopian Imagination*
MPAA (Motion Picture Association of America), 172, 198
Mr. Hoover and I (1989), 80, 82
MRSA (methicillin-resistant Staphylococcus aureus, a hospital superbug in the UK), 274
MTV campaigns in 2004 election, 298
Muller, Robert (veteran air force pilot), 115
Murdoch, Rupert (owner of Fox network), 238, 240
Murrow, Edward R., 22
My Pet Goat, 94, 178–80, 185–89, 191
My Son John (1952), 115
MySpace generation, 294
myth of objectivity (of newsmagazines), 81

Nader, Ralph, 5, 193
Nanook of the North (1922), 107
Nashville (1975), 28
Nation, The, 37
National Guard, 6, 94, 129, 162, 209
National Health Service (NHS), 273
National Review Online, 289
National Rifle Association (NRA), 12, 19, 35, 59, 64–67, 69, 87, 88, 115, 143, 145–48, 245
NBC, 82, 169, 203, 204, 233, 235, 236, 238, 239, 249
Neroni, Hilary, 65
Nevsky, Alexander (1938), 159
New Deal, 108, 225
New German Cinema, 109
Newlywed Game, The (1966), 84
New Yorker, The, 133
New York Stock Exchange, 22, 238
New York Times, 30, 32, 42, 71, 169–71, 176, 181, 183, 287, 294, 300
news, as manufactured commercial product, 233
newsmagazines, TV, 233, 235–37, 240, 242, 243, 249
Moore's vs. others, 234
and myth of objectivity, 248
satires of, 14
NHS. *See* National Health Service
Nichols, Bill, 11, 127, 128, 151, 186
Nichols, James (brother Terry Nichols), 65, 66, 88, 116, 143
Nielsen ratings, 238, 240
Night and Fog (1955), 11, 109. *See also* Resnais, Alan
9/11 attacks, 94, 157, 159
1984 (1949 Orwell novel), 13, 128, 196, 205–7, 210, 211, 219
Nixon, President Richard, 14, 15, 17, 19, 20, 34, 36, 69, 73, 80, 94, 225, 247
No End in Sight (2007), 8, 205
nonfiction, 8–9, 10, 80, 92, 97, 105–10, 114, 120, 127, 129, 149, 167–168, 241, 256, 258–59, 272. *See also* documentary
North American Free Trade Agreement, 237
Nosferatu (1922), 160

Not the Nine O'Clock News (Satirical British TV show), 262
NRA. *See* National Rifle Association
Nyberg, Chuck (Hormel Executive VP), 131

Obama, Barack, 3, 6, 16, 21, 45, 70, 100, 295, 296, 301, 302
 and Facebook friends, 302
 as redactor, 302
 and rhetoric of "change," 301
 and social media, 302
Observer, The (British newspaper), 268
Official Fahrenheit 9/11 Reader, The, 35, 93, 95, 150
Oklahoma City bombing, 66, 88, 116, 143, 160
online activism, 291, 294, 299, 302
O'Reilly, Bill, 38, 45, 223, 288
O'Reilly Factor, The (1996–), 5, 249
Orwell, George, 13, 14, 206, 207, 209, 210
Oscoda, Michigan (home of Strategic Air Command), 88
Owens, Tamarla (mother of Kayla Rolland's shooter), 67, 68

PAC. *See* Political Action Committee
Palast, Greg (author), 190, 200
Pantagraph, The (Bloomington, IL newspaper), 158, 190, 192
Pariser, Eli (MoveOn PAC campaign director), 16, 286, 288–90, 295, 297, 302
Patriot Act, 41, 94, 118, 208
Peacework, 35
Peeno, Linda (former health insurance executive), 9, 62, 69
Peterson, Alan (filmmaker, *FahrenHYPE 9/11*), 13, 119, 179, 184, 186, 187, 189, 191, 192, 194–96.
Pets or Meat: The Return to Flint (1992), 113
Pew Research Center, 298
Phelps, Fred (Topeka, KS preacher), 239, 247
Pierce, Julie (featured in *Sicko*), 63
Pilger, John (British filmmaker), 256, 257
Pittsburgh Post-Gazette, 285, 288
Plow That Broke the Plains, The (1936), 156
plugged-in society, 282
Plumbers for Obama, 6
Point of Order (1964), 87, 101
political action committee (PAC), 280, 301
political activism
 and models of, 297, 300
 and online petition, 299
political discourse, 51, 112, 232, 233, 235, 240, 250
political entertainment television, 231–51
Politically Incorrect (TV show), 235, 249, 250
political mimesis. *See* Gaines, Jane
politiques des auteurs, 29
Porton, Richard, 21
power elite, opposition to. *See* Williams, Raymond
Power of Nightmares, The (2004), 257, 271. *See* Curtis, Adam
Prelude to War, 149–64. See *Why We Fight* series
Primetime (TV show), 233
public sphere, 16, 233, 279, 282–83, 297
 and the Internet, 283

Rafferty, Kevin (documentary filmmaker), 83, 254
Rafko, Lay Lani Rae, 58.
Reagan, President Ronald, 57, 84, 225
 administration, 11, 80, 99, 131, 175, 225
 and Bush era, 132
 and revamping the New Deal, 225
Real Time with Bill Maher (2003–), 5, 6
redaction/redactor, 15, 16, 284, 285, 292, 293, 300, 302
Regan, Donald, 21
religious Right, 162
Republican National Committee, 175
Republican National Convention, 6
Republican Party, 45, 172, 296
Republic Windows and Doors, 22
Resnais, Alan, 11, 109
Rhoads, Kelton (psychologist), 184, 199
Rice, Condoleezza, 157, 176, 189
Rich, Frank, 20, 42
Riefenstahl, Leni, 12, 156
Right (wing), 38, 51, 108, 173, 212, 215, 296
 agenda, 93, 94
 power structure, 208
Riis, Jacob (photographer), 133
River, The (1938), 156
Rivera, Geraldo, 142
Rivethead: Tales from the Assembly Line, 31, 33, 236. *See also* Hamper, Ben
Robinson, Sally, 65, 75
Rock, Chris (comedian), 88, 116

Rock the Vote (2004 MTV campaign), 298
Rocky Mountain Health Plan, 20
Rodney King video, 188
Roger & Me (1989), 3, 4, 6–8, 10, 11, 17, 20, 22, 27, 28, 30–36, 39, 46, 51–58, 60–63, 67, 79, 80, 82–88, 93, 98, 105–9, 111–13, 115–17, 119, 127, 128, 133–37, 139, 141, 142, 144, 151, 152, 170, 174, 196, 202, 223, 224, 236, 247, 258–60, 262, 264, 265, 272, 287
  as impetus for TV series, 235
Rogers, Ray (featured in *American Dream*),128
Rogers, Will, 86
Rolland, Kayla, 35, 54, 59, 60, 63, 64, 66–69, 89, 245, 246. See also *Bowling for Columbine*
Ronson, Jon, 37
Roosevelt, President Franklin D., 99, 150, 176, 193
Rostow, Walt, 114
Rota, Nino, 21
Rotha, Paul, 150, 164
Rouch, Jean, 109
Rove, Karl, 173
Ruiz, Raoul, 30
Rumsfeld, Donald, 95, 112, 118, 157, 176, 177
Rushkoff, Douglas (media analyst), 294
Rush to Judgment (1967), 87, 101
Russo, Sal (Move America Forward chief strategist), 172

Sacramento Bee, 289
Sahl, Mort, 33
St. Petersburg Times, 183, 253
Salesman (1968 Maysles film), 155
Salk, Jonas, 22
Salon, 203, 214
Salter Street Films (Canadian producer of *The Awful Truth*), 240
Saltzman, Joe, 150, 158, 159
Sammon, Bill, 177–84, 186, 187, 195
San Francisco Chronicle, 298
Santorum, Rick (ex-U.S. senator), 210
Sarasota Herald-Tribune, 177
satires of newsmagazines, 14
Saturday Night Live (1975–), 14, 296
Saudis, investments by, 156
Savage Productions (producer of *Fahren-HYPE 9/11*), 175
Schankula, David (Moore's Web page editor), 285
Schechter, Danny (filmaker, *Counting on Democracy*), 190
Schickel, Richard, 34
Schutz, Charles, 243
Schwarzenegger, Arnold, 40, 45, 57
Scorecard.org (online database of local environmental statistics), 291
Scorsese, Martin, 28, 39
Scott, A. O., 169
Seattle Times, 300
Second Amendment, 66
second bill of rights, 22, 99
Secular Blasphemy (English-language blog written by Jan Haugland), 203
Shah of Iran, 146
Sharrett, Christopher, 12, 56, 58, 69
Sherk, William (music scholar), 162, 166
Sherman's March (1986), 11, 111, 196
Sicko (2007), 3–5, 9, 11, 14, 17–20, 22, 27, 36, 38, 44, 45, 51, 52, 54, 55, 60–65, 67, 69–71, 74, 79, 98–100, 223–25, 227, 244, 247, 255, 273, 274, 301
  empathy in, 224
  as left-liberal provocation, 223
  and Malke, Becky, whistle-blower featured in, 19, 63
  and Moore visiting Canada, Great Britain, France, and Cuba, 226
  and origin of current U.S. health care malaise, 225
  review in *Time Out*, 274
  and welfare state vs. Communist subversion, 225
Sight & Sound, 37, 258,
Simon, Ray (author, *Mischief Marketing*), 281
Simpsons, The, 5, 238
sit-down strike of 1937, 62
Situation Room, The (2003–), 44, 50
60 Minutes (1968–), 14, 233, 234, 248
  and reporters' roles, 242, 244
Slacker Uprising Tour, (Moore comedy sketches in 2004), 4, 10, 297
slavocracy, 147
Smith, Donna and Larry (featured in *Sicko*), 61
Smith, Gavin, 40, 41
Smith, Roger, GM CEO, 7 44, 54–56, 83, 87, 88, 112, 135, 136, 138, 174
Smothers, Tom, 58, 141

Snyder, Steven, 45
Society of the Spectacle (1973), 111
Solanas, Fernando, 109
Soros, George, 193
South Central (LA), 89
South Park (1997–), 89
Speaking Directly (1974), 111
Spears, Britney, 118, 119, 157
spin, age of, 58, 173, 251, 268, 278, 299
Spurlock, Morgan, 7, 111
Stafford, Roy. See *Media Student's Book, The*
Stallone, Sylvester, 30, 40, 57
Standard Operating Procedure (2008), 8
Starr, Kenneth (former special prosecutor), 243
Starr, Paul (sociologist), 225
Star Wars (1977), 17
Stecco, Larry (attorney in Flint, MI), 84
Steve Haugen. *See* Savage Productions
Stewart, Jon, 15, 24, 58, 249
Stiff, James, 184
Stone, Matt, 117
Strategic Air Command, 88
Straub, Jean-Marie, 109
Structural Transformation of the Public Sphere, The (1962). *See* Habermas, Jurgen, and the public sphere
Stupid White Men (2000), 5, 38, 141, 281
Sullenberger, Captain Sully, 21
Summers, Larry (economic advisor to President Obama), 100
Sundance film festival and submissions of documentaries, 106
Super Bowl, 280
Super Size Me (2004), 7, 111
Supreme Court, 178, 278
Swift Boat Veterans for Truth, 195

Taliban, 88, 163, 195
Tampa Tribune, 183
Tanaka plan, 159
Tarantino, Quentin, 170
Tauzin, Billy (congressman), 19, 71
Taxi Driver (1976), 28
Taxi to the Dark Side (2007), 8
Taylorism, 139
Telegraph (UK), 183, 268
television news, 235
television newsmagazines. *See* newsmagazines
television series of Moore's. See *The Awful Truth; TV Nation*
TerreBlanche (leader of the Afrikaner fascists), 265
Terry Nichols (suspected terrorism coconspirator), 88, 116, 143
That Was The Week That Was, 15, 260
Theroux, Louis, 15, 236, 261
Thin Blue Line, The (1988), 91, 187
Third Cinema, 109
This Divided Nation (2005), 119
Thomas, Mark (UK satirical humorist), 15, 262, 263
  and left-wing convictions, 263
Thomson, Desson, 171
Thorburn, David. See *Democracy and New Media*
Time Out (magazine), 45
  review of *Sicko*, 274
Times (of London), 256
Times Square, 236, 240, 241
Tiomkin, Dimitri, 162
tomandandy (musical group), 237
Tookey, Christopher, 267
Toplin, Robert Brent, 108
Tose-Rigell, Gwen (principal at Booker Elementary School), 187, 188
Touching the Void (2003), 258
Triumph of the Will (1934 Leni Riefenstahl film), 12
Trotsky, Leon, 141
Truffaut, Francois, 207, 218
Truman Show, The (1998), 266
Turan, Kenneth, 171
Turkle, Sherry, 294, 301
TV Nation (1994–1995), 5, 14, 113, 141, 231, 233, 235, 236, 238, 240, 244, 247–49, 260, 261
  and airing in UK, 260
  and appeal to British critics, 260
  and correspondents on, 236, 241
  and Emmy nominations, 240
  and examples of segments, 238, 239
  and move to Fox network, 238
  and music by group tomandandy, 237
  and Nielsen ratings, 238
  and opinion polls reported, 241
  and origin of title, 236
  and polling agency, 236
  and segments not aired, 239

TV Nation (*continued*)
and similarities to *Monty Python's Flying Circus,* 260
and similarities to *That Was The Week That Was,* 15, 260
and storytelling techniques, 244
and use of specialists, 247
20/20 (TV newsmagazine), 233
2004 election, 278
and information dissemination, 279
results, 298
TWTWTW. See *That Was The Week That Was*

UAW (United Auto Workers), 134
UK
critics on *Fahrenheit 9/11,* 269
critics on Moore, 268
and impact of Moore's work, 255
satirical humorists, 262
Uncovered: The Whole Truth About the Iraq War (2003), 13, 177, 186, 194
United Mine Workers, 130
Unocal oil company, 193
UN resolution, 195
Unprecedented (2002), 190
USA Today, 73, 102, 207, 253, 254, 305
U.S. News & World Report, 298

Vast Left Wing Conspiracy, The (2006), 289
VCRs, 29
Veiller, Anthony (Capra film narrator), 154
veriscope, 168, 181, 186
Vernon, Florida (1981), 91
Vertigo (1958), 21
Vertov, Dziga, 92, 168, 176, 194
Vietnam War, 80, 114, 146
violence
in America, 146
American vs. Canadian in *Bowling for Columbine,* 147
as assertion of masculine identity, 68
causes of, 145
juvenile, 146
Violence: Reflections on a National Epidemic (1997), 65
Virginia Tech shootings, 20, 308

Walker, Rob (journalist), 300
Wall Street, 17, 20, 22, 100, 241
meltdown, 17, 20
Walmart, 93
Walter Reed hospital, 169
War at Home, The (1979), 206
War Comes to America (Capra film), 155, 162
Warner Bros., 6, 7, 27, 85, 265
war on terror, 94, 210, 217, 263
Warren Commission, 87
Washington Post, 171
Washington Times, 177, 179
Watanabe, Maria (featured in *Sicko*), 61
Waugh, Thomas, 108
Wayne, John, 39
weapons of mass destruction, 95, 119, 157, 168, 173
Weather Underground, 80
Webcore, 281
Weekend Update (segment on *Saturday Night Live*), 14
Weekly Standard, The, 38
Weinstein, Bob, 169
Weinstein, Harvey, 42, 43, 169, 172, 225, 287
Weinsteins, 170, 171
welfare-to-work system, 67
Welles, Orson, 111
Wertmüller, Lina, 30
Westmoreland, William, 114
When Louis met . . . (2000–2002), 261, 262
When We Were Kings (1996), 258
White House, 14, 16, 69, 70, 159, 171, 173, 177, 179, 194, 206, 213, 244, 289
Why We Fight (2005), 8, 164
Why We Fight series (of Frank Capra, 1943–45), 12, 149, 151, 153, 156, 158, 161, 163
and effects on attitude change, 163
Williams, Linda, 53
Williams, Raymond, 296
Wilson, Bruce, 119
Windsor, Ontario, 142, 145
Winston, Brian, 55, 74
Winston (protagonist in novel *1984*), 206
Wired magazine, 280, 298
Wiseman, Frederick, 106
Wolff, Daniel, 43
Wolfowitz, Paul, 176
World Trade Center, 41, 160, 169, 178, 180, 187, 188, 193, 196

Worthington, Minnesota (Armour plant location), 132
WTC. *See* World Trade Center
www.boxofficemojo.com, 4
www.michaelmoore.com, 15, 195, 278–82, 284–87, 294, 300–302
www.moorelies.com, 174, 190, 195
www.moorewatch.com, 173, 195, 288
www.moorexposed.com, 174

Yippies, 101
  and influence on Moore, 232
York, Byron, 289
You Don't Know Jack, (online game), 280
Young, Neil (singer), 97

Zola, Émile, 171. See also *J'Accuse*